Comparing Public and Private Schools

Volume 1: Institutions and Organizations

The Stanford Series on Education and Public Policy

General Editor: Professor Henry M Levin, School of Education, Stanford University

The purpose of this series is to address major issues of educational policy as they affect and are affected by political, social and economic issues. It focuses on both the consequences of education for economic, political and social outcomes as well as the influences of the economic, political and social climate on education. It is particularly concerned with addressing major educational issues and challenges within this framework, and a special effort is made to evaluate the various educational alternatives on the policy agenda or to develop new ones that might address the educational challenges before us. All of the volumes are to be based upon original research and/or competent syntheses of the available research on a topic.

School Days, Rule Days: The Legalization and Regulation of Education *Edited by David L Kirp, University of California, Berkeley, and Donald N Jensen, Stanford University.*

The Incompetent Teacher: The Challenge and the Response *Edwin M Bridges, Stanford University.*

The Future Impact of Technology on Work and Education *Edited by Gerald Burke, Monash University, Australia, and Russell W Rumberger, Stanford University.*

Comparing Public and Private Schools

Volume 1: Institutions and Organizations

Edited by

Thomas James and Henry M. Levin

 The Falmer Press

(A member of the Taylor & Francis Group)
New York, Philadelphia and London

USA The Falmer Press, Taylor & Francis Inc., 242 Cherry Street, Philadelphia, PA 19106-1906

UK The Falmer Press, Falmer House, Barcombe, Lewes, East Sussex, BN8 5DL

First published 1988

Library of Congress Cataloguing in Publication Data is available on request

ISBN 1-85000-039-5
ISBN 1-85000-040-9 (pbk.)

Jacket design by Caroline Archer

Typeset in 11/13 Bembo by
Imago Publishing Ltd, Thame, Oxon

Printed in Great Britain by Taylor & Francis (Printers) Ltd, Basingstoke

Contents

Contents

Preface

This volume had its origins in the Project on Comparing Public and Private Schools of the Institute for Research on Educational Finance and Governance (IFG), School of Education, Stanford University. As a National Research and Development Center funded by the National Institute of Education, IFG proposed to compare public and private schools as organizations. The main focus was to ascertain how the two sets of schools are similar and differ and what each can learn from the other. The chapters in this volume and Volume 2 on school achievement were presented at the Conference on Comparing Public and Private Schools in October 1984.

We wish to thank Gail MacColl of the National Institute of Education who showed an interest in this project that far exceeded that of the usual program officer. She read and commented on all of the papers and provided unusually helpful suggestions to ensure balanced coverage of the topics. We also wish to thank Jay Chambers, John Chubb, Jody Encarnation, John Meyer, Richard Scott, Joan Talbert, and Terry Moe for their contributions to the overall research project. The views represented in this volume are those of the authors alone and do not represent the institutions with which they are affiliated, Stanford University, or the National Institute of Education.

1 Introduction

Thomas James and Henry M. Levin

The 1980s will be remembered as a decade of American educational reform. Responding to deteriorating educational results and setbacks in the international economic position of the United States, over two dozen reports have been issued by various national commissions and agencies calling for an overhaul of American schools. The states have responded with major changes including increases in mandatory courses in the sciences, mathematics and English at the secondary level as well as minimum competency standards for graduation. Other reforms include alteration in the criteria for teacher certification, implementation of higher teacher salaries and merit pay, and renewed attention to administrative leadership.

Nevertheless, something is missing from the discussions of educational reform. The recommendations for improving American education are limited to public schools. They are 88 per cent solutions, since 5 million of the 43 million students at the elementary and secondary levels attend private schools. Schools educating one of every eight students in the nation have been virtually ignored in the attempt to reshape American educational policy. A 100 per cent solution must recognize the overall system of American schools among fifty states and 15,000 local school districts, most under public sponsorship, but a significant proportion sponsored privately.

Neglecting the role of private schools in national and state educational reform is a long-standing tradition in American educational policy. For this reason, private schools have enjoyed an ambiguous status in discussions of the nation's schools. On the one hand, attendance at a private school satisfies state compulsory attendance laws. This basic right of private schools to exist in a predominantly public system was affirmed by the U.S. Supreme Court in *Pierce* v. *Society of Sisters* (1925), a ruling which also reaffirmed the power of the states to establish regulations for private schools, within constitutional limits. On the other hand, private schools are only minimally regulated in most states. These schools are often viewed as being beyond the purview of public policy, their mission unrelated to the goals of the public schools.

Much of this neglect has been closely connected with the social history of schooling in the United States. Historically, private schools developed separately from, and often in opposition to, the public schools. Outside the legal structure established for public education, the private sector evolved along diverse lines of educational practice and institutional design, including a large share of religious, especially Catholic, schools. Participation in private schools did not go unchallenged in the history of American education, as the anti-Catholic agitation leading to the *Pierce* case attests. Independent of public authority to some extent, and proud of their autonomy, private schools in the past remained less known to the larger world around them than public schools, and less understood by the educational research community. Private schools were less frequently counted, less scrutinized by the public eye in all of its forms — from media attention to political debate, from reform commissions to research and the gathering of statistics. This kind of institutional privacy still persists in some parts of the private sector — for example, among the Christian fundamentalist schools that have grown so rapidly during the last decade.

Several recent developments in the 1980s have begun to bring private schooling more frequently into public policy discussions. Attempts to reconsider the role of government in financing education have led to proposals for tuition tax credits and educational vouchers, policies that would more fully unify the funding of public and private schools. Educational vouchers represent an approach by which the government would give parents a tuition voucher that could be used to purchase education at any approved school, public or private. The goal would be to create an educational marketplace in which public and private schools compete for students. Advocates suggest that such a financing scheme would increase educational choice and school effectiveness, as schools compete among themselves for students and their vouchers. Although the voucher plan was proposed by Milton Friedman in 1954 and has been discussed for the last three decades, even appearing briefly as an experiment by the US Office of Economic Opportunity, only in recent years has it entered policy deliberations as an active concern with a constituency behind it.

Tuition tax credits represent a way for parents to obtain subsidies for private schooling through a provision for reducing their tax payments to state or federal governments by some portion of tuition paid to private schools. This approach has been under discussion at the federal level since the mid-1970s, and a similar policy — a state tuition tax deduction — is presently operating in the state of Minnesota. That plan, which has been approved by the US Supreme Court and is discussed in the chapter by Darling-Hammond and Kirby in this volume, allows parents to deduct from taxable income a specified portion of educational expenses, whether for public or private schools.

Support from the Reagan administration has lent momentum to discussions of tuition tax credits and vouchers, but the recent currency of these approaches has also been linked to political concerns for providing financial assistance to parents who send their children to private schools as well as a more general quest for greater educational choice. Whatever the cause for their new-found celebrity, these proposed policies highlight the fact that the educational system of the United States includes both public and private sectors, and both must be considered in framing policies for education.

The neglect of private education in discussions of school policy is ending for other reasons as well. After substantial declines in the 1960s and early 1970s, enrollments in private elementary and secondary schools have stabilized, and over the past few years they have represented a slightly rising proportion of total school enrollments in the nation. Accompanying this relative growth is the contention, forwarded in a major national study (Coleman, Hoffer and Kilgore, 1982a) that private schools produce higher levels of student achievement than public schools with comparable students. The study became a source of debate over its statistical techniques, and other researchers using the same data as well as data from other sources found very small or no differences in student achievement between public and private schools. However, the report and the ensuing debate established the relevance and legitimacy of studies that compare public and private schools and that use the results of such studies for thinking about overall educational policy for the nation. In fact, an important focus of the debate was the degree to which public schools could adopt private school practices such as a disciplined school environment and increased homework to obtain higher student achievement.

New Research on Public and Private Education

Because of the relevance of private schools to public policy discussions, researchers at Stanford University initiated a series of activities in the early 1980s that eventually led to this book and its companion volume on educational achievement in the public and private sectors. These activities took place under the auspices of the Institute for Research on Educational Finance and Governance (IFG) in Stanford's School of Education with financial support from the National Institute of Education.

First, IFG sponsored a conference on tuition tax credits in Washington, DC, in October 1981. The purpose was to understand the implications of using tuition tax credits to provide public funds for private schools. Co-sponsored by the National Institute of Education and the National School Finance Project, this conference featured a debate between Chester Finn, who helped to draft the Packwood-Moynihan tuition tax credit proposal for Congress, and Albert Shanker, President of the American Federation of Teachers. Researchers presented fifteen papers at the conference. Coming out of several academic disciplines and offering different modes of policy analysis, these papers embodied new research findings on tuition tax credits and interpretations of related background issues (James and Levin, 1983).

Even before the 1981 conference, IFG initiated a complementary activity aimed at greater understanding of schools in the private sector. In December 1980 the Institute started a research project using its interdisciplinary team of scholars to build a comparative data base on public and private schools and to conduct a number of studies drawing from that base. The purpose of the activity was to examine differences in patterns of decision-making, internal structures of control, and resource allocation in schooling organizations in the public and private sectors. Focusing on the San Francisco Bay Area, the project resulted in close analysis of some key issues touching upon current policy discussions of public and private schools.

A third and more recent effort was a project entitled 'The Organization and Performance of Private Schools', through which IFG attempted to relate organizational structures and practices more precisely to educational outcomes such as student achievement. To accomplish this end, IFG collaborated in the collection of follow-up data by the National Opinion Research Center for the High School and Beyond survey. What has been gained through this enquiry is rich information on teacher characteristics and other school features, making possible a more refined analysis of the determinants of achievement in public and private schools.

Finally, IFG sponsored a second conference — out of which came the chapters in this volume — on 25–26 October 1984, to delve more deeply into the question of what public and private schools can learn from each other. Father Timothy Healy, President of Georgetown University, delivered the keynote speech, and the participants represented a spectrum of interests and opinions across the public and private sectors. The group included researchers, policymakers, school leaders and practitioners.

At the conference, researchers working on the forefront of comparative study of public and private education presented fourteen papers examining critical issues of current interest. The majority of the papers were written under the auspices of IFG and were funded by the National Institute of Education. Four of the papers came from other NIE projects that produced research highly relevant to the topic of the conference. One paper was written under the auspices of the National Opinion Research Center and the University of Chicago. The discussion cut across sectors, interest groups, and professional cultures. Just as the papers explored issues common to separate traditions of education, the conference succeeded in generating dialogue among people who routinely have few opportunities to communicate with each other and to articulate their common aims.

Despite professional differences, the participants found no difficulty agreeing on the most fundamental matters. No matter what the auspices of the school, educators share a common interest in the cultivation of learning, 'the contained explosion of young minds', as Father Healy put it in his keynote speech. Healy's speech captured some of the most salient themes of the conference. He drew upon the analogy of public and private higher education to find common ground. 'In a curious American way', he suggested, 'both sides make a system'. Even when there is competition, the partisans of each sector 'know in their hearts that they are two sides of the same coin, and that each needs the other to thrive'. Discerning that this is the reality for elementary and secondary education as well as for higher education, Healy told the group he found it odd that leaders of the public system worry about competition from private schools, 'like the elephant complaining that the mouse's weight will break the bridge'.

Healy argued that public schools can learn from private schools. One important lesson after two decades of program innovation in public schools is the necessity of maintaining a coherent curriculum. Second, many private schools can show the way in learning how to avoid compromising the educational process in the classroom. Acknowledging some of the recent reform studies that point to similar conclusions, he mentioned smaller classes, homogeneous groupings of students, high expectations, more streaming of students in basic subjects, designating master teachers, strengthening the role of the principal, and the need for something analogous to religious commitment, an 'excitement, spiritual fulfillment and richness' in the devotion of teachers to their work.

Healy further urged public school leaders to observe the ways that private schools turn teachers into 'a faculty' who experience a sense of corporate responsibility and cohesive leadership. A sense of unity must become pervasive in the life of the school. For the faculty, who infuse life into learning, the pride of belonging to the teaching profession can be enhanced through closer relationships with other educational institutions, particularly with local colleges and universities.

Public and private schools must stand together on the most basic needs for improving education, Healy argued. First and foremost, he cited adequate teacher salaries as a common goal across school sectors. To this goal he added the need to reduce the intervention of courts and lawyers in the operations of schools. Further, there should be a more flexible interpretation of compulsory education laws for adolescents. Healy ended his speech by urging all those seeking better schools in both sectors to persevere in quest of 'the integration of our society' through educational opportunity for minority groups.

It soon became clear in the IFG conference that many different questions must be addressed to discover what a comparison of the public and private sectors can teach about schooling needs and policies. To begin with, what is 'public' and what is 'private' in schooling today? Does the distinction influence the nature of the school and its educational practices? These questions are more complex than might appear on the surface, partly because all schools mix public and private interests. From an institutional perspective, how strong are current trends toward privatization in schooling? Are they related to long-term trends toward greater secularization of education in the public sector? And what draws people to public or private schools? If public subsidies are expanded to include private institutions on a larger scale than at present, what will be the effect on schooling in both sectors?

Such questions inevitably open the door to others that require responsible discussion and considerable information. What do parents think about when they choose a school? Are enrollments in the two sectors changing significantly, or is the situation relatively stable? Within the private sector, exactly where are the largest changes occurring, and what do these changes mean for education as a whole? More fundamentally, are private schools better than public schools? Do they generally produce higher levels of academic achievement? If so, how — and how much?

Approaching the public-private distinction from another angle, how do the two sectors compare in serving the aims of social equity and equal educational opportunity? Are the disparities in family income of parents greater within one sector than the other, and how do the two sectors compare overall? Does one exhibit greater tendencies toward segregation? How does segregation come about differently within various kinds of schools in each sector?

From a research standpoint, while posing such questions it is also necessary to ask what is significant and what is misleading when quantitative differences are found between the public and private sectors. Are the quantifiable differences the right ones to be looking at to understand the identity of public and private schools? For example, is the profession of teaching distinctly different in public and private schools? How do salaries compare, and what do the differences mean? Does the composition of the teaching force reveal any differences that show who tends to teach in public and private learning environments?

More broadly, how does the organization and authority of schooling differ between the two sectors? What can this contrast tell us in general about the educational program likely to be offered in public and private schools? And speaking of authority, would proposals for greater public subsidies of private education lead to greater regulation by public authorities? If enacted, would such proposals make private education more 'public'?

Beyond such questions lie other issues that received attention in the papers and discussion of the conference. Many people are wondering how today's schools, whether public or private, can recapture the cohesion, the face-to-face moral universe, of small communities. Some see private schools as the 'common schools' of today, the place where moral instruction and civic learning occur with greatest intensity. Others see private schooling as inherently divisive. How do the two sectors prepare citizens for participating in a democracy? Equally important, how has each created obstacles to the achievement of that aim? How can social policy help to enhance family choice and at the same time improve democratic participation through education? What can the two sectors learn from each other about renewing moral education and civic learning? And how can the lessons of cooperative understanding between the two sectors be spread widely to build a positive and sustaining education for children throughout the country in all kinds of schools?

What Can Public and Private Schools Learn from Each Other?

It was a concern with integrating our knowledge of public and private schools into an overall picture of the educational system that motivated the preparation of a unified set of papers on public and private schools, the conference at which they were discussed, and the two volumes in which the papers are published. Although at one level, public and private schools are in competition with each other, at another level they represent different problems. For example, public schools must educate highly heterogeneous populations that live in a particular area. In contrast, private schools address the needs of students who are necessarily more homogeneous by virtue of the fact that their parents have selected particular schools with a specific religious, philosophical or academic orientation. Public schools must educate the students who live in their attendance districts including the handicapped, bilingual, gifted, disadvantaged and those from many different religious or political backgrounds. Private schools may choose to educate any combination of these, but usually are designed to appeal to students from particular religious or philosophical origins, or displaying uniformly high levels of academic proficiency. What can each sector learn from the other, both in meeting the needs of specific groups of students and in serving diverse populations?

Beyond this, private schools represent a wide variety of pedagogies, educational styles, clientele, teacher policies and so on. They can be seen as representing a wide range of experiments in organizing education, from highly structured academic and religious institutions to alternative or free schools. In contrast, public schools are more constrained by the public laws under which they operate and the sheer size of school districts, so they generally have less autonomy in providing the variety that naturally occurs among private schools in a market setting. What can each learn about differences in pedagogies, teacher selection and remuneration, and organizational styles and their implications for learning?

Finally, there are the unified themes that both groups of schools share. Both seek greater popular support for education and increased parental support for the educational achievement of their students.

Yet, each has approached this task in a different way. Clearly, both sectors have a shared interest in obtaining maximum national and community support for education, and there is surely a dialogue and the potential for a unified strategy in obtaining this end.

In order to compare public and private schools, one must have a clear understanding of what is public and what is private. Normally, the distinction between the two types is interpreted as one of sponsorship. If schools are sponsored by government authorities, then they are considered to be public; otherwise, they are considered to be private. But it might be more productive to think of public and private *education* in a more fundamental sense. Public education is that which serves the larger society and private education is that which serves the individual and family. Using this distinction, it is not at all clear that private schools provide only private education or that public schools provide only public education. For example, both types of schools are likely to provide some background on political institutions and citizen obligations. To the degree that this instruction contributes to preparation for civic responsibility, both are contributing to 'public' education. Likewise, both provide services to students and families that are 'private' in nature. Private schools offer a unique religious, philosophical or academic orientation that families believe is in their private interest. But, many suburban public schools also provide a unique academic orientation that serves individual or family needs. Both groups of schools furnish services such as music instruction that would appear to be forms of 'private' education.

The difference between private and public schools is hardly as distinct as the categories imply. Probably, the private schools provide a larger component of private education and a smaller component of public education than the public schools. In many respects the differences in 'publicness' of what the two types of schools do is substantial (see the chapter by Levin in James and Levin, 1983). But a pure public-private distinction in terms of educational services is hardly synonymous with the public-private distinction in school sponsorship. Conference participants saw this as a major area for future research and evaluation.

A second area of debate is the issue of what constitutes a democratic approach to the organization and provision of education. To some, the notion of democracy in education is tantamount to the practice of having common schools, which were governed through democratic processes by representatives of those who were being educated as well as the larger society that was funding education. To others the application of democracy to education means the establishment of a free market of educational choices funded by the state, much like a voucher system. They view the free market as the epitome of democracy, even though the government would serve as a funding agency rather than as a provider of education. Others yet view democracy in education as embodying various combinations of these themes such as providing increased choice within the public sector or between public and private sectors, while retaining the government sponsorship of schools.

What seems most clear is that there is little consensus among researchers, public policy analysts, and representatives of public and private schools on the principle of democracy as applied to the provision and organization of education. Some see educational vouchers and tuition tax credits as fostering democratic traditions and view the present public schools as a government monopoly in the provision and organization of education. But others regard the government 'monopoly' as a rhetorical term, with public education being constituted of thousands of school districts and school governing boards and tens of thousands of different public schools.

New Perspectives on the Public-Private Debate

In some measure the vitality of the discussion of such issues at the IFG conference was due to a set of papers prepared for the conference and contained in the two volumes that came out of the conference. The papers were substantive and analytical, offering new information or insights on the various comparative aspects of public and private schools.

This book is the first of two volumes on *Comparing Public and Private Schools*. It provides a series of original papers that focus on institutional and organizational issues. In the second volume (Haertel, James and Levin, 1987), we present several related papers addressing the question of whether public or private schools produce higher academic achievement. That volume includes chapters by Thomas Hoffer; Andrew M Greeley; James Coleman; Karl Alexander and Aaron Pallas; and J Douglas Willms, along with an interpretive chapter by Edward Haertel. The main conclusions of those chapters are that measured differences in academic achievement between public and private schools are heavily conditioned by the assumptions and statistical methods that are used for analysis. Perhaps the major contribution of these studies is that they advance the methodological debate and raise important issues regarding how we might view studies of public-private differences in achievement. The volume provides a clear understanding of the strengths and limits of the debate as well as lucid discussions and interpretations of the statistical findings.

In the present volume we have organized the chapters under three themes: the institutional context of public and private schooling, the nature of choice in schooling organizations, and minority groups in public and private schools. These chapters share an assumption that policy discussions at all levels of educational governance can be improved through a better comparative understanding of public and private schools in the United States.

Focusing on the institutional context, the enquiry begins with an attempt to overcome past neglect by describing as accurately as possible the private sector of American education. Bruce S Cooper addresses this task in a chapter on the changing universe of private schools. Tracing the shifts in enrollments and numbers of schools across numerous categories of affiliation in the private sector, Cooper reveals the dynamic growth and adaptability of these institutions and the diversity of publics they serve. One of the most notable findings is the profound shift in private schools from a group that was predominantly Catholic and urban in 1960 to one that is much more diverse in terms of sponsorship and location. Cooper also suggests that the growth of private schooling is likely to continue, signalling an important change in public attitudes toward the education of their children.

While Cooper emphasizes the composition of the private sector, James S Catterall chooses instead to compare public and private schooling in the aggregate. Directing his analysis toward general patterns of equity instead of descriptive characteristics, Catterall compares such things as family income and racial balance between the two sectors, finding that private school participation increases with family income and that there are proportionately more whites in private schools than blacks or Hispanics. The implication is that public subsidies are likely to bring greatest benefit to those groups that are now participating disproportionately in private schools. His chapter also questions many current assumptions about expansion of the private sector and whether there will be a trend toward substantially greater growth in private school enrollments over the next few years.

Of course, policy can have a large impact on where people choose to send their children to school. New financial policies — such as tuition tax credits — provide some examples with as yet untried potential. A more familiar kind of policy whose effects have profoundly shaped education in the two sectors is that associated with religion. In a chapter on the treatment of religion in public schools and its impact on the resurgence of private schools, Patricia M Lines argues that the imposition of values in public schools and the progressive secularization of these schools under public authority have influenced the growth of private schools. Beginning with an historical argument that traces legal and institutional changes in schooling, she concludes by examining recent trends in litigation and legislation. She calls attention in the public-private debate back to the central issue of values and pluralism in family choices on how to educate children.

Another issue related to the institutional context is the overall organization of the two sectors and what difference this makes for education. Taking a broad view of the problem, Estelle James compares the two systems across different nations, viewing them as alternative ways of organizing the production of desired social goods. Using categories of economic analysis that emphasize supply and demand of educational services, she explains why private education arises and how it endures as a distinct way of organizing schools in different countries. She finds that the demand for private schools is determined by a shortage of places in public schools and/or a desire to obtain education that is different from what the public schools offer. These explanations are supported by the data for the several countries that are evaluated.

One way to expand the base of reliable information on the differences between the two sectors is to understand more deeply the factors that influence their governance and structure. In a chapter dealing with organization within the public and private sectors in the United States, W Richard Scott and John W Meyer find that the environment of public schools is more complexly organized but also more fragmented than is the environment of private schools. First offering a conceptual framework and then conducting an empirical enquiry using the six-county data from the IFG sample of the San Francisco Bay Area, they find that the governance of public education is more elaborate, largely because it is more interconnected with external influences above the level of the individual school, than is the governance of private education. The difference has tended to produce, simultaneously, both more complexity in administration and less coherence in programs among public schools.

In a related chapter, Joan E Talbert asks the question of whether private schools are useful models for improving school effectiveness. Reflecting upon the differing organization of the public and private sectors, Talbert summarizes the research literature on effective schools, then compares school sectors to see whether their organization offers the conditions necessary to produce school effectiveness. Apart from striking differences in selectivity and organizational environments, she also observes that the public and private sectors rely upon different kinds of authority to maintain themselves as institutions. In general, the organization of public schools presents greater obstacles than that of private schools in achieving school effectiveness.

Parental choices reflect a host of judgments about public and private schools. One critical area of concern is the teaching force — and with good reason, since teacher salaries represent the majority of educational expenditures. Recognizing that comparative research into the status of teachers across the two sectors of schooling is badly needed, one of the chapters makes some initial advances using information from the IFG data set developed in the San Francisco Bay Area. In a study of patterns of compensation for teachers in public and private schools, Jay G Chambers confirms that public school teachers earn more than private school teachers. He offers some reasoning for why these differences exist, while also probing more deeply into the patterns of variation within different parts of the private sector. Much of the difference in teachers' salaries between public and private schools is shown to be related to higher levels of education and experience of public school teachers. Chambers concludes that public funding for private education would have the effect of more nearly equalizing teachers' salaries between the two sectors.

Craig E Richards and Dennis J Encarnation approach the labor market in education from a different standpoint. In their chapter they ask what determines where minority teachers work. Basing their empirical study upon the IFG data from the San Francisco Bay Area, they find that the strongest determinant of minority employment across sectors is the proportion of minority students in the schools. Also important is the overall size of the school, continuing increase in the number of teachers employed, and the presence of categorical aid programs for specific educational services. Further analyzing the data to distinguish the patterns of black and Hispanic employment, they reiterate that racial composition of the student body is the most important factor in minority employment for both groups. But they also note that varying historical experiences in entering the labor force for the two groups have resulted in differential opportunities. Finding that the relationship between client characteristics and minority teacher employment is less salient among private schools — also, proportionately fewer minority teachers are employed in the private sector — the authors suggest that the public schools have a greater need to maintain legitimacy in view of the public they serve. They do this by carrying out educational and employment reforms, particularly where large minority constituencies are involved.

Asking how parents choose one school over another, Linda Darling-Hammond and Sheila Nataraj Kirby study a jurisdiction where public support of private school choices does exist on a small scale. They try to understand the 'choice-making behavior' of parents when confronted with greater incentives for choosing between the two sectors, and they analyze whether public-school parents would transfer to private schools in greater numbers if public subsidies made it more attractive for them to do so. The chapter focuses on public policy and private choice in Minnesota, reporting on a survey the authors conducted of parents in that state. Minnesota has a functioning program, approved by the US Supreme Court in *Mueller* v. *Allen* (1983), that provides tax deductions for private and public school expenses. They find that race, income and the extent to which people know about the deduction have little relation to schooling choices, but that attitudes, tastes and the availability of free transportation are important influences on the choices that parents make in educating their children.

Exploring the issue of how minority status is reflected in individual choices and student populations in the private sector, two chapters examine the participation of blacks in private schools. In a study of patterns of racial segregation in the nation's big cities, Robert L Crain draws upon data from Chicago and Cleveland to show how Catholic schools sometimes reinforce and sometimes help to overcome racial isolation. He finds greater segregation at the elementary level among urban Catholic schools. The level of racial segregation in Catholic secondary schools, he suggests, probably represents what would occur under an unrestricted system of voluntary student transfers in public schools within the major urban areas. Challenging the interpretation of Coleman, Hoffer and Kilgore (1982a) on the influence of private schooling on racial segregation, Crain finds overall that private schools do contribute to segregation, but that they also offer signs of encouragement for reducing racial isolation in schools and communities.

In another study of school choice and minority students, Barbara L Schneider and Diana T Slaughter have examined survey and census data from the Chicago area to provide an explanation of recent patterns of change in the participation of black students in urban private schools. Additionally, the chapter prepared for this volume reports on an ethnographic study of such schools and the families that choose them, offering insight into the values of parents and the character of the schools. After differentiating the types of private schools — elite, alternative, and sectarian — being chosen by black families in increasing numbers, Schneider and Slaughter draw upon life history interviews to explain how school climate and the educational goals of black families interact to form distinctly different school choices.

Despite the variety of issues illuminated by these studies, the new research on public and private schools leaves many questions unanswered. What has been done so far constitutes only the beginning of a range of studies that needs to be made to understand the two sectors in comparative perspective. Complementing other new and useful research along these lines (see, for example, Levy, 1986a and 1986b), the purpose of this foray into selected issues has been to help improve the dialogue about school reform with a broader base of reliable information and interpretation. By bringing together analyses from a variety of perspectives, the goal has been to compare the two sectors in illuminating ways, and to discover more about the reality of schooling institutions in the two sectors and their implications for public policy.

Perhaps most important as a suggestion for the future, the conference itself was characterized by a constructive emphasis. An unspoken assumption prevailed — that both sectors have a role to play in American education, but that each needs to be understood in greater depth as it relates to the public interest. A better understanding of what public and private schools can learn from each other is part of the larger challenge of meeting this nation's pressing demand for quality education in a diverse citizenry. There needs to be not only a closer study of school life and organization, but more cooperation between disparate groups that share a common interest in education. Though not sufficient in themselves, these are necessary conditions for a renewal of public commitment to schooling in all its forms.

PART I
THE INSTITUTIONAL CONTEXT

2 The Changing Universe of US Private Schools

Bruce S. Cooper

Introduction

For all its importance to nations, families, and educators[1], precious little is known about private education in the US. This research represents the latest effort to examine the size, composition, location, and developments in private elementary and secondary education.[2] It analyzes the trends in all types of private schools, relating these changes to wider conditions in education, both private and public. What types of private schools have increased or decreased in size and number? Where? And why have some kinds of schools in some regions increased while others shrank in enrollment and number of schools over the same period. These shifts are then applied to social and political changes, making some initial interpretation possible.

The purpose of this chapter is to analyze trends in private schools of all types. In particular, the chapter attempts to present the following:

1 Reliable enrollment figures.
2 Reliable information on the number of private schools by type.
3 Regional differences.
4 Projections of enrollments through 1990.
5 Important factors which explain growth and change.
6 Wider trends in private school composition.
7 Speculations about the impact of socio-political change on private schooling in the US.

Methods

Counting private schools is a difficult business. Many are new, unaffiliated, small, and relatively unknown. Others include not only school-age children but also pre-schoolers, kindergarteners and after-school enrollees, making exact measures of size difficult. Still others refuse to report their whereabouts to authorities, much less such vital statistics as pupil names, program characteristics, and the number of graduates.

Despite these limitations, using three different approaches we were able to create a picture of non-public schools in the US between 1965 and 1985, one useful in drawing certain conclusions. First, in 1982, to locate some of the most difficult schools — particularly the exclusive Evangelical Christian schools — McLaughlin and Cooper[3] conducted a door-to-door exploration in 22 counties in the states of California, Illinois, Iowa, Louisiana, Massachusetts, Minnesota, New Jersey, Tennessee, Texas and Washington. This method involved spending days in sample counties, studying the telephone *Yellow Pages*, calling each school, visiting, talking with private and public school officials, and comparing the extant list of schools held by the National Center for Education Statistics (NCES) with the actual schools: some had closed, moved, changed names; others had never before been found and recorded; others had been miscategorized by the National Center. In all, we found after generalizing from a population in the twenty-two counties of 1/35th of the nation to the total country that NCES had under-calculated the number of Christian Evangelical schools by 26 per cent and underestimated all private schools by 18 per cent.

Second, we established that the NCES and the US Department of Education's Office of Private Education have recently taken account of the earlier discovery of unknown schools and included them into the new estimates of the non-public school sector. On this basis they have constructed the 1984 data, which are included in this study.

Third, we also contacted the heads of national private school associations who provided up-to-date and particular data on the schools under their aegis. In analyzing the number, size, and location of these schools by type, we found that NCES used some categories which we found too broad; for example, they record 'Jewish' while we preferred 'Orthodox Jewish', 'Conservative Jewish', and 'Reform Jewish'. The Center tended to divide the Christian academies among churches, such as Methodist and Baptist, while we lumped them together by 'Evangelical' and by their national affiliation (Association of Christian Schools International, American Association of Christian Schools, and Accelerated Christian Education Schools). Moreover, since some private school associations are affiliated with the Council of American Private Education, a national voluntary group of private schools organizations, we also used some of their membership units to present our data.

This study presents, first, a group-by-group, type-by-type analysis of groups of private schools in the United States. The micro-trends are important to give a sense of the variety and complexity of the non-public school landscape. Then, we shall present some macro-trends: the ties between changes in overall non-public education and wider social and political factors.

Micro-Trends

Roman Catholic Schools

The largest system of non-public schools in the US is operated by the Roman Catholic Church. Historically, millions of Catholics confronted prejudice and open hatred in the Protestant-dominated public schools in the nineteenth and twentieth centuries. As Harold A Buetow explains, 'Those with nativist proclivities adopted social Darwinism to relegate Catholic immigrants to the role of the most unfit' (Buetow, 1970, p. 46).[4]

To escape such denigration, the Church opened over 5000 new parochial schools between 1880 and 1920, to accommodate a burgeoning Catholic population which increased from 6 to 19 million souls in only forty years. By 1965, some 13,292 Catholic schools were teaching 5.66 million students. In eighty-five years (1880 to 1965), school numbers leaped by 490 per cent, from 2246 to 13,292 schools, while pupils grew from 405,000 to 5.66 million in the same period, a jump of 800 per cent (see table 1).

Since 1965, however, the number of schools and students has declined steadily. Peaking at 5.66 million, Catholic school enrollments reached a low of 2.96 million by 1984/85, a total percentage dip of 48 per cent in two decades. The number of schools operated by the church also declined, though less precipitously, from a high of 13,292 schools in 1965 to 9401 in 1984/85, a slip of 30 per cent. These declines are significant, not only for what they tell us about changes in the Catholic community but also for their impact on private school statistics generally.

Table 1: Over a Century of Catholic School Growth and Decline, 1880–1983

Year	Pupil Enrollment	Elementary Pupils	+	Secondary Pupils	Percentage Change over Previous No.	Number of Schools	Elementary Schools	Secondary Schools	Percentage Change Over Previous Entry
1880	405,234	NA		NA	—	2,246	same	NA	—
1890	633,238	—		—	+56	3,931	3,194	737	+68
1900	854,523	—		—	+35	5,012	3,811	1,201	+28
1910	1,237,250	—		—	+45	7,405	5,856	1,549	+48
1920	1,925,616	1,795,700		129,916	+56	8,103	6,551	1,552	+ 9
1930	2,464,522	2,222,600		241,921	+28	10,046	7,923	2,123	+24
1940	2,396,329	2,035,200		361,129	— 3	10,049	7,944	2,105	+ 0
1950	3,066,419	2,560,819		505,600	+28	10,778	8,589	2,189	+ 7
1960	5,288,705	4,373,403		915,302	+72	10,892	10,500	2,392	+ 1
1964	5,662,328*	4,505,620*		1,066,740	+7	13,296*	10,879*	2,777*	+22
1965	5,582,354	4,492,100		1,090,254*	— 1	13,292	10,879	2,413	+ 0.32
1970	4,363,600	3,355,500		1,008,100	—22	11,262	9,307	1,955	—18
1975	3,415,000	2,525,000		890,000	— 0.001	9,993	8,340	1,653	+ 5
1980	3,106,378	2,269,300		837,000	— 0.4	9,560	8,043	1,516	—16
1982	3,094,521	2,266,432		828,089	— 0.4	9,494	7,996	1,498	— 0.7
1983	3,027,312	2,225,289		801,023	— 2.2	9,432	7,950	1,482	— 0.7
1984	2,963,210	2,180,160		788,049	— 1.9	9,401	7,937	1,464	— 0.3
1985	2,902,008	2,120,008		782,000	— 2.2	9,340	7,891	1,449	— 0.67

* Peak amount for enrollment or number of schools.
Sources: A Statistical Report on US Catholic Schools, 1978–79, Washington, D.C., National Catholic Education Association, p. 3.
A Statistical Report on US Catholic Schools, 1984–85, pp. 8, 12.

In 1965, 85 per cent of children in private schools were attending those operated by Catholics; hence, when one thought 'private', one usually heard 'Catholic'. Now, the mix has changed as Catholics declined and other non-public schools grew. Today, only 54 per cent of all pupils in private sector schools attend those sponsored by the Catholic Church. Reasons for this drop are many, including (a) the relocation of the Catholic community out of the cities where parishes were strongest and schools most numerous;[5] (b) the general decline in the Catholic family birthrate, in part because of affluence and assimilation; and (c) the loss or religious tone in some Catholic schools, along with the great decline in teaching priests, sisters and brothers (religious).

In the last four years, however, Catholic schools show signs of stability. First, the rate of decline has nearly stopped; there was only a 1.9 per cent decline between the 1983/84 and 1984/85 school years in pupils and a mere 0.3 per cent fewer Catholic schools. The future for Catholic schools in the US has improved; the commitment is still there, as witnessed by the growth in several areas of the country.[6] When this slow leakage in size and numbers will stop is not clear. It appeared in 1982 that the decline had bottomed out at a 0.4 per cent enrollment dip, but in 1983, the drop was 2.2 per cent and in 1984 1.9 per cent.

Lutheran Schools

The second largest category of affiliated private schools belongs to the various synods of the Lutheran Church. Founded on the teachings of Martin Luther, who insisted that Christians learn to read, not only for religious reasons, but for civic and economic ones as well, these schools sought to create 'able, learned, wise and upright cultivated citizens' (Luther, 1963, p. 9). In the US the Lutheran groups came from Sweden, Germany, Holland and Austria, founding their own church schools as early as 1600 (Beck, 1963).

As shown in table 2, the Lutherans run some 2500 schools for about a quarter of a million pupils. Most of the students (71 per cent) attend schools run by churches of the Missouri Synod, followed by Wisconsin Evangelical and American Lutheran Church synods. Like other Protestant school groups, Lutherans have increased their numbers in the years since 1965; pupil totals are up from 208,209 in 1965 to 280,559 in 1984, a leap of 35 per cent in enrollments. The number of schools has climbed from 1896 in 1965 to 2480 in 1984, up 31 per cent. So while Roman Catholic enrollments dipped by 46 per cent between 1965 and 1984 (48 per cent by 1985), Lutheran schools grew by a third, most markedly among the American Lutheran Church, up 256 per cent, from 8795 in 1965 to 31,284 pupils in 1983/84.

Table 2: US Lutheran Schools, by Type and Level: 1983

	Elementary		Secondary		Total	
	Schools	*Pupils*	*Schools*	*Pupils*	*Schools*	*Pupils*
Lutheran Church, Missouri Synod	1542	181,666	61	16,493	1603	198,061
American Lutheran Church	374	31,284	2	333	376	31,617
Wisconsin Evangelical Lutheran Church	372	31,126	18	4,414	390	35,540
Lutheran Church in America	40	8,555	6	813	46	9,368
Association of Evangelical Lutheran Church	21	4,296	—	—	21	4,296
Evangelical Lutheran Synod	16	848	—	—	16	848
Church of the Lutheran Confession	19	517	2	28	21	545
Church of the Lutheran Bretheran	3	106	1	113	7	219
The Protestant Conference (Lutheran) Inc.	3	65	—	—	3	65
Total by Category:	2390	181,568	90	22,194	2480	280,529

Sources: Statistical Report, Elementary School Statistics, Report 01, 02, The Lutheran Church — Missouri Synod, Board of Parish Services, Information Bulletin 33883, 1982–83; Community Lutheran High Schools, Report 25083, 1982–83.

Parochial schools have become an integral part of Lutheran church life, with about a third of all churches having their own day schools. A recent church report states that 'Lutheran schools are a mission of the church' (Board of Parish Education, 1983, p. 3).

Jewish Day Schools

The development of Jewish all-day schools reflects changes in the American Jewish community, starting with the very first synagogue which opened such a day school in 1731. Since then, with the arrival of Eastern European Jews, both Orthodox *Yeshivot* (Torah academies, Talmud-Torahs) and the newer multicultural modern day schools have opened in large numbers (Schiff, 1966).

Today, Jewish schools can be divided roughly into Orthodox, Conservative (also called Solomon Schechter Schools after the former president of the Jewish Theological Seminary), and the newest, the Reform day schools. In 1965, the US had a total of 73,112 children in Jewish day schools, a number rising to 100,202 by 1984, a jump of 37 per cent in nineteen years. The number of these schools also grew, but faster (by 66 per cent). In 1965, there were 345 schools; by 1984, 572, with each group increasing: Orthodox, 55 per cent more schools; Conservative, 258 per cent; Reform, 40 per cent. Numbers of pupils by group also grew: Orthodox by 25 per cent; Conservative, 245 per cent; and Reform, 87 per cent (see table 3).

Table 3: Jewish School Growth by Group, 1965–83

	1965/66	1970/71	1975/76	1980/81	1982/83	% Growth/Decline 1965 to 1983
Total Jewish						
(a) *Schools*	345	417	483	542	572	66
(b) *Pupils*	73,112	83,106	91,513	96,178	100,202	37
Orthodox Jewish						
(a) *Schools*	321	378	427	477	497	55
(b) *Pupils*	68,800	75,221	82,203	84,201	86,321	25
Conservative						
(a) *Schools*	19	34	50	59	68	258
(b) *Pupils*	3,489	7,042	7,965	10,546	12,341	254
Reform Jewish						
(a) *Schools*	5	5	6	6	7	40
(b) *Pupils*	823	843	1,345	1,431	1,540	87

Sources: Jewish Educational Services of North America, New York; Torah Umesorah (the National Society for Hebrew Day Schools); United Synagogue of America, Commission of Education; and Union of American Hebrew Congregations, Department of Education, 1984.

This growth indicates a change in traditional support by Jews for public education, though this issue of 'abandoning' the public schools is still debated (Syme, 1983) as Jews continue to search for religious identity and assimilation into American life. Jewish day schools play a vital role in this effort to be Jews and Americans.

Seventh Day Adventist Schools

Among Protestant groups, the Seventh Day Adventist is among the most active, fastest-growing and evangelistic. In the US, the first Seventh Day Adventist schools opened in 1852. Today, 1324 schools enroll 81,507 pupils; this includes forty coeducational boarding high schools. These data are up from the 1965 levels of 884 schools (27 per cent increase by 1983) and 64,252 pupils (up 49 per cent between 1965 and 1984) (see table 4).

Table 4:   Growth in Seventh Day Adventist Schools, 1965–83

	1965/66	1970/71	1975/76	1980/81	1982/83	Percentage growth form 1965–83
Students	64,252	72,106	74,938	74,615	81,507	27
Schools	884	994	1,115	1,280	1,324	49

Source: Seventh Day Adventist Church, National Headquarters, Department of Education (K-12), 6840 Eastern Avenue, N.W., Washington, D.C.

These increases parallel the developments in the US church. Like the Roman Catholics, the Seventh Day Adventists have a long-term commitment to schooling, not only in the US but around the world (Seventh Day Adventist Church, 1965). Like Catholics, the Adventists take an international view of religious and educational life, showing strong growth and development.

National Association of Independent Schools (NAIS)

Thus far, the private schools discussed have been religious in sponsorship. The member schools of the NAIS, an Association with headquarters in Boston, are known primarily for their academic excellence, elite clientele, and their ability to get their students into prestigious colleges (the Ivy League, for example). Some NAIS members are religiously affiliated as well, particularly the Episcopalian and Roman Catholic schools run by religious orders.

Many of the preparatory schools were founded at the turn of the century (such as Groton, Hotchkiss, Lawrenceville), though a few trace their origins to the century before (Andover and Exeter academies).[7] These well-known boarding schools make up a small but important segment (23 per cent) of all NAIS member schools, with only 15 per cent of the pupils, while *day schools* comprised 251,713 out of 294,985 total students in NAIS schools in 1980.

Table 5 shows the breakdown of private, independent schools: coeducational, boys only, girls only, day and boarding. Between 1965 and 1984, enrollments jumped from 199,329 to 336,797, or 69 per cent, while numbers of member schools went up from 697 to 837, or 25 per cent. Between 1969 and 1980, all-boys schools dropped by 49 per cent, all-girls by nearly 10 per cent, with more all-boys schools becoming coeducational than did girls-only schools. In the same

Table 5: *Enrollment Trends 1969-70 Through 1979-80 All Nais Schools, Continental US*

	69-70	70-71	71-72	72-73	73-74	74-75	75-76	76-77	77-78	78-79	79-80	69-70 to 79-80 % Change
Total												
Total N of Students	235,330	241,599	249,228	255,409	262,600	263,950	265,766	272,759	264,795	285,122	294,985	+25.3%
Average ($\bar{x}$) N Students/School	336	336	343	354	360	363	368	373	373	377	381	+13.4%
N of Schools	701	718	726	721	730	728	722	732	709	757	774	+10.4%
Coed Schools												
Total N of Students	137,091	158,045	169,335	183,798	196,902	204,945	208,124	215,627	187,509	204,977	214,645	+56.6%
Average ($\bar{x}$) N Students/School	350	344	352	367	374	377	380	384	374	377	383	+ 9.4%
N of Schools	392	460	481	501	527	543	548	561	502	544	561	+43.1%
Boys Schools												
Total N of Students	65,342	53,315	49,509	44,626	40,492	35,772	34,385	33,855	36,342	36,515	35,814	-45.2%
Average ($\bar{x}$) N Students/School	339	344	346	343	343	334	347	349	363	365	362	+ 6.8%
N of Schools	193	153	143	130	118	104	99	97	100	100	99	-48.7%
Girls Schools												
Total N of Students	32,897	30,239	30,384	26,985	25,206	24,233	23,257	23,277	34,272	36,842	37,486	+13.9%
Average ($\bar{x}$) N Students/School	284	294	298	300	297	299	310	315	346	351	357	+25.7%
N of Schools	116	103	102	90	85	81	75	74	99	105	105	- 9.5%
Day Schools (> 95%)												
Total N of Students	148,909	155,430	165,946	175,314	183,153	199,531	201,802	198,382	200,563	219,712	218,260	+46.6%
Average ($\bar{x}$) N Students/School	370	373	385	400	407	417	423	418	422	422	420	+13.5%
N of Schools	403	417	431	438	450	478	477	474	475	521	520	+29.0%
Boarding Schools (> 50%)												
Total N of Students	47,508	45,169	40,994	40,361	39,893	38,701	36,907	40,588	38,736	41,233	43,272	- 8.9%
Average ($\bar{x}$) N Students/School	228	217	213	215	214	216	213	225	231	238	243	+ 6.6%
N of Schools	208	208	192	188	186	179	173	180	168	173	178	-14.4%
K-12 Schools (Including Pre-School)												
Total N of Students	122,653	128,234	131,358	139,292	143,855	144,682	146,852	152,622	143,853	153,458	157,864	+28.5%
Average ($\bar{x}$) N Students/School	467	473	479	501	510	522	534	543	541	546	564	+20.8%
N of Schools	263	271	274	278	282	277	275	281	266	281	280	+ 6.5%
Elementary Schools												
Total N of Students	31,953	32,387	36,695	36,480	37,504	39,142	39,224	36,513	34,155	42,884	46,442	+45.3%
Average ($\bar{x}$) N Students/School	237	236	258	261	266	266	271	250	253	245	251	+ 5.9%
N of Schools	135	137	142	140	141	147	145	146	155	175	184	+36.3%
Secondary Schools												
Total N of Students	80,524	80,978	81,175	79,637	81,241	80,126	79,690	83,624	78,438	85,427	87,242	+ 8.3%
Average ($\bar{x}$) N Students/School	266	261	262	263	265	264	264	274	284	296	294	+10.5%
N of Schools	303	310	310	303	307	304	302	305	276	289	297	- 1.9%

Source: National Association of Independent Schools (1984) Boston, MA.
N = Number

period, elementary day-coeducational schools increased by 36 per cent; secondary coeducational schools dropped by 2 per cent during the same period, indicating a shift in the independent school sector.

Thus, the overall make-up of independent schools has greatly changed: from boarding to day school, from single-sex to coeducation, and from more secondary to more elementary schools. The growth of local, day-independent coeducational schools, indicates the rising need for easily accessible elite private schools that were once only available for boarding students. This trend continues, with a 14 per cent increase between 1980 and 1983. And as pressure rises to gain access to elite colleges and jobs, the demand for NAIS schools will probably grow, particularly for local independent schools.

Episcopal Schools

Episcopalians started some of the nation's most prestigious private schools, such as St. Paul's and Groton, though the church leadership nationwide has put little money or energy into such schools. Today, in a number of communities, church clergy and laypeople have cooperated in starting elementary Episcopal schools, often growing from a church kindergarten or preschool.

Between 1965 and 1983, for example, the number of Episcopal day schools rose from 347 schools with 59,437 pupils in 1965 to 527 schools with 78,214 students, a jump of 32 per cent in enrollment and 52 per cent in number of schools (see table 6). As the new mini-baby boom continues, these schools, which offer local, parent-controlled, and high quality programs, seem in a good position to grow, not only for members of the Episcopal church but for people in general (already, over 75 per cent of students in Episcopal schools are *not* Episcopalians, in contrast to the Catholic church schools with 17 per cent non-Catholics in attendance).

Table 6: Growth of Episcopal Schools, 1965–83

	1965/66	1970/71	1975/76	1980/81	1982/83	Growth (1965–83)
Student Enrollment	59,437	74,892	76,436	76,388	78,214	32%
Number of Schools	347	459	438	320	527	52%

Sources: National Center for Education Statistics, 1984; National Association of Episcopal Schools, 815 Second Avenue, New York, NY 10017.

Comparing Public and Private Schools: 1

Greek Orthodox Schools

In the last fifty years, the number of Greek Americans in the US increased to almost 2 million, and their day schools have grown as well. In 1965, for example, there were thirteen Greek Orthodox day schools in the US with a total attendance of 2205. By 1984, the number of schools almost doubled to twenty-three schools in seven states, and a total of 7590 pupils. In this period, the schools grew in number by 77 per cent, student enrollments by 24 per cent — a great change since 1907 when the Socrates School of Chicago, America's first Greek Orthodox day school, opened.

Each school is attached to a church or cathedral and is supported by the entire Greek-American community. To date, only three high schools have been opened, requiring Greek Orthodox families to place their children in public or other non-Greek secondary schools. Perhaps new schools will be opened, including additional high schools.

Table 7: The Development of Greek Orthodox Day Schools in US, 1965–83

	1965/66	1970/71	1975/76	1980/81	1982/83	Growth (1965–83)
Student Enrollment	2205	3655	3600	6654	5590	24%
Number of Schools	13	18	19	21	23	77%

Source: Greek Orthodox Archdiocese of North and South America, 1983, 10 East 79th Street, New York, NY 10021.

Friends (Quaker) Schools

The Society of Friends founded some of the first private schools in the nation: William Penn himself chartered Friends Select School in 1689. By 1985, the number had grown to sixty-nine schools, with 15,901 enrolled, an increase from 1965 when 10,878 pupils attended thirty-six Quaker schools (see table 8). Friends Schools, then, grew by 77 per cent in number of schools and 27 per cent in enrollment.

Table 8: Growth of Quaker Day Schools, 1965–83

	1965/66	1970/71	1975/76	1980/81	1982/83	Growth (1965–83)
Pupils	10,878	13,706	13,801	13,522	13,853	27%
Schools	36	41	47	51	53	77%

Source: National Center for Education Statistics and Friends Council on Education, 1507 Cherry Street, Philadelphia, PA 19102.

Mennonite Schools

Another of the 'peace' churches (along with the Quakers and Brethren), the Mennonites are followers of the Swiss priest, Huldren Zwingli (1484–1531), an early Anabaptizer (Krallbill, 1978, p. 52). They, like the Quakers, sought religious freedom in Penn's Wood (Pennsylvania). By 1984, some 10,906 children attended 113 schools (7801 pupils in ninety-three elementary schools; 3105 in twenty secondary schools). These numbers were down 18 per cent in pupils and 59 per cent in numbers of schools from 1965/66, in part because of the withdrawal of Amish schools from the Mennonite statistics. Between 1970 and 1984, however, there has been steady growth in enrollment (from 7368 to 10,906) and schools (from eighty-nine to 113). The recent data seem to show a renewed interest in Mennonite education in the US, as shown in table 9.

Table 9: Mennonite School Enrollments, 1965–83

	1965/66	1970/71	1975/76	1980/81	1982/83	Percentage
Totals						
Pupils	13,256	7368	8079	9765	10,906	−17.73
Schools	279	89	93	99	113	−59.50
Elementary						
Pupils	10,947	5172	5589	6778	7,801	−28.74
Schools	267	75	78	81	93	−65.17
Secondary						
Pupils	2,309	2196	2490	2987	3,105	+34.47
Schools	12	14	15	18	20	+66.67

Sources: National Center for Education Statistics, 1984; *Mennonite Yearbook and Directory* Volume 75, 1984; James E. Horsch, Editor, Mennonite Publishing House, Scottsdale, PA.

Special Education Schools

Changes in federal laws and state/local regulations have greatly increased the demands for private schools for children with special intellectual, physical and emotional problems. If the local public schools cannot supply an appropriate school for a special needs child, the family under Public Law 94–142 and other legislation may seek placement in a private, specialized school, even in another state. With public support, then, many of these schools are privately run but publicly financed.

Longitudinal data are not yet available, though it is known that about 300,000 such children are served by about 2600 privately-run schools, some boarding, for special children in 1983; only a few are attending schools affiliated with the National Association of Private Schools for Exceptional Children. These schools play a significant role in helping children who cannot function in the traditional school. Also, since they are heavily subsized, they are an interesting model of total state support, useful perhaps to policymakers and others interested in state-private school relations.

Alternative Schools

In the 1960s, a number of families sought progressive, 'free' school educations, ones that were 'open', 'child-centered', and non-competitive (National Center for Education Statistics, 1983).[8] Today, some twenty years later, while many of the free and freedom schools of the 1960s have closed, a number of these still exist and have contact with the Alternative Schools Network in Chicago. The Network produced a list of 128 existing private free schools in 1983, down from 467 such schools in 1975, the peak year. While many closed, and some joined the public school system as alternative or magnet schools, a number survived and have even become larger and more established.

Military Schools

Prior to the Vietnam war, a number of families sought military academies for the education of their sons (and now their daughters). During the 1960s and 1970s, it appears that many of these academies either closed or went 'civilian', dropping many of the trappings of military life (commandants, usually a general, cadets, etc.). Though exact longitudinal data are not available, discussions with the Association of Military Colleges and Schools indicate the existence of thirty-six military schools, mostly in the South and Midwest, of which ten are coeducational, with girls as day students (they go home at night) and boys as boarders. Total enrollment was about 10,000. Today, these schools appear to be more popular as discipline and patriotism seem more acceptable in US education.

Calvinist Schools

Calvinist schools are affiliated with Christian Schools International, formerly the National Union of Christian Schools. Brought to the US by the Dutch, Calvinist churches and schools are today associated with Christian reform congregations, and are run by 'parent societies', *not* churches. As shown in table 10, Calvinist schools lost ground between 1965 and 1975; though by 1983, they had climbed back to a higher total of 382 schools and 74,541 pupils, up from the 1975 low of 211 schools, 48,585 students. Overall, from 1965 to 1983, however, Calvinist schools showed a 78 per cent growth in number of schools and a 45 per cent increase in enrollments.

Table 10: Growth Among Calvinist Day Schools, 1965–83

	1965/66	*1970/71*	*1975/76*	*1980/81*	*1982/83*	Growth (1965–83)
Schools	234	222	211	217	382	+78%
Students	51,240	51,182	48,585	51,845	74,541	+45%

Sources: Christian Schools International, *Directory 1983–84*, 3350 E. Paris Avenue, S.E., P.O. Box 8709, Grand Rapids, MI 49508; Dr Michael T. Ruiter, Executive Director; and the National Center for Education Statistics, 1983.

Evangelical Christian Schools

The explosion of interest in Fundamentalist Christianity has led to a phenomenal growth in Evangelical Christian schools, some claiming that they open at the rate of one per day. This break with public schools is important, since these Protestants had long been loyal supporters of the local public system. Such a break with the past signals, according to James C Carper, 'a collapse of consensus concerning the basic nature and function of our institutions and the values, traditions, and purposes undergirding them' (Carper, 1983, p. 135).[9] Parents now see public schools as too secular and un-Christian, and are seeking refuge in their own Fundamentalist academies with other 'born-again' families.

Exact data over time are not available. From our survey and search in twenty-two sample counties, extrapolated to the entire nation, we came up with 10,741 Fundamentalist schools, with a total enrollment of 912,985 in 1983/84. These figures tend to concur with surveys by other scholars,[10] and the numbers have continued to increase in the last three years, putting the number close to a million children in nearly 12,000 schools more recently. These schools tend to be small, decentralized and totally autonomous: that is, not usually affiliated with a national body.

Assembly of God

A sect of Evangelical Protestants, this group now reports having 200 schools with 10,212 pupils in 1984, according to NCES. Again, we have no reliable long-term data on these schools, though we assume that they have many of the qualities of other Fundamentalist schools.

American Montessori Schools

Montessori schools began as primarily a pre-school program, which recently has expanded into the primary and elementary grades. Based on the philosophy and practices of Maria Montessori, these schools have expanded from 485 to 640 schools between 1983 and 1985, with an estimated elementary school population increase from 40,000 to 50,000.

Mega-Trends

What do these changes mean for private education and for the future of schooling in the US? What patterns and trends emerge from these data? Here are the major changes that these data illustrate.

From Catholic to Diverse

It seems clear that the American private school sector has been re-defined in the last two decades or so. What was previously a Roman Catholic, ethnic, and immigrant phenomenon, with nine out of ten children in that sector attending Catholic schools in 1960, has now become highly diverse. As shown in table 11, while Catholic schools decreased in number by 30 per cent and showed losses of 46 per cent in enrollments from 1965 to 1983, the non-Catholic private schools showed extensive growth: leaders included Jewish schools 66 per cent, Lutherans 31 per cent, Adventists 49 per cent, Greek Orthodox 77 per cent, Fundamentalist 223 per cent in number of schools and even stronger showings in pupil growth: Lutherans 35 per cent, Jews 37 per cent, Episcopal 32 per cent, and Evangelical 627 per cent. In fact, only the Mennonite and Roman Catholic schools registered a loss, while the other types of private schools expanded.

Table 11: The Demographic Diversity of US Private Schools by Type (1965–83)

	1965/66 Students	1965/66 Schools	1970/71 Students	1970/71 Schools	1975/76 Students	1975/76 Schools	1980/81 Students	1980/81 Schools	1982/83 Students	1982/83 Schools	Percentage growth/decline: 1965 to 1983 Students	Percentage growth/decline: 1965 to 1983 Schools
1. Roman Catholic	5,574,354	13,292	4,361,007	10,841	3,363,979	11,352	3,106,378	9,560	3,027,317	9,432	−46%	−29
Lutheran Total:	(208,209)	(1,896)	(202,362)		(212,908)		(140,701)		280,539	(2,480)	+35%	+31
2. Amer. Lutheran Church	8,795	147	9,926	154	16,121	159	25,873	318	31,284	376	+256%	+155
3. Missouri Synod	171,966	1,364	163,386	1,207	165,604	1,225	182,684	1,460	198,061	1,603	+15%	+18
4. Evangelical Lutheran	—	—	—	—	—	—	5,111	—	5,144	37	—	—
5. Wisc. Evang. Lutheran	27,448	239	29,050	255	31,183	304	32,144	—	35,550	391	+30%	+14
Jewish Total:	(73,112)	(345)	(13,106)	(417)	(91,533)	(483)	(96,173)	(543)	(100,202)	(572)	+37%	+66
6. Orthodox Jewish	68,800	321	75,221	378	82,203	427	84,201	477	86,321	497	+25%	+55
7. Conservative Jewish	3,489	19	7,042	34	7,965	50	10,546	59	12,341	68	+254%	+258
8. Reform Jewish	823	5	843	5	1,345	6	1,431	7	1,540	7	+87%	+40
9. Seventh Day Adventist	64,252	884	72,106	994	74,938	1,115	74,615	1,280	81,507	1,324	+27%	+49
10. Independent NAIS	199,329	697	221,216	769	277,406	774	294,985	809	336,797	873	+69%	+25
11. Episcopal	59,437	347	74,892	459	76,436		76,388	320	78,214	527	+32%	+52
12. Greek Orthodox	2,205	13	3,655	18	13,603		5,311		7,590	23	+24%	+77
13. Friends (Quaker)	10,878	36	13,706	41	13,801		13,522	51	13,853	53	+27%	+47
14. Mennonite	13,256	276	7,368		8,079		9,705	99	10,906	113	−18%	−39
15. Special Education	NA		NA		7,853		101,213		298,999	2,600	—	—
16. Alternative	125		13,142	625	23,498	895	—		11,592	128	—	+0.4
17. Military	NA		NA		13,609		12,117	520	9,792	36	—	—
18. Calvinist (CSI)[a]	51,240		51,182	222	48,585	211	51,845	217	74,541	382	+45%	+78
19. Evangelical[b]	110,300		254,211		344,200		759,425	7,459	912,985	10,741	+627%	+223
20. Assembly of God	3,110		7,462	60	21,921	155	9,343	160	10,212	173	+228%	—
21. Montessori	—		—		—		40,000	485	50,000	640	—	—
							Total:		5,305,041	30,097		

Notes
[a] Christian Schools International
[b] Evangelical is a category of self-confessed, 'born again' Christian schools, such as Baptist, Methodist which have indicated a Fundamentalist ideal.
Sources: National Center for Education Statistics, The Condition of Education (1983); National Catholic Education Association.

An analysis of the various parts of the private sector provides a look at the changing make-up of non-public school types in the US. Table 12, for example, shows the growth in the non-Catholic private schools (row 3), in contrast to the drop in the Catholic schools, a loss of 46 per cent for Catholics versus a 186 per cent increase in non-Catholic private schools. The total private sector enrollments shrank because of the size and contraction of Catholic schools. The relationship among types was also restructured, as table 13 illustrates.

Table 12:   *Private School Enrollments Totals by Type, 1965–1983*

	1965/66	1970/71	1975/76	1980/81	1982/83	Change (1965–83)
Total Private Schools:	6,369,807	5,365,415	4,592,349	4,764,946	5,305,041	−17%
Catholic Schools:	5,574,354	4,361,007	3,363,979	3,106,378	3,027,312	−46%
Non-Catholic Schools	795,453	1,004,408	1,228,370	1,748,568	2,277,729	+186%

Sources: National Center for Education Statistics, 1984; in addition, data from national groups and other surveys.

Table 13:   *Distribution of Private Schools and Students Among Sectors, 1983*

By type	Students	Percentage of total sector	Schools	Percentage of total sector
Roman Catholic	3,027,312	57	9,432	31
Protestant Church Related	1,470,347	28	15,816	53
Jewish Sponsored	100,202	2	572	2
No Religious Affiliation	707,180	13	4,277	14
TOTAL:	5,305,041	100%	30,097	100%

Schools with religious versus no religious affiliations:

	Students	Percentage sector	Schools	Percentage sector
Religious affiliation:	4,597,861	87%	25,820	86%
No religious affiliations:	707,180	13%	4,277	14%

Source: National Center for Education Statistics, 1984.

Comparing Catholic, Protestant, Jewish and Not Religiously Affiliated, one sees that 57 per cent of private *enrollments* are Catholic (down from 88 per cent in 1960), while Protestant-sponsored schools reached 28 per cent, Jewish 2 per cent, and Not Religiously Affiliated 13 per cent. The data are even more graphic when examining numbers and percentage of private *school* types: Catholic, 31 per cent; Protestant now 53 per cent, the largest; Jewish, 2 per cent; and not affiliated with religion, 14 per cent. Hence, the majority of private schools in the US have a Protestant affiliation, although the Protestant schools are much smaller in size than the Catholic ones. The former have an average enrollment of less than 100 students. It is also worth noting that only 13 per cent of the pupils and 14 per cent of the schools are not religiously related. It is clear, then, that American private schools are now predominantly religious and Protestant — not Catholic as was once the case.

The private school picture is now more diverse with a greater balance among the variety of religious, social and ethnic and class groups, twenty-one different types, most of which have grown recently. It seems obvious, too, that religious reasons are most prominent in explaining the sponsorship and attendance at non-public schools, with 86 per cent of the schools attended by 87 per cent of the nation's private school pupils going to religiously sponsored schools. Hence, we can no longer read 'Roman Catholic' when one hears 'private', though Catholic schools were still enrolling 57 per cent of the pupils, in only 31 per cent of the private schools, in 1983.

From Eastern and Urban to Everywhere and Rural

Private schools are no longer located predominantly in ethnic, urban and industrial centers of the East and Great Lakes. Christian academies are found in many small towns previously unacquainted with non-public schools. Tables 14 and 15 show schools and pupils by state in 1980. California now has more private schools than New York, though New York has more pupils in private schools and many.more Catholic schools: New York, 1907 schools, 1085 Catholic; California, 2415 schools, only 731 Catholic. As for enrollments, table 15 shows New York leading but slightly with 580,000 students, of whom about 500,000 are in Catholic schools. The South, long a place with very few non-public schools, has seen these schools mushroom. North Carolina, for one, has nearly 300 private schools, but again, few Catholic ones: thirty-eight Catholic (13 per cent), seventy-five Baptist

Table 14: Approximate Distribution of Private Schools by State, 1980

	TOTAL [a]	Not Church-Related	Total Church-Related	Baptist	Catholic	Christian	Episcopal	Jewish	Lutheran	Seventh Day Advntst.	Other Church-Related
UNITED STATES	20,764	4,722	16,042	1,075	9,509	651	320	386	1,534	1,083	1,484
Alabama	249	94	155	33	53	13	4	1	13	15	23
Alaska	36	4	32	4	7	7	0	0	2	8	4
Arizona	221	93	128	6	54	9	4	4	19	16	16
Arkansas	114	29	85	7	35	2	4	0	3	20	14
California	2,415	860	1,555	127	731	152	38	35	146	141	185
Colorado	228	70	158	16	68	6	1	6	22	26	13
Connecticut	333	94	239	1	198	4	8	9	5	7	7
Delaware	82	22	60	9	30	4	1	1	0	2	13
District of Columbia	93	40	53	2	39	1	5	0	0	2	4
Florida	824	303	521	105	184	35	32	17	45	44	59
Georgia	334	154	180	58	37	22	2	4	5	32	20
Hawaii	114	37	77	8	36	6	5	0	5	10	7
Idaho	46	2	44	1	13	2	0	0	5	18	5
Illinois	1,318	236	1,082	28	769	24	2	16	175	32	36
Indiana	482	38	444	31	228	20	2	3	56	20	84
Iowa	287	17	270	5	171	2	0	1	26	17	48
Kansas	185	26	159	1	111	6	1	1	22	11	6
Kentucky	286	41	245	20	190	10	2	1	1	10	11
Louisiana	437	108	329	18	248	4	15	1	11	15	17
Maine	113	59	54	9	25	6	0	1	0	5	8
Maryland	371	89	282	9	190	8	12	10	19	18	16

State											
Massachusetts	513	155	358	3	317	4	3	11	0	14	6
Michigan	883	93	790	64	393	21	3	4	164	63	78
Minnesota	483	39	444	21	250	17	2	2	116	17	19
Mississippi	168	80	88	11	47	5	8	0	0	10	7
Missouri	558	68	490	9	334	8	1	2	69	17	50
Montana	78	11	67	3	26	1	0	0	4	15	18
Nebraska	227	8	219	2	130	2	1	1	64	15	4
Nevada	38	8	30	3	14	3	0	1	3	5	1
New Hampshire	102	35	67	10	38	5	3	0	0	3	8
New Jersey	829	180	649	10	553	10	3	27	11	14	21
New Mexico	110	33	77	7	38	8	1	2	2	10	9
New York	1,907	415	1,492	42	1,085	20	26	173	51	40	55
North Carolina	293	109	184	75	38	14	6	2	7	24	18
North Dakota	64	7	57	0	39	0	0	0	5	10	3
Ohio	871	64	807	22	619	22	1	12	35	25	71
Oklahoma	82	10	72	2	32	6	5	1	7	12	7
Oregon	183	41	142	6	63	8	1	17	6	45	12
Pennsylvania	1,627	273	1,354	47	899	59	13	2	16	26	277
Rhode Island	117	28	89	1	77	1	2	1	1	0	5
South Carolina	203	91	112	40	29	15	7	0	5	4	11
South Dakota	108	28	80	2	32	7	1	4	11	11	16
Tennessee	290	89	201	40	52	8	7	8	7	47	36
Texas	659	93	566	40	289	13	62	0	63	48	43
Utah	26	8	18	0	9	0	0	0	3	5	1
Vermont	62	39	23	1	14	1	2	2	0	5	0
Virginia	361	159	202	46	70	7	20	1	11	22	24
Washington	330	77	253	17	96	20	3	0	22	54	40
West Virginia	85	5	80	14	44	6	0	1	0	13	3
Wisconsin	909	56	853	35	458	17	1	1	268	28	45

Source: National Center for Education Statistics, 1984.

Table 15: Enrollment in Private Elementary and Secondary Schools by Affiliation of Schools and by State, 1979–1980

States	Grand Total	Non-Church Related Private	Total: Church-Related	Roman Catholic	Non-Catholic Religions
	5,084,030	820,360	4,263,670	3,315,010	948,660
Alabama	62,709	24,683	38,026	14,720	23,306
Alaska	3,815	583	3,232	1,029	2,203
Arizona	40,986	11,848	29,138	18,308	10,830
Arkansas	19,424	6,196	13,228	7,223	6,005
California	513,709	103,134	410,575	362,690	47,885
Colorado	36,750	7,757	28,993	17,120	11,873
Connecticut	88,404	21,005	67,399	41,780	25,619
Delaware	33,374	4,282	19,022	14,723	4,299
District of Columbia	21,703	4,836	16,867	12,314	4,553
Florida	204,988	60,084	144,904	94,208	50,696
Georgia	82,538	49,483	33,055	13,297	19,758
Hawaii	47,146	13,165	34,981	18,069	16,912
Idaho	8,859	377	8,482	2,189	6,293
Illinois	356,463	28,782	328,681	278,240	50,441
Indiana	100,934	7,433	93,501	83,237	10,267
Iowa	85,237	1,352	83,885	44,790	39,095
Kansas	33,889	3,814	30,075	28,810	1,265
Kentucky	89,728	11,033	78,795	60,226	18,569
Louisiana	158,923	30,178	128,745	112,098	16,647
Maine	17,540	8,002	9,538	8,733	805
Maryland	106,948	18,359	88,589	68,168	20,421
Massachusetts	138,343	28,405	109,938	104,720	5,218

Michigan	15,588	195,883	129,220	211,471
Minnesota	4,841	84,828	64,418	89,669
Mississippi	30,338	19,780	11,342	50,118
Missouri	8,837	117,482	96,124	126,319
Nebraska	1,367	37,207	30,163	50,574
Nevada	844	5,655	4,309	6,499
New Hampshire	8,866	14,855	11,238	22,721
New Jersey	23,483	206,415	188,876	229,898
New Mexico	5,143	12,884	9,217	18,027
New York	70,894	508,976	428,881	579,870
North Carolina	24,605	33,473	9,323	58,078
North Dakota	1,571	9,088	8,220	10,659
Ohio	14,284	274,083	227,880	288,367
Oklahoma	2,218	14,118	9,381	16,336
Oregon	4,059	33,789	14,287	27,848
Pennsylvania	39,575	372,080	314,389	411,655
Rhode Island	3,843	27,232	25,018	31,075
South Carolina	24,435	24,384	9,883	48,819
South Dakota	1,780	9,116	6,882	10,896
Tennessee	20,784	50,833	18,185	71,617
Texas	17,894	130,940	99,765	148,834
Utah	1,682	3,803	3,088	5,485
Vermont	2,284	4,281	4,062	6,565
Virginia	26,807	48,282	33,080	75,089
Washington	8,901	47,048	37,386	55,949
West Virginia	840	11,758	8,466	12,598
Wisconsin	8,060	158,201	110,014	166,261
Wyoming	750	1,894	1,387	2,654

Source: US Department of Education, National Center for Education Statistics, 1980. Revised figures.

schools, fourteen Christian academies, twenty-four Seventh Day Adventist. Thus, the states with newer and rising private school statistics are less likely to have large Catholic school populations.

This dispersion of non-public schools into virtually every community with 10,000 people, in every state and region has implications for public policies. No longer can legislators and bureaucrats ignore the pleas for help from private schools. The public may no longer sit by quietly; they may demand more involvement and choice. Public schools too are forced to confront the loss of patrons to private schools.

From Decline to Growth

There can be little doubt that the diversification and growth of private education in the US signals a change. The non-Catholic private sector grew by over 87 per cent in the last fifteen years, with an overall leap from 0.795 million to 2.27 million — up 186 per cent. This growth shows a vigor at the local level, since many or most of these schools are the result of grass-roots community and family effort, not the 'top-down' work of national or regional associations. The private school enterprise is growing, expanding, becoming more diverse and more available to all children in the US. Families everywhere have shown interest.

Figure 1 indicates the enrollment growth and decline starting in 1965 and projected through 1990. School types are grouped by Roman Catholic, non-Catholic private, and total private schools. If the Catholic sector recovers and shows net gains — or even holds constant — and other schools continue their climb, the total private school sector should reach 5.95 million pupils by 1990. Already, the segment of children attending private (versus public) schools has risen from 9 per cent in 1975 to 12 per cent in 1984. So as public schools lose population (down 14 per cent in ten years), the private schools, particularly the non-Catholic portion, are growing. This realignment has important implications for three groups in society: private schools, parents, and policymakers.

Figure 1: Private School Enrollments by Group 1965/1966-1989/1990

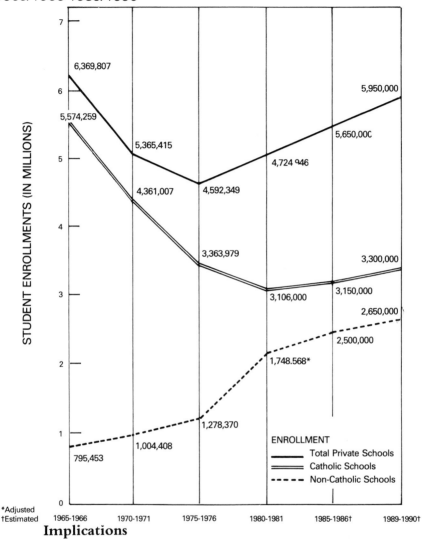

STUDENT ENROLLMENTS (IN MILLIONS)

6,369,807

5,950,000

5,574,259

5,365,415

5,650,000

4,724.946

4,361,007   4,592,349

3,363,979

3,300,000

3,106,000   3,150,000

2,650,000

2,500,000

1,748.568*

1,278,370

ENROLLMENT

1,004,408

795,453

——— Total Private Schools
=== Catholic Schools
- - - - Non-Catholic Schools

*Adjusted
†Estimated   1965-1966   1970-1971   1975-1976   1980-1981   1985-1986†   1989-1990†

Implications

For Private Schools

Changes in the demography of private schools have important implications for various groups in the US. Private schools — their
national, regional, and local leadership — should understand that they
are now part of a burgeoning, vital national movement, one reaching
into almost every hamlet, region, and religious community. Already
in some places, one sees a growing awareness among private schools
of their common identity and concerns: the need for public funds,
dealing with the attempt of states to regulate and control these

41

schools, the effort to attract students, and the relationship with local education authorities. Associations, within and across private school sponsors, are emerging, from the Council for American Private Education (CAPE) in Washington, DC, to separate religious associations (for example, National Catholic Education Association) to newcomers like the Southeastern Association of Christian Schools.

The formation of private school affiliations signals a new phase in private education, a time when their influence grows, and when these schools can find support and help. The exact nature of these relationships and associations is yet to be investigated systematically. Research on the formation, activities, and influence of the growing private sector is a fruitful area of study. As the number of new, unassociated schools increases, what are the ways in which other similar schools reach out and communicate with these schools? What is the nature of relationships among private schools and the authorities? And what happens to the newer-type Christian academies, and other private schools as they increase in size and structure? Do they tend, as they become older and more established, to associate with one another and to form organizations for cooperative efforts? These and other questions need exploration, as we come to understand the increase in non-public elementary and secondary schools.

For Parents

Parents appear to be presented with a larger number of options in schooling their children both in terms of kinds of private education and in location. In turn, parents may be treating both the private and public schools as a kind of 'educational marketplace', selecting among numerous types of schools in both sectors, depending on the needs, talents, abilities, and expectations of their children.

This change in parental outlook has come about in part because more public schools are adopting private-school techniques of advertising, attempting to attract talented and able children, and representing themselves to the public clearly and forcefully. Private schools, meanwhile, are seen more and more as a 'public good', an available choice to an increasingly broad group of families. In effect, then, the dividing line between 'private' and 'public' diminishes with private schools fulfilling public services and public schools being more competitive and special. This merging is bolstered somewhat by the sense that all education is both *private* (a commitment to personal growth and development) and *public* (contributing to the commonweal, economic productivity, and national expansion). Public 'magnet schools' in large cities are often exclusive, even elite programs, taking the most academically talented students, or the most artistically talented, the best athletes, and most committed. Private schools, too, have this magnet quality, using many of the same criteria for admissions.

The changing make-up, size and location of private schools in the US clearly signals that more parents everywhere are seeking private alternatives, are exercising their rights to select among private (and public) schools. And in so doing, they are creating more options for families. Today, even within the same family, one sees siblings attending a variety of private and public schools, depending on (a) family resources; (b) the talents, abilities, and needs of the children; (c) the availability of options; (d) the preferences of the children themselves; and (e) the values and beliefs of the parents. Such a mix, diversity, and availability for families are certainly new developments in American life. This state of universal diversity has been reached in many locations, if our data on the spread of private schools are any indication. Growing entrepreneurship, drive, and receptiveness among parents, churches, synagogues, and communities have offered more options to families and their children than ever before.

While we have evidence that families are exercising choice among numerous public and private school options, additional research is necessary on how families balance costs, distance, programs, religious values, and academic qualities in selecting schools for their children. Buying education is the largest single activity that society accomplishes — consuming more funds than any other government service except health; yet we know very little about how the key decision-makers — parents — reach their determination as to schools. And as more private schools are available, the options grow. With the availability of public support for non-public schools, family choice could become more important in the years to come.

For Politicians and Policymakers

Finally, this restructuring, expansion, and newfound strength of US private schools has implications for the political process. Groups traditionally committed to public schools (Fundamentalist Christians, Jews, the middle class) appear to be using private schools more extensively. For example, more than 100,000 Jewish children are now in Jewish all-day schools, and nearly a million pupils attend Fundamentalist Christian academies. Both groups were bedrock supporters of the local public schools as roads to equality of educational opportunity. Their appeal to private options cannot easily be ignored by politicians.

Much research needs to be done to trace the political power of private education in shaping the laws that govern the way private schools are regulated, funded, and operated. Already, we see the states creating offices of non-public education, within state departments of education. Private schools are being granted greater autonomy in some places, often a response to the lobbying of private school groups for control over their own destinies. Yet, in other places, states and their private schools become locked in struggle, with the courts called in to settle the issue. In Ohio, for example, a fundamentalist school refused to follow the extensive state regulations, arguing that to be in compliance would rob the Christian school of the freedom and time to carry out its religious mission. The US Supreme Court, in *Whisner*, ruled that in balancing the responsibility of the state against the freedom of the school to maintain its unique program, the school could ignore some of the state requirements, if they obviated the nature of the religious program and thus the school.

Once certain policies are established, how do they affect the operation and quality of private schools? For example, since Minnesota has a 'tuition tax deduction' scheme in effect, what impact is that form of aid having on the composition and resources of non-public schools in that state? By implication, we could learn about possible results of such a program nationwide under a policy of federal tax support for participants in private schooling.

As the political power and unity of private schools grows, and as private *and* public school groups begin to realize that they have much in common (resources for children), perhaps they can work together to lobby for better financing of schools at state and national levels. The image of the leaders of, say, the National Catholic Education Association and the National Education Association, marching on Capitol Hill for increased help for schools — all schools — is not too far-fetched. A combined public-private front for education — just the way private and public universities work now — has tremendous possibilities.

The US is a different place, educationally and socially, because of the introduction of private schools into virtually every community. What had once been ethnic and Catholic now takes on a universal, small-town Southern and Western flavor. The spread of non-public schools reminds us of the energy and vision that built the common public schools in the nineteenth century: local folks starting schools for their children in their local communities, schools reflecting their own beliefs and values. And this new energy and dedication to non-public schools may indicate a shift in political power, public funding, and general public concern — and the probability of greater public scrutiny and regulation of private schools. These trends have just begun; they require deliberation and study. But we see already how changes in private schools have altered the nation's educational landscape, the allegiances of families, and the religious, spiritual, not to mention the academic, life of children.

Notes

1 A number of important books and articles have appeared in the last few years on private education, public policies, and related issues. See GAFFNEY, 1981; ERICKSON, 1969; KRAUSHAAR, 1972; and CARPER and HUNT, 1984.

2 Prior systematic efforts include ERICKSON, NAULT and COOPER, 1978; see also NATIONAL CENTER FOR EDUCATION STATISTICS, 1981, 1982, 1983, pp. 63, 65, 67 and 71 (1981 edn), 45, 53 and 55 (1982 edn), and 17 and 19 (1983 edn); and McLAUGHLIN and BAKKE, 1981.

3 See also ERICKSON, 1986; and McLAUGHLIN, 1981 and 1983.

4 See also, McCLUSKY, 1969; BURNS and KOHLBRENNER, 1937; and SANDERS, 1976.

5 For a treatment of this controversy, see GREELEY and others, 1976; GREELEY, 1982; COLEMAN, HOFFER and KILGORE, 1981; CIBULKA, O'BRIEN and ZEWE, 1982; and MANNO and COOPER, 1983.

6 In 1983, for example, there was net growth in both schools and pupils in a number of areas. The elementary level saw increases in twenty-one dioceses/archdioceses, twelve states, and one region. Secondary school growth occurred in twenty-seven (out of 165 dioceses) and eleven states. For an analysis, see COOPER *et al.*, 1983.

7 The history of Hotchkiss School is most informative; it was started by the leadership of Yale College to secure a steady flow of elite, well-educated children, through a gift from Maria Hotchkiss. It was originally to be called Yale Preparatory School, but was named after the Hotchkiss family.

8 For treatments of the free school movement, see DUKE, 1978; COOPER, 1969; GRAUBARD, 1972; and COOPER, 1973.

9 See also LANOUETTE, 1977; LOWRIE, 1971; and OSTLING, 1977.

10 Carper, too, estimated a total of some 900,000 children in Evangelical Christian schools.

3 Private School Participation and Public Policy

James S. Catterall

This chapter probes patterns of enrollment in American private elementary and secondary schools. Persistent controversy over the numbers and characteristics of private schoolers is one source of interest. Another is the importance of such information for discussions of public policies involving non-public schools. My hope is to remap some of these disputed territories.

I begin with a brief discussion of why private schools have captured legislative and research attention, and identify a number of questions central to the concerns of these communities. I then discuss a comprehensive and longitudinal picture of the diverse private school sector in the United States and offer an interpretation of what the reported trends may mean for potential public policy enactments; at issue is our understanding of such proposals as tuition tax relief, public vouchers for private schools, and other forms of assistance and regulation. I then address several characteristics of school participation in the United States, particularly the incomes and racial and ethnic backgrounds of families who enroll their children in private as opposed to public schools. Also provided is information about tuition costs for private schools and recent tuition trends in comparison to changes in price and income levels. And I discuss regional patterns of school participation. I conclude with some thoughts about a research agenda which would augment what is reported here.

Why Private School Research

Events over the past few years have encouraged the efforts of re-searchers and their sponsors to understand more fully the world of private schools in the United States.[1] Of most importance are consistent efforts in the Congress and at the state level to provide some sort of financial assistance to private schools. Proposals for tuition tax benefits have passed state legislatures and the United States Senate and are supported by the Reagan Administration (Catterall, 1983a). A tuition tax deduction in Minnesota was recently upheld in the US Supreme Court (*Mueller v. Allen*, 1983). Education voucher plans have had less success but seem to crop up periodically, most often as proposed voter initiatives (Catterall, 1984). In addition, aid to private schools in the form of textbooks and transportation or other assistance is provided in some thirty states and is on the agenda in others. Along with public assistance, the regulatory relations between governments and private schools are of current legislative interest, an example being proposals which would limit the tax-exempt status of private schools for one reason or another.

Also engendering interest in private schools has been our national preoccupation with 'excellence in education', which was spawned by, or at least coincided with, the issuance of numerous critical national commission reports and published research-based indictments in the early 1980s.[2] While for the most part not an explicit suggestion of these reports, the idea that our nation's private schools might provide their public cousins with hints about effective schooling has gained some followers. James Coleman's recent comparisons of public and private schools, and the heated controversy surrounding his conclusions, have fueled interest in verifying such beliefs.[3]

Critical Questions in Private School Research

It should surprise noone that policymakers and others grappling with these events have faced less than perfect information when questions are raised. What would the effects of specific proposals be? Who would benefit? What would they cost? Who would pay? What alternatives would serve similar ends? Numerous questions important to policy decisions seem to result more in controversy than consensus as they are posed. We simply have not been focusing on private schools long enough to have refined our information-gathering techniques, nor have we devoted substantial resources to such efforts until recently. Private schools also exhibit varying tendencies to want to remain private — which makes some of our data collection an individualized and problematic process.

I argue in this chapter that information fundamental to understanding many of the critical questions in private school policymaking and research lies in just who participates in our private schools. Basic questions of efficiency and cost, equity, and school effectiveness hinge on who our private school clientele are, who may be considering private over current public choices, and why private school choices are made. The connections between enrollments and these questions are straightforward.

The costs of aid schemes as diverse as tuition tax credits, tuition vouchers, and textbook loans would be expected to vary directly with the size of the eligible private school population. And future costs would depend on private school enrollments in future years. So both current numbers and also past and projected trends in private school enrollments are important information for policy analysts. We also need to know what the effects of policy proposals might be on parental decisions to enroll their children in private versus public schools. Private school aid proposals are likely to have encouraging effects on private school enrollments, since they generally act to reduce what parents must pay for private school attendance, or to reduce the costs of maintaining private schools. The first result makes private schools more affordable for larger numbers of families; the latter, other things being equal, has a dampening effect on what schools must charge for a given set of offerings.

Primary questions of benefit of public policies for private schools are also tied to current and projected enrollment characteristics. A tax credit, tuition voucher, or other form of material assistance would go first to those in private schools now, since these families have already made decisions to attend private schools; and newly provided government help, per se, is not likely to change their minds. (Accompanying government regulations and consequent changes in private schools might suppress or enhance enrollments, however.) So we must know who attends private schools — children living where, and with what backgrounds, and attending what types of schools — to know something of the pattern of benefits of proposed policies. An awareness of trends in these areas would lead to informed assessment of future patterns of benefits.

Finally, since our private school world is so diverse, and since specific parts of that world may have distinctly different patterns of interaction with our governments (for constitutional or other reasons), we need some fine-grained detail in our understanding of private school participation in our society. Publicly assisting or regulating private schools can be considered in some monolithic abstract, but doing so hides much of what we might like to know about specific policy creations. For example, what sorts of education would be encouraged or discouraged and for whom by proposed schemes? Or would participation in assistance plans be constitutional for all schools or only for some of them because of church affiliations or specific practices of given schools? I turn now to some facts and figures which inform such questions.

Beyond the 'Universe' of Private Schools

I begin where another contributor to this volume leaves off in his discussion of the universe of American private schools. Table 1 catalogues Bruce Cooper's estimates of private school attendance, and also shows patterns of total school enrollments, both private and public, for purposes of comparison (Cooper, 1985). The first year shown, 1965/66, recorded an all-time high in American private school enrollments, about 6.4 million; ten years later, 1975/76, marked the end of a steady enrollment decline which followed the earlier peak, and also marked the beginning of a period of sustained private school growth which has continued to the present time; figures for 1980 and 1983 confirm the renewed popularity of private schools in our society. These estimates benefit from Cooper's sampling of geographical regions and canvassing of school associations for an exhaustive count of schools and pupils across the nation. The current total, roughly 5 million youngsters in private schools, exceeds US Census Bureau estimates of private school enrollments by about 18 per cent for reasons which he discusses, and it is probably a more accurate accounting (see the chapter by Cooper in this volume). However, even though more than 12 per cent of school children are now reported to be in private schools, present enrollments in the private sector are nearly a fourth lower than their historical high of twenty years ago.

Over these same years, private and public school enrollments have behaved very differently. While private schools were losing nearly 30 per cent of their clients in the ten years after 1965, total school enrollments inched up by about 3 per cent and public school enrollments gained almost 8 per cent. Beyond 1975, the trends reversed themselves. Private school enrollments have increased by about 14 per cent, while total enrollments dropped by 14 per cent and public school enrollments declined by more than 17 per cent.

Table 1 also presents figures for particular types of schools. Several points deserve comment. Twenty years ago, the Catholic schools enrolled 87 per cent of the nearly 6.5 million private school

Table 1:   Enrollments in Private American Schools and All Schools, Selected Years, by type of
School (1000s)

Type of School	1965/66	1975/76	1980/81	1982/83	Percentage changes 1975–82
Roman Catholic	5574 (87% of total)	3363	3106	3027 (58% of total)	−10
Lutheran	208	213	240	281	+32
Jewish	73	91	96	100	+10
Evangelical	110	344	759	913	+165
Other religious affiliates	236	267	229	272	+2
Total Affiliated	6201 (97%)	4278	4430	4593 (87%)	+7
Non-Affiliated Indep. NAIS*	199	277	295	337	+22
Special Education	NA**	8	101	299	+3637
Other***	NA**	37	24	21	−43
Total Non-Affiliated	199 (3%)	322	420	657 (13%)	+104
Grand Total Private	6,400 (100%)	4,600	4,850	5,250 (100%)	+14
Total K-12 Enrollment	48,430	49,791	43,742	42,590	−14
Private (% of total)	13.2	9.3	11.1	12.3	

Notes:
*   Includes some schools with religious affiliations, mostly Protestant.
**   No data available.
*** Includes military and alternative schools (Casper definition).
Sources: Cooper, B. (1985). 'The Changing Universe of US Private Schools', Report P/NP-
12, Stanford University, Institute for Research on Educational Finance and
Governance, November Total enrollments from US Bureau of the Census, October
Population Surveys (cited in Noell, 1984) and NCES, *The Condition of Education*,
(1984), p. 14.

children in the United States, while religious schools together
accounted for 97 per cent of all private attendance. Due largely to a
precipitous and continuing decline in Catholic school enrollments,
religious schools now enroll 87 per cent of our private school youngsters, while Catholic schools account for only 58 per cent. The decline
of Catholic schools and the rise of just about every other type of
school over the two decades have resulted in what appears to be an
increasingly diverse private school sector, with stronger religious
school contingents in non-Catholic denominations, and steady growth
of non-affiliated schools. Among other things, this means that
although private schools are not so absolutely dominated by religious

institutions as they once were, private schooling in America is still very much a religious phenomenon, and public policy connections between governments and private schools will, for the foreseeable future, include significant issues of church-state relations. This is consistent with findings that religious inclinations rank highly as reasons why private schools are chosen (Gratiot, 1979).

We also see in table 1 that the evangelical Christian schools have grown rapidly, approaching a million youngsters and now second in size only to the Catholics among our types of schools. And another substantial contributor to private school growth in recent years is the rise of private special education schools which now enroll nearly half of all non-affiliated private school children.

Implications of These Patterns

The most salient features of American private school life seem to be its increasing popularity, particularly when viewed alongside public school enrollment declines, and its increasing diversity, which Cooper discusses at length in his chapter. More importance is probably attributed to the increasing privatization of schooling in recent years than to other specific trends in our world of private and public schools. Our data indeed show an increase in the fraction of American youngsters choosing private schools. Here I offer some observations about both global and specific patterns outlined above.

Analysts have suggested that a critical source of support for education, America's economically advantaged families, are increasingly opting for private schools; some claim that private schools have generally grown to the point where societal consensus undergirding current public schooling arrangements is seriously threatened.

To begin, for purposes of examining who may be leaving public schools for what reasons, it is justifiable to think about the nation's children involved in special education programs as a distinct group. New laws have made private special education services more available to all children, often at public expense when locally available public services are not deemed appropriate (Hartman, 1981). Any general trend toward choosing private as opposed to public schools should probably not be confused with movements to private special education services which are generally supported by the same public authorities.

Table 2 outlines an interpretation of enrollment shifts to private schools in recent years. The actual increase in regular private school enrollments over the past seven years amounts to about 350,000 pupils nationwide. As such, enrollments in these private schools have increased by about 50,000 pupils, or by about 1 per cent per year. Even if all of this increase were to represent public schoolers switching to private schools, the fraction of current public school children involved amounts to about a tenth of one per cent. Also shown in table 2 are analogous figures based on estimated increases in private school enrollments over the past two years; if the estimates presented are accurate, private schools have recently gained pupils at a higher pace — about 100,000 pupils per year. Even this amounts to no more than two or three tenths of a per cent of public schoolers 'abandoning' their schools. The flow of youngsters from public to private schools appears to be a trickle and not a flood.

Table 2: *'Flight' to American Private Schools, 1975/76 to 1982/83 (excluding special education)*

School year and change measures		Enrollments (in 1000s) and enrollment changes
I 1975/76 private enrollments		4,600
1980/81 private enrollments		4,750
1982/83 private enrollments		4,950
II 7-year change: 1975–82	Numbers	350
	Percent	7.6
	Annualized Change	1.1%
III 2-year change: 1980–82	Numbers	200
	Percent	4.2
	Annualized Change	2.1%
IV Public school population 1982/83		37,385(a)
Projected additional private schoolers		
per year — 7-year trend		50,000
— 2-year trend		100,000
V Fraction of public schoolers		
switching to private schools		
per year — 7-year trend		.0013
— 2-year trend		.0027

Sources: Calculations from Table 1; (a) US Bureau of the Census, Current Population Reports, 1982 (cited in Noell, 1984), p. 17.

There is an additional reason to suspect that even the observed and small growth of private schools over the past few years may not be sustained with its current strength into the future. Clearly, the dominant element in the growth of private schools has been the growth of the evangelical Christian schools. In fact, without the roughly 600,000 additional Christian schoolers enrolling over the past seven years, the absolute growth of regular private education during this time (by about 300,000 pupils) would be turned into a loss of similar magnitude.

I contacted representatives of the nation's two largest Christian school associations — the American Association of Christian Schools and the Association of Christian Schools International — to check on their impressions of their schools' growth.[4] Feelings were mixed about the likely continuance of recent pupil gains in these schools. On the one hand, it was reported that requests for association assistance in establishing schools continues at high levels, and that the numbers of potential clients — the nation's 50 million or more practicing Protestant evangelicals — have only begun to be tapped for participation in Christian schools. On the other hand, some slowing down of growth in this sector was reported. Reasons cited were the exhaustion of the pool of families most ready to establish new schools and a decline of interest in the establishment of Accelerated Christian Education (ACE) type schools. These latter schools are based on a packaged set of curriculum materials and require very little in the way of specialized facilities, equipment or personnel. Both associations report a trend toward more teacher-centered and traditional types of education within the Christian schools, and these schools are more difficult to establish. Our data show a slight deceleration of Christian school growth — down to an added 77,000 children per year in the past two years from 83,000 in each of the previous five — but this change is probably smaller than our errors of estimate for these figures. There is no question, however, that in percentage terms there has been a dramatic decline in the growth of Christian school enrollments, from nearly 25 per cent per year in 1976 to about 9 per cent in 1983.

The fact remains that public schools have lost pupils in recent years and private schools have grown. If these patterns are sustained into the future, the private sector will hold increasing shares of the school market, and the societal importance of public policies for private education will be enhanced commensurately. We do know, on the basis of currently known demographics, that the numbers of school-age children will begin a sustained period of increase in 1985 (Plisko, 1984, p. 14). By 1992 total enrollments will have increased by about 5 per cent. As I point out when I suggest a research agenda, the school choice patterns of the families contributing to the current surge of childbirths will have much to do with upcoming changes in the comparative sizes of the public and private school sectors.

Characteristics of Private School Participation

In previous sections, I have described overall enrollment patterns and trends in American private schools. Here I examine patterns within the larger picture. Where are the private schools, what are the backgrounds of families who send their children to them, and what do families pay for private schools? Most of the data for these presentations have been obtained from the October reports of school enrollments compiled annually by the US Census Bureau. These data reflect the results of annual surveys of samples of American families. As mentioned earlier, the total private school enrollments estimated in these surveys seem to undercount actual figures by about 18 per cent. Nevertheless, the methods used to gather information have been uniformly applied over the past dozen years, and these data adequately reveal general distributions and trends in private school participation. No attempt has been made to gauge the nature of any bias introduced by this undercounting on our estimates of family characteristic distributions. Cooper's work seems to suggest that it is the smaller, newer schools which are neglected in attempts to estimate enrollment, and that the evangelical Christian schools and their families might be underrepresented in the Census Bureau data (see the chapter by Cooper in this volume). Just why families patronizing these schools might be systematically undercounted or less responsive to surveys in the Census Bureau's sampling strategies is unknown.

Elementary Versus Secondary Participation

Private schooling is more popular at the elementary than secondary levels. As shown in table 3, higher percentages of youngsters at lower grade levels attend private schools — varying from over 14 per cent of kindergarteners and more than 11 per cent of first through sixth graders, down to about 7 per cent of high schoolers. Why this pattern exists may have something to do with the fact that private elementary schools are much cheaper (see subsequent section) and for reasons of curricular simplicity easier to establish by such institutions as church parishes; it may also be due to parental desires for specific educational experiences in their children's early years to provide a foundation for public secondary school experiences. In any event, public policies which have an impact on private schools generally will have larger effects on elementary schooling than on secondary schooling, other things being equal.

Table 3:   *Private Enrollment by Type of School and Level (in thousands), 1979*

Type of School	K	1–6	Grade Level 7–8	9–12	Total
Public	2,593	18,306	6,450	13,994	41,343
Private	432	2,374	735	1,122	4,663
Private (%)	14.3	11.5	10.2	7.4	10.1

Source: US Bureau of the Census, Current Population Reports, Series P-20, No. 360, Table 14, October 1979.

Geography and Private School Participation

Private schools are not evenly distributed across the United States, nor are they distributed precisely according to where school-age children live. Table 4 shows that private schools are disproportionately popular in the Northeast and North Central regions of the country, and less prevalent in the South and the West. Whereas the Northeast has about 23 per cent of school-age youngsters, it houses 31 to 34 per cent of the nation's private schoolers. Similar figures for other regions are shown, with the South being most underpopulated by private schools — having 31 to 33 per cent of the country's youngsters and only 25 per cent of the private school children.

Table 4:   *Private Versus Total School Enrollment Distributions by Region and Level of School, October 1979*

Region and level of school	Total enrollment share (%)	Private enrollment share (%)
Elementary		
North east	23	31
North central	27	30
South	33	25
West	17	14
	100	100
High School		
North east	23	34
North central	28	28
South	31	25
West	18	13
	100	100

Source: US Bureau of the Census, Current Population Reports, Series P-20, No. 360, Table 14, October 1979.

Regional distributions of private school attendance are more finely dissected in table 5. Here I show not only major geographical regions of the country, but also the community types — central city, suburb, and non-metropolitan areas — and their counts of private school youngsters. I also show figures for both 1979 and for 1982, since an interesting shift may be occurring.

Across the United States, central city families enroll disproportionately high shares of their children in private schools — 16 and 14 per cent in the two years shown versus a national private school enrollment percentage of about 10 per cent. Where private school utilization is high, such as in the Northeast, central city private school attendance rates are commensurate — as high as 20 per cent in 1979. In contrast, non-metropolitan areas of the South and West show private school enrollment shares as low as 3 and 4 per cent of all school children.

These general patterns held up over the three-year period shown (and have been evident throughout recent history), but a curious trend is suggested in table 5. In all four regions of the nation, the fractions of youngsters attending private schools in the central cities decreased, while the shares in private schools in suburban areas have gone up. Overall, the percentage of central city children in private schools dropped from 16 to 13.7 per cent, while the suburban fraction went from 10 to 11 per cent. This is probably directly tied to recent closings of Catholic schools (a city phenomenon) discussed by Cooper, perhaps due to the diminishing incidence of school busing for desegregation in the cities, and perhaps also a result of the proliferation of evangelical schools (a suburban phenomenon).

Such geographical distributions do not have dramatic importance for public policy decisions about private schools. But the prevalence of private schools in our urban centers may be important to public deliberations concerning our city schools. These systems are consistently featured when the educational fortunes of our minority and poor youngsters are debated, or when issues of shifting school tax bases are raised.

Origins and Incomes of Private Schoolers

Private school children come from all backgrounds, but the frequency of attendance is tightly linked to family origins and is positively tied to family income. Table 6 shows the fractions of children from white, black, and Hispanic families who attended private schools in 1979 and 1982. Slightly more than 11 per cent of white children attend private schools, while only 4.4 per cent of black children and 8.7 per cent of Hispanic children do so. The fraction of white and Hispanic children

Table 5: Total and Private Elementary and Secondary Enrollments, and Private Enrollment Shares, by Region and SMSA* Status: 1979 and 1982

Region SMSA* Status	1979			1982			Increase (decrease) of private percentage share
	Total school enrollments	Private school enrollments	Private enrollment share (per cent)	Total school enrollment	Private school enrollment	Private enrollment share (per cent)	
US Total	42,981	4,231	9.8	41,534	4,149	10.0	0.2
Central city	11,106	1,774	16.0	10,969	1,502	13.7	(2.3)
Suburb	17,329	1,732	10.0	16,599	1,827	11.0	1.0
Non-metro (Not in SMSA)	14,546	725	5.0	13,966	819	5.9	0.9
North east	9,734	1,220	12.5	8,774	1,171	13.3	0.8
Central city	2,894	588	20.3	2,615	461	17.6	(2.7)
Suburb	4,582	473	10.3	4,131	515	12.5	2.2
Non-metro	2,259	160	7.1	2,828	195	6.9	(0.2)
North central	11,198	1,287	11.5	10,743	1,260	11.7	0.2
Central city	2,768	479	17.3	2,605	471	18.1	0.8
Suburb	4,584	574	12.5	4,449	566	12.7	0.2
Non-metro	3,846	235	6.1	3,690	223	6.0	0.1
South	14,482	1,126	7.8	13,782	1,024	7.4	(0.4)
Central city	3,450	429	12.4	3,398	299	8.8	(3.6)
Suburb	4,437	418	9.4	4,091	420	10.3	0.9
Non-metro	6,595	279	4.2	6,292	305	4.8	0.6
West	7,567	597	7.9	8,236	693	8.4	0.5
Central city	1,994	279	14.0	2,350	271	1.5	(2.5)
Suburb	3,726	266	7.1	3,929	326	8.3	1.2
Non-metro	1,846	52	2.8	1,957	96	4.9	2.1

* SMSA = Standard Metropolitan Statistical Area.
Source: US Bureau of the Census, October Current Population Survey, 1979 and 1982.

in private schools inched up over the three-year period shown, while the fraction of black children decreased. Also shown are divisions of these populations between church-related and non-church-related schools. All three groups send close to 90 per cent of their private school youngsters to church-affiliated schools, so no one group exceeds another in its relative preference for one type as opposed to the other.

Table 6: Enrollment Rates of Private Elementary and Secondary Schools, by Race/Ethnicity and Church Affiliation: October 1979 and 1982

Total, by church affiliation	Total		White		Black		Hispanic	
	1979	*1982*	*1979*	*1982*	*1979*	*1982*	*1979*	*1982*
Total	9.8	10.0	10.8	11.2	4.9	4.4	8.4	8.7
Church-related	8.3	8.4	9.1	9.3	4.2	3.5	7.5	7.6
Not church-related	1.4	1.4	1.5	1.5	0.5	0.5	0.7	0.7

Note: Detail may not add to total because of non-response.
Source: US Bureau of the Census, October Current Population Survey, 1979 and 1982 (cited in Noell, 1984).

Table 7 also shows patterns of private school attendance for the three groups, this time with the addition of enrollment rates by income category. For all groups — whites, blacks, and Hispanics — the propensity to enroll children in private schools, church-affiliated or not, increases almost uniformly with family income. Overall, percentages of children in private schools range from about 3 per cent for families with less than $7500 in annual income to 31 per cent for children from families with incomes exceeding $75,000. Both blacks and Hispanics show smaller private attendance rates than whites at low income levels, and higher rates at high income levels. Reported private school percentages are between 60 and 70 per cent for these groups at the highest income levels, as opposed to about 30 per cent reported for white families. Interestingly, table 7 shows these high income, minority private school attendees to be confined to church-related schools, but this is no doubt an artifact of the Census Bureau's small annual samples. Table 8 shows the percentage distributions of families across income levels for public and private schools for 1979. Private school families crowd the higher income ranges, while public school families are more evenly distributed.

These figures document that private schools in the United States (i) continue to serve higher than average income families; and (ii)

Table 7: Enrollment Rates in Private Elementary and Secondary Schools, by Income and Race/Ethnicity: October 1982

Family Income	Total			White			Black			Hispanic		
	Total	Church related	Not church related	Total	Church related	Not church related	Total	Church related	Not church related	Total	Church related	Not church related
All	10.0	8.4	1.4	11.2	9.3	1.5	4.4	3.5	0.5	8.7	7.6	0.7
Less than $7,500	3.3	3.0	0.2	4.4	3.9	0.3	1.7	1.5	0.1	2.9	2.6	0.3
$7,500-$14,999	6.1	5.5	0.4	7.2	6.6	0.5	3.0	2.3	0.2	5.3	4.8	0.5
$14,999-$24,999	10.0	8.4	1.2	10.7	9.0	1.2	5.9	5.0	0.7	12.2	10.7	0.5
$25,000-$34,999	13.5	11.6	1.6	13.8	11.9	1.6	9.9	7.3	1.9	15.5	13.0	2.0
$35,000-$49,999	13.2	11.0	1.7	13.1	10.9	1.6	12.2	8.4	3.2	27.7	25.4	2.3
$50,000-$74,999	16.6	13.0	3.2	16.3	12.6	3.2	22.3	21.8	0.5	12.2	12.2	0.0
Greater than $75,000	31.0	19.9	11.1	30.2	19.0	11.2	69.3	69.3	0.0	64.1	64.1	0.0
Not reported	13.0	9.2	2.5	13.4	9.5	3.0	10.1	6.8	0.0	13.0	10.1	1.3

Source: US Bureau of the Census, Current Population Survey, October 1982 (cited in Noell, 1984).

Table 8: Percentage Distribution of Families by Income (in $1000) in Public and Private Schools, 1979

Control of school	$0–5	$5–10	$10–15	Income 15–20	$20–25	$25+	No report	Total
Public	8.7	14.5	17.8	15.1	15.0	20.7	8.0	100.0
Private	2.6	5.7	12.5	15.4	17.1	37.3	9.3	100.0

Source: Current Population Reports, Table 14; author's calculations. Figures are for October 1979.

continue to serve higher fractions of children from white as opposed to minority families. As I have pointed out elsewhere, this suggests that policies which involve mainly existing private school families will have comparatively greater impacts on higher-income and whiter Americans (Catterall, 1983b).

Tuition Costs at Private Schools

Annual fees paid by families for private school attendance range from under $500 per year at many church-related elementary schools to about $10,000 per year at others. Table 9 shows median tuition levels at the elementary and secondary levels for both church-affiliated and non-affiliated schools. The median fee at church-related elementary schools was $569 in 1982 — the cost at non-affiliated schools was a substantially higher $1755 per year. Secondary school costs were roughly double these amounts — $1307 and $3415 respectively. The tuition charges at private schools increased substantially between 1979 and 1982, with the highest increases reported for church-related schools. The church-related elementary school median increased by 74 per cent during this time, while the median fee for church-related secondary schools increased by nearly 46 per cent. Fees at non-affiliated schools rose about 32 and 40 per cent at the elementary and secondary levels respectively, if the increases of the median elementary school tuition and mean secondary school tuition shown are a good indicator of overall changes.

Also shown in table 9 are trends over the same time period in consumer prices and family incomes in the United States. With the exception of the church-related elementary schools, whose fees increased by 74 per cent, the increases in median tuitions were roughly comparable to changes in the urban and services-component consumer price indices, which were up 33 and 45 per cent. The tuition increases

Table 9: Private School Tuition Compared to Price and Income Levels: 1979 and 1982

	1979	1982	Percentage change
Median Tuition			
Elementary			
Church-related	$ 327	$ 569	74.0
Not-related	$1,329	$1,755	32.1
Secondary			
Church-related	$ 898	$1,307	45.5
Not-related*	$2,446	$3,415	39.6
Consumer Price Index			
Urban:			
Total CPI-U	217.4	289.1	33.0
CPI-U services component**	244.9	355.3	45.1
Median Family Income			
All families	$21,503	$26,019	21.0
Familes with two children	$23,000	$27,745	20.6

* Mean tuition.
** Service-less-rent component of the CPI-U.
Sources: Current Population Survey; Bureau of Labor Statistics; Bureau of the Census; National Education Association. (Cited in Noell, 1984).

for both levels and both types of schools, however, managed to outstrip growth in family incomes during this time, which increased by a more modest 21 per cent.

Table 10 displays the distribution of tuition levels for affiliated and non-affiliated elementary and secondary schools reported for 1982. At the elementary level, the vast majority of church-affiliated schools charge less than $1000 per year, with nearly half charging $500 or less. Non-affiliated elementary schools seem to be offered at all tuition levels — with roughly comparable numbers of families paying fees at each level shown. At the secondary level, the patterns are similar save the expected shift toward higher cost categories. In addition, a large share of non-affiliated schools, 35 per cent, charge more than $3000 per year.

Tuition levels are potentially important for public policy decisions regarding private schools. For instance, some of the effects of a small tax credit, such as the $300 per year credit for half of tuition proposed by President Reagan, can be assessed with this information. Such a credit would offset half of the tuition needed to attend a majority of the nation's church-affiliated elementary schools, but would be less significant for church-related high schools and even less so for non-affiliated schools because of their comparatively high costs. If tuitions continue to grow at the rates reported here, the effect of a $300 tax credit would be reduced substantially for all participant

Table 10:   Tuitions at Private Schools by Level and Affilation: October 1982

	Percentage of Families Paying					
	$0–500	*$501–1000*	*$1001–1500*	*$1501–2000*	*$2001–3000*	*Over $3000*
Elementary						
Church affiliated	47	39	9	3	2	1
Non-church	4	22	20	14	21	18
Secondary Schools						
Church affiliated	4	34	42	12	3	4
Non-church	5	18	20	12	9	35

Source: US Bureau of the Census, Current Population Survey, October 1982 (cited in Noell, 1984).

families from year to year — and if such a plan should be enacted, there would undoubtedly be sustained pressure from beneficiaries to increase the credit to keep up with increases in tuition costs. This, in turn, would affect the costs of maintaining the tax credit from year to year.

Another implication of these trends is that private schools seem to be becoming a relatively more expensive item for American families. If tuitions continue to progress faster than family incomes, the increasing cost burden could have a depressing effect on enrollments in private schools. Some evidence for this already taking place is provided by the fast increasing church-related school tuitions shown here and the continued reductions of Catholic school enrollments shown earlier. I do not attempt to establish a causal link between these two trends in this analysis, but such a possibility is at the very least plausible.

Finally, the distribution of various tuition charges evident in table 10 raises some questions about how a public education voucher might interact with private schools. Most voucher designs would make public certificates redeemable for some set amount available to participating youngsters, and in turn to their chosen schools. Setting a voucher value at any specific unitary level would have interesting effects. According to the distributions shown, most schools would either have more money than they are accustomed to collecting per youngster by virtue of an education voucher — perhaps a great deal more — or less than they currently charge for tuition — perhaps a great deal less. This raises some important questions. How would financial windfalls be spent by schools which receive them? Would private schools participate in a program if vouchers do not fully cover tuition charges? Would expensive schools demand the right to charge fees in excess of voucher stipends? And how would the answers to these question bear on other assessments of the effects of a voucher design, such as important questions of efficiency and equity?

Conclusions

In this chapter I have presented a variety of estimates regarding private school participation in the United States. These were based on information for the 1982/83 school year and selected previous years. In each section, I have pointed to potential policy implications of the figures and trends presented; so I will not restate these in full here.

The overall view of enrollments in the multitude of American private schools presented is a more complete picture of this world than has ever been available. In the decade following 1965, private schools suffered a 30 per cent decline in pupil numbers, accounted for mainly by reductions in Catholic schools. This trend turned around in 1975, but only about a fourth of the nearly 2 million in lost enrollments has been restored. Within this trend, Catholic schools continue to lose pupils each year, while nearly every other type of school — most of them affiliated with a church or religious group — is growing slowly. The evangelical Christian schools are a glaring exception, adding about 80,000 pupils per year since 1975 and now enrolling nearly 1 million children.

The overall current growth of private school enrollments in the United States is slow — about 2 per cent per year if private special education schools are not considered. (I argue that this exclusion is appropriate.) This suggests that no more than two-tenths of a per cent of current public school pupils are annually switching to private schools. At the same time, public school enrollments have been declining by about 2 per cent per year. The confluence of these two trends has yielded an upward creep of the percentage of American youngsters enrolled in private schools, now exceeding 12 per cent.

My examination of other qualities of private school participation in the United States included the levels of schooling subscribed, the geographical distributions of private schools, the family backgrounds of private school patrons, and tuitions paid for private school attendance. Private schools continue to be more prevalent at the elementary than secondary grade levels. They are more popular in the North East and North Central sections of the country than the South and West. And they are most commonly found in our central cities and comparatively scarce in non-metropolitan areas. In recent years, there has been a decline in fractions of central city children attending private schools and a small increase in the share of children in our suburbs attending them. White families frequent private schools at rates more than twice those of black families in the United States — 11 per cent of their children attending private schools versus about 4.5 per cent. Hispanic families fall in between these enrollment rates. Participation in private schools is highly and positively dependent on family income, for all types of schools and for families of all backgrounds. The tuitions their client families pay vary tremendously, from a few hundred dollars at church elementary schools to thousands of dollars per year at others. Tuitions increased between 1979 and 1982 on a par with consumer prices, but at rates greater than increases in family income.

There appear now to be fewer reasons for disagreement on the facts of private school participation in the United States than on what to make of them or about how specific policy proposals might alter patterns of participation. The past ten years have seen great improvements in the detail and completeness of the sorts of data presented here. The National Center for Education Statistics (NCES) has made efforts to find hidden schools, the Census Bureau has added questions about private school tuitions to its annual surveys, school associations seem to be keeping better track of their constituent enrollments and have evidenced some willingness to be counted when researchers come knocking. Most of the figures covered here are not controversial and are not in particular need of refining. Existing patterns of private school participation by school level, broad school types, family characteristics, and geographical region are widely accepted and our abilities to detect changes in them somewhat trusted. And our data on tuition patterns fit our intuitions rather well.

Future Research on Private School Participation

Unfortunately, the comprehensive picture drawn together by Cooper and displayed at the outset in our discussion is not automatically reproduced and updated from year to year. It has been pieced together from a variety of information sources. It would be helpful to have a picture as complete as this on a year to year basis. But without a commitment on the part of NCES or others in the education research community, we are not likely to have one. This is one suggestion for future research attention which grows from this discussion. It is more a request for institutionalizing comprehensive and detailed data gathering than it is a plea for original research, however.

One particular attribute of future private school participation warrants special vigilance over the coming years. I mentioned that our total population of school age youngsters will begin to climb in 1985. Since this increase is the result of higher birth rates, elementary grade levels will feel it first and high schools will not be affected until the early 1990s. In fact, in the ten years beyond the latest patterns discussed in this chapter, the nation's population of youngsters in kindergarten through grade eight will increase by 11 per cent while high schools will decrease by 12 per cent in their enrollments (Plisko, 1984, p. 3). When we consider that far more families subscribe to private elementary schools than to private high schools, this demographic trend guarantees that overall percentages of children opting for private schools in the United States are likely to increase in the next seven or so years. This would hold even if families continue to choose private and public schools at given grade levels in proportions similar to those now evidenced. If tastes for private elementary schooling should expand, growth of private schools will be all the more dramatic. So pupil counts in the coming years will be interesting to watch.

Another and related factor may bear on school selection in the near future and could be the object of research attention. Since many of the added enrollments may come from families who have had children recently for the first time, their school choice patterns are worth examining. These families may or may not conform to the historical behaviors described here. And since some of these may be families who have put off having children until their careers and lives were more settled and established, they may because of this find private schools more financially feasible as an option.

Finally, there are more general reasons to identify school selection patterns as worthy of future research attention, apart from what I have said of coming population trends. How and why families choose schools and the results of their choices have long been a source of insight into what we want in the education of our children and how we believe these interests can be met. Such behavior also provides something of a barometer on the effectiveness of our public schools. And since we are in the midst of concerted efforts to 'reform' our schools in the directions of stiffer graduation standards and higher demands for competence in their personnel, our private school selection behavior will be that much more interesting to watch over the next few years.

Notes

1 See, for instance, COOPER, MCLAUGHLIN, and MANNO (1983).
2 Among these are NCEE (1983) *A Nation at Risk: The Imperative for Educational Reform*; BOYER (1983) *High School: A Report on Secondary Education in America*; COLLEGE BOARD (1983) *Academic Preparation for College: What Students Need to Know and Be Able to Do*; GOODLAD (1984) *A Place Called School: Prospects for the Future.*
3 See COLEMAN, HOFFER and KILGORE, 1981.
4 These interviews were conducted by telephone in July of 1984. The information reported reflects expressed opinions of individual leaders.

4 Treatment of Religion in Public Schools and the Impact on Private Education

Patricia M. Lines

This chapter traces the major historical changes in treatment of religious values in public schools and the corresponding development of new private schools.[1] Although the evidence is far from complete, there is much to support the theory that, when they alter their treatment of religion, public schools lose some pupils and gain others. Most of all, it appears that public school values have a major impact on the formation of new private schools. When public school values were Protestant, a vigorous Roman Catholic school system emerged; when public school values became secular, a strong Protestant (Christian) private school movement emerged. While Roman Catholic schools served 90 per cent of the private school population for most of this century, by the 1985–86 school year they served less than half. Yet the total private school population has held fairly steady, due largely to the formation of new Christian schools. Tension between public and private educators accompanied the growth of both Roman Catholic schools a century ago, and new Christian schools today. This tension can be traced in turn to the tension between cultural pluralism and the desire to establish a common cultural base.

An Overview: Public School Values Over Time

Public school treatment of religious values has gone through three overlapping stages of development. First was an evangelical Protestant period, beginning with the development of public education and lasting well into the nineteenth century. Next came a relatively brief period of non-denominational religious emphasis, an emphasis that never completely permeated American public education before it was overtaken by the third and current era of secular education. Non-

67

denominationalism still persists, particularly in the 'Bible Belt' (a term that describes an ideological orientation and not a geographical area) where political leaders sometimes continue to call for ecumenical prayer at the start of the school day or the posting of religious material such as the Ten Commandments. But the public schools have become officially secular and mostly so in practice.

From the beginning of the nineteenth century until today, public schools have changed in many other ways as well. Along with changes in religious orientation, they have begun to favor enquiry over rote learning, to emphasize student development over acceptance of authoritarian sources, and to extend the range of study to include sexuality, evolution, drugs and alcohol. Public schools of today often provide opportunities for children to discover information and ideas that many people would prefer to restrict to a family setting. The reason that these changes are controversial seems closely bound up with the religious beliefs and religious sensitivities of a diverse population.

The Religious Prototype for Public Schools

The European schools on which early American schools were patterned had a clear religious mission. Church-operated schools were the original norm, followed by government schools that were similar in orientation. The founders of the state-operated schools, moreover, were able to compel attendance — using the powers of government to pursue their personal vision for education. As early as 1524, for example, Martin Luther urged the rulers of German cities to establish schools and compel attendance[2] and, over the next forty years, several rulers did in fact heed Luther's advice. The purpose of these public schools was to foster Lutheranism, to suppress religious dissent and to rear good citizens (Rothbard, 1974, p. 12). Luther's idea spread. In the mid-sixteenth century, as ruler of Geneva, John Calvin established a number of public schools and compelled attendance, an example Holland followed in the early seventeenth century (*ibid*, p. 13).

Like the Europeans before Luther, the early Americans relied almost exclusively on church-operated schools. These first American schools considered themselves 'public', because they educated children and in other ways served the public good (Katz, 1975, p. 22). Bernard Bailyn, in *Education in the Forming of American Society*, has observed that 'the very idea of a clean line of separation between "private" and "public", was unknown before the end of the eighteenth century'

(Bailyn, 1972, p. 11). Family training and apprenticeships based on sixteenth century English poor laws[3] also played an important role, but the churches led explicit schooling efforts.

As Bailyn observes, the church schools did not limit themselves to religious instruction, but 'furthered the introduction of the child to society by instructing him in the system of thought and imagery which underlay the culture's values and aims' (*ibid*, p. 18). After giving up an attempt to convert the Indians, colonists turned their missionary fervor inward: 'For the self-conscious, deliberate, aggressive use of education, first seen in an improvised but confident missionary campaign, spread throughout an increasingly heterogeneous society and came to be accepted as a normal form of educational effort' (*ibid*, p. 39). Thus, Bailyn notes that

> [s]ectarian groups, without regard to the intellectual complexity of their doctrine or to their views on the value of learning to religion, became dynamic elements in the spread of education, spawning schools of all sorts, continuously, competitively, in all their settlements, carrying education into the most remote frontiers (*ibid*, p. 40).

These proselytizing church-run schools, pursuing both educational and religious goals, became prototypes for the early American government school.

The Religious Public School and Compulsory Education

Colonial America ultimately followed Europe's lead and organized government-run, *religious* schools. The idea of compelling attendance also emerged fairly early. By the seventeenth century, American laws often compelled education, explicitly citing both religious and economic needs.[4] In 1642, only a year after the Massachusetts Bay Colony began passing laws for its own governance, it enacted a compulsory literacy law (Records of the Governor ..., 1642)[5], enforced by apprenticing the truant to a master who would provide the required instruction (*ibid*, p. 7). The purpose, as in Luther's time, was to assure that children understood 'the principles of religion and the capital law of the country' (*ibid*, p. 6). Massachusetts enacted an amended law in 1648, which set specific fines for non-compliance and expanded on the religious goals: a child should understand the capital laws and learn an orthodox catechism.[6] The amendments also required boys to be apprenticed until age 21 (girls until age 18) and provided for payments to masters from the town treasury (Charters and General Laws, 1644, chapter 88, section 1).

Other New England colonies followed suit.[7] The Plymouth Colony, in 1671, decided to fine parents and masters who failed to comply and, as a last resort, to place children in suitable apprenticeships (The Book of General Laws, 1685, chapter 5, section 1, p. 13). In 1650, Connecticut modeled a law on the 1648 Massachusetts law, following it almost word for word (Jernegan, 1918, p. 749).

Not all colonies followed the Massachusetts example. Rhode Island resisted the trend (*ibid*). In 1683 Pennsylvania adopted a poor law modeled after English law: everyone not gainfully employed was required to serve an apprenticeship.[8] The south, which proceeded at a slower pace, adopted laws resembling the English poor laws — requiring apprenticeships for certain children, particularly the poor and illegitimate.[9] Not until the beginning of the eighteenth century did any true education laws appear in the south; those that appeared required only literacy (Butts and Cremin, 1953, p. 105).

Outside the south, interest in education waned in the latter part of the seventeenth century. Requirements were reduced until by the beginning of the eighteenth century, no laws remained to compel education in New England (Jernegan, 1931, p. 115; Edwards and Richey, 1947, p. 59).[10] Historians attribute the diminished interest in education to social and economic dislocation following the Indian Wars of 1675–76, the general scattering of the population into rural areas, the emphasis on material development in frontier conditions, and growing religious tolerance (Jernegan, 1931, p. 115; Edwards and Richey, 1947, pp. 108–9). Before educational institutions could fully rebuild, they suffered another blow: the American Revolution, which totally disrupted the operation of most schools (Cubberley, 1920, pp. 653–5).

Following the Revolution, the United States became intensely interested in education as a means of eradicating class distinctions and fostering the values of the new nation. In 1789 the new state of Massachusetts enacted a statewide school law requiring all towns of at least fifty families to support a school for at least six months per year. Larger towns had even larger responsibilities, and rural areas were included within district systems.[11]

The compulsory education laws as we know them today were developed in a period beginning in 1852 and ending in 1918. In 1852, Massachusetts, again the leader (Rothbard, 1974, p. 14)[12] mandated that any person responsible for a child send the child to school for twelve weeks a year, six of which were to be consecutive. Vermont,

New Hampshire and Connecticut soon followed suit. As in the colonial period, Rhode Island lagged behind other New England states, perhaps because it had been established as a religious haven, had only a weak central government, and emphasized individualism (Jernegan, 1919, p. 39). But by 1900, more than thirty states and the District of Columbia had adopted compulsory education laws. As in colonial days, the southern states were the last to act, passing compulsory education laws between 1900 and 1918 (Kotin and Aikman, 1980, pp. 25–6; Umbech, 1960).

Public schools of the nineteenth century espoused the same missionary goals as their private predecessors. As Michael Katz (1975) has observed, 'it is in fact impossible to disentangle Protestantism from the early history of the common school. . .' (p. 37). Most historians of American education tend to agree (Cremin, 1980, pp. 50–105; Tyack and Hansot, 1982; Westerhoff, 1978; Edwards, 1941, pp. 2–4). To take just one example of this bias, more than 120 million McGuffey Readers, containing a strong Protestant orientation, were sold between 1839 and 1920 (Westerhoff, 1978, p. 14). Other textbooks were openly anti-Catholic; *The New England Primer* is a famous case in point (McCluskey, 1969, pp. 234–5). Moreover, class and race bias were pervasive (Katz, 1975, p. 40). The early public schools served only the very poor and were to this extent altruistic, but they also helped assure the stability of the upper class.[13] Advocates of public schools hoped to teach youth 'proper subordination' and 'to confide in and reverence their rulers' (Fischer, 1964; Rothbard, 1974, p. 15). Katz observes that the urban public school system was 'founded to cope with the problems of urban living, among which the threat of the urban poor had high priority' (Katz, 1975, p. 40).

The Impact on Private Education

Religious, class, and race bias all worked together to alienate Roman Catholics. In many ways, the establishment of Protestant public schools and the enactment of compulsory attendance laws helped give birth to Roman Catholic schools. Many events contributed. Great waves of Catholic immigrants arrived throughout the nineteenth century. Within fifty years, Catholics went from a tiny minority to the single largest religious denomination in the nation (Dolan, 1975, pp. 1–2). Both religious and class biases spawned anti-Catholic sentiments. While prior generations of Catholics in America were generally affluent and Anglo-American (*ibid*, pp. 1–4), the newcomers were poor, and mostly Irish and German, with some Slavs, Italians and others. Too poor to leave the vicinity of Ellis Island, most settled in New York City where they lived in overcrowded, unsanitary conditions.[14] They migrated north, south and west only after gaining some small economic base.

The compulsory education laws were in place by the time of the immigration to New York and secondary migration to other parts of the country. Laws designed to enlighten poor Protestant immigrants were now applied to the newcomers. They understood the biases present in the new public system (*ibid*, p. 3). Thus, the working class and Catholics (often the same people) led the opposition to the development of public education. The New York Workingmen's Party opposed the establishment of public schools (Rothbard, 1974, p. 17), while Catholics developed their own schools. The bitterness of this debate led to the famous 1844 riot in Philadelphia over which version of the Bible should be used in the public school program.[15]

In response, Catholic leaders attacked the Protestant nature of the public schools, not only for the sake of Catholic children in those schools but also as an argument for state aid to the new Catholic schools. One official response was a new state law in 1842, which removed control of the public schools from the crusading Public School Society and attempted to secularize instruction (Dolan, 1975, p. 39; Cremin, 1980, p. 168): the idea of private school aid was rejected.

Catholic leaders obtained more immediate relief with their alternative response: to bring most Catholic children into Catholic schools. Prior to this time private schools were scattered among many denominations — Jewish, Lutheran, Episcopal, Quaker, to name a few.[16] Roman Catholic schools were very few, probably because of the small numbers of Catholics — only 1 per cent of the population by the end of the Revolution (Lee, 1967, p. 225). The first Catholic elementary school, St. Peter's in New York, was founded in 1800 (Dolan, 1975, p. 102). It even received financial assistance from the state until 1824 (*ibid*, p. 104). The first free coeducational Catholic school was founded in 1809 (Lee, 1967, pp. 255–6). By mid-century, Catholic schools were growing as fast as public schools. In 1884 the Third Plenary Council of Baltimore declared its goal: 'Every Catholic child in a Catholic school' (McCluskey, 1967, p. 233). The political efforts to stop the development of public education failed; the private education efforts endured. From the middle of the nineteenth century until the mid-1960s well over 90 per cent of the children in private schools were in Roman Catholic schools.[17]

Public Reactions to Successful Catholic Schools

One public response to the new schools was hostility. While the emergence of Catholic schools might have been seen as a clear benefit to overcrowded public schools hard pressed to accommodate the large numbers of new immigrants, some people also saw the new schools as a threat to public schools. Also, substantial numbers of people saw the generally poor and overcrowded new schools (Lee, 1967, pp. 255–6) as undesirable, and even unpatriotic.

Thus, in the 1920s, a number of states sought to impose restrictions on private schools. The restrictions were not aimed exclusively at Catholic schools, but at German-language and Japanese-language schools as well. Oregon even attempted to abolish all forms of private education. In 1922 the Klu Klux Klan, which had infiltrated the Scottish Rite Masons, campaigned successfully for a statewide referendum that modified Oregon's compulsory education law to require attendance at public schools only. The Klan exploited not only anti-Catholic sentiments but also anti-German sentiments fanned by popular reaction to the Great War.[18] In a decision often hailed as a 'bill of rights' for private schools, the Supreme Court struck this law down in *Pierce v. Society of Sisters*, in 1925.

Following the tension of the 1920s, private schools enjoyed a period of relatively peaceful coexistence with public schools. Most of them resisted state standards for a while but in the end strove to meet them, wishing to be viewed as excellent by any standard, even a government stardard. By the 1960s, most private schools had accepted most state requirements for their operation.

The Non-denominational Movement

The second response from public leaders was to reform public schools to make them more acceptable to religious minorities by replacing traditional Protestant values with non-denominationalism. As early as 1817, Thomas Jefferson submitted a draft of an 'Act for Establishing Elementary Schools' to the General Assembly of Virginia which provided that 'no religious reading, instruction or exercise, shall be prescribed or practiced inconsistent with the tenets of any religious sect or denomination (Padover, 1943). In general, Jefferson favored non-denominational religious observances for public school, believing that there was a body of religious principles 'common to all sects' that could be taught (Costanzo, 1961; Butts, 1955, p. 182).[19] Had Jefferson's ideas received rapid and widespread acceptance, the history of the Roman Catholic school movement might have turned out differently.

Horace Mann advocated a somewhat similar position. Giving up, temporarily, a promising political career to become Secretary of the newly-created Massachusetts Board of Education in 1837 (Cremin, 1957, p. 3), Mann was in a position of considerable influence. Motivated in large part by religious zeal, he strove to find a common denominator for all religious views. The difficulty of such an endeavor is illustrated by the preference Mann showed for a pan-Protestant approach.[20] Mann was, in fact, a Unitarian, as were seven of the ten members of his Board (Glenn, 1984),[21] and his public position coincided with his private beliefs. As Lawrence Cremin (1951) has wryly observed, Mann

> ... came increasingly to believe that certain common principles could be culled from the several sectarian creeds and made the core of a body of religious doctrine on which all could agree. For Mann, these were the great principles of 'natural religion' — those truths which had been given in the Bible and demonstrated in the course of history. The fact that this new corpus of knowledge closely resembled his own optimistic, humanistic Unitarianism did not seem to trouble him. Nor did questions about 'which version of the Bible' from Catholic and Jewish citizens. If the Word of God — personified in the King James Bible — were taught without comment, how could that conceivably be sectarian? If the Fatherhood of God were taught as the foundation of the brotherhood of men, how could that be sectarian? (p. 13)

Others also called for reform. Horace Bushnell, one of Hartford's leading ministers, prepared a lengthy tract on how to make public schools acceptable to Catholics. He argued that '[i]t is the responsibility of Protestants to do all they can to render it [the public program] acceptable to Roman Catholics, and the responsibility of Roman Catholics to respond by joining in the common venture instead of demanding their own schools (Bushnell, 1953).

George Cheever, another advocate of compulsory education, exemplifies another view also typical of the era:

> We are in great danger from the dark and stolid infidelity and vicious radicalism of a large portion of the foreign immigrat-

ing population... How can we reach the evil at its roots, applying a wise and conservative radicalism to defeat the working of malignant, social, anti-Christian poison? How can the children of such a population be reached, except in our free public schools? (Cremin, 1951, p. 47)

Jefferson and Mann were successful, but not in their lifetimes. The non-denominational movement slowly gained ground, particularly in the east. The 1870 edition of the McGuffey Reader was dramatically altered. In the words of John Westerhoff, 'Calvinistic theology and ethics have been replaced by American middle-class civil religion, morality, and values' (Westerhoff, 1978, p. 19). Meanwhile, other education leaders were taking the non-denominational movement one step further, and urging secularization of the public schools.

The Move Toward Secularism

In 1899, John Dewey published *The School and Society*, advocating a system of public education in which religion would have little or no place (Dewey, 1965). Cremin finds that the book marked a turning point: 'By the turn of the century a revolution was clearly at hand, and progressives found themselves with a growing body of theory to support the pedagogical reformism they so dearly espoused' (Cremin, 1964, p. 91). In 1918, the United States Bureau of Education published its famous *Cardinal Principles for Secondary Education*. The development of 'ethical character' in students was one of seven objectives, but no mention was made of religious training (U.S. Bureau of Education, 1918). In 1919, Stanwood Cobb formed 'The Association for the Advancement of Progressive Education' (PEA) (Cremin, 1964, p. 240). The PEA endorsed non-sectarian principles for education, including freedom for children to develop naturally, student interest as the motive for learning, the teacher as a guide, not a task-master, the scientific study of pupil development, greater attention to all that affects children's physical development, and cooperation between school and home (Cremin, 1964, pp. 242–5).

All of these were harbingers of the move to secular education, but sectarian influences remained. As late as 1955, for example, a Buddhist parent in Massachusetts was convicted under the compulsory school attendance law for attempting home instruction; he had objected to the reading of the 23rd Psalm and recitation of the Lord's

Prayer in the public school (*Commonwealth v. Renfrew*, 1955). But non-denominational sentiments had generally prevailed by the mid-twentieth century. Typical of the treatment of religion was the 'Regent's Prayer' mandated by the state of New York as an opening ceremony for all public schools. It was non-denominational, although theistic: 'Almighty God, we acknowledge our dependence upon Thee, and we beg Thy blessings upon us, our parents, our teachers and our Country.'[22] Protestant views may still have permeated rural and small-town public schools, but in eastern and urban areas, opposition was growing to even this much religious orientation in public schools.

The shift toward secular schools accelerated after the courts stepped in, armed with the First Amendment to the US Constitution. It declares that '*Congress* shall make no law respecting an establishment of religion...' Prior to the twentieth century, most jurists believed that it applied to Congress, and not state government, and preferred to leave issues concerning religion in public schools to state officials. In 1925, however, the Supreme Court extended the principles of the First Amendment to the states, reasoning that due process requirements of the Fourteenth Amendment (which expressly applies to states) incorporated first amendment rights (*Gitlow v. State of New York*, 1925). This decision gave the opponents of religion in public schools a powerful legal weapon.

Finally, in 1962, the US Supreme Court ruled that officially mandated prayer in the public schools was unconstitutional (*Engel v. Vitale*, 1962). The following year, the Court ruled that the Bible could not be read in school as a religious exercise, although it could be studied for its literary, historic and social value (*School District of Abington Township v. Schempp*, 1963).

As is sometimes the case in major social issues, the Court was somewhat ahead of its time. Thus, response to its decisions was mixed. While President J F Kennedy urged Americans to support the Court's decision, other public officials ignored the Court's mandate and failed to take steps to end prayer in the schools (Dolbeare and Hammond, 1971). Some parents instructed their children to pray in school on their own. When a New York school principal stopped kindergarteners from reciting a simple grace before cookies and milk, parents went to court. The US Court of Appeals for the Second Circuit upheld the principal's decision in 1965 in *Stein v. Oshinsky*.[23] Troubled by the case and seeing it as a restriction on individual prayer, Senator Everett Dirksen of Illinois sought passage of a constitutional amendment to clarify this and similar court decisions. The

Dirksen amendment ultimately failed, and the issue largely disappeared from national politics for more than a decade.

Religion and the Public School of Today

Political support for religion in the public schools seems on the rise again, and the issue has reappeared before the Supreme Court in the past five years. The result has been reaffirmation of the constitutional demand for secular public schools. In 1980 the Court struck down a Kentucky law enacted in 1978 that required posting of the Ten Commandments, finding that the purpose was to promote religion and not the discussion of social, historic, literary or other secular aspects of the commandments (*Stone v. Graham*, 1980). In early 1982 the Supreme Court struck down a Louisiana law calling for voluntary prayer in the schools, and in 1985, the Court struck down an Alabama law calling for silent prayer (*Treen v. Karen B.*, 1982).[24] The only ruling in the other direction is limited: in 1981, in *Widmar v. Vincent*, the Court upheld the right of college students to meet for religious purposes., Basing its analysis on the right to freedom of speech, the Court ruled that once a university became an 'open forum' by making facilities available for a wide variety of activities, it could not then selectively close the forum based on content of what was said.[25]

Thus, today, the *Protestant* orientation of the public schools has completely vanished and the non-denominational religious orientation is limited. Where strong political efforts are being made to continue a prayer as part of the daily program, such as in Alabama, that prayer is an ecumenical prayer acceptable to many theistic religions.[26] This limits potential religious objections, but some remain. Such a prayer may fail to utilize a required convention, may fail to be religious enough for some, or may not be acceptable to non-theistic religions.

In other areas of the country, particularly in urban school districts, education leaders have written policies on how to deal with major holidays. For example, policies adopted in such diverse locations as Sioux Falls, Cedar Rapids and Seattle recommend the presentation of secular aspects of holidays and cautious educational treatment of any religious material. These policies incorporate Supreme Court standards for dealing with religious material, requiring, among other things, a secular purpose. Santa Claus is welcome at Christmas assemblies; sacred music must be presented in a context that emphasizes its educational, historical or cultural value. Such policies typically require attention to holidays of all major religions. *Daily* attention to religious matters is not contemplated.[27]

Further, even relatively innocuous practices that some people regard as religious in nature, such as a moment of silence, are under fire. For example, when the New Jersey Civil Liberties Union filed a lawsuit challenging a state law calling for a moment of silence, state officials, including the Governor and Attorney General, refused to defend it.[28] As another example, students have had to go to court to preserve their right to student-initiated religious activity, an activity that the Court has found protected by the First Amendment's guarantee of free speech, in some circumstances.[29]

The Impact on Private Schools

Many Catholics now seem to regard public schools as safe for their children; some Protestants do not.[30] In fact, the change in the religious orientation of public schools coincides with shifts within the private school population; the Catholic school population has declined and the Protestant school population has increased.

Cause and effect are problematic, and researchers have forwarded many reasons for the decline in the Catholic school population.[31] But the people who have founded new fundamentalist Protestant schools in the past decade explicitly cite disagreement with the secular nature of the public school. The fundamentalist school movement gets its impetus from the religious beliefs of its adherents. Many who are dismayed by the secularization of public schools want to reform public programs. Others accept the secularization of the public schools and seek to found new schools with a strong religious emphasis. They believe that these schools should not obtain approval from the state, arguing that the school is an extension of the church and that teachers are like missionaries or pastors. The significance of the point is illustrated by the fact that a fact-finding panel in Nebraska, appointed by the governor, began its report by describing this set of beliefs (Governor's Christian School Issue Panel, 1984, p. 1). This idea has been attributed to David Gibbs, a pastor and an attorney involved in some of the litigation on this issue.[32] However, the idea is now widely accepted by participants in the movement.[33]

Shifts Within the Private School Population

As noted above, secularization of the public school program and major shifts within the private school population are taking place simultaneously. To be sure, the total private school population remains relatively small and constant compared to the public school population (figure 1). However, dramatic internal changes have taken place. Figure 2 shows private school enrollments broken down between Catholic and non-Catholic populations. While the Catholic school population has declined,[34] the non-Catholic private school population has more than doubled from 1965 to 1975[35] and may have tripled or quadrupled.[36]

This increase reflects, in large part, the growth of new fundamentalist schools. Included with the new schools are some older schools — Lutheran, Jewish, Seventh Day Adventist and others,[37] and some new secular schools, such as Montessori and communal schools.[38] Home instruction is also on the rise.[39] Nonetheless most observers agree that the largest growth is in the Christian school movement (Nordin and Turner, 1980; Cooper, McLaughlin and Manno, 1983, p. 97).

Litigation and New Private Schools

The new schools have opposition from many quarters, just as Catholic schools did up through the 1920s. To be sure, some new schools offer cause for concern. They may have inadequate physical facilities, poorly qualified teachers, or too few teachers. Some educators are concerned that a few schools may be teaching political views that diverge sharply from the mainstream of American democratic thought. But many are simply new.

In any case, public officials who view these schools as inadequate have been using compulsory education laws and other legal tools to require them to meet state standards or to shut down. Litigation over state regulation of private education has increased sharply in the past several years. More amicable forms of conflict resolution have broken down. Tension between public officials and new private schools sometimes runs quite high.

In Nebraska, for example, in a much publicized case, dealing with a Faith Baptist Church in Lewisville, a local judge ordered a church door to be padlocked except during hours of worship, to enforce a court order closing the school operated on church premises.

Figure 1: Public and Private School Enrollments

Trends in enrollment in public and private elementary/secondary schools: 1899-1900 to 1985-86

In millions

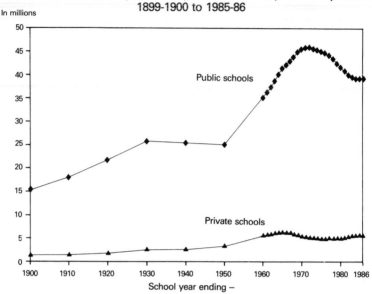

School year ending –

Figure 2: Private School Enrollments

Trends in enrollment in Catholic and other private schools: 1929-30 to 1985-86

In millions

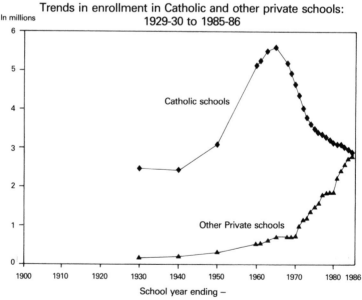

School year ending –

Source: U.S. Department of Education, Center for Statistics, Digest of Education Statistics, 1985-86 (forthcoming), and unpublished date. See Appendix.

The churchmen responded with sit-ins and other forms of passive resistance. Many were arrested. Other state officials and other churchmen continued to negotiate, but the impasse was not broken until the governor and legislature acted. Nebraska now has a new law, discussed below.

Earlier, in North Carolina, a Christian school that lost a court battle responded by successfully seeking legislation lowering standards for those private schools that did not desire state approval. The bitterness of the battle with state administrators left its mark, however, as the Christian school lobby also managed to persuade the legislature to place the responsible officer in the governor's office rather than the state department of education.

A quantitative measure of this tension might be the frequency of litigation. Typically, people do not invoke judicial intervention except when they are unable to resolve differences through discussion, negotiation or political processes. The legal process is expensive, time-consuming and emotionally painful. The positions of the parties harden and become inflexible. Frequently, even clear winners are emotionally exhausted. In short, an increase in litigation over an issue of public policy indicates not only that policy changes are in the wind but also that the changes have not won a social consensus.

Figure 3 shows actual reported cases involving regulation of private education. These cases were infrequent before the 1950s. But the number sharply increased in the 1970s and again in the 1980s. If the exponential increases of the early 1980s continue throughout the decade, four to five times more cases will be brought in the 1980s than in the 1970s. (Figure 3 provides data only in the first three years of 1980, and does not attempt any projections for the remainder of the decade.)

One explanation for the increase could be a general increase in population coupled with a deterioration in other dispute resolution processes. However, this cannot account for the extraordinarily sharp increase in regulation cases while two kinds of truancy cases (shown for comparison) increased only slightly. It seems likely that a combination of events triggered the change. Most obvious is the belief of many leaders of fundamentalist Christian schools that the school is an extension of the church and therefore not subject to state regulation. Many fundamentalist pastors and congregations view compromise as a religious defeat, rather than a political stratagem. Many state officials meet this stubbornness with equal stubbornness. One might also speculate that the data reflect a change in the application of laws written in most cases over a century ago to deal with children who

Figure 3: Litigation Under Compulsory Education Laws and Other Laws Regulating Private Schools

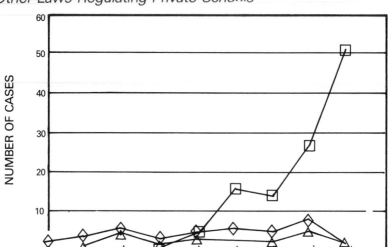

DECADE BEGINNING

☐ REGULATION △ PROTESTS ◇ TRUANCY

Regulation cases are those involving the adequacy or appropriateness of the private program of education. Truancy cases are those in which parents failed to enroll a child in any education program and had no legitimate reasons for doing so. 'Protests' are truancy cases in which parents withdrew a child from a public school because of a religious or philosophical disagreement with the public program, and failed by the time of prosecution to enroll the child in a private program.

Cases for the 1980s are actual and not projected.

For Source of Data see 'Compulsory Education and Regulation of Private Education: A Review of Litigation', LEC-83-8 (briefs of reported cases dealing with compulsory education and other forms of regulation of private education); available from the Education Commission of the States, Denver.

avoided education altogether. The data may also reflect a general increase in state board regulation, pursuant to general compulsory education laws, and the growing ability of state boards to enforce regulations.[40] There has been a trend towards setting standards for schools, rather than merely requiring attendance.[41]

Judicial resolution of the conflict is likely to be slow in coming. Litigation has not, to date, yielded any unified legal theory. Courts uphold state standards as often as they strike them down. Generally, though, courts will balance the state's interest in regulation (which must be designed to assure that children are self-sufficient and capable citizens), with first amendment freedoms for individuals (Lines, 1983).

Clearly, some minimal standards will pass constitutional muster. Requiring reports on enrollment, for example, is generally upheld by the courts. Teacher certification requirements, on the other hand, have been upheld in some states and stricken in others. Of course, a decisive case or series of cases from the Supreme Court could settle much of the matter, as it did in the *Pierce* and related cases in the 1920s. Courts typically rule narrowly, however, and the range of issues presented in various states is unlikely ever to be fully addressed by the US Supreme Court (*ibid*, pp. 214–17).

Trends in Legislation

In the final analysis, it is for legislatures to decide how much they wish to accommodate dissenting groups and at what cost to uniformity in education standards. In fact, state legislatures have been more responsive to the recent problems of private schools than have the courts. At least twelve states have adopted legislation in recent years to expand the range of choice available in the private education sector. Most of these provide for some alternative method of approval of those private schools not wishing to undergo full state regulation.[42]

In addition, three states deregulated in other ways. South Dakota recently exempted children from the compulsory education law if they receive 'competent alternative instruction for an equivalent period of time, as in the public schools' (South Dakota, 1983). Arizona has made it clear that home instruction is permissible (aiding Christian fundamentalists interested in correspondence courses) as long as teachers and children are periodically tested (Arizona, 1983). Finally, New Hampshire has not altered its statute but has administratively determined to accept required information on church stationery in lieu of reports on state forms. Christian school officials in that state have found this agreeable.

In Nebraska, where polarization has been greatest, Governor Robert Kerrey appointed a four-member panel to recommend new policy. The panel presented a strong set of recommendations that included deregulation of Christian schools and annual testing of students as a means of assuring accountability (Governor's Christian School Issue Panel, 1984). The legislature subsequently adopted a law that authorizes 'instruction monitors' in private schools, provided that they either submit credentials for reviews or take a nationally standardized test. Poor credentials or test scores do not necessarily lead to state disapproval of the school, however.[43] Most Christian schools appear ready to comply with the new law.

There appears to be no countervailing trend away from accommodation and towards stricter legislative standards. In states that do not regulate private schools at all, there is some interest in requiring reporting of data, but efforts to obtain this minimal requirement have failed. The only exception, perhaps, comes with the unintended consequences of recent efforts to improve education nationwide by increasing the length of the school day or the school year under compulsory education laws: such laws increase expenses for *all* schools.

Sources of Tension

Public schools at the beginning of the twentieth century reflected Protestant values; today they reflect mostly secular values. The first and last periods of public school development profoundly affected non-public schools. The Protestant orientation of the early public schools directly motivated Roman Catholic immigrants who settled in the United States in the nineteenth century to found Catholic schools. In recent times, the official secularism of the public schools has motivated some fundamentalist Protestants to found their own private schools. The resulting shift in private school population from Catholic to non-Catholic schools has been dramatic.

Public response to the emergence of a strong private school movement has sometimes been hostile, affecting Catholic schools in the nineteenth and early twentieth centuries and fundamentalist Protestant schools now. This hostility gave rise to an attempt to close down private schools in the early part of this century. Today it gives rise to a sharp increase in litigation over standards and other aspects of the operation of private schools. A legislative trend toward accommodating private schools has been evident in the 1980s, and it should ultimately lessen litigation and reduce tension between the new schools and state officials.

Public educators who fear private schools seem to feel that they are either too good or not good enough. What is the source of this conflict? Do private schools and public schools compete, and, if so, what are the stakes? Given present policies on public assistance to private education, private schools and home instruction do not offer substantial competition for public dollars. They even relieve financial pressure on the public schools, at least on a large scale. Yet as long as there is pressure to change those policies, private schools remain potential competitors. Further, in small school districts, a sudden exodus of forty children to a new school can have a substantial impact on state aid. All in all, however, financial competition is only a possibility or is limited to narrow geographic areas.

Some non-public schools compete with public schools in educational excellence. The newest private schools, however — the ones most likely to meet public opposition — are also most likely to be substandard (as measured by resources). For example, Catholic schools were severely underfunded in the nineteenth century. Even in recent times, they have suffered from inferior facilities and faculty; they have never rivaled public schools in such things as expenditures per pupil, science facilities, or counseling.[44] Many of today's new private schools have similar problems, which the current move for greater excellence in public programs may exacerbate (Euchner, 1983; Council for American Private Education, 1983). They may have difficulty meeting stiffer standards such as a longer school day or school year. Even if such changes are limited to public schools, private schools will feel a competitive pressure to make the same offering. In short, based on things money can buy, private schools do not compete. Public schools are relatively well endowed and they charge no tuition.

Some would argue that non-public schools produce better results. The Coleman report claims, based on test scores, that Catholic high schools, on the average, do a better job teaching some subjects (Coleman, Hoffer and Kilgore, 1982; Greeley, 1982).[45] While this assertion has received its share of criticism, one can say, at minimum, that some private schools have served their populations well. Students in Catholic schools, representing over 90 per cent of the private school population until the 1960s, have succeeded against poverty and prejudice. An immigrant population built an education system that today provides an alternative for over three million children. Andrew Greeley has found adult Catholics who attended Catholic schools are somewhat better off educationally and economically, and have fewer racist sentiments, than Catholics who attended other schools (Greeley and Rossi, 1966; Greeley, 1977, p. 112; Greeley, McCready and McCourt, 1976, pp. 255–7).[46] In income and education, Catholics have moved ahead of Lutherans and Baptists, although they still lag behind Jews, Episcopalians and Presbyterians (Greeley, McCready and McCourt, 1976, p. 44). He points out that adult Irish Catholics under 40 have graduated from college at a rate second only to Jews and enjoy an income level second to none (*ibid*, p. 74). In this new generation, Italian Catholics are second only to Irish Catholics in income. The selective and limited evidence about children in the new Christian schools permits no similar conclusions for them, but the evidence (on achievement tests) that does exist tends to be favorable.[47]

The fact that the most dramatic changes in private school population have occurred during changes in public school values suggests that the most serious competition is over values. Both in the nineteenth century and now it appears that a substantial number of individuals choose private schools because of religious beliefs. Then, as now, the values reflected in the public schools influenced this choice.

Giving priority to values rather than physical facilities is particularly common among the new Protestant fundamentalist schools. Typically, these schools are located in church basements. They cannot afford much in the way of salary for the teachers. They often refuse to obtain state accreditation. Teachers refuse to obtain teaching certificates, even when they are certifiable[48] and even when it is required by law. This has not deterred the families who chose these schools, because they have an overriding concern that their religious values be reflected in their child's school.[49]

Most educators who take a strong position against the new schools say they base this position on standards, not values. But a public ideal expressed by Horace Mann seems also to have its influence:

> ... the tendency of the private school system is to assimilate our modes of education to those of England, where churches and dissenters — each sect according to its own creed — maintain separate schools, in which children are taught, from their tenderest years to wield the sword of polemics with fatal dexterity; and where the gospel, instead of being a temple of peace, is converted into an armory of deadly weapons, for social, interminable warfare. Of such disastrous consequences, there is but one remedy and one preventive. It is the elevation of the common schools.[50]

Mann's observation still rings true. Many modern day educators decry the private school that appears to march to a different drummer. They see these schools as wielding 'the sword of polemics' and they see the public school as the one best remedy. The conflict goes on, and the choice remains: should the education system in America nurture the growth of a pluralist or a homogenous society?

Appendix

The sources for figures 1 and 2 are as follows:

Year	Public	Catholic	Non-public Non-Catholic	Total Private
1919–20	21,579,316[5]	1,925,527[1]		1,699,481[5]
1929–30	25,678,000[5]	2,464,467[1]	186,517[E]	2,651,044[5]
1932–33				2,026,625[2]
1939–40	25,433,542[5]	2,396,305[1]		
1940–41			205,000[E]	2,611,047[2]
1959–60	36,086,771[5]			5,674,943[5]
1960–61		5,253,791[1]		5,236,480[2]
1965		5,574,000[7]	615,548[6]	5,560,000[6]
Fall 1969	45,618,578[5]			5,500,000[5]
1970–71	45,900,000	4,363,566[1]		5,143,182[2]
1975		1,433,000[6]		
1976–77	44,317,000[3]	3,404,386[4]	1,661,782[4]	5,167,000[3]
1977–78	43,577,000[3]	3,322,803[4]	1,718,999[4]	5,140,000[3]
1978–79	42,611,000[3]	3,251,583[4]	1,820,000[7]	5,084,297[2]
1980–81	41,000,000[8]		2,000,000[7]	
1981–82			2,280,000[7]	
1982–83		3,026,000[7]		
Fall 1983	39,300,000[8]	3,200,000[8]	2,600,000[8]	
Fall 1985	39,513,000[9]	2,821,000[10]	2,879,000[E]	5,700,000

[E] Estimated, based on other figures in this chart. Note that there are serious discrepancies between school populations reported from different sources. As a result, the non-public, non-Catholic figure would appear to be a negative amount on line 1.

[1] NCES, Digest of Educ. Stat., 1982, Table 42, p. 50 (this may exclude kindergarten).

[2] NCES, Private Schools in American Education, Jan. 1981, Table A, p. 15.

[3] *Ibid*, Table B.

[4] *Ibid*, Table E-4, p. 52 (enrollments in other religious schools and unaffiliated schools were added).

[5] NCES, note 1, Table 3, at 8, includes K-12.

[6] Department of Health, Education and Welfare, National Center for Education Statistics, Statistics of Public Elementary and Secondary Day Schools 6 (1976).

[7] Based on an estimate by Bruce S. Cooper, Donald H. McLaughlin and Bruno V. Manno, extrapolating from a sample of twenty-one counties. They estimate the growth rate for non-Catholic private school pupils at 100,000 per year. Cooper and McLaughlin, and Manno, (1983) 'The Latest Word on Private School Growth', *Teachers College Record* 85 pp. 88–98. Total private school population generally experienced a small decline from 1965–66 to 1975–76, but began increasing after that date. Cooper *et al.* project a continued increase through 1990 for both Catholic and non-Catholic schools, although the projected increase in Catholic enrollments are based upon an assumption that the decline in enrollment has bottomed out, and that areas that are showing strong growth will continue to grow. *Ibid*, pp. 91–92 and figure 1, p. 96.

[8] NCES, Private Elementary and Secondary Education, 1983: Enrollment, Teachers, and Schools. Washington, DC, US Department of Education, 1983.

[9] NCES. Digest of Education Statistics, 1987, Table 2, p. 8.

[10] *Ibid.*, Table 45, p. 56.

Notes

This chapter was prepared when the author was Director of the Law and Education Center at the Education Commission of the States, Denver, Colorado; she is now with the US Department of Education. The views expressed in the chapter are her own and are not intended to represent the US Department of Education.

1 For a discussion of the constitutionality of regulating private schools, see LINES, 1983.
2 See letter to German Rulers, 1524. Luther urges that 'the civil authorities are under obligation to compel the people who send their children to school ... because in this case we are warring with the devil...' The context of the tract is discussed by Bruce (1928). See also Letter to Elector John of Saxony, 1529, in Smith and Jacobs (1913).
3 For example, Statute of Artificers, 1563 5 Eliz. I, c. iv.
4 Bailyn cites a stream of laws in the mid-seventeenth century 'ordering all towns to maintain teaching institutions, fining recalcitrants, stating and restating the urgencies of the situation' as evidence of 'fear of the imminent loss of cultural standards, of the possibility that civilization itself would be "buried in the grave of our fathers"', (Bailyn, 1972, p. 27).
5 The law also required knowledge of a trade. See Jernegan, 1918, pp. 735–6, for a copy of the law.
6 This is found in the Book of the General Laws..., 1648. See Jernegan, 1918, pp. 740–1, for a published copy of the law.
7 See Public Records..., pp. 520–21; Records of the Colony..., 1858, pp. 583–4; and The Book of the General Laws of the Inhabitants of New Plymouth, 1685, chapter V, sec. 1, p. 13.
8 See, for example, Laws of the Province of Pennsylvania, 1683, c. CXII.
9 See, for example, Laws of Virginia, 1642–43, Act 43; and 1646, Act 27.
10 See also Public Records, Colony of Connecticut, 1678–89, pp. 251 and 427–8; Act of 1691, (Mass.) Acts and Resolves, vol. 1, pp. 27 and 99; Public Records, Colony of Connecticut, 1678–89. pp. 427–8; Privy Council Acts of 1695 (Aug. 22); see Laws of New Hampshire, vol. III, 2d Sess. 1766, c. 14, p. 140.
11 See Acts and Resolves of Massachusetts, 1789, chapter 19.
12 See [Mass.] st. 1852, c. 240, secs. 1, 2, 4.
13 For example, the New York Public School Society was formed in 1805 to promote free schools for the very poor — those not provided for by any religious society. The early free schools of Pennsylvania were only for the poor, and not until 1830 did the legislature decide to open them up to all children (KATZ, 1975, p. 14). In 1837 and 1838 the idea of universal public education was introduced at the Pennsylvania state constitutional convention, and lost (KATZ, 1975).
14 In mid-century New York, in one Irish ward, one of five adults died in a period of thirty-two months; in another, one in seventeen persons died in a year (1854) (DOLAN, 1975, p. 39).
15 In May, a Protestant society favoring the King James version of the

Bible held a meeting in Kensington, an Irish working-class area, to protest a school board decision to allow Catholic children to use the Douay version; shots rang out; at least one Protestant was killed. In the end, several blocks of the district were burned (WEISBERGER, 1970, p. 172).

16   See, for example, WINTER, 1966.

17   See figure 2 in the text.

18   See Meyer v. Nebraska, 262 US 390 (1923); Farrington v. Tokushiga, 273 US 284 (1927). See also JAMES, 1982.

19   For the view that Jefferson opposed support of any religion, see DAVIS, 1955, p. 80. The phrase 'common to all sects' is from the report in an 1818 document on the curriculum of the University of Virginia, in which Jefferson urges that religion be placed within the province of a professor of ethics and that there be no professor of theology (PADOVER, 1943, p. 1104; COSTANZO, 1959, pp. 101–2).

20   In 1846, in response to a widespread public debate triggered by the will of Stephen Girard of Pennsylvania, establishing a school for orphans on condition that no religious personnel teach there, Mann said, 'The whole influence of the Board of Education from the day of its organization to the present time, has been to promote and encourage, and, whenever they have had any power, as in the case of the Normal Schools, to *direct* the daily use of the Bible in school' (CREMIN, 1951, p. 198). Cremin notes that Mann meant the King James Bible (CREMIN, 1951, p. 13).

21   Glenn argues that Mann was imposing a Unitarian point of view on the formerly evangelical Protestant schools. Cremin, who has provided considerable detail on the rift among Protestants, especially Congregationalists, feels that at bottom Mann's view were not too different from the 'evangelical conceptions of the day' (CREMIN, 1951, p. 140).

22   The prayer is quoted in Engel v. Vitale, 370 US 421 (1962).

23   For a discussion of the response to this and similar cases, see generally, LAUBACH (1969).

24   See Treen v. Karen B., 102 US 1267 (1982), *aff'ing per curiam* 653 F.2d 897 (5th Cir. 1981); Wallace v. Jaffree, 105 S. Ct. 2479 (1985).

25   Widmar v. Vincent, 454 US 263 (1981), prohibiting university officials from refusing space to students who planned a religious meeting.

26   See Jaffree v. Wallace, 705 F.2d 1526 (11th Cir. 1983), *aff'd* 104 S. Ct. 1704 (1984).

One of the many Alabama laws found unconstitutional had been championed by former Governor Fob James, who at one point risked contempt of court charges for urging Alabama citizens to ignore court orders prohibiting prayer in the schools. The invalid law would have allowed teachers, including college professors, to 'lead willing students in prayer', and it suggested a prayer written by the governor's son, then a law student:

Almighty God, you alone are our God. We acknowledge You as the Creator and Supreme Judge of the world. May Your justice, Your truth, and Your peace abound this day in the hearts of our countrymen, in the counsels of our government, *in the sanctity of*

our homes and in the classrooms of our schools *in the name of our Lord.* Amen.
Ala. Act 82–735 (1982) (emphasis in the original).

27 The Cedar Rapids, Iowa, school district adopted written guidelines for the study of religious history and traditions in the public school program. The guidelines use Supreme Court language for determining valid teaching activity and specify that '(1) the activity must have a secular purpose; (2) the activity's principal or primary effect must be one that neither advances nor inhibits religion; and (3) the activity must not foster an excessive governmental entanglement with religion'. The district permits the schools to observe religious holidays and include materials in the school program that bear on 'historical and contemporary significance' of religious holidays. The instruction must be unbiased and objective, and selection of holidays must 'take into account major celebrations of several world religions, not just those of a single religion'. Such programs must be 'educationally sound and sensitive to religious differences. . .'. The policy resembles that upheld by the US Court of Appeals for the Eighth Circuit in Florey v. Sioux Falls School Dist., 619 F.2d 1311 (8th Cir.), *cert. denied* 101 S. Ct. 409 (1980).

28 A federal district court judge ultimately struck the law down. May v. Cooperman, 572 F. Supp. 1561 (D.N.J. 1983). It is the only case in which a moment of silence, established in a law that does not by its terms mention prayer, has been struck down. Among other things, the court found an unconstitutional intent based upon statements of key sponsors of the bill. The decision raises the strange possibility of an identical law being upheld in sister states, because of a different legislative record.

29 For example, Widmar v. Vincent, 454 US 263 (1981). See also Bender v. Williamsport Area School Dist., 563 F. Supp. 697 (MD Pa. 1983); Lubbock Civil Liberties Union v. Lubbock Ind. School Dist., 669 F.2d 1038 (5th Cir. 1982); Collins v. Chandler Unified School Dist., 644 F.2d 759 (9th Cir. 1981), *cert. denied*, 454 US 863 (1981); Brandon v. Board of Education, 635 F.2d 971 (2d Cir. 1980), *cert. denied*, 454 US 1123 (1981).

30 Even before the current Christian school phenomena, Otto Kraushaar had observed that: 'Even the nondenominational independent schools generally owe their origins to founders who evinced a strong desire to transmit nonsectarian but nonetheless distinctly Protestant, middle class moral and religious ideals, but with strong emphasis also on superior academic attainments' (KRAUSHAAR, 1972, p. 6).

31 One major reason, some suggest, is increased income of Catholic families (NAULT, ERICKSON and COOPER, 1977, pp. 16–21). As Catholics become more affluent, they move to the suburbs, and choose other kinds of schools. In another study, the decline is attributed to complex factors:

> It may be clear, years from now, that the serious Catholic school enrollment setbacks during the ten years under study are best explained by . . . a stunning combination of profound challenges, each of which reinforces the negative impact of all the

others. To mention just a few: it was a massive fiscal shock, for a system subsidized enormously for decades by the contributed services of nuns, priests, and brothers, to have the supply of these religious teachers diminished drastically, to have the costs of the remaining religious teachers increase three-to-four fold, and to replace most of them with 'lay' teachers whose salaries were astronomical by comparison. No other non-public school group faced the massive city-to-suburb migration that Catholics have recently undergone, coupled with the refusal of church leaders to replace old city schools with new suburban ones. (One can hardly attend a non-existent school!) But perhaps most fundamentally, no other non-public school group underwent the startling, rapid shifts in philosophical outlook that the second Vatican Council symbolized. The doctrine that provided the old reasons for Catholic schools were largely swept away or reinterpreted. (ERICKSON, NAULT, COOPER and LAMBORN, 1976)

See also, COOPER, MCLAUGHLIN and MANNO (1983).

32 'Does David Gibbs Practice Law as Well as He Preaches Church-State Separation?', *Christianity Toady* 10 October, 1981, pp. 48–51.

33 Cases where this kind of argument was offered into evidence include State v. Faith Baptist Church, 107 Neb. 802, 301 N.W.2d 571 (1981), *appeal dismissed for want of a substantial federal question*, 102 S. Ct. 75 (1981); State v. Shaver, 294 N.W.2d 883 (ND. 1980); State v. Kasuboski, 87 Wis. 2d 407, 275 N.W.2d 101 (Wis. App. 1978); Hill v. State, 381 So.2d 91 (Ala. Crim, App. 1979), *reversed on other grounds*, 381 So.2d 94 (Ala. 1980); Hill v. State, 410 So.2d 431 (Ala. Crim, App. 1981) (same parties; convictions upheld after procedural defects corrected); Iowa v. Moorhead, 308 N.W.2d 60 (Iowa 1981); State v. Riddle, 285 S.E.2d 359 (W. Va. 1981).

34 See figures 1 and 2 in the text and authorities cited at note 31.

35 See figure 2 in the text. The Bureau of the Census estimates that enrollment in non-Catholic, non-public schools increased from 615,548 to 1,433,000 between 1965 and 1975, but these are probably only the more formal and accredited schools.

36 It seems likely that the largest growth is in attendance at unapproved schools. These small unaccredited schools often do not seek and do not want state approval, and probably do not want to be counted by the Census Bureau. Many of these unauthorized schools are fundamentalist Christian schools, which as a matter of faith reject state authority over their operations and refuse even to provide information on themselves. See COOPER, MCLAUGHLIN and MANNO, 1983.

In contrast the public school population has declined from approximately 45,900,000 in 1970, to 42,600,000 in 1978, to 41,204,093 in fall 1980; and to 40,984,093 by fall of 1981 US Department of Health Education and Welfare, National Center for Education Statistics, Statistics of Public Schools (fall, 1970, 1971); Statistics of Public Elementary and Secondary Day Schools (fall, 1978, 1979); NCES, Digest of Education Statistics 1982, Table 2, p. 7.

37 Interview with Carl Fynboe, then private school liaison for the

Washington Department of Public Instruction, 7 April 1983.

38 See for example, Santa Fe Community School v. New Mexico Board of Education, 85 N.M. 783, 518 P.2d 272 (N.M. 1974).

39 Up until recently the late John Holt (whose Boston-based organization, Holt Associates, continues to provide support services for home instruction) had estimated over 10,000 families educated their children illegally at home. However, a survey of just a few suppliers of home instruction materials for grades K-8 suggests that about 50,000 children are receiving home instruction, using such materials. Many more suppliers exist, and many parents develop their own materials, suggesting that some 100,000 to 200,000 children in grades K-8 are home-schooled. From 120,000 to 260,000 are in grades K-12 (Lines, 1987).

40 For a discussion of this phenomenon, see Wiley, 1983; and Murphy, 1980. They attribute much of the new power of state boards to growth in federal programs.

41 Compare the discussion of compulsory education laws in Kotin and Aikman, 1980, with Lines, 1983. During this brief period the focus of these laws shifted from regulation of truants to regulation of schools.

42 Georgia recently adopted a law to relieve pressure on private schools: S.B. 504, signed into law in May 1984. North Carolina established two levels of state approval. One implies state review of school standards; the other is approval only for purposes of compulsory attendance laws. North Carolina General Statutes, sec. 155C–547 through 115C–555 (Cum. Supp. 1983). Alabama exempts church schools from its normal requirements for approval. Ala. Code sec. 16–28–3 (Supp. 1983). So does Tennessee, Tenn. Code sec. 49–5201 (1982). Vermont's new law has made it clear that the state board has no authority to expand upon statutory standards. The earlier law required 'equivalency' as determined by the state board of education. See Vt. Stat. Ann. sec. 1121 (1974) (prior law). The new law strikes this provision and sets forth some minimal statutory requirements. Vt. Stat. Ann. secs. 906 and 1121 (supp. 1983). For background, see State v. LaBarge, 134 Vt. 276, 357 A.2d 121 (1976). Colorado adopted a law specifying that its state board has no jurisdiction over the 'internal affairs of any non-state or parochial school' although these schools must meet some attendance and basic education requirements. H.B. No. 1346, signed 3 June 1983 (to be codified as Colo. Rev. Stat. sec. 22–33–110). Mississippi has adopted a law prohibiting *any* regulation of private schools. Louisiana has repealed all state requirements for teachers in private schools. See La. Rev. Stat. Ann. sec. 17:411 and 17:7(8) (West Supp. 1981) (prior law, requiring teacher certification).

43 L.B. 928, signed into law on 10 April 1984.

44 The Head of the Education Department at Notre Dame University evaluated Catholic schools with concern:

> [B]roadly considered, government schools are typically superior to Catholic schools at every level — with, of course, many notable exceptions. Administrators, teachers, and guidance workers in government schools are typically better prepared professionally than their Catholic school counterparts. The

pupil-teacher ratio in Catholic schools, particularly at the elementary level, is frightfully high. There is an almost unbelievable shortage of qualified guidance counselors. Too high a percentage of Catholic secondary schools are not regionally accredited. (LEE, 1967, p. 264)

He also observed that

Government schools have always taken the lead in all spheres of professionalization, especially in experimentation, in guidance, and in instructional services. Catholic schools generally have lagged behind, criticizing government schools for their innovational practices and ending up by tardily accepting these improvements. (*Ibid*, p. 258).

However, these schools probably are getting better. Moreover, a substantial number of people *think* they are better. In a 1974 survey, 34 per cent of those who said they sent their children to Catholic schools did so primarily because they felt the children would receive a better education; 19 per cent did so primarily to assure religious instruction; 18 per cent hoped mainly for more discipline (GREELEY, McCREADY and McCOURT, 1976, p. 227).

45 Following the criticism, and after additional data became available, Coleman and his colleagues analyzed the data again, finding significant effects for basic language and mathematics skills (HOFFER, GREELEY and COLEMAN, 1984). For critiques, see *School Research Forum*, April 1981 (published by Educational Research Service).

46 Of course, socioeconomic characteristics of Catholics attending Catholic schools may influence their education and income attainment. In fact, the richest and poorest Catholics do not attend these schools; the middle income are more likely to do so (GREELEY, 1977, p. 112).

47 The scant amount of testing evidence indicates that unapproved alternatives can be educationally adequate. One source of data comes from a handful of litigated cases, where 'before and after' scores from standardized tests were introduced into evidence. For example, in re Rice, 204 Neb. 732, 285 N.W.2d 223 (1979); State v. Shaver, 294 N.W.2d 883 (N.D. 1980). In one, a court found that a child kept in an unapproved school had made 'remarkable progress' compared to her level of development in the public school. In re Rice, *supra*. In State v. Faith Baptist Church, the celebrated Nebraska case, the court considered some evidence — testimony of a parochial school teacher — that the children were receiving an adequate education but rejected it as irrelevant and not grounded on adequate expertise. 107 Neb. 802, 301 N.W. 2d 571 (1981), appeal dismissed 454 US 803. Testing data from a Los Angeles home tutorial movement indicate that the children in the tutorial program scored higher than children in the public schools, but there were no controls for socioeconomic status of the parents, and pretest data were not available (WEAVER, NEGRI and WALLACE, 1980).

48 See for example, North Dakota v. Revinius, 328 N.W.2d 220 (N.D. 1982). Teachers were certifiable, but refused to obtain certificates for religious reasons. See also State v. Nobel, Nos. S 791-0114-A and S

791–0115–A (Mich. Dist. Ct., Allegon County, 12 December 1979) (same home instruction case).

49   This is not to say that the new schools reject accountability: many of the leaders in this movement have asked, in lieu of state certification requirements, for nationally standardized testing of their children to assure education accountability. They have requested testing in lieu of more onerous requirements during litigation. See, for example, State v. Whisner, 47 Ohio St.2d 181, 351 N.E.2d 750 (1976); State v. Faith Baptist Church, 107 Neb. 802, 301 N.W.2d 571 (1981), *appeal dismissed for want of a substantial federal question*, 454 US 803 (1981). Fundamentalist leaders also lobbied for this solution in North Carolina, Nebraska and other states, as an alternative to more onerous regulations.

50   Horace Mann, First Annual Report (1837). A published copy can be found in CREMIN, 1957, pp. 29, 33.

5 The Public/Private Division of Responsibility for Education: An International Comparison

Estelle James

Introduction

To what degree do different countries rely on the private sector in their provision of education? How can we explain the diverse choices made by different societies and for different levels of education? This chapter presents findings from my international study of the public/private division of responsibility for education and other quasi-public goods. Both statistical analyses and intensive case studies are used, for the dual purpose of hypothesis formation and hypothesis testing. In the broader work of which this chapter is one part, I also examine what difference the choice of public versus private management makes, with respect to variables such as funding, quality, cost, efficiency and distribution of services (James, 1982, 1984, 1986 and 1987; James and Benjamin, 1984).

The wide disparity in public/private enrollment ratios across countries and levels is presented in table 1. We see there that the relative size of the private sector varies from 1 per cent to 98 per cent at the primary level, from 2 per cent to 91 per cent at the secondary level. The range at higher educational levels is also substantial, although not quite as wide.

How do we explain the great diversity? Is the choice of system by a country a random event, or are there underlying forces which enable us to predict its choice? Part I argues that the relative size of the private sector is determined by excess demand and differentiated demand for education, emerging from a collective choice process, and by the supply of religious entrepreneurship in the society and industry in question. The demand-side variables, initially set forth by Weisbrod (1975 and 1977) and developed further in this chapter, view the

Table 1:   Relative Role of the Private Sector in Education

	Percentage private primary (1)	Percentage private secondary (2)	Percentage PVT sec divided by percentage PVT prim
Selected modern industrial societies			
Australia	10	26	1.3
Belgium: Flemish	63	72	1.1
French	32	48	1.5
England and Wales	5	8	1.6
France	15	21	1.4
Germany	2	9	4.5
Ireland	98	91	0.9
Italy	8	7	0.9
Japan	1	15*	15.0
Netherlands	69	72	1.0
New Zealand	10	12	1.2
Sweden	1	2	2.0
USA	18	10	0.6
Selected African and Asian Countries			
Hong Kong	92	72	.8
India	25	49	2.0
Indonesia	15	34	2.3
Kenya	1	60	60.0
Nigeria	31	45	1.5
Singapore	35	28	0.8
Selected South American Countries			
Argentina	17	30	1.8
Brazil	12	43	3.6
Colombia	15	47	3.1
Chile	17	20	1.2
Ecuador	17	30	1.8
Paraguay	15	33	2.2
Peru	13	13	1.0
Uruguay	16	16	1.0
Venezuela	11	21	1.9
Selected Central American Countries			
Costa Rica	3	6	2.0
El Salvador	4	29	7.3
Mexico	5	26	5.2
Nicaragua	12	43	3.6
Panama	5	19	3.8

*Data include upper and lower secondary. Figure for upper secondary is 28 per cent.
Note: All countries for which I could get data for percentages of private, primary and secondary, have been included. Data is for varying years between 1973 and 1980, as noted under 'Sources'.

Sources:
%Private, Primary and Secondary, European countries except Sweden 1978, 1979 or 1980: Neave, G. (1953) *The Non-state Sector in the Education Provision of Member States of the European Community: A Report to the European Community,* Brussels.

%Private, Primary and Secondary, Sweden, 1978: Marklund, S. (1979) *Educational Administration and Educational Development,* University of Stockholm, Institute of International Education.

%Private, Primary (1975, 1976 or 1977) and Secondary (1977), South and Central America: *America En Cifras, 1977,* Washington, DC, O.A.S., 1977, pp. 118–40.

%Private, Primary and Secondary, US, 1980: *Digest of Educational Statistics,* Washington, DC, National Center for Educational Statistics, US Dept. of Education, 1982, p. 13.

%Private, Primary and Secondary, Australia, 1978: Sherman, J. (1981) 'Government finance of private education: A review of the Australian experience', *School Finance Project Working Paper,* Washington, DC, US Dept. of Education, p. 3.

%Private, Primary and Secondary, Japan, 1980: *Nombusho,* Tokyo, Ministry of Education, 1981, pp. 1, 3, 15 and 18.

%Private, Primary, African/Asian Countries and New Zealand, 1973 or 1974:   *UNESCO Statistical Yearbook,* 1975.

%Private, Secondary, African/Asian Countries and New Zealand, 1977: *Education Statistics of New Zealand,* Wellington, Department of Education, 1978; *Hong Kong Annual Digest of Statistics,* Hong Kong, Census and Statistics Dept., 1978; *Fourth All-India Educational Survey,* New Delhi, National Council of Educational Research and Training, 1978; *Indonesia Education Sector Survey Report,* IBRD Report No. 443-IND; *Educational Trends* 1973–77, Nairobi, Central Bureau of Statistics, p. 72. *Statistics of Education in Nigeria,* Lagos, Federal Ministry of Information, 1972, data for 1972; *Yearbook of Statistics, Singapore 1977–78,* Singapore, Dept. of Statistics, 1977.

I am indebted to Daniel Levy who provided me with most of the data on South and Central America.

private sector as a market response to a situation where large groups of people are dissatisfied with the amount or type of government production.[1] I argue that two different patterns of private education have developed, depending on whether it is motivated by excess demand or differentiated demand. The former is more likely to be the source of private sector demand in developing countries, the latter in advanced industrial societies. In both cases, a supply-side variable, the availability of (religious) educational entrepreneurs, adds further power to our explanation of the differential growth of the private sector and also sheds light on why much private production in education is non-profit, why much non-profit production is in education.

Part II applies this theoretical model to several countries I have studied — the US, Japan, Holland, India and Sweden. Demand-and-supply-side variables are used to analyze why the size of the private sector in education varies widely by state or province within each country. The results are consistent with our hypotheses. More tentative evidence suggests that the same framework will help in understanding the role of the private educational sector in other countries as well.

Three caveats should be mentioned at the outset. First, the definition of 'private' is by no means clear-cut in a situation where many 'private' schools are heavily funded and regulated by the state. 'Source of funding' and 'degree of decision-making authority' may then yield different public-private categories, and many mixed rather than polar cases (see James, 1987). Second, I have modeled private sector growth as a response to government decisions about amount and type of public education. While I have suggested some of the forces influencing government behavior, I am unable to explain it fully, given the absence of a generally accepted theory of the state. It is certainly possible that government production depends partially on what is happening in the private sector, i.e., causation may run both ways.

Relatedly, majority voting and the median voter theory is used as my hypothetical collective choice mechanism. In the real world, however, different people have different degrees of political power; for example, certain groups don't vote, are underrepresented in the legislature, have fewer economic resources to invest in influencing decisions, and sometimes police or military power rather than free elections are the basis of the government. Then, the outcome will depend on the preferences of the ruling coalition, which may not include the median voter or represent the majority will. In the following pages, 'ruling coalition' can be substituted for the term 'median voter' to explain how the preferences of a dominant group or individual affects public/private choices. A logical but difficult next step would be to predict which group becomes dominant, and to simultaneously determine government and private sector behavior.

Part I: Determinants of the Private Sector in Education Demand Side Explanations: Excess Demand

Private production has been a response to an excess demand for education and other quasi-public goods in the face of a limited government supply. Weisbrod (1977) has shown that, with a given tax structure, if government satisfies the median voter (in order to maximize its votes in a two-party democracy), some people will have a 'left-over' demand for public goods which they will attempt to satisfy privately (pp. 51–77). While developed for the case of pure collective goods, this model can easily be adapted to the case of quasi-public goods, such as education, i.e., goods which, in fact, get parcelled out and from which people can be excluded. The basic idea is that people will vote to expand the public school system so long as their probable (external plus private) benefits from expansion exceed their tax shares and cannot be purchased more cheaply in the private market; but if the capacity chosen by the majority is less than full enrollment some people with high benefits may be left out and will enter the private sector.[2] I develop this model more precisely for the two cases of uniform tax shares and varying tax shares, first assuming equal and then unequal costs of production for the two sectors.

Case I: Uniform Tax Shares

Consider the decision about how many secondary school places a government should provide. Each incremental space may end up being occupied by your own child or by someone else's child. Thus, for each space every family receives a marginal benefit, B, which can be decomposed into an 'external' component EXTB, i.e., that accruing from the probable education of others, plus a 'private' component PRB, accruing from the probable education of your own child. PRB includes both the private investment and consumption benefits of education. EXTB may stem from the desire to have a literate citizenry, to instill patriotism and other common values, and to develop a core of educated people to help the government and the economy run smoothly.

Suppose there are n families in the population, each with one child, and m school places, with all children having an equal chance of getting in , i.e., the ranking of different children is not known ahead of time. Then, the expected private benefit PRBi to the ith family of the $(m + 1)^{th}$ space is $\left(\dfrac{n - m}{n}\right)\left(\dfrac{1}{n - m}\right)bi = \dfrac{b_i}{n}$, and the expected external benefit $EXTB_i^m = \dfrac{n - 1}{n} EXTb_i^m$ where:

$B_i^m \quad = PRB_1 + EXTB_i^m$

$b_i \quad$ = the private benefit of school attendance by the ith child

$EXTb_i^m$ = the external benefit to family i if another family's child occupies the $(m + 1)^{th}$ space

$\left(\dfrac{n - m}{n}\right)$ = the probability that the ith child did not get into the 1st m place

$\left(\dfrac{1}{n - m}\right)$ = the probability that i will be admitted to the $(m + 1)^{th}$ place, if he applies

$\dfrac{n - 1}{n}$ = the probability that another child will end up occupying the $(m + 1)^{th}$ place

Note that, while b_i may differ for different people depending on their incomes and taste for education, for a given family, i, b_i and PRBi are constant for all levels of potential public school size up to n, the point of full enrollment. However, $EXTB_i^m = \dfrac{n - 1}{n} EXTb_i^m$ may be downward sloping, i.e., the benefit i derives from the education of another incremental person may decline as the number of people already educated rises. In that case, B_i will also be downward sloping.

Let us make the following simple assumptions. People are risk neutral, hence act on the basis of expected values. The size of the public sector is determined by majority vote (the median voter) and non-price rationing is used, if public capacity < n. Admission to private schools is also possible, is strictly by price-rationing, and the size of the private sector is large enough to clear the market. Tuition = P covers the cost of private education while taxes are used to finance public education, each family having the same tax share T for each marginal public school place. Thus, public funding implies public production and private production is also privately financed; publicly funded private systems are not an option in this model. We assume at first that $T = \frac{p}{n}$, i.e., government and private sector have equal marginal production costs.

In this model, each family votes for an expanded public system so long as $T \leq \left(EXTB_i + \frac{b_i}{n}\right)$ and also $T \leq \left(EXTB_i + \frac{p}{n}\right)$, i.e., so long as the tax cost is less than the marginal benefit, which is either $\left(EXTB_i + \frac{b_i}{n}\right)$ or $\left(EXTB_i + \frac{p}{n}\right)$, whichever is smaller. Since $T = \frac{p}{n}$, the second inequality is satisfied whenever $EXTB_i \geq 0$. Consequently, only the first inequality matters in case I; all those with high Bs (due to high income or high taste for education) will vote for more education, those with low Bs for less. Under the median voter theory, if the majority of people have $B_i \geq T$ at n, as in figure 1, the public school system will be large enough to enroll the entire population, and there will be no leftover demand for the private sector.[3] On the other hand, if the median voter prefers a smaller size public sector, such as E* in figure 2, some children will not be able to attend public school; those excluded whose private benefit $b_i > P$ will seek other alternatives, creating a left-over demand for private education.[4]

It is useful to ask: why do we have public schools at all, under these conditions? If $EXTB_i = 0$ for everyone, and private schools are available, the majority would either strictly prefer 0 or would be indifferent between 0 and n as the size of the public system; since, in the latter case, the minority would be made worse off by n, it should be able to convince (bribe) the majority to choose O, hence no public schools. However, if $EXTB_i > 0$ for some people, the majority may wish to set a floor on the size of the overall system, rather than leaving it to individual decision-making. The ability of the median voter to set this floor for a public system, in the presence of externalities, is the only (positive) rationale for its existence, under uniform tax shares and equal production costs. As we have seen, the floor may not accommodate everyone with private benefits greater than tuition, leaving room for a private sector as well.

Case II: Varying Tax Shares

Once tax shares vary for different people, the situation becomes more complex. Suppose, for example, taxes are a positive function of

Figure 1: Public and Private School Enrollments

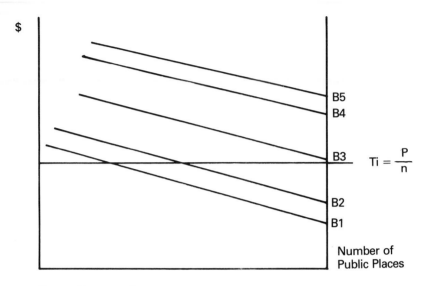

Source: See appendix.

Figure 2: Private School Enrollments

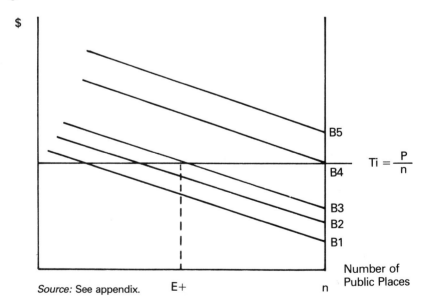

income. Since $T_i > P$ for some i when tax shares vary, the second inequality tells us that these high-tax families will prefer a small public sector, unless they derive large externalities from the education of others. Consequently, some high income people who would have voted for a large public system in case I may vote against it in case II. This limitation on government production of quasi-public goods is one potential consequence of a progressive tax system. On the other hand, some low-tax, low-income people may switch their votes in the opposite direction. Thus, when tax shares vary, the desire for redistribution is another rationale for a public system and the resistance of those being redistributed from is a limiting force on its size. The net impact of differing tax shares on equilibrium capacity of the public sector depends on the relative size of these switching groups. A full enrollment system is more likely to result if taxes are concentrated in a small group of (wealthy) people, whose perceived externalities are large, and if $T_i \leq \frac{p}{n}$ for the majority. The prevalence of large public systems suggests that these conditions exist in many countries, especially at the primary level. However, if taxes are high relative to benefits and tuition for the median voter, $E^\star < n$ and once again, some people with $b_i > P$ will be left over for the private market.

Case III: Private Production Cheaper Than Public

In cases I and II the groups voting for 'more' government production do so because of the externality thereby generated or because their T_i is low relative to B_i and P; in this sense, they are being 'redistributed to'. The number of people preferring a large public system, hence the probability of this outcome, decreases if public production is more costly than private production, i.e., if $\Sigma\ T_i > P$.

In another paper, I discuss some of the reasons — bureaucratic rules, above-market civil service wages, etc. — that may lead to higher costs in the public sector (James, 1987). A particularly important reason is the deadweight loss from taxation, including the cost (and sometimes the impossibility) of implementing an effective tax collection system. Lower private costs also result from the religious nature of entrepreneurship in the private sector, as discussed below. The higher $\Sigma\ T_i$ is relative to P, the more people whose $T_i > \left(\text{EXTB}_i + \frac{p}{n}\right)$ at n, leading the median voter (or ruling coalition) to choose a smaller quantity of government production and leaving a greater excess demand for the private sector to fill.[5]

Excess-Demand-Driven Private Sectors in Developing and Modern Countries

My empirical studies of private educational sectors indicate that the 'excess demand' model applies in developing countries, where small-scale production and subsistence agriculture, industries with a low return to education, still predominate, but contrast sharply with the growing urban areas where the private return is high. The difficulties in raising tax revenues in rural subsistence economies, and the reluctance of the urban upper class to subsidize a large public sector from which others will benefit, leads to a coalition of low demanders and high taxpayers that effectively restricts the supply of government schools in many developing countries.

One might expect this coalition of low demanders and high taxpayers to be strongest at the secondary level. At the primary level, where private benefits are substantial in rural as well as urban areas and where externalities are most often perceived, the group of low demanders may be relatively small. At the university level, high taxpayers may be willing to pay a disproportionate amount of the public bill, if they also get disproportionate access. At the secondary level, however, rural benefits may be lower and costs per student higher than for primary and access not as income-biased as for university; hence the low demanders and high taxpayers form a coalition to restrict government production. At the same time, as primary school graduates increase, and as the incentive to acquire higher education (often heavily subsidized) rises, many urban middle and working class families become anxious to send their children to secondary school, even if they must pay themselves. By the above reasoning we would predict that the private sector will be relatively small at the primary level, much larger at the secondary level, and the two would not be highly correlated, in developing countries where excess demand is the moving force. We would expect to find a somewhat smaller (though still substantial) private sector in higher education as well. Indeed, this prediction is roughly consistent with table 1, where the relative role of private education is much larger at the secondary than the primary level [median (percentage private secondary)/ (percentage private primary) = 2.0] and the correlation between the two is low ($r^2 = .32$) for the group of developing countries from Africa, Asia and Latin America.

Among industrialized countries, Japan best fits the 'excess demand' model at both the secondary and higher levels: over one-quarter of all high school (upper secondary) students and three-quarters of those in universities attend private institutions. While Japan today can hardly be characterized as a developing country, it has made the transition to a modern industrial state more rapidly and recently than most Western countries and its large private education sector may be a legacy of earlier periods. In addition, Japan has, since the end of World War II, been controlled by the conservative Liberal Democratic Party (LDP), which has maintained the lowest rate of government expenditure and taxation among modern developed countries. This policy of limited government production, as applied to education, meant that only the minimum quantity deemed necessary for national purposes was provided publicly, while everything else was considered a consumer good, left to private enterprise. It is hardly surprising that the supporters of the LDP (top managers, small shopkeepers, farmers — i.e., groups with a low taste for education or high tax shares) constituted a majority coalition benefiting from this policy of limited public spending on education. However, demand far exceeded the limited government supply, as evidenced by high application rates, low acceptance rates, and the large number of ronin — students who, having failed the entrance exam to universities the first time round, spend a year or two 'cramming' and try again. (This phenomenon is also found in other countries, such as India). Thus, private funding and management of secondary and higher education flourished, particularly in the years after World War II (see James and Benjamin, 1988).

It is instructive to contrast the Japanese with the Swedish case, since the party in Sweden during this period, the Social Democratic Party, is the mirror image of Japan's LDP. The SDP's working class constituency wanted — and got — a redistributive tax structure combined with a high quantity of government service, a vast expansion of education and other social services provided by the government at the expense of upper and middle class taxpayers. In Sweden, 90 per cent of each cohort now stays in school until age 18 and one-third go on to higher education, proportions which are very similar to those in Japan, but almost all are accommodated in government institutions (James, 1982, p. 48). Clearly, there was no leftover demand for the private sector.

Does the ability to tax as well as the median voter's willingness to spend on education (and other quasi-public goods) increase with economic development, leaving less leftover demand for the private sector? We would expect the group of low demanders to decline with development, given the income elasticity of demand for education and the higher rate of return to education in urban, industrial areas. Thus, the number of government-funded school places should increase, reaching full enrollment at the secondary and possibly higher levels. In the case of Japan, as agriculture shrank and the urban working class grew, the LDP did indeed find it necessary to form new coalitions in order to maintain itself in power. Spurred by declines in its electoral majority during the 1960s, the LDP undertook a major reexamination of its policies in the fields of education and social welfare, culminating in a decision to increase expenditures in these areas. However, the increase took the form of subsidies to the well-established private sector rather than increased government production; sectoral shares were deliberately stabilized (James and Benjamin, 1988). Since the subsidies covered only a part (up to 30 per cent) of private sector costs, but played a crucial role in keeping many institutions alive, a larger number of people reap their benefits than would have been the case if the same amount of money had been spent on the full funding of new public school places. Presumably, this was deemed to be in the vote-maximizing interest of the LDP.

In other words, a third alternative exists to the two set forth above, the possibility of partial government support to private schools, and indeed, this often plays an important role (see James, 1987). Thus, a shift from private to public financing does not necessarily imply a shift from private to public production, particularly if the coalition in power is able to keep the public financing partial. The total shift occurred earlier in England and Sweden but has not occurred in Japan and does not appear to be an inevitable consequence of development.

Differentiated Tastes: Another Demand Side Explanation

A second demand-side model views private production of quasi-public goods as a response to differentiated tastes about the *kind* of service to be consumed (rather than differentiated tastes about *quantity*), in situations where that differentiation is not accommodated by government production. The private sector would then grow larger if (i) peoples' preferences with respect to product variety are more heterogeneous and more intense, usually due to deep-seated cultural (religious, linguistic, ethnic) differences; (ii) this diversity is geographically dispersed so it cannot be accommodated by local government production; (iii) government is constrained to offer a relatively uniform product, the median voter's preferred choice; and (iv) the dominant cultural group is not determined to impose its preferences on others; hence private production is a permissible way out. The 'differential demand' model appears to explain the development of private educational production in modern industrial societies, and is often associated with large government subsidies.

Economic models usually assume that local governments provide quasi-public goods, that people will move to a geographic community offering the kinds of services they prefer, and those with like tastes will therefore congregate together to get the product variety of their choice. The hypothesis proposed here is that barriers to mobility often stop this process at a point where considerable heterogeneity still exists within a local political unit. Yet, economies of scale and standardization or other political constraints prevent the local government from satisfying this diversity. Private production is then based on a 'community of interest', and constitutes an institutional mechanism for responding to diverse tastes without incurring movement costs or overcoming other movement barriers. For example, clients may be drawn from a number of localities who share a preference for a particular type of service, even though they wish to live in different neighborhoods for other reasons.

In countries where cultural groups are concentrated in different geographic areas (as in Switzerland) local government production achieves the desired diversity. In countries where a dominant group seeks to impose its language or values on others, private schools may be prohibited or restricted; this was the position of Holland and France during earlier anti-clerical periods. The 'melting pot theory' and the general belief in assimilation of minorities to majority values led to the 'common school' movement in the nineteenth and twentieth century US; the growth of Catholic private schools was a response by a group that did not want to be fully assimilated. However, the 'cultural heterogeneity' model best explains the development of the private sector in countries such as Holland and Belgium today (as discussed at length in James, 1984).

Dutch society has long been characterized by deeply felt cultural (religious) cleavages. In particular, control over their own education was particularly important to the Catholics and Calvinists (orthodox Protestants) who constitute approximately 50 per cent of the population. These two groups formed a political coalition at the turn of the century which, after much battling, succeeded in bringing about state subsidy of private schools, a principle embodied in the 1917 Dutch constitution (James, 1984; Geiger, 1984). In the years to come out only education but most other quasi-public goods, such as health care and social service, were to be produced by private organizations, though financed mainly by the state (Kramer, 1982). Similar cleavages along linguistic and religious lines may be found in Belgium.

In India, too, private schools and colleges are often differentiated by language (associated with region of origin), religion (Moslem, Parsee, Sikh) or caste group. The same is true of Malaysia (Chinese and Indian minorities). In Israel, most private schools are run by and for very orthodox Jewish groups, who are dissatisfied with the secular public schools.

Since densely populated urban areas will be characterized by greater diversity, with a market large enough to support several schools, the cultural heterogeneity argument leads us to expect private provision of education to be positively associated with urbanization and density indices. This is one of the hypotheses that will be tested below.

More generally, I would expect differentiated demand rather than excess demand to be the moving force behind large private sectors in modern industrial societies, particularly those which have a large private primary sector. Desire for cultural homogeneity is likely to be greatest at the primary level, for this is the age at which linguistic ability and religious identification develop, and values are formed. It is also true, however, that residential segregation in public systems may accomplish this purpose better at the primary than the secondary level, since the catchment area is often larger for the latter. The partially counter-acting effect of these two forces could easily lead to a relatively large private primary sector, but a relatively small disparity in private sector size at primary and secondary levels, in societies where differentiated demand is the raison d'etre for private education. These predictions are roughly consistent with table 1, where the private sectors at primary and secondary levels are close in relative size [median (percentage private secondary)/(percentage private primary) = 1.25] and highly correlated ($r^2 = .96$) for the group of modern industrial countries, excluding Japan.

Differentiated Demand: Quality

Differentiated preferences about quality, one group demanding a 'better' product than the median voter choice, may also lead to the development of a private alternative. Our earlier discussion about capacity of the public school system assumed that quality, as indicated by per student spending (PSS) was fixed. Actually, however, cost per student is a variable, and societies, especially developing ones, face a quantity-quality trade-off.

To analyze this choice, assume that each country has a total public educational budget, EDBUDG, which depends on its income, ability to tax, and taste for education. Since EDBUDG = Q · PSS, for any given EDBUDG a country can choose to spend more on quality (PSS), less on quantity (Q), leaving some unsatisfied demand for quantity (as discussed above); or it can choose to satisfy the entire zero-price demand, n, allowing quality to fall to EDBUDG/n, often leaving some unsatisfied demand for quality (see figure 3). In general, the upper classes would prefer quality, the working classes quantity, assuming that the income elasticity of demand for educational quality is higher than that for educational quantity. The political power and coalitions formed by different groups, then, determine the quantity-quality combination just as they determine the total EDBUDG chosen by each country.

Secondary and higher education in Japan fit the first model; the public system is the high cost, high quality system. On the other hand, some Latin American countries and parts of India fit the second model, with the public system, especially at the primary and secondary levels, providing quantity for the working class while higher income people purchase better quality education in the private market. Still a third model features both high quality and high quantity. This, of course, implies a large educational budget and is an option available only to wealthy countries, such as Sweden, where the private educational sector is negligible.

What, then, is the impact of public school quality on private sector size? Complicating the empirical analysis of this issue, as we shall see in Part II, is the endogeneity of quality choices, the fact that public quality may be correlated with other variables, such as per capita income, that directly determine private sector size. If we perform the mental experiment of holding income constant, I would expect variations in the quality variable to have different effects in excess demand and differentiated demand countries.

In differentiated demand countries, when there is no excess de-

Figure 3: Supply of Public School Places – The Quantity-Quality Trade-Off.

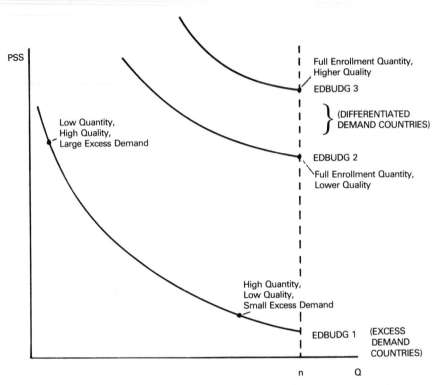

mand (public school capacity maintained at n), higher PSS does not affect the number of available public school places, but necessarily implies a higher EDBUDG, and hence should unambiguously reduce the number of people who flee to the private sector seeking quality education. In contrast, in excess demand countries, two forces are at work: a higher PSS decreases the number who choose private education for quality reasons, hence should lead to a smaller private sector. On the other hand, if EDBUDG is held constant, greater public quality implies lower public quantity, given the quantity-quality trade-off, hence should lead to a larger 'mass' private sector (see figure 3). Public sector quality and private sector size will consequently be negatively or positively correlated depending on which of these two effects dominate. I would conjecture that the number of people willing to pay for private education on quality grounds, when public education is available, is relatively small, while a larger number will pay for private education if no public alternative is open to them. Therefore, I would expect the second effect to dominate and public quality to be positively related to private sector size, when EDBUDG is held constant but public sector size is not (for example, in some excess demand countries), and negatively related under the opposite conditions (in differentiated demand countries). I would also expect the negative effect to approach zero for countries where the public sector is already considered the high quality sector, so that the marginal impact on enrollment of further quality improvements is negligible. The statistical results from the US and Japan, presented in Part II, are consistent with my expectations for differentiated and excess demand countries, respectively.

In any event, it appears that the private sector cannot generally be considered higher in quality than the public sector and the demand for quality does not explain the existence of large private sectors. This is partly because the public system can be and has been structured in many countries to accommodate differentiated preferences about quality; for example, selective schools, internal tracking, residential segregation are commonly used to keep those with an effective demand for quality within the public system. Also, in our above analysis of the quantity-quality trade-off, the public sector is sometimes deliberately chosen to be small and high in quality. On the other hand, a high quality private sector was shown to develop when the public sector was large and low cost; the private sector will then, by definition, be relatively small. Indeed, the 'quality' of these prestigious private schools stems in part from their scarcity and selectivity, which also help explain the important role they play in the economic and social structures of their countries.

I would hypothesize that the larger the private sector the less likely it is to be the high quality sector preferred by the upper classes, the more likely it is to stem from excess demand or cultural differentiation rather than quality considerations. As supporting evidence: the private higher educational sectors in Colombia and Brazil, which have over 50 per cent of total enrollments, are largely excess-demand driven, while those in Venezuela and Mexico, which have less than 15 per cent of total enrollments, represent a demand for superior education; quality considerations play an important role in US secondary education (10 per cent private) while cultural differentiation is more important at the primary level (18 per cent private) (see the following section on statistical testing); and the public/private ratios of educational Gini coefficients in Japan are positively related to relative size of the private sector, increasing from primary to secondary and reaching unity at the university level, where most enrollments are private (James and Benjamin, 1988).

Supply Side Explanations and the Theory of Non-profit Organizations

Who starts private schools and why? Ordinarily, we do not ask this question in the theory of the firm. We assume that enterprise founders are an anonymous group of people seeking profits and willing to start a new business wherever a profitable opportunity presents itself. Since we 'know' their objective, profit maximization, any further information about their identity, tastes and motives is irrelevant.

In situations where education is characterized by huge excess demand, we do indeed find many ordinary profit-maximizing private schools, the Philippines and parts of South America being prime examples. However, more commonly, private schools are established as non-profit organizations, i.e., as organizations which cannot distribute a monetary residual. It is useful then to ask why private schools are often non-profit, what are the motives of the founders (in the absence of a profit motive and reward), and what factors determine their availability? As we shall see, non-profit educational entrepreneurs often have special non-pecuniary objectives and access to low-cost resources which enable them to compete effectively both with government and for-profit schools. I conjecture that differences across countries in the supply of non-profit entrepreneurs exert a potentially powerful influence on the size of the private educational sector and provide empirical evidence to support this hypothesis.

Disguised Profits, Prestige and Political Power

One potential motive for founding schools is the possibility of earning profits or, in areas where non-profit status may be a legal requirement for schools and universities, disguised profits. There is a popular belief in many countries (for example, Japan, Colombia) that disguised profit distribution takes place. Although called 'non-profit' these organizations are, allegedly, really profit-making entities. The illegal ways of distributing profits are only rarely brought to light, as when student places or professional appointments are 'sold' to families giving large gifts to the school's administrator or 'kickbacks' are given to influential people after successful equipment sales. The legal ways are more interesting but very difficult to detect. For example, the founder may become the headmaster and be paid a salary beyond the market wage, i.e., beyond what he could earn elsewhere; he is, in effect, receiving monetary profits, albeit in disguised form. Even more valuable disguised profit distribution is said to take place in non-monetary, hence non-taxable form — expense accounts, free houses and cars (James and Benjamin, 1988, p. 16). These opportunities for earning profits seem to be particularly prevalent in excess demand countries.

Benefits to founders may also take an intangible form: perpetuation of a family name on a school, status and prestige from being connected with an important institution. In effect, by creating these status distinctions (and therefore exacerbating prestige inequalities) a society is increasing the coinage at its disposal and using some of it to pay for non-profit entrepreneurship. These motivations are common in the US, and in other countries where non-profits are found. In Sweden, on the other hand, private philanthropy is actually frowned upon as a source of undesired status differentials.

A related benefit to school founders in many countries, particularly excess demand countries (for example, Japan, India, Kenya), is the political support they gain in a local community. The community may be beholden to an individual who starts a school there; in addition, he gains a potential cadre of student and teacher supporters. Thus, political ambition is often pointed to as a motivation of non-profit private school founders.

Religious Motivation

However, another motivation seems much more potent when we observe that most founders of private schools (and other non-profit organizations) are 'ideological' organizations — political groups (as in colonial countries such as India and Kenya before independence), Socialist labor unions (as in Swedish adult educational associations), and, first and foremost, organized religion. Universally across countries, religious groups are the major founders of non-profit service institutions. We see this in the origin of many private schools and voluntary hospitals in the US and England, Catholic schools in France and Latin America, Calvinist schools in Holland, missionary activities in developing countries, services provided by Moslem *waqf*s (religious trusts), etc.

Usually these are proselytizing religions, but other religious/ideological groups often must start their own schools as a defensive reaction (for example, the 'independence schools' in Kenya and the caste-dominated schools in India were started partly to provide an alternative to the Western mission schools). These non-profit founders concentrated on education because schools are one of the most important institutions of taste formation and socialization. The non-profit form was chosen because their object was not to maximize profits but to maximize religious faith or adherents, a goal which was often not compatible with profit-maximizing behavior. For example, religious schools may wish to charge a price below the profit-maximizing level in order to keep members within the fold and/or attract new believers.

Typically, these ideological groups have their own 'school systems', horizontally and vertically integrated sets of schools which cater to a particular group; and often the systems (although not each school in it) are 'inclusive' rather than 'exclusive', i.e., having places for all their members or prospective members in the quantity-quality trade-off. Also, in the past they had access to low-cost volunteer labor and donated capital, so their costs of production were lower than those of government or secular profit-maximizing schools (see James, 1987). Their lower cost and potentially more rapid supply response meant that people were more likely to vote for a smaller public sector and excess or differentiated demand were more likely to find an outlet in the private non-profit sector in countries with strong independent, proselytizing religious organizations competing for clients.

These conditions were obviously satisfied in Holland in the early twentieth century, when 95 per cent of all private schools were started by religious groups; and in Latin America in the same period, when Catholic universities were started in reaction to the secular ideology of the public universities. They are present in countries with a history of missionary activity, as in Japan, India and Kenya. On the other hand, they are absent in Sweden, the country which, as observed earlier, has a very small private educational sector. The Church of Sweden, to which 95 per cent of the people nominally belong, is an established church with little opposition, closely tied to and financially dependent on the government. Historically, the church has relied on government funding and, in return, the government has the right to make decisions about Church procedures and personnel. In effect, the Church of Sweden could be viewed as part of the Swedish government, with neither the need for nor the ability to supply a competing service. Thus, both demand and supply-side variables would predict a small private sector in Sweden, and that is exactly what we find.

Part II: Statistical Testing of Demand and Supply Effects

Methodological Problems

Statistical testing of the demand and supply side hypotheses presented above is not an easy task. Ideally, if we were attempting to explain the differential size of the private non-profit sector across a large number of countries, we would need information, for each country, on the amount of government and private production; the quality, religious and linguistic orientation and differentiation of public schools; various indicators of quantity and quality demanded; the degree of cultural heterogeneity within the population, including the strength of religious and linguistic identification; the availability of (ideological) entrepreneurs; and the amount of governmental subsidy to existing and prospective private schools.[6]

In practice, these data are exceedingly difficult to obtain. Data gaps and definitional differences from one country to another make cross-national statistical analysis problematic, in general. In this case, uniform data are often not available on degree of (religious and linguistic) differentiation within the public system or government subsidies to the private system. In addition, objective measures do not exist for some of the subjective variables we would want to include, such as 'intensity of preference' for religiously differentiated schools. For example, the Catholics and Calvinists strongly wanted their own privately controlled schools, and made this their major political objective in Holland, a country which is almost 100 per cent Christian; similarly, the very orthodox Jews wanted their own schools in Israel, a Jewish state. These two countries would not show up as very heterogeneous by international standards, yet the subjectively felt heterogeneity and desire to achieve more homogeneous groupings was obviously great.

Moreover, as noted above, the definition of 'public' versus 'private' is by no means an unambiguous concept. We really have a continuum of public and private funding and control, with different countries representing different points on this continuum. For example, in Ireland the majority school system, attended by almost everyone, is funded by the government but managed by autonomous boards dominated by the Catholic Church; this system is often called 'private' but could just as easily be labeled 'public'. In Italy, whose school system is usually called 'public', the influence of the Catholic Church is likewise strong. In both cases, a dominant cultural group and a set of potential religious entrepreneurs have substantial decision-making power in government-funded schools, which are variously termed public or private, leaving little space (either of supply or demand) for a truly independent system.[7]

To reduce these problems in statistical testing, I have focused on differences in private sector size across states or provinces *within* several of the countries studied, including Holland, India, Japan, Sweden and the US. The advantage of this approach is that definitions are more uniform within countries, and some of the variables that are most difficult to measure, such as degree of differentiation in and religious control of the public schools and subsidies to the private schools may be relatively constant across states or provinces in a given country. Therefore, we are left with a smaller set of more easily quantifiable variables.

The public/private division of responsibility for education (%PVT) was taken as my dependent variable; this differs greatly both within and across countries. In the case of the US, Holland and India this was measured as 'percentage of schools that are private'; in the case of Japan, 'percentage of total enrollments in private schools' was the counterpart available statistic. Somewhat different models were used for each country, because of data availability or because the relevant models (underlying raison d'être for the private sector) seemed to vary. However, whenever possible a common set of variables — per capita income, density, urbanization, per student spending in public schools and religious variables — were tested. Per capita income was taken in some cases (for example, Japan) as an indicator of excess demand, in other cases (for example, the US) as evidence of ability to pay for differentiated private education. Density and urbanization were included as indicators of heterogeneous demand within a geographically limited area. Per-student spending was used as a proxy for public school quality and the quality motive for attending private school. (However, the high positive correlation between per-capita income and per-student spending complicated the interpretation of this variable in several cases.) Religious variables, as discussed above, capture both demand and supply side effects. Differential rates of government subsidy across states and provinces were not used because these data were not available; in addition, it was hoped that the variation within a country was not great. Most of the data pertain to 1979 or 1980, except for India where the latest available figures were for 1970 or 1971. All the variables tested appear to influence private sector size in most cases, although per-capita income (demand) and 'religion', which includes both supply and demand effects, do so with the greatest consistency. A list of symbols and data sources appears in the appendix.

Japan (Secondary Level)

It was hypothesized that the driving force behind the private sector in Japan was excess demand, combined with entrepreneurial availability. For reasons developed by James (1986) James and Benjamin (1988) differences across the forty-seven prefectures (states) in excess demand were expected to be positively related to per-capita income (PCI) and negatively related to the supply of public school places (PUB), the latter depending on the size of the public school budget, EDBUDG, and the quantity-quality trade-off. Both demand and public supply turned out to be highly significant. A dummy for the presence of pre-World War II Christian higher schools (CHRSCH), and a continuous variable, the percentage of Christian clergy relative to population (CHRCL), were taken as alternative indices of (religious) entrepreneurial availability; the latter was sometimes significant, the former always significant and yielded the highest R^2. Density and urbanization variables — population per square kilometer (DENS) and percentage of population in dense areas (% DENS) were also used. These were both significant when added as a second variable (to CHR) and sometimes but not always when added as a third or fourth variable (to CHR, PCI and EDBUDG), suggesting that they operate largely through their correlation with these variables.

I also tested the effect of PSS (which is determined by each prefecture, despite the high degree of centralization of other aspects of the Japanese educational system). To the degree that some people opt for the private sector because of low quality in the public sector, we would expect PSS to exert a negative influence on %PVT, as it does in the US. On the other hand, I have argued that the private sector in Japan stems from excess demand, not from heterogeneous demand. In fact, the public sector in Japan is generally considered the high quality sector and is usually filled to capacity. People do not opt out to get higher quality so the direct impact of PSS on %PVT is expected to be negligible. Thus, if PSS has any impact on %PVT, this operates indirectly through its effect on public quantity and not through people's direct demand for quality. We have seen that a higher public quality may stem from a higher EDBUDG, or may signify a choice of quality over quantity along a given EDBUDG. The former implies a high public quantity supplied and hence a low %PVT, while the latter implies a low public quantity supplied and hence a high %PVT. I would expect the latter effect to dominate and %PVT to be a positive function of PSS of EDBUDG is controlled, while these effects would cancel each other out if EDBUDG is not controlled. Actually, I found that when PSS was included as a third variable (with PCI and CHR) it did not have a significant effect, but when EDBUDG was added, PSS became significantly positive, as expected.

Our best result, corrected for the heteroscedasticity which was initially present,[8] and consistent with our hypothesis, was:

$$R^2 = .92$$

%PVT = 6.49 + .015PCI + 3.9CHRSCH − 0.017EDBUDG + 0.04PSS
       (0.73) (3.44)*   (2.01)**   (4.73)*   (2.84)

(In all regressions numbers in parentheses are t-statistics, * indicates significance at 1 per cent level or better, ** at 15 per cent level or better *** at 6 per cent level using one-tailed test. Note that R^2s are for transformed variables and should not be taken as a measure of the explanatory power of the original variables in the case of the US and Japan).

Holland (Primary Level)

As discussed above, religious demand and supply, especially among Catholics and Calvinists, was hypothesized to be the raison d'être for the private sector here. Thus differences in %PVT across the 11 Dutch provinces should be positively related to the percentage of Catholics and Calvinists (CATH + CAL in the population of each province). In addition, for reasons given above, per capita income (PCI) and population density (DENS) were expected to exert a positive influence on %PVT. Data on per student spending in public schools were not available; however, this probably does not vary much by province since most costs (for example, teacher salaries) are determined and paid centrally.

Our results were consistent with our hypothesis. (CATH + CAL) was highly significant; a regression with this variable alone yielded an R^2 of .82 (James, 1984a). PCI and DENS were each significant when used as a second variable. When both were included, however, neither was significant; this was undoubtedly due to the high correlation (.92) between them. Our best regression with (CATH + CAL) and PCI was:

$$R^2 = .89$$

$$\%PVT = -.72 + .83(CATH + CAL) + .00009PCI$$
$$(1.83) \quad (8.17)\star (2.57)\star\star$$

India (Primary and Secondary Levels Combined)

In India it was hypothesized that heterogeneity, excess demand, religious entrepreneurship, and quality considerations would all be at work. Regressions were run for the sixteen regular states, with Bihar excluded for the reason given below. Tribal states and union territories were excluded because their decision-making structure was assumed to differ and we did not have complete data sets for them. Variables used were: percentage of the population that is Christian (CHR), population density (DENS), per cent of population living in urban areas (URB), per capita income (PCI), per student spending in public schools (PSS) and literacy rate (LIT). CHR was viewed as a supply-side variable, since it indicated presence of Christian missionaries. LIT was viewed as a historical variable — since high literacy stems from early educational activity in the state, which was likely to be private, given the paucity of pre-independence public schools.

When all these variables were included in the regression, none was significant by the t test although the F test indicated that the set as a whole was significant, a finding which indicates multicollinearity among the variables. Based on my theoretical expectations as well as my findings in other countries, I decided to start with CHR and try adding each of the others, alternatively, as a second variable. All these 2-variable models were indeed significant, with CHR and LIT yielding the highest R^2. Interestingly, the sign on PSS was positive, which I believe stems from its high positive correlation with PCI. However, when I tried to add a third variable the F test indicated it should not be added, in each case. Apparently, all these variables are highly correlated and exert a common influence on %PVT. Results from the equations with CHR, LIT and CHR, PCI were:

$$\%PVT = 2.63CHR + .02PCI \qquad R^2 = .49$$
$$(4.07)\star (2.83)\star$$

$$\%PVT = 1.79CHR + .42LIT \qquad R^2 = .54$$
$$(2.39)\star\star (3.23)\star$$

The state of Bihar was included at first but was subsequently excluded because it was an extreme outlier: our explanatory variables predicted a small private sector (approximately 10 per cent), but in 1971 (the year for which we had data from all states) Bihar actually had a very large private sector (77 per cent). Thus, Bihar was throwing off the relationships which held for the other sixteen states. Significantly, in 1972 the Bihar government took the unprecedented action of nationalizing most of the private schools; in effect, our equation had truly predicted their action.

Sweden (Primary and Secondary Levels)

Because of the miniscule size of the private sector in Sweden, and the absence of private schools in some parts of the country, we could not do a statistical analysis of differences across Swedish provinces. However, we may simply note that most of the private secondary schools are vocational schools, connected to, and partially supported by, particular trades or enterprises. Of the thirty-five private primary schools in Sweden, twenty-four are in the two largest cities (Stockholm and Gothenburg), nine have a (minority) religious affiliation, eleven follow a foreign curriculum and teach in a foreign language, and ten practice the special Waldorf (Rudolph Steiner) pedagogy (James, 1982), all roughly consistent with my model.

US (Primary and Secondary Levels)

I have saved the US for last, since this merits the fullest discussion, several other studies also being available here. In the US, I conjectured that cultural heterogeneity and religious entrepreneurship would be the major forces determining private sector growth. Regressions were run separately for the elementary and secondary levels using the following independent variables, with each of the fifty states the unit of observation: percentage 'Catholic' in population (CATH), percentage 'black' in population (BLK), population density (DENS), degree of urbanization (URB), per capita income (PCI) (as evidence of ability to pay for differentiated education), per student spending in public schools (PSS) (as evidence of their quality). My key results, corrected for heteroscedasticity, were:

(i)   Elementary level:

$R^2 = .65$

%PVT = -10 [+] .4CATH + .3BLK + .002PCI + .0003PSS $-$ .007DENS
    (1.76)   (3.87)★ (2.39)★★ (2.03)★★ (.15)   (1.10)

(ii)   Secondary level:

$R^2 = .61$

%PVT = -7 [+] .3CATH + .1BLK + .001PCI + .01DENS $-$ .002PSS
    (1.71)   (5.42)★ (2.46)★ (2.13)★★ (2.83)★ (1.60)★★

We observe that 'Catholic', 'black', and 'per capita income' are significant for both levels, consistent with the cultural/ethnic heterogeneity and religious entrepreneurship models of private school formation. The Catholic variable was taken as evidence of a desire for religious homogeneity by Catholics, living in a religiously heterogeneous society, while the black variable signifies a desire for racial homogeneity by whites, living in a racially mixed society.

Beyond this simple observation, somewhat different structures are operating for elementary and secondary levels. The coefficients of these variables are larger at the primary level, suggesting that parents are more concerned with the cultural setting and value formation of young children. On the other hand, population density and per-student spending in public schools play a significant role at the secondary but not the primary level. Apparently, parents are more likely to send their children to a private school to avoid a low quality public high school, and denser areas are needed to support more than one high school in a given area, given economies of scale. In both cases, 'urbanization' was significant when PCI was not in the equation, but was not significant together with PCI: multicollinearity precludes separating out these effects.

My findings may be compared with those of several other studies, which have tried to explain variations in %PVT in the US. Two of these studies — by Gemello and Osman (1983) and by Sonstelie (1979) — drew on data for the state of California in 1970. Gemello and Osman found that differences in %PVT across school districts and census tracts was positively related to PCI, CATH and BLK; this was consistent with my observations for nationwide data. The effect of their PSS variable was ambiguous, possibly because of its correlation with PCI. The most important difference between their findings and mine, perhaps stemming from the differences in our data bases, is that they observed similar structures operating at the primary and secondary levels, whereas I found differing structures, with desire for cultural and racial homogeneity more important in primary schools, quality considerations more important in secondary schools.

Sonstelie, in explaining differences across census tracks in Los Angeles County, does not disaggregate between these two levels and hence does not throw light on this issue. However, his significant variables are quite comparable to mine and those of Gemello and Osman: CATH, percentage of minority students, and median family income all exert a positive influence, PSS and percentage Spanish a negative influence (the last sign, somewhat surprising, is explained by a complex pattern of correlations described by Sonstelie).

A study by Frey (1983) based on more recent nationwide data, estimated separate demand and supply equations for private school enrollments in 1976–78, by state. Frey found evidence, as I did, that different structures may be operating at the elementary and secondary levels, with CATH significant in the demand equation for the former but not the latter. PCI seems to be significant at both levels. Frey also includes a private tuition effect, which has the expected negative sign in his demand equations. Variables such as BLK, URB and DENS are not included in his regressions, nor is PSS, which he treats as caused by, rather than causing, %PVT. The many studies he reports on the latter point show very mixed results in sign, but almost all are small in magnitude. In his supply equations, percentage of private teachers from religious orders and tuition are both positive and significant at the secondary level, consistent with my interpretation of religion as a supply-side as well as a demand-side variable.

Conclusion

In summary, I have offered a theory which explains the size of the private sector in education as depending on three variables: (i) excess demand, stemming from a political coalition which limits government production below full enrollment levels; (ii) differentiated demand, arising from deep-seated religious or linguistic diversity, in the face of a relatively uniform government product; and (iii) the supply of non-profit entrepreneurship, often religious, to start the private schools. I hypothesize that excess demand will lead to a large private sector at the secondary and university levels, uncorrelated with that at the primary level, while differentiated demand leads to private education at the primary level, highly correlated with that at the secondary level. This allows us to distinguish between excess demand countries, which tend to be developing countries and those with differentiated demand, which tend to be modern industrial societies. The fragmentary evidence available seems consistent with this hypothesis. The differential availability of (religious) entrepreneurship explains why the private supply response varies across countries, often taking the non-profit form.

To test this model, regression analyses were conducted attempting to explain variations in size of the private sector across states within several countries: the US, Japan, Holland, India and Sweden. In all cases the religion variable turns out to be highly significant. While this combined both a demand and supply effect in Holland, Sweden and the USA, in India and Japan, where many people who attend Christian schools are not Christians, we are probably observing primarily a supply-side phenomenon. Per-capita income is also generally significant as an indicator of excess demand and/or the financial ability of parents to purchase a preferred differentiated type of education for their children. Density and urbanization appear to be correlated with 'percentage private', but this effect often disappears when PCI is included, suggesting that these three variables are exerting a common influence. Per-student spending in public schools plays a very limited role, except in US secondary schools. Also of interest is the importance of historical factors; i.e., the early founding of private schools. This shows up, for example, in the importance of the 'literacy' variable in India and 'presence of pre-World War II Christian schools' in Japan. It suggests that once private schools are founded they disappear only with a long lag, even if the initial conditions disappear.

These results are all roughly consistent with the hypotheses given above concerning the impact of demand and supply variables, and, perhaps most important, the role of religious entrepreneurship in determining relative size of the private sector in education. Although the five countries considered here differ greatly in terms of stage of development, political system, cultural values and size of the private educational sector, they are remarkably similar in terms of the variables determining the geographic distribution of private schools within each country. This suggests that these same variables, properly framed, may explain international differences in role of the private sector in education, and exploring this hypothesis is the next step in my study.

Appendix
List of Symbols

%PVT (US, India, Holland) = Percentage of schools that are private
%PVT (Japan) = Percentage of total enrollments that are in private schools

PCI	= Per-capita income (in currency of country)
DENS	= Population density (per square mile US, kilometer elsewhere)
%DENS	= Percentage of population living in densely populated areas
URB	= Percentage of population living in urban areas
PSS	= Per-student spending in public schools
CHR	= Percentage of population that is Christian
CHRSCH	= Presence of pre-World War II Christian higher schools
CATH	= Percentage of population that is Catholic
CATH + CAL	= Percentage of population that is Catholic or Calvinist
BLK	= Percentage of population that is black
EDBUDG	= Spending in public high schools per hundred population
LIT	= Percentage of population that is literate

Data Sources and Years for Regression Analysis

US

%PVT (1980), *Digest of Educational Statistics, 1982*, National Center for Education Statistics, US Govt. Printing Office, Washington, D.C. p. 13.
PSS (1980), *ibid.*, p. 81.
PCI (1980), *Statistical Abstract of the US*, 1982–1983, US Dept. of Commerce, Census Bureau, p. 2.
DENS (1980), *ibid.*, pp. 10–12.
URB (1980), *ibid.*, pp. 10–12.
BLK (1980), *ibid.*, pp. 10–12.
CATH (1980), *Churches and Church Membership in the US*, compiled by Quinn, Anderson, Bradely, Goetting, Shrive, Glenmary Research Center, Atlanta, GA, 1982, table 3.

India

%PVT (1970), *Education in India*, Government of India, 1970–71.
PSS (1970), *ibid.*, pp. 130–2, 308–12.
PCI (1970), *Statistical Abstract*, Government of India, 1977.
DENS (1971), *Census of India*, Government of India, 1971 p. 28.
URB (1971), *ibid.*, p. 68.
LIT (1971), *ibid.*, p. 138.
CHR (1971), *ibid.*, p. 130.

Japan

%PVT (1980), *Summary of Educational Statistics*, Mombu tōkei yōran, Ministry of Education, Tokyo, 1982, pp. 126–81.
PCI (1979), *Japan Statistical Yearbook*, Tokyo, 1982, p. 545.
PSS (1979), *ibid.*, p. 644.
DENS (1981), *ibid.*, p. 6.
%DENS (1980), *ibid.*
EDBUDG (1979), *ibid.*, p. 644.
CHRCL (1980), *Japan Statistical Yearbook*, Tokyo, 1982, pp. 16, 670–1.
CHRSCH (1932), *Christian Education in Japan*, Report of the Committee on International Missionary Council, 1932

Holland

%PVT (1979), *Statistiek van gewoon lager onderwijs*, Central Bureau of Statistics, The Hague, 1980, p. 14.
PCI (1979), Data supplied by Central Bureau of Statistics.
DENS (1981), *Bevolking der gemeenten van nederland*, op *1 Januari 1981*, Central Bureau of Statistics, The Hague, 1981, table 5.
CATH & CAL (1977), *Voortgezet onderwijs en verzuiling e.g. Ontzuilingin in Nederland, 1953–78*, KASKI rapport no. 3661, The Hague, 1981.

Sweden

Location and type school from: *Fristående Skolor För Skolpliktiga Elever,* Stockholm, Swedish Government Education Dept., Report SOU, 1981, 34, p. 23.

Notes

A slightly revised version of this chapter appeared in *Economics of Education Review,* 6 (1987), 1–14.

1 The private sector is also viewed as a mechanism for providing more, different or better education by GEIGER (1984) and LEVY (1984 and 1986).

2 At the origin of an educational system, before the benefits of formal education are widely recognized, government production may be zero. Private schools may then be started, as a market response to the excess demand of people who perceive their benefits to be positive. Public schools will be started when this is seen to be in the interest of the group with dominant political power, as described in the text.

3 To simplify the exposition I assume that everyone derives some positive benefits from education and is willing to attend a free public school, hence full enrollment $= n$. If the majority of the population prefer a full enrollment public system because their $B_i \geq T$, they are able to impose their will on the minority, since a system which accommodates n will then be built and used.

   Note that if $EXTB_i$ were not downward-sloping, each person would have a horizontal benefit curve, hence would vote for either n or 0 public production (depending on whether his taxes $\gtrless$ his benefit), and the private sector would be either 0 or 100 per cent. An interior solution, therefore, requires a downward-sloping $EXTB_i$, an upward-sloping T_i, or a declining probability of admission, hence a declining PRB_i. A downward sloping $EXTB_i$ may stem from the belief that, once a minimum core of educated people is available, the remaining labor market needs can be met by less educated groups, if necessary.

4 Recall that $\dfrac{n-1}{2}$ people prefer less public education than $E^\star$ and $\dfrac{n-1}{2}$ prefer more. If everyone has equal access, $\dfrac{n-1}{2}\left(\dfrac{E^\star}{n}\right)$ of the available places will go to those preferring less and a similar number to those preferring more. Therefore, $\dfrac{n-1}{2} - \left[\dfrac{n-1}{2}\dfrac{E^\star}{n}\right] = \dfrac{n-1}{2}\dfrac{n-E^\star}{n} \sim \dfrac{n-E^\star}{2}$ people having $\left(EXTB_i + \dfrac{b_i}{n}\right) > \dfrac{P}{n}$ won't get into the public schools. Assuming that $EXTB_i$ is a relatively small component of marginal benefits many of these people will also have $b_i > P$ and will bring their excess demand to the private sector.

5 Of course, this approach leads us one step further back to ask: what

determines the tax system? Once the tax system is viewed as an endogenous variable, the same coalitions that determine the distribution of taxes may simultaneously determine the quantities of government services, thereby complicating the analysis. For example, the tax burden may be heavily concentrated, by a ruling group, on those too powerless to limit taxes or government production. The group which benefits may then opt for generous provision of public services paid for by the minority — until this process is halted by the disincentive effect of taxation or the possibility of 'exit' (emigration). Along similar lines, if a high tax, low benefit coalition is powerful enough to limit government production, why don't they also reduce taxes for the former? Perhaps the high tax shares they are paying reduces the effective opposition of outside groups and thereby helps to keep them in power. For a discussion of related issues see SPANN (1974).

6 The existence of government subsidies constitutes a fourth variable (besides excess demand, differentiated demand and availability of ideological entrepreneurs) determining the equilibrium size of the private educational sector. The presence of government subsidies implies an alternative other than those set forth in the demand-side models depicted above — public funding of private production. In fact, substantial government subsidies are usually found in countries with large private educational sectors, so they cannot be ignored. While the correlation between subsidies and private sector size is clear, it is less clear which is cause and which is effect, whether the subsidies should be viewed as exogenous or endogenous, an independent variable or a response to excess and differentiated demand as well as pressures from private suppliers. Here, I simply note their existence and importance, deferring further discussion of their causes and consequences to another paper (JAMES, 1987).

7 As another example of a hybrid organization, consider the case of the Kenyan 'harambee school', which is built with volunteer contributions of money and labor from local communities, often has a teacher whose salary is paid by the central government, therefore faces regulations over criteria for admitting students, and is sometimes managed (at the request of the community) by a mission group, one of the few groups with educational managerial experience. Is this private or public, secular or religious?

8 Heteroscedasticity was initially present and was corrected by an appropriate transformation of the independent variables. The transformation involves dividing all the data for the state i by $\sqrt{w_i}$ where $w_i = \dfrac{1}{PUB + POP}$ $(1 - \%\overline{PVT})\%\overline{PVT}$. For a discussion of this problem and the technique for resolving it see GOLDBERGER (1964) and ZELLNER and LEE (1965). The correction was made for the US and Japan, but not for India and Holland, because of data limitations $\%\overline{PVT}) = $ predicted $\%\overline{PVT}$.

6 Environmental Linkages and Organizational Complexity: Public and Private Schools

W. Richard Scott and John W. Meyer

Introduction

We can now discern a gradual shift in the direction of studies pursued by organizational researchers generally and studies of educational systems more specifically. The shift involves increasing attention to the external context as a basis for explaining internal features of organizations. Early signs of this development may be found in the emergence of general systems theory in the 1950s, but clear and strong efforts to revise organizational models did not appear until well into the 1960s. These contributions, most notably by Katz and Kahn (1966) and by Thompson (1967), served to effect a change in the dominant perspectives from closed to open systems models stressing the interdependence of organizations and environments. (For a detailed review of these changes, see Scott, 1987.)

A second change, a more modest adjustment in course, is currently underway as attention is shifting from technical aspects or views of organization-environment interdependence to more institutional views of this relation. Earlier emphases on the distribution of requisite resources and/or information in the environment and the strategies employed by organizations to secure them (Dill, 1958; Lawrence and Lorsch, 1967; Pfeffer and Salancik, 1978) have begun to be supplemented by approaches that stress that environments are more than stocks of resources and technical know-how. Environments as contexts supplying legitimacy and meaning coded in cultural symbols; environments as political systems comprised of more and less dominant interest; contending; environments as storehouses containing the remnants and survivors of earlier times and processes; environments as stratified and differentiated labor markets; environments as increasingly structured systems of organizations — these are among the new images that are shaping the current agenda of organizational research. (See, for example, Meyer *et al.*, 1978; Karpik, 1978; Rogers and Whetten, 1981; Baron and Bielby, 1980; Meyer and Scott, 1983b; DiMaggio and Powell, 1983.)

This chapter continues and extends this more recent emphasis by focusing on the environment of schools, noting the extent to which that environment is itself organized, and attempting to discern what effects these more general organizational frameworks have on the structure and operation of particular organizations within them, for example, individual schools and school district offices. The organizational environment of schools may be expected to vary by place (for example, across national systems or among the several states within a society), by time, by type of school (for example, elementary, secondary) and by auspices (for example, private and public). We focus here on differences between private and public school systems.

Private and public organizations differ in a number of respects. We emphasize the extent to which these labels are associated with distinctive administrative contexts or organized environments. We argue that some of the differences in the internal organization between public and private schools can be attributed to differences in the structure of their environment. Although the potential range of environmental variables to be examined is substantial, we limit attention here to selected properties of administrative systems and funding arrangements. *Our general predictions are that organizations operating in more complex and conflicted environments will exhibit greater administrative complexity and reduced program coherence.* The evidence regarding environmental arrangements and their organizational consequences comes from two sources: a review of the existing literature on school organizations and their environments, and data gathered through a small-scale survey of public and private schools in one area of California.

All of our own data and the other studies reviewed pertain to the United States. Important changes have occurred within this country in recent years in the organizational environments of schools — particularly schools in the public sector. We briefly review these changes in the next section, first for public schools and then for private, and attempt to conceptualize the environments of schools in terms that highlight their organizational significance. Then we examine associated characteristics of educational organizations, in particular, their administrative components at varying system levels: districts, schools and the nature of administrative work. Finally, we examine the effects of environmental complexity on the educational goals and programs of schools.

The Environments of Public and Private Schools

Public School Environments

The environment of public schools in the US has become increasingly complex and disorganized over the past few decades. A series of reforming and centralizing forces have created many new sets of legitimate authorities over the public schools without integrating them with one another or with previous authorities. At the same time, a growing number of varied stakeholders and claimants whose rights are explicitly defined in law are entitled to representation and due process. Attempting to characterize the particular shape and form of the evolving order, we argue that the environments of schools are increasingly centralized, federalized, and fragmented.

Centralization

There is little doubt that the public school system has become more centralized over the past few decades. Historically, decision-making in the educational sector has been highly decentralized in this country. It has traditionally been the case that local educational authorities — school districts and individual schools — have dominated educational decision-making. Most state departments of education have, until quite recently, been small, weak and ineffectual. And, until the 1960s, the federal government took virtually no role in elementary and secondary education, recognizing the rights of state and local agencies in educational governance.

This situation changed dramatically in 1965 with the passage of the Elementary and Secondary Education Act. Aimed primarily at achieving greater equity for disadvantaged groups, this legislation introduced a strong federal voice into educational affairs. Subsequent legislation extended services to additional groups — e.g., educationally handicapped and bilingual students — or attempted to stimulate educational reform and innovation — for example, creation of the Teacher Corps and grants to improve state and local planning. Although at its peak level in the late 1970s, federal aid accounted for only 9.2 per cent of total educational revenues, most observers agree that the use of categorical funding targeted to the support of particular groups and programs allowed the federal government to exercise a disproportionate influence on education (see Berke and Kirst, 1975; B. Levin, 1977).

Moreover, it appears that the federal presence has stimulated and strengthened state educational authorities both directly and indirectly. Directly, states were not only delegated power to supervise the implementation of the federal programs but were allocated federal funds to augment their staffs to perform these functions. As a consequence, state education departments have grown dramatically: 'they have doubled and tripled in size since the mid-1960s and the amount they receive from the federal government for their administrative budgets has grown to an average of 40 per cent of the total' (Murphy, 1981, p. 127). In recent years they have declined somewhat as federal appropriations have been reduced under the Education Consolidation Improvement Act of 1981, but the long-term growth has been sustained relative to the sixties and seventies. Indirectly, the increased size and power have attracted more competent and aggressive personnel at the state levels who have been able to both encourage and benefit from the political efforts of the 1980s to use block grants and other revenue sharing proposals to return more power and discretion to the state level.

While the federal role in financing education did not change appreciably during the decade of the 1970s, the states' contributions have increased relative to local funding. Funds controlled by states increased from about 39 per cent of the total expenditures for schooling in the early 1970s to about 45 per cent by the end of the decade, bringing them to a par with local revenues (Sergiovanni *et al.*, 1980). These trends have accelerated during the 1980s as states have continued to oversee the distribution of federal funds and to increase their funding and programmatic authority in relation to local education agencies.

Thus, beginning at the national level, but continuing now at the level of the states, new administrative units have emerged and grown within the educational sector, shifting some types of decisions formerly made within a local community to the state or national level.

Federalization

To argue that new decision centers have emerged is not necessarily to conclude that former authorities have atrophied. The authority of local educational systems and the influence of local interests have not been displaced but only supplemented by the growth of power at the state and national levels. One set of authorities has been layered over another, with each claiming legitimacy to make some types of educational decisions — the federal agencies basing their claims on overriding 'national interests', the states standing on their constitutional grounds, and the communities affirming continuing faith in the 'religion of localism', a dogma with many adherents in the realm of education. Thus, increasing centralization of educational authority at the state and federal levels has been associated with federalization: 'the explicit establishment of independent authorities with both separate responsibilities and overlapping jurisdictions' (Scott and Meyer, 1983, p. 134). This doctrine within education receives legitimacy and support from its congruence with wider political beliefs prevalent in the US regarding the need to divide and juxtapose powers in order to prevent their abuse (see Grodzins, 1966; Scott, 1983, p. 171).

The practice of pitting educational authorities against each other at various levels is characteristic not only of administrative agencies but also of the system of courts, an institution that has played an increasingly active role in education since the early 1950s. Beginning with the landmark *Brown* decision of 1954, both the federal and the state courts have become involved in every major area of education policy (see B. Levin, 1977; Kirp and Jensen, 1986).

Fragmentation

In addition to the complexity generated by the existence of multiple uncoordinated layers of educational authorities, additional complexity is associated with the fragmented nature of educational authority. Fragmentation refers to the extent to which authority is 'integrated or coordinated at any given level' of the educational sector (Scott and Meyer, 1983, p. 145). The independent operation of courts and agencies is a prime example of fragmentation at each level — national, state and local — as well as of federalization — the lack of integration across levels.

Numerous observers have called attention to the extent of fragmentation that characterized educational administration at all levels in the early 1980s. Sergiovanni and his colleagues (1980) have described fragmentation at the federal level:

> One could, in fact, question whether it is even accurate to speak of 'federal policy' in education. Certainly there is no single center of planning and coordination within our nation's capital. Programs which bear upon education emerge,

rather, from literally dozens of agencies and congressional committees. (p. 162)

They note that in addition to the Office of Education, located at that time within the Department of Health, Education and Welfare, and the independent National Institute of Education,

> There are countless pockets within other agencies and departments that exercise control over highly significant programs. The Office of Civil Rights has been instrumental in enforcing desegregation guidelines. Head Start, Follow Through, and Upward Bound programs make their home in the Office of Economic Opportunity. Dependents' schools on overseas military bases are administered by the Department of Defense, and many Indian children attend schools administered by the Bureau of Indian Affairs within the Department of Interior (p. 164).

As might be suspected, the fractured character of state education agencies is not unrelated to fragmentation at the federal level. Consistent with predictions that organizational structures tend to reflect the characteristics of the environments to which they relate, McDonnell and McLaughlin (1982) report:

> During their time of greatest growth, most state departments developed organizational structures that matched that of ED/ USOE (Department of Education, formerly the US Office of Education) and faithfully replicated, unit for unit, federal program categories. (p. 24)

Moreover, linkages among governmental levels take a variety of forms that add to the complexity and fragmentation confronting any particular layer (Berke and Kirst, 1975, p. 224). In addition, in the period under consideration, different officials associated with distinct offices were engaged in monitoring compliance. The interpretations of the rules and regulations by US Office of Education officials was found to sometimes vary from that of HEW auditors working out of ten HEW regional offices (see Goettel, 1976).

Summary

Some societies have developed highly centralized and unified ministries of education in which the chain of command is clearly defined from the top down with the local school systems functioning as 'branch offices' (Meyer, 1983a). Public education in the United States has not followed this model, and while centralizing processes have been evident in recent decades, they have not replaced local powers, nor have they succeeded in overcoming the divisions among authorities competing with one another at each level. The resulting system is one of considerable complexity and disorder.

Private School Environments

Discussion of the environment of private schools is rendered difficult by three conditions. First, much less information is available about private schooling in this country than about public education. There are questions about the accuracy of existing data on the number of private school students and schools — rather fundamental facts — and private schools have been surprisingly neglected by organizational researchers up to the present time (see Erickson, 1983). Part of the responsibility for the present lack of accurate information lies with the schools themselves, some of which are small and short-lived while others wish to avoid surveys.

A second barrier to understanding is posed by the great variety of private schools. While Catholic schools — which themselves vary in type from parish and diocesan to those of specific religious orders — make up about half of the population (and account for about 65 per cent of the students), a large variety of other types of religious schools comprise an additional 30 per cent while the remaining 20 per cent are independent or secular in orientation. Moreover, the composition of the population of private schools has been changing, with Catholic schools declining precipitously since the mid-1960s, while high-tuition independent schools have experienced steady growth, and fundamentalist schools have grown rapidly during the past decade (Erickson, 1983).

Third, private schools receive varying levels of public support and are subject to varying degrees of public regulation. Thus it is incorrect to distinguish too sharply between the environments of public and private schools. Estimates are that, on the average, non-public schools receive approximately 26 per cent of their total income from government, about half of which is derived from indirect tax deductions or exemptions and the other half from direct program expenditures (Sullivan, 1974, p. 93). The latter programs include transportation, textbooks, and health and welfare services available in many of the states and compensatory education, child nutrition, instructional materials and aid to handicapped students from the federal government. While most private schools take advantage of the tax benefits, a smaller number receive direct categorical aid, virtually all of which is designed to serve targeted student populations (Encarnation, 1983).

The same dimensions used to characterize the environments of public schools can be employed to describe those of private schools. The blurring of boundaries between public and private systems is ignored in this discussion, but will be considered later. Also, it is important to note that environmental variation for private schools is related strongly to school type.

Centralization

Private schools vary in the extent to which decision-making has been centralized. Some, like Catholic and Lutheran schools, belong to hierarchical systems, while others belong only to loosely organized federations, such as the National Association of Independent Schools, and still others operate as completely independent units. Little research has been done on governance in private school systems (see Bridges, 1982).

Federalization

Private schools may experience federalization since they are subject to control exercised by both local and state authorities. Although there is great variation across the fifty states, private schools are subject to state regulation in such areas as minimum educational standards, attendance reporting, licensure and teacher certification (O'Malley, 1981). Other agencies regulate private schools as a business subject to 'state and local building, fire, health, sanitation, child welfare, and zoning codes' (Encarnation, 1983, p. 188). Private schools applying and qualifying for more direct forms of public aid, such as textbook or compensatory educational programs, are subject to review by public authorities. Because the programs are defined as benefiting targeted student populations, the great majority of them are not administered by the private schools but by public school districts (*ibid*).

Private schools vary by type in the degree to which they participate in larger private educational systems and hence are subject to additional controls at more than one authority level. Catholic schools no doubt represent the most highly developed system of private education with the possibility of control exercised at the parish and diocesan levels. Most other private school systems are much less complex. In general, it appears that the extent of federalization experienced by private schools is relatively low, since although multiple authorities exist, they do not overlap greatly in jurisdiction.

Fragmentation

Similarly, private schools appear to be confronted by less fragmented environments than their public counterparts. Sources of funds are fewer and programmatic authority is more likely to be located at the school level. What variation exists is likely to be associated with the receipt of public funds, as discussed below.

Environments and Educational Organizations: Predicted Relations

The pattern of fragmented and federalized centralization that characterizes the educational sector in the US provides the environment within which individual educational organizations must function. What are the consequences of this type of environment for educational organizations? We have argued that several organizational effects are expected (Meyer, 1983c; Scott and Meyer, 1983), two of which are emphasized here.

Administrative Complexity

A widely accepted proposition in open-systems theory is that organizations located in more complex and uncertain organizational fields will exhibit more complex internal structures. When the environmental units take the form of funding and regulatory bodies, organizational complexity is likely to develop particularly at the administrative level, where boundary-spanning activities are centered. Even more particularly, when the external pattern exhibits centralization of funding flows combined with fragmentation and competition among regulatory bodies, we expect to see environmental controls exercised through accounting and statistical mechanisms. The result within organizational units will be an expansion of the numbers of accountants, bookkeepers and clerks hired. We would also expect general administrators to report spending more time in tracking and overseeing the functioning of those programs linked to special funds and reporting requirements. Specific hypotheses to be tested are:

(a)   School organizations exposed to an increased variety of funding and programmatic authorities are expected to have larger administrative components than those relating to less complex environments.

(b)   School organizations exposed to an increased variety of funding and programmatic authorities are expected to have a higher proportion of business, accounting and financial personnel in their administrative staff than those relating to less complex environments.

(c)   General administrators in school organizations exposed to an increased variety of funding and programmatic authorities are expected to spend a greater proportion of their time overseeing such programs than general administrators in school organizations relating to less complex environments.

(d)   Federal funds and programs, because they are more likely to be fragmented and federalized than comparable state funds and programs, are expected to generate larger administrative components in school organizations than state programs.

(e)   Public school organizations are expected to exhibit larger administrative components than private schools because of the relatively greater complexity of the fiscal and regulatory environments they confront.

Curricular Coherence

As more authorities emerge within an arena claiming the right to speak on behalf of particular groups or interests, it becomes increasingly difficult for those who administer a specific organization to retain control over its policies and programs (Meyer and Scott, 1983a; Meyer, 1983b). Authorities in education at higher levels do not completely displace the authority of officials at lower levels, but can impose some policies and programs on local jurisdictions. In this manner, local administrators are less completely in control of the educational programs they are expected to manage: some of the complexities and inconsistencies of environmental groups are built into the structure of local organizations with the result that these programs are expected to be less coherent, less unified, less 'rational' than those of similar organizations less subject to these pressures. Our specific hypotheses are:

(a)   Officials in school organizations exposed to an increased variety of funding and programmatic authorities are expected to share more decision-making authority with external groups than officials in organizations relating to less complex environments.

(b) The curricular goals of school organizations exposed to an increased variety of funding and programmatic authorities are expected to be more elaborated and less coherent than the goals of organizations relating to less complex environments.

(c) Public school organizations are expected to exhibit more elaborate and less coherent goals than private schools because of the greater complexity and fragmentation of their environments.

Environments and Educational Organizations: Evidence

Preliminary Concerns

Before reviewing evidence relating to these predictions three preliminary issues require brief attention: the issue of organizational levels; alternative explanations for our dependent variables; and the nature of our sample of public and private schools.

Organizational levels

School organizations vary in the extent to which they are components of hierarchical structures with different organizational units located at higher or lower levels of the system. When a multiple level system exists, an important question to be addressed is where, at what level, are the predicted organizational effects likely to be manifested? If complex and conflicted environments are expected to be associated with administrative complexity of the component organizational units, which units are most likely to be affected? It is possible to argue either that *all* organizations will be affected or that only some levels will be affected, forms at one level serving to manage or absorb complexity in the environment. We can offer no theoretical basis for selecting among these competing possibilities and so will simply observe and report on the empirical situation in the US educational sector.

Alternative explanations

Our perspective focuses attention on environmental sources of administrative complexity and curricular coherence. More conventional organizational arguments view administrative complexity as primarily the product of *internal* characteristics, either size (see Blau, 1970) or technical complexity and interdependence (see Thompson, 1967; Galbraith, 1973). We control for the effects of organizational size on administration in assessing our own propositions. We assess technical or instructional complexity and interdependence only through the distinction between elementary and secondary schools or the number of grades included within the school organization.

Public and private school study

Data on a sample of public and private schools, public school districts and Catholic school dioceses in the six county San Francisco Bay Area were collected in the spring of 1981 by an interdisciplinary team of researchers at the Institute for Research on Educational Finance and Governance, Stanford University. Since the study was expected to serve multiple objectives, its design was complex. Chambers and Lajoie (1983) provide a description of the study objectives and general design (see also Gilliland and Radle, 1984). Table 1 reports sample size and return rates for public schools and districts and for the various categories of private schools surveyed. Return rates for the entire sample averaged only about 30 per cent, with significantly lower rates characterizing public middle and elementary schools, independent schools (not associated with a parish or diocese), and other types of private religious schools.

For purposes of our analyses, respondent schools were divided into three categories by auspices: public, Catholic, and private. Catholic independent schools are being assigned to the private category since their organizational environments are similar to those of private schools. Four categories of schools were identified by grade level: elementary, middle, secondary, and comprehensive. These categories and the numbers of schools in each are reported in table 2. As is clear from table 2, the middle school is primarily a public school form, while the comprehensive school is a private school type. Also, private schools were more likely than either public or Catholic systems to combine junior and senior high programs into a single school type.

Most of the data reported in this chapter are based on questionnaires mailed to schools and district offices. Differentiated but com-

Comparing Public and Private Schools: 1

Table 1: Sample Size and Return for Schools and Districts

Type	Sample size	Number returned	Percentage returned
Public Schools			
High School	153	49	32
Junior high/middle	82	20	24
Elementary	299	61	20
Public School Districts			
District offices	110	49	45
Private Schools			
Secondary			
Catholic parochial	16	6	38
Catholic independent	20	4	20
Other religious	8	2	25
Non-religious	17	9	53
Elementary			
Catholic parochial	151	69	48
Catholic independent	5	1	20
Other religious	62	15	24
Non-religious	56	15	28

Source: Gilliland and Radle (1984), tables 8 and 9.

Table 2: Number of Responding Schools and Grades by School Categories

Categories	Number of schools	Mean number grades
Elementary		
Public	61	6.5
Catholic	69	8.4
Private	31	8.2
Middle		
Public	20	2.7
Catholic	1	2.0
Private	1	2.0
Secondary		
Public	49	4.0
Senior high	(48)	(3.9)
Combined senior and middle	(1)	(6.0)
Catholic	7	4.3
Senior high	(6)	(4.0)
Bombined senior and middle	(1)	(6.0)
Private	16	4.7
Senior high	(11)	(4.0)
Combined senior and middle	(5)	(6.2)
Comprehensive		
Private	9	12.8

Source: Gilliland and Radle (1984) table 14.

140

parable survey instruments were prepared for each type of school included within the study (see Chambers and Lajoie, 1983). A survey form was mailed to principals and superintendents with the request that it be completed by the recipient or a person designated by him or her as knowledgeable in the areas covered. Initial return rates were disappointingly low, but were somewhat improved by telephone follow-ups. Data on Catholic diocesan activities were collected by interview.

Administrative Complexity

District level

The administrative staffs within public school districts have certainly grown. Rowan (1981) reports that:

> In 1932, the earliest year for which records on the number of administrators in the public school system are available, there were only .23 local administrators per district. By 1970 that number had increased to 6.8 administrators per public school district. (p. 47)

By 1982, in our six county sample of school districts in the San Francisco Bay Area, the average number of administrators was 12.80. What factors are associated with this increase?

Of course, the consolidation movement has contributed to district size: as larger territories with more schools are created, the number of administrators per district is likely to increase. It is also possible that the work performed within schools — the 'technology' of schooling — has become more complex requiring more administrative input. While this is possible, there is little evidence to suggest that district administrators are closely connected with the instructional work of schools. Indeed, what evidence we have suggests the opposite (see Hannaway and Sproull, 1978–79). Another possibility is that the work confronting school districts is not so much how to manage students as how to manage schools themselves, and that schools as organizations have become more complex over time, and perhaps also more interdependent, requiring more administrative attention and coordination. It is clear that considerable administrative growth at the district level is related to such internal organizational changes. In virtually all districts, the budgeting process has become more highly centralized; and in most districts, critical personnel decisions are made at this level. Note, however, that these types of changes are largely a result of change in school environments, not of internal processes. Thus, budget decisions are more centralized largely because a greater proportion of school funds come from outside the district, and districts are held accountable according to standards set and enforced by these external authorities. And personnel decisions are more centralized partly in response to the pressure of professional associations and unions and to state licensure requirements that are external to any specific district.

In order to focus attention on effects of environmental changes on the administrative structure of school districts, we and our colleagues at Stanford have carried out several empirical studies. The first, based on data collected in a survey of twenty elementary school districts in the San Francisco Bay Area in 1975 (see Cohen *et al.*, 1979, for details of sampling procedures), was conducted by Rowan (1981). After controlling for district size, measured by average daily attendance, Rowan found a strong positive association between the amount of special federal and state funds received per student and size of district administration, measured as the number of full-time equivalent (FTE) administrators per student. These effects were much greater than those associated with measures of internal district complexity (whether the district was administering only elementary schools or was unified, managing both secondary and elementary schools) and of interdependence (whether there existed a district-wide reading program).

A second study, conducted by Bankston (1982), examined in depth a single large school district in an urbanized location within the San Francisco Bay Area. For the fiscal year 1979–80, the district received 8 per cent of its funding from the federal government, 69 per cent from the state, and the remainder from local sources. Combining both state and federal special programs, 20 per cent of the district's funding came from categorical programs while 80 per cent was received as general aid. While only one-fifth of the district's income was associated with categorical programs, one-third, seventeen of fifty-three central district officers, were funded by these programs. And although only 8 per cent of the funding was derived from the US Department of Education, Bankston estimated that about 30 per cent of the required annual reports were directed to this source. Finally, not only the activities of the administrative staff but their titles and the structural differentiation of the district office reflected the patterning of external funding packages and reporting requirements. Thus, Bankston's descriptive study, although based on a single case, provides

strong evidence in support of the view that school district organization is shaped by the structure of its administrative environment.

A third study, also conducted by Rowan (1982), utilized data
from a random sample of thirty city school districts that existed in
California in 1930. Using published data at five-year time intervals,
Rowan analyzed changes over time in the composition of district staff.
He observed that

> The most pronounced tendency of districts in the sample
> was to differentiate positions with business and personnel
> functions. The proportion of districts with these specialities
> rose from 0% in 1930 to 83% with business positions and
> 67% with personnel positions in 1970. Such a marked pat-
> tern of growth reflects not merely the growth in scale of
> operations within school districts, but also an increased con-
> cern with financial accountability and with credentialing and
> labor management contingencies. (p. 49)

These results are consistent with our arguments that changes in the
organizational environments of schools are associated not simply with
larger administrative components within educational organizations
but also with the addition of certain types of administrative personnel,
in particular, business and accounting specialists.

Turning now to the data from our private/public study, we
examine first the results based on survey responses from forty-nine
public school districts. Questionnaires were mailed to superintendents
who were asked to respond personally or to locate a knowledgeable
associate who could do so. As the principal measure of environmental
complexity, respondents were asked to indicate from a list of twenty-
two federal and state programs all those in which the district currently
participated. The number of external programs in which the district
was involved was regarded as an indicator of environmental fragmentation. The locus of the programs — whether federal or state —
was taken as an indicator of environmental centralization. The average
Bay Area district reported participating in 11.1 programs (for a description see Gilliland and Radle, 1984, pp. 41–4).

Throughout these analyses, our primary measure of administrative complexity is simply the number of full-time equivalent (FTE)
administrators in the district. Administrators reported as 'part time'
were considered as 0.5 administrators. We avoid administrative ratios
to eliminate the problems of definitional dependency (see Freeman and
Kronenfeld, 1974).

Multiple regression was used to determine which factors were associated with size of the district's administrative staff and to assess the relative impact of each factor. Table 3 reports, in both standardized and unstandardized regression coefficients, representative results for three equations (columns 1–3). We note that size, whether measured in total district enrollment or in number of schools within the district, was highly associated with size of district administration, as expected. The greater effect of number of schools is consistent with the expectation that district size is more a function of complexity in managing schools than students.

Table 3: Factors Affecting Size of Public District Administration

	1	2	3
Constant	−5.614	−5.672	−5.801
Size			
Enrollment	.875** .0011 (.000071)		
Number of schools		.8866** .658 (.042)	.907** .674 (.039
Internal complexity			
Unified district	−.019 −.606 (1.759)	−.059 −1.868 (1.762)	
High school district			.129** 5.584 (1.859)
External complexity			
Fragmentation (number of public programs)	.146* .631 (.263)	.161** .698 (.259)	.124* .536 (.220)
R^2 =	.91	.92	.93

Note: First listing in table for each variable is standardized regression coefficient (beta). Second listing is unstandardized coefficient. Third listing, in parentheses, is standard error of the estimate.
*$p = < .05$
**$p = < .001$

Two more direct measures of complexity within the district are whether the district was unified or restricted to either elementary or to high schools. Like Rowan (1981) we found no effect on number of district administrators or whether the district was unified; but districts administering high schools — known to be larger and more complex systems than elementary or middle schools — were observed to have larger administrative staffs. In sum, internal complexity as represented by number of schools and by the complexity of the individual schools themselves, was found to increase district administration over and above that associated with numbers of students enrolled.

With respect to our central concern, we found that environmental fragmentation, as measured by the number of public programs in which districts participated, was consistently and significantly associated with larger district administrative staffs. Related results (not reported in table 3) showed no differences between the effect of participation in special state programs or federal programs, an index of centralization. The combined effects of size, internal complexity and environmental complexity accounted for approximately 90 per cent in the observed variance in number of administrators among public school districts (see table 3).

Administrators are not the only types of personnel within district offices. Two other general categories of staff include non-administrative professionals and classified personnel. The first category includes various types of personnel providing support services to schools including counselors, social workers, librarians, psychologists and resource specialists. These personnel are located at the district level because they provide only 'staff' services to teachers and students or because they serve more than one school. Classified staff includes secretaries, bookkeepers, clerks and similar administrative support personnel. The only significant predictor of numbers of classified staff at the district level was size, whether measured by district enrollment or number of schools. The measures of internal and environmental complexity were not significantly associated with the size of the classified staff. To our surprise, the number of professional staff at the district level was significantly associated not only with the district size measures but also with the number of publicly funded local, private-school programs — but not the number of public programs — administered by the district.

In summary, it appears that school districts are strongly influenced in their size and composition by involvement in public programs. After taking into account the size and internal complexity of the district, the larger the number of public programs managed, the larger the number of administrators.

County level

In addition to district administrative development, other public administrative staff are located within the office of the county superintendent of schools. We did not attempt to examine developments at this level systematically but call attention to it as another important locus of administrative services for schools. In order to obtain some sense of the scale of operations at this level and the types of services provided, we conducted interviews with officials in two Bay Area county offices, one in a smaller county encompassing sixteen school districts, and the other in a larger county encompassing nineteen districts. The smaller county office contained a staff of sixty-five professionals and 191 clerical workers. The types of functions reported included the administration of development centers for handicapped students and court schools; the provision of in-service classes for teachers and other professionals, such as training in computers; and the performance by contract of specific functions for schools, such as training workshops and payroll services. In addition, the larger of the county offices reported that they provided liaison with private schools, the county serving as the 'representative of the SEA', collecting private affidavits every fall and occasionally serving as an intermediary between private and public schools for joint programs.

Diocesan level

Turning now to the private sector, only one type within our sample, the Catholic parochial schools, were organized into a larger system at the 'district' level — the diocese. (One other non-religious private school in our sample reported that it belonged to a statewide regional system.) All of the parochial schools in our sample were incorporated within one of three systems — two diocesan and one archdiocesan. Interviews with school administrators located in each of these offices revealed the presence of very small administrative staffs. In the smaller diocese, only two full-time administrators and one part-time clerical person exercised oversight for a system containing thirty-two schools — twenty-eight elementary and two secondary. In the second diocese, four full-time administrators, four secretaries, a bookkeeper and an accountant managed fifty-seven elementary schools and four secondary schools. And in the larger dioceses, seven administrators and two clerical persons administered a system containing ninety-four schools — seventy-five elementary and nineteen secondary.

Given the size of these central offices, it is not surprising that diocesan administrators reported carrying out primarily staff functions — collecting system-wide data on academic performance and teacher qualifications and credentials, conducting training workshops, and consulting on curricula. All these offices reported having at least informal contact with the independent private Catholic schools within their areas. The diocese takes almost no fiscal responsibility for parish schools which are funded from fees, collections and fund-raising activities. No state funds were received, and any federal funds were administered by public districts and routed directly to qualified schools. Parochial schools were reported to be receiving ESEA Title 1 (now Chapter I) funds, ESEA Title IV-B (now part of Chapter II) library and learning resource funding, ESEA Title VII (also part of Chapter II) bilingual education funds, and National School Lunch Program funds. While not involved in the administration of these programs, two of the three diocesan officers reported conducting regular on-site inspections of those schools participating in publicly-funded programs.

In sum, by comparison with the public system, private schools are much less likely to be organized at a regional or district level, and those that are exhibit only relatively small and rudimentary administrative staff functioning at this level.

School level

Another of our colleagues, Ann Stackhouse (1982) utilized data from a survey of a 10 per cent sample of US secondary schools conducted in 1977 by NIE (see Abramowitz and Tenenbaum, 1978) to test hypotheses similar to those we have advanced. Stackhouse expected fragmentation within the environment of secondary schools to increase the size of the administrative component of the school. The primary measure of fragmentation was similar to our own: the number of types of special categorical funds from which a school was receiving funds. The two primary measures of administration were the number of general administrators and the number of specialists (for example, special education teachers, resource teachers, media specialists) on the staff of the school. After controlling for school size, region and urban location, her findings were that fragmentation (but not centralization) in the funding environment of secondary schools was significantly and positively related to the number of specialist personnel but not to the number of regular administrators.

Turning to our own study of public and private schools, we first categorized the sample into seven relatively homogeneous classes, by level and type: three classes of elementary schools — public, Catholic and private; public middle schools; and three classes of secondary schools — public, Catholic and private. Recall that the category of Catholic school refers only to those schools with direct ties to the local Catholic hierarchy, that is, to parochial and diocesan schools. Independent Catholic schools were assigned to the private school category.

As table 4 demonstrates, enrollment varied greatly by both level and school type. Secondary schools were, on the average, from two to three times larger than elementary schools; and public schools were, on the average, from two to three times larger than private schools. Catholic schools were intermediate in size between public and private schools; and middle schools were sized between elementary and secondary schools.

Table 4 also contains information on staffing ratios. The category of administrator was defined to include principals or heads, assistant administrators or vice-principals, instructional or program administrators, and general or business administrators. The category of professional included teachers, counselors and psychologists, social workers, librarians, nurses, chaplains, resource specialists and other types of student support services professionals. Size of both types of staff was calculated as the number of full-time staff members plus half the number of part-time members.

Table 4: Average Number of Students and Number of Students per Administrative and Professional Staff, by School Type and Level

Level and Type	N	Average enrollment	Students/ administrator	Students/ professional
Elementary				
Public	60	386	358	23
Catholic	66	296	204	31
Private	27	185	129	16
Middle				
Public	19	784	320	19
Secondary				
Public	46	1446	326	24
Catholic	7	715	194	21
Private	16	325	92	12

Source: Based on Gilliland and Radle (1984) table 21.

There was a slight tendency for staffing ratios to be higher in the more complex types of schools: secondary and middle schools had more administrators per student than did elementary schools, and Catholic and private (but not public) secondary schools had more teachers per student than did elementary schools. But these differences by level were overwhelmed by the staffing differences by type of school. The private schools in our sample had, on average, almost three times as many administrators per student as did the public schools, and the Catholic schools, nearly twice the number of the public schools. Similarly, private schools contained a significantly higher number of professional staff per student than public schools, with Catholic schools being intermediate. The only exception to these general patterns was that Catholic elementary schools in our sample contained fewer professional staff members per student than did public elementary schools.

Although the relative differences in staffing ratios by school type were substantial, the absolute numbers of administrators at the school level were small. The typical elementary school in our sample contained between one and one-and-a-half administrators: 1.07 for public schools; 1.45 for Catholic schools, and 1.43 for private schools. The average middle school contained only 2.45 administrators. And the average high school contained between three-and-a-half and four-and-a-half administrators: 4.43 for the public secondary school, 3.68 for the Catholic schools and 3.53 for the private high schools in our sample.

Parallel to our examination of the factors affecting size of administration at the district level, we examined similar regression equations at the school level. As expected given the staffing patterns just described, dummy variables used to indicate a Catholic or a private school were significantly associated with a larger administrative component. Similarly, a dummy variable to indicate secondary vs. elementary school — an indicator, among other things, of internal organizational complexity — was significantly associated with size of administration, with secondary schools having more administrators. Given these differences, we sought to determine, for a given type and level of school, whether school size and complexity of the school's external environment were associated with size of administrative staff. Two measures of size were employed: number of students enrolled and number of grades within the school. No attempt was made to directly measure internal school complexity (although number of grades can be regarded as an indicator of complexity as well as of size). Rather, we attempted to control for this variable by distinguishing between and conducting separate analyses for elementary, middle and secondary schools. Two measures of external environment were employed, both indicators of fragmentation. First, as with districts, we determined for each school the number of public programs in which it was currently participating. Second, we asked an informant in each school to rate the degree of integration or coordination of federal and state programs and reporting requirements.

Table 5 is similar in form to table 3 in that each column represents a regression equation including the variables listed in the rows. In order to control for school type and level, separate equations were estimated for each type of school examined. Catholic secondary schools are omitted because of the small number of these schools in our sample. Given the exploratory nature of this analysis and the small numbers involved for some of the schooltypes, we identify associations significant at the .10 level as well as the .05 and .001 levels.

Table 5:   Factors Affecting Size of School Administration

	Elementary schools			Public middle schools	Secondary schools	
	Public	Catholic	Private		Public	Private
Constant	.014	.869	−.169	3.751	1.856	1.347
Size						
Enrollment	.644***	.260	.919***	−.239	.464**	.369
	.003	.003	.013	−.002	.002	.001
	(.0005)	(.0016)	(.0015)	(.0022)	(.0005)	(.002)
External complexity						
Fragmentation (number of public programs)	.100	.290*	.029	.676*	.278*	.572
	.027	.272	.039	.516	.221	.887
	(.035)	(.149)	(.168)	(.284)	(.111)	(.769)
Perceived Integration	−.009	−.287*	−.149	−.492	−.382**	.310
	−.003	−.105	−.103	−.484	−.533	.252
	(.035)	(.055)	(.086)	(.360)	(.196)	(.423)
R^2 =	.47	.24	.90	.27	.43	.53

Note: First listing in table for each variable is standardized regression coefficient (beta). Second listing is understandardized coefficient. Third listing, in parentheses, is standard error of the estimate.
   * $p = < .1$
   ** $p = < .05$
   *** $p = < .001$

Size of school as measured by enrollment was generally associated positively and significantly with size of school administration although there are exceptions. Turning to the measures of environmental complexity, number of public programs was positively associated with size of administrative staff across all the types of schools studied, but this association was statistically significant only for public middle and secondary schools and for Catholic elementary schools. Further, as expected, perceived integration in the administrative and reporting requirements imposed by participation in state and federal programs was negatively associated with size of the school's administrative staff. Five of the six coefficients were in the expected direction but only two — those for public secondary and Catholic elementary schools — were statistically significant.

Other data pertaining to the composition of the support staff for administrators indicated that public and Catholic, but not private, schools that participated in a larger number of public programs employed higher proportions of accountants and bookkeepers to other types of supporting staff members. Moreover, these results held just for all public and for federal programs, not for state or local programs.

Overall our results on increasing demands by the external environment on the time of school administrators are consistent with a number of recent studies based on detailed observations of the principal's work profile. Thus, based on his in-depth study of the work activities of a single elementary school principal, Wolcott (1973) noted that in his 'representational role' the principal performed an important interface function, mediating between the demands of the school system bureaucracy and the regulatory environment on the one hand and the school's client community on the other (see also Morris *et al.*, 1981).

Summary

To summarize the school level findings, we found substantial differences in size of the administrative component by type and level of school, with private and then Catholic having larger ratios of administrators to students than public schools and secondary and middle schools having slightly larger ratios of administrators than elementary schools. The differences associated with type appear to reflect both the smaller average size of the Catholic and private systems and the absence of any substantial intermediate buffering structure such as the district office represents for the public system. Participation in public programs was observed to be associated with more elaborate administrative components for Catholic elementary and for public middle and secondary schools. And the perception that state and federal program requirements were well integrated was associated with reduced administrative components in both Catholic elementary and public secondary schools.

Complexity and organizational level

It appears that we have an empirical answer to the question: at what level, does organizational structure become more elaborate and complex to deal with environmental pressures? For the case of the public school system, we found that administrative complexity is generated at both the district and school level (not to mention the state level where, as noted, educational agencies have expanded enormously in recent years). While school district offices do expand and function to manage and, partially, to mediate between individual schools and state and federal program requirements, they do not completely absorb these demands. That individual school administrators both expand in number and/or devote increasing amounts of time to managing such external demands is not surprising when one reviews the extensive descriptive literature detailing the processes by which specific federal or state programs are implemented at local levels within individual schools (see, for example, Weatherley, 1979; Hargrove *et al.*, 1981). The view of individual schools directly confronting and responding to a fragmented regulatory and funding environment in addition to responding to these pressures more indirectly as mediated by superordinate structures reinforces an image of educational organizations as loosely-coupled systems (see Weick, 1976; Davis *et al.*, 1977).

Curricular and Goal Coherence

We turn now to the second general empirical issue posed in this report. It is argued above that public schools are likely to have less organizational coherence than are private schools. This idea is not related to a conception that private schools are somehow more successful than public ones — indeed, any reasonable reflection would suggest that in purely organizational terms, private schools have statistically lower chances of stability and survival than do public ones. Private schooling systems face continuing and crucial problems of funding and market survival on a scale far beyond that of public schooling. But in a sense it is just that difference in their environments that leads to our main hypothesis. Public schooling is provided by its environment with something close to a monopoly situation in the community, and is highly protected and funded by a network of superordinate organizations and rules. It obtains this monopoly, however, at a considerable cost in internal organizational consistency. Public schooling is under great legal, organizational, and political pressure to meet the full range of 'needs of the community' as these are defined by disparate groups internal to the local community, by state organizations and their penumbra of legitimated interest groups, and now by organized interests and programs at the national level.

Public schooling maintains its organizational strength by giving up autonomous authority to the widest variety of disparate environmental groups.

Private schools do not have these benefits, nor the associated resources. They have to try to find in their environments some niche to occupy that will make them successful — some more specialized set of environmental groups that will see in them special virtues sufficient to overide their extra costs. Attempting to play to the full range of environmental supports is in this case almost always a mistake: it is more important to organize around a distinctive and unified set of goals which will make a special appeal to a limited constituency (see the chapter by James in this volume).

We examine our general argument empirically in three distinct ways: there is no very definite way to establish the coherence of an organization's goals, and much inconsistency and disagreement in the literature on the subject. First, we consider the direct reports of the school administrators to questions about the importance of various goals to their programs. One may question the meaning of such verbal accounts, but modern thinking on the subject treats the concept of organizational goals as referring more directly to official organizational rhetoric than to more hidden and supposedly 'real' goals inferred by researchers from participants' behavior. Using the verbal reports, we directly compare public and private schools.

Second, using the same data, we look at the factors affecting schools' goal depictions. We know that public schools face more plural environments than do private ones: does this account for some of the differences among the goals they define?

Third, we shift to data describing patterns of influence over school decisions, rather than goals themselves. Do private schools have more internal control over their own policy decisions than public ones? It seems reasonable to infer from data on this question to the issue of goal coherence in general.

Administrator Verbal Reports

Our school survey contained a series of questions about school program goals. The intention was to see whether public school administrators tended to report a wider range of clearly distinct programmatic purposes. Table 6 reports the distribution of school responses on the goals questions. Schools are classified by level, since elementary school purposes tend naturally to differ from the issues mentioned at the secondary school level. For each type of school, the proportions subscribing to each of the goals in the list is given.

Table 6: *Reported School Programmatic Emphasis of Public, Catholic and Private Elementary and Secondary Schools (table entries are percents reporting emphasis on each goal)*

	Elementary Schools			Secondary Schools		
	Public	*Catholic*	*Private*	*Public*	*Catholic*	*Private*
Vocational preparation	2	12	6	53	29	19
College preparation	10	19	35	86	86	100
Basic skills	98	97	90	90	71	62
Critical thinking	62	76	90	39	86	81
Respect for authority	67	93	65	39	86	50
Social development	55	72	74	41	71	38
Self-esteem development	88	93	97	57	86	50
Religious values	5	97	48	2	100	50
N (= 100%)	60	67	31	49	7	16

The relevant comparisons are those between public, Catholic and other private schools within school-level categories. Turning first to the elementary school level, we find some differences among types of schools, but little that is relevant for our analysis. Schools generally espouse broad educational goals — linked to quite general standards of citizenship and competence. Some private schools emphasize college preparation, but this is not really sharply distinct from the broad general standard. Very few schools of any sort mention vocational preparation. We had hoped that a stress on basic skills might denote a distinct emphasis on more remedial work, but by the time of our survey this too had become a stock phrase embraced by every type of school. Private schools emphasize more goals having to do with broad socialization, and Catholic ones especially mention respect for authority and religious values. But although types of schools at the elementary level vary a little in the package of qualities they want to build into their products, none of their survey responses reflect the differences in coherence we were attempting to measure.

The data at the secondary level reflect similar variations. But here we find additional results. Almost all the schools report an emphasis on college preparation. But the public schools combine this with a very different emphasis — on vocational preparation. They are also more likely to report a program emphasis on basic skills than are Catholic and other private secondary schools.

The general findings here clearly illustrate our hypothesis. Catholic and other private secondary schools focus their programs on building the college-bound middle class person. Public schools tend to add to this goal a very different emphasis on serving students who will probably end up in working class positions in society. The finding reflects a truism about American public education — for the most part, public schools can do little to choose their constituencies or the purposes appropriate to them.

Effect of Public Programs

As a second analysis we can carry the finding noted above one step further. The distinct goal-emphasis public secondary schools add to those of private schools is the direct acknowledgement of the goal of vocational preparation. Does this simply reflect the fact that public schools have much more diverse student constituencies than private ones? Or is it more that public schools are immersed in an organizational environment which makes necessary the organizational adaptation to vocational training as an explicit purpose? We use involvement in more state and federal funding programs as an indicator.

Table 7, restricted to our secondary school sample, reports the relevant data. It reports a multiple regression analysis predicting which secondary schools describe vocational education as one of their special programmatic emphases. We include, as independent variables, the following factors: the proportion of the school's students who are from ethnic minority groups; the number of special state or federal programs funding the school (reflecting our main hypothesis); and dummy variables indicating whether the school is Catholic or other private. Enrollment size is also included as a control variable.

Table 7: *Multiple Regression Analysis of Factors Affecting a School Emphasis on Vocational Preparation: Secondary Schools Only*

Independent Variables	Slopes	Standard Errors	T
Enrollment	−.0001	.0001	−1.4
Catholic	−.14	.25	−.6
Other Private	−.15	.23	−.6
Percent minority students	.005	.003	1.6
Number of funded public programs	.06	.025	2.2*
Constant	.27	.24	
R^2	.26		
N	64		

* $p < .05$

We already know that Catholic and other private schools tend not to espouse the goal of vocational education. The question here is whether this effect can be accounted for by the distinctive population served by public schools or by their involvement in public programs requiring programmatic conformity. The further question answered by table 7 is whether vocational education is more affected by the actual presence of low status minority students, or whether it is the school's involvement in formal public programs that is the crucial factor.

The data answer both questions convincingly. When the other factors are held constant, Catholic and other private schools no longer differ significantly from public ones. And second, the school's subscription to a programmatic emphasis on vocational preparation is affected significantly by involvement in public programs: the actual presence of more minority students has an insignificant effect. The data thus suggest that the formal acknowledgement of educational goal, quite distinct from the standard image of desirable secondary education is indeed affected by the organizational environment, and that this accounts for the difference between public and private schools. Curriculum goal complexity reflects the organizationally complex environment.

The Direct Influence of Environmental Groups on School Policy

We now consider a more indirect way of discussing the programmatic goal coherence of public and private schools. Our instruments contained a number of items asking about influence within the school's decision-making process of both internal and external groups. We can compare public and private schools on this dimension.

One set of questions asked administrators simply to report the number of external organizations that made on-site inspections of their school. Almost all of these were inspections in connection with various specially-funded public programs. Naturally, the public schools were more likely to receive such inspecting visits — 78.4 per cent of the public schools received one or more on-site inspections compared with only 56.9 per cent of the private and Catholic schools. In itself, this finding suggests the openness of the public schools and their programs to external control and to the expectation of such control.

We also asked a series of questions about which groups influenced school decision-making. The questions asked about five major decision areas (budget, admissions, teacher hiring and firing, and curriculum). For each, we asked respondents to indicate the relative influence on a scale from 0 (none) to 4 (high) of various internal and external parties (parents, teachers, internal administrators, and external governing bodies).

In table 8, we simply report the mean percentage of decision-making influence exercised by external agents. For public schools, external agents are defined as the state department of education, the school district or school board, school advisory council(s) and committee(s), and the PTA. For Catholic and private schools, the external agents are the administrative system office, the local governing board, the pastor or rabbi, and the parent gruop. The percentage of influence exercised by external agents is calculated as the sum of the influence scores for these groups over the five decision domains divided by the sum of the influence scores for all groups.

The data show that public schools report more influence in the hands of external groups than do Catholic or other private schools, in which most decision-making influence is in the hands of groups in the organizational structure itself. The findings for Catholic schools may come as some surprise to readers unfamiliar with this system, but are borne out by our more qualitative observations. In the Catholic system, neither diocesan or parish leaders routinely intervene in the operation of the local schools, and very few other groups are in any position to do so.

Summary

We find evidence that public schools, at the secondary level, report less goal coherence than private ones. In addition to the standard educational goals related to broad definitions of education, they often also report emphasizing vocational education. This emphasis is a response to their involvement in public funding programs, which obviously carry this emphasis.

We also find that in reporting influence over school decision-making public schools report much more involvement of external groups — a process that sustains the high level of support public schools receive in this country, but that also lowers their ability to maintain a coherent internal structure. As we have noted in other contexts (for example, Meyer and Scott, 1983a), the internally decoupled character of public schooling is intimately related to its close linkages with a complex organizational environment.

Table 8: *Mean Percentage of Decision-making Influence Accounted for by External Agents[a], by Educational Sphere and Grade Level[b]*

			Educational Sphere and Grade Level				
	Public elementary	*Catholic elementary*	*Private elementary*	*Public middle*	*Public secondary*	*Catholic secondary*	*Private secondary*
Mean percentage of decision-making influence exercised by external agents	52.5	46.5	37.8	45.6	48.5	41.7	29.9
(N)	(60)	(66)	(31)	(18)	(49)	(6)	(16)

[a] Excluding Catholic and private middle schools (n = 2) and private comprehensive school (n = 9). See Gilliland and Radle (1983): pp. 28–31 for a discussion of the manner in which educational sphere and grade level categories were assigned.

[b] Respondents were asked to assess the degree of influence (on a 5-point scale) exercised by each of six positions or groups over five decision-making domains (see text for description of positions and domains). For public schools, external agents are defined as the state department of education, the school district or school board, the school advisory council(s) or committee(s), and the PTA; for Catholic and private schools, external agents include the administrative system office, the local governance board, the pastor or rabbi, and the parent group. The mean percentage of influence exercised by external agents was calculated by dividing the sum of the influence score of these positions over the five domains by the sum of the influence scores for all groups over the five domains.

Conclusion

We have compared public and private schooling organizations, with the argument that their differing organizational environments should produce quite different organizational arrangements even though in many respects their internal tasks are similar. We find substantial differences in two areas. First, public schooling has a much more elaborate organizational structure than does private schooling. It is not necessarily a larger organizational structure, in terms of ratios of administrators to students, but it is certainly much more complex. Catholic and private schooling systems have high ratios of building level administrators to students, but above this level very little administrative structure. This reflects their funding and controlling environment. Public schooling has complex and expanding structures running above the school level. And it is exactly these organizational levels that expanding environmental controls from state and national levels have acted to foster in recent decades: the complex fundings, programs, and requirements in which public schooling is immersed create pressures that generate much administrative expansion.

We also find evidence that the internal organizational coherence of public schooling is affected by this same process. The involvement of the public schools in an environment with diverse pressures from so many organizational levels provides many resources for the public schools, but also immerses them in a complex and inconsistent, controlling environment. Public schools are in a sense collections of organizational structure from a very complex and increasingly organized environment, rather than highly bounded and internally coherent organizations in their own right. They are immersed in, and interpenetrated by an organized environment, not simply affected by it.

Acknowledgements

The research for this chapter was supported by funds from the National Institute of Education (Grant No. NIE-G–83–0003). The analyses and conclusions do not necessarily reflect the views or policies of this agency. The private/public survey was designed and conducted in collaboration with other researchers at IFG, principally Jay Chambers, Dennis J Encarnation and Joan Talbert. Mary Bankston, Lauren Edelman and Douglas Roeder participated in designing the survey instruments for the school and district study. Mary Bankston played a key role in coordinating the collection of the data. Data files were created primarily by Edward M Gilliland and Janice Radle with the assistance of Kendyll Stansbury. And Edward M Gilliland and Janice Radle implemented most of the analysis on which this chapter is based. Our project officer at NIE, Dr Gail MacColl, provided continuing support and helpful feedback throughout the performance of this project.

7 Conditions of Public and Private School Organization and Notions of Effective Schools

Joan E. Talbert

The current reform movement in US public education is bolstered by claims that private schools do better than the public schools. Documents such as the highly publicized report of Coleman, Hoffer and Kilgore (1981; see also 1982a and 1982b) have credited the private sector with superior academic productivity, higher-quality school life, and more effective administration. Apart from offering a rationale for increased public support of private education, these assessments call for an upgrading of public schools. They suggest that the private schools offer a model of effective school organization, emphasizing traditional curricula and management roles.

Significantly, the Coleman, Hoffer, and Kilgore study (hereafter CHK) and subsequent comparisons of school effectiveness in the public and private sectors[1] do not analyze school organization. What CHK call school 'policy' variables in their study are measures of student behaviors and perceptions, such as time spent on homework and how frequently peers cut classes. The data sets do not include measures of administrative policies and practices needed to reach conclusions about organizational differences between more and less successful schools. In short, school organization is a 'black box' in these studies of private and public school effectiveness (Rossi and Wright, 1982).

The notion that stricter administration of private schools accounts for overall differences between the public and private sectors in academic performance and school climates rests upon two shaky assumptions. First, it assumes that administrative policies and practices are the central means by which private schools establish desirable academic and social environments. This assumption has been challenged by numerous critics of CHK, largely in terms of private schools' capacity to select academically committed students and families and to establish value communities through selection processes and school traditions. Second, the argument assumes that school administrative policies and practices differ significantly across the sectors, with private schools generally having tighter control systems. This assumption conflicts with a convincing argument that shared values and norms may substitute for administrative controls, thus enabling private schools to achieve order with limited rule structures and minimal direct management (Salganik and Karweit, 1982).

The conclusion that public schools would benefit by emulating private school organization requires two further assumptions: that schools are not organizationally constrained by being in one sector or the other, and that local administrative strategies effective in the private sector are also effective in the public sector. These assumptions are questionable in the light of recent claims that school organization is qualitatively different across the sectors. The literature points to sector contrasts in student selection, educational goals, governance, and types of authority and organization.

This chapter examines the implications of different conditions of school organization for school effectiveness in the public and private sectors of education. How do the organizing frameworks of private and public schools facilitate or inhibit program, administrative and social-system features associated with effective schools? Might effective administrative roles differ across the school sectors due to their unique organizational conditions and the local resources and problems generated by these conditions?

Apart from these substantive assessments, the chapter provides an analytic framework for comparing school sectors organizationally, for tracing implications of particular organizational features for school effectiveness, and for considering administrative strategies relevant to different conditions of school organization. The framework integrates the 'effective schools' literature and recent organizational comparisons of school sectors. The former literature points to school features associated with successful public schools and bridges descriptions of sector differences in school organization and evaluations of sector differences in school effectiveness.[2]

A brief summary of the effective schools research provides a backdrop for subsequent comparisons of private and public school organization. The next section highlights organizational conditions which distinguish the school sectors. It reviews arguments and evidence that these conditions make a difference for local school features and discusses in more detail my claim that public and private schools display three alternative 'types' of authority and organization (Talbert, 1984). The next section traces implications of the distinct conditions of public and private school organization for each of the school features deemed productive in the effective schools literature. The final section raises issues and offers some cautions regarding conclusions warranted by this integration of literatures.

Effective Schools in the Public Sector

'Effective schools' studies have aimed to determine features of public school programs, administrations and social systems that are conducive to school success. The typical research strategy has been to identify more and less successful schools and note the features which distinguish them. The studies are quite diverse, apart from this commonality. They have used a range of success criteria, including various measures of academic performance levels and gains and indicators of school life quality like staff morale and safety. They also have used a variety of study designs: outlier studies, case studies, program evaluations and multivariate analyses of survey data. Further, the studies lack a common theoretical framework and their data cover different combinations of school organization variables (see Purkey and Smith (1983) for a more thorough analysis of the effective schools research).

Despite the problems of integrating findings from such diverse studies and cautions against making causal inferences from these cross-sectional analyses (cf. Rowan, Bossert and Dwyer, 1983), the effective schools research has generated considerable consensus on productive school features. The literature provides the framework for school improvement programs across the United States (cf. Neufield, Farrar and Miles, 1983; Purkey and Smith, 1983).

The school features enumerated in table 1 are those which have distinguished successful schools across a number of studies and which have come to be regarded as productive. This summary includes some features isolated by many studies and other features isolated by a few studies representing different designs or effectiveness criteria.[3] The table groups features according to their organizational or social system referents and indicates the studies and literature reviews which emphasize each school feature as effective.

The crude conceptual framework of the line of research is apparent in this summary of its findings. First, the researchers have used different labels to describe roughly the same phenomenon (for exam-

Table 1: *Administrative and Program Features and Social-System Conditions Identified with Successful Schools*[a]

Level	Feature	Research Base
Administrative and Program	Clear goals/common purpose among staff/emphasis on basic academic skills	Weber (1971); Trisman et al. (1976); HEW* (1978); Austin (1979); Brookover and Lezotte (1979); Rutter et al. (1979); ECE (1980); Glenn (1981); Levine and Stark (1981); Edmonds (1979 and 1981); Tomlinson (1980); Purkey and Smith (1983); Neufield, Farrar, and Miles (1983)
	Administrative autonomy	Berman and McLaughlin (1977); HEW (1978); Hunter (1979); Purkey and Smith (1983)
	Coordination of resources and activities	Wellisch et al. (1978); Glenn (1981); Levine and Stark (1981); Purkey and Smith (1983)
	Joint planning by staff/collegiality	Trisman (1976); Armor et al. (1976); Glenn (1981); Levine and Stark (1981); Purkey and Smith (1983)
	Staff development/in-service training	Armor et al. (1976); ECE (1980); Glenn (1981); Levine and Stark (1981); PDK (1980); Purkey and Smith (1983)
	Clear principles and guidelines for student behavior	HEW (1978); Brookover et al. (1979), Rutter et al. (1979); Purkey and Smith (1983)

	Strong administrative leadership/instructional leadership	Weber (1971); Armor *et al.* (1976); Trisman *et al.* (1976); HEW (1978); Wellisch *et al.* (1978); Austin (1979); Brookover *et al.* (1979); ECE (1980); Tomlinson (1980); Glenn (1981); Levine and Stark (1981); Edmonds (1979 and 1981); PDK (1980); Tomlinson (1980); Purkey and Smith (1983); Neufield, Farrar, and Miles (1983)
	Frequent/careful review of student progress	Weber (1971); Austin (1979); Hunter (1979); Levine and Stark (1981); Edmonds (1979 and 1981); Purkey and Smith (1983); Neufield, Farrar, and Miles (1983)
	Schoolwide recognition of student success	HEW (1978); Brookover *et al.* (1979); Brookover and Lezotte (1979); Wynne (1980); Purkey and Smith (1983)
Social System	Sense of community/discipline and order/teacher-student rapport	Weber (1971); Armor *et al.* (1976); Trisman *et al.* (1976); HEW (1978); Austin (1979); Wynne (1980); Glenn (1981); Edmonds (1979 and 1981); Purkey and Smith (1983); Neufield, Farrar, and Miles (1983)
	High expectations for student success	Weber (1971); Armor *et al.* (1976); Trisman *et al.* (1976); Austin (1979); Brookover *et al.* (1979); Brookover and Lezotte (1979); Hunter (1979); Rutter *et al.* (1979); ECE (1980); Glenn (1981); Edmonds (1979 and 1981); Purkey and Smith (1983); Neufield, Farrar, and Miles (1983)
	Parent contact and involvement	Armor *et al.* (1976); Brookover and Lezotte (1979); Austin (1979); PDK (1980); Purkey and Smith (1983)

*US Department of Health, Education and Welfare (1978).

Note: [a] Studies and literature reviews which isolate the feature as conducive to school effectiveness are indicated in the third column. Literature reviews which include the feature in conclusions are included in parentheses.

ple, 'clear goals', 'common purpose among the staff', and 'emphasis on basic academic skills'). Table 1 combines features which seem to have a common empirical referent and indicates some of the labels used by different researchers. Second, the features isolated by the studies vary in how much they are empirically independent of others. For example, 'school administrative autonomy' is relatively distinct from other features, while 'clear principles and guidelines for student behavior' and 'discipline and order' may be highly related empirically, though they are theoretically distinct. Third, the features have been specified at different levels of abstractness. For example, 'staff development and inservice training' is relatively concrete, while 'sense of community' and 'strong administrative leadership' are quite abstract. The leadership variable is so abstract and subject to alternative interpretations that it is meaningless as a criterion for evaluating school administrators.

Sector Contrasts in Conditions of School Organization

Recent comparisons of public and private schools point to basic organizational conditions which distinguish the sectors: selection principles (McPartland and McDill, 1982; Salganik and Karweit, 1982), goal frameworks (Salganik and Karweit, 1982) and governance conditions (*ibid*). These analyses suggest that qualitative differences in the organization of public and private schools offer better chances for private schools to establish desirable program, administrative and social-system features.

After reviewing this literature, I develop the argument that schools organize according to three different types of authority and report data consistent with the view that public, religious and non-religious private schools are organizationally distinct from one another.[4] This analysis suggests that particular organizational structures and strategies are more or less valued and legitimate across types of US schools.

Selection Principles

McPartland and McDill (1982) have argued that the jurisdictional principle of student selection in the public sector influences the nature and success of schools' academic programs and their social climates. They emphasize that students with different socioeconomic origins, academic aptitudes and interests are differentiated organizationally in the public school system. Students are segregated by residence into different schools and by academic aptitudes into different courses, and their curricula and instruction differ in emphasizing academic or non-academic goals. In effect, public school effectiveness is a matter of demographic concentrations of students: schools with substantial portions of academically disadvantaged students exhibit diminished academic productivity and commitments.

Salganik and Karweit (1982) provide a complementary assessment of the importance of voluntarism in defining private schools' social and organizational systems. They contrast the school sectors in terms of government control in the public sector and voluntarism in the private sector. In this view, compulsory student selection is one manifestation of government control in the public sector; and the 'unwilling clientele' it generates has negative effects on public schools' internal processes and climate. In contrast, voluntarism in the private sector assures private schools' legitimacy and respect. These authors portray voluntarism as the source of value consensus and mutual trust among constituents; traditional authority (obedience to persons in lieu of elaborate policy and rule structures); a sense of efficacy among teachers, principals and students; commitment to school success; and a stable identity over time.

In sum, the principle of student selection is an organizational condition which distinguishes school sectors and which influences internal structures and cultures. Voluntarism in the private sector should promote social system features associated with effective schools, while compulsory attendance and patterns of residential seg-regation yield divergent levels of academic performance and commit-ment among the public schools.

Educational Goals

Goal competition and conflict are pervasive in US education and present special problems for public schools. The public schools must accommodate competing mandates for academic excellence and educa-tional equity and are open to institutional fads and trends which alter priorities for public education. As commonly noted by analysts of public school organization, these dynamics generate complex prog-rams and administrations and 'loose coupling' (cf. Bidwell, 1965; Weick, 1976). In contrast, the private schools are constrained by tradition, size and often by religious auspices to a limited range of educational goals, thus maintaining greater program coherence within the private sector.

The public schools' capacity to establish local, delimited goals has been constrained increasingly over the past century. Trends toward greater rationalization and legalization in education have formalized a wide range of educational norms and values and have undermined local schools' autonomy (for analyses of these developments see Bailey, 1981; Cohen and Neufield, 1981; Meyer, 1981; Tyack and Hansot, 1982). National and state laws and educational programs responsive to special interest groups and particular educational values establish the multiple, conflicted goal framework of US public education at the local school level.

In short, goal coherence is highly problematic for schools in the complex environment of US public education (cf. Salganik and Karweit, 1982). This condition of school organization distinguishes the public from the private sector; and it has been explicitly linked to effective schools and implicitly related to social-system conditions deemed effective, such as a local sense of community.

Governance Frameworks

Salganik and Karweit (1982) have argued that government control of public schools and voluntarism within the private school sector have profound effects on school organization and efficacy. Voluntarism and self-governance establish the legitimacy of a private school and assure value consensus, traditional authority, efficacy and high levels of commitment among local constituents. Almost conversely, government control — combined with conflicted goals and fragmented governance — establish the legitimacy of public schools but foster rational-legal authority and bureaucratic selection, disagreement over values, low efficacy and low levels of commitment among local school constituents (pp. 153 and 156).

These authors highlight contrasts between public schools' rational-legal authority and private schools' traditional authority. This distinction between types of organizational authority derives from Max Weber's work (tr. 1947) and is defined as a difference between relying upon rules and their enforcement (rational/legal authority) and relying upon obedience to persons (traditional authority) as the basis of control in the organization. Salganik and Karweit argue that traditional authority derives from a sense of community in private schools and allows school heads to assume the kind of symbolic leadership role which, in turn, promotes social integration. They argue that rational-legal authority is established for the public schools by government control and is the source of proliferating laws, administrative structures and accountability systems at higher levels of the public school system. They note important local consequences of these 'rationalizing' trends in the public sector: narrowed scopes of authority for teachers, cast as implementers of programs, and principals, cast as administrators of programs, policies and rules determined elsewhere; and disciplinary laws and rules which undermine student commitment (pp. 157–8; see also Wise, 1979). In short, Salganik and Karweit argue that the contrasting governance of public and private schools is the source of different kinds of organizational authority and tendencies in school organization which allow private schools to be more effective, at least on quality-of-life criteria.

W. Richard Scott and John Meyer (in this volume) have empirically assessed effects of complex, fragmented governance structures on local school administration and programs. They argue that the trends in US public education toward centralization, federalization and fragmentation become manifest at the local level in highly complex, disorderly organizational environments and various internal adaptations (see also Meyer and Scott, 1983a). Using data from the survey of the Institute for Research on Educational Finance and Governance (IFG) at Stanford University, they compared environmental complexity for public and private schools and found that the public schools showed (a) more complex higher-level administrative structures; (b) less goal coherence at the secondary level; and (c) less autonomy of school staffs in making decisions. Further, the local environmental complexity generated by a school's participation in externally funded programs apparently increased the size of the internal administrative component and the total administrative time devoted to these additional programs. These effects were observed among both public and private schools, though the levels of private school participation in such government-funded programs are much lower.

This analysis does not posit qualitative differences in the governance conditions of public and private schools, as have Salganik and Karweit. Nevertheless, the empirical observations support a distinction between public and private schools' governance structures and suggest that public schools' complex and fragmented administrative environment constrains two features associated with effective schools: decision autonomy and goal coherence. The public schools' wider participation in federal and state educational programs also may limit these schools' capacity to coordinate their programs and resources and to establish collaborative staff relations, two additional features identified with effective schools.

Alternative Types of Organization

Should we view these organizational contrasts between the public and private school as relatively independent of one another; or do they reflect different 'logics' of organization established within the school sectors? For example, do conditions of public school organization — the jurisdictional principle of student selection, multiple and competing educational goals, government control through fragmented administrative structures — follow a common logic?

Salganik and Karweit (1982) favor the latter, 'syndrome' view of organizational differences between the school sectors, positing government control and voluntarism as the source of numerous features distinguishing private and public schools. The organizational logics derive from the requirements and opportunities for legitimacy presented by the schools' governance conditions, according to their argument. This analysis may overemphasize structural sources of the sector differences in school organization. Particularly in light of current theory on schools as 'institutional' organizations, developed through observations of public schools, we might explore the possibility of institutional sources of organizational differences between public and private schools.

Institutional theory on school organization argues that organizations like schools, which lack clarity or consensus on goals, outcome standards and effective 'technologies' necessary for technically rational organization, gain legitimacy by becoming isomorphic with organizational structures established as legitimate in their environments (cf. Meyer and Rowan, 1977). In other words, schools are supported by their constituents if they conform to institutionalized 'models' of organization: if they look like proper schools and display control systems deemed effective.

The environment of US schools is dominated by complex organizations operating under rational-legal norms. The 'rational-legal', or 'bureaucratic', model of organization is established for public schools partly by government control, which subjects the schools to administrative structures and routines of local, state and federal bureaucracies. The model also is enforced by powerful local constituencies of public schools, many of whom are accustomed to the technical rationality of business firms, and by current public mandates for greater accounta-

bility within the school system. In effect, public schools are legitimized according to their display of rational, bureaucratic organization.
Meyer and Rowan (1977) have traced implications of this mandate for
the schools' educational programs and administrative structures; Sal-
ganick and Karweit (1982) have traced implications for local authority
relations and social-system conditions.

While we would expect all schools to conform to established
notions of proper school programs, for example, teaching the 3 Rs in
age-graded classes, the private schools may embrace different models
of authority and organization. In fact, we can identify types of organizational authority alternative to the rational-legal model enforced
upon public schools and propose that private schools obtain legitimacy by conforming to these alternatives. If the principle of isomorphism is a reasonable account of the bureaucratic features of public
schools, the principle may also explain organizational differences between public and private schools. The remainder of this section develops the argument and offers supporting evidence, which suggest
that the legitimacy and support of private and public schools depends
upon their being organizationally distinct.

Institutionalized models of organization

Max Weber (tr. 1947) defined alternative models of authority and
organization which, I will argue, are institutionalized in US society
by different kinds of organizations and serve as alternative bases for
school administrative organization and legitimacy. First, it is worth
reviewing Weber's distinction between rational-legal and traditional
models of authority and organization, as the alternative values and
norms they represent are often lost amidst bemoanings of 'over-
rationalized' organization; and the survival of the traditional model
among modern organizations often is ignored.

The bureaucratic model of organization emerged in antithesis to
the traditional organization of pre-industrial society. In traditional
society, organization was based upon the authority of individuals to
govern by virtue of their birthright or ordainment. Organization was
simple, based in a hierarchy of individuals' authority and communities
of dedicated followers. Loyalty was cemented by familial affiliations
or by economic dependency, but the system rested upon norms of
deference and obedience. The model of rational-legal organization
emerged at an historic moment when economic productivity depended upon neutralizing traditional loyalties. New organizing norms
aimed to establish and legitimize 'culture-blind' organizations in

which: goals and criteria of effectiveness would be objectively defined; effective divisions of work would be established; authority would be located in positions within a hierarchy; individuals would be recruited, evaluated, and rewarded according to competence standards rather than according to their family, friendship or other personal ties to the organization.

Elements of these two ideal types of Weber's theory can be found in most modern organizations; yet they are institutionalized as alternative principles of authority and organization structure. The rational-legal model is widely established among US organizations; yet the traditional model of authority and organization is maintained by many religious and other voluntary organizations.

Weber's typology of authority includes a third type, charismatic authority. However, charismatic authority has not been institutionalized as an organizational model given tensions between charismatic leadership and organizational control (cf. Swidler, 1979) and tendencies toward bureaucratic or traditional models of organization beyond the life or charisma of the leader. Recent organizational research and theory suggests that a fourth type of organizational authority has been established as legitimate and viable by various new modes of organization in the US. W. Richard Scott (1981) labels this alternative the 'authority of goals' (pp. 286–90). Organizations for which common goals are the basis of control challenge the principle of hierarchical control common to both bureaucratic and traditional organization and bureaucracy's reliance on formal policies and rules. Scott identifies various forms of organization and labels for this new, goal-based type of authority: 'value rationality' (Satow, 1975), 'collectivist-democratic' organization (Rothschild-Whitt, 1979), 'clan' systems (Ouchi, 1980), 'management by objectives' (Swanson, 1980). These kinds of organizations commonly rely upon participants' commitments to specific operational values and goals and avoid organization structures which might inhibit individual contributions to the collective good.

Presumably, heads or representatives of such organizations have no special authority beyond that associated with goals and accomplishments of the organization and their ability to integrate members and clients around those values. Professional credentials may be represented, linking the organization with a rational-legal model; or personal attributes may symbolize collective values, linking the organization with a traditional model; but neither kind of borrowing from other authority models may be evident, as with cooperatives which prize their democratic structure and process as an organizational goal. Such organizations gain legitimacy mainly through constituencies' demand for their goals and for the model of organization they represent as an alternative to the bureaucratic or traditional models. In a climate of disaffection with bureaucracy, for example, the popular sentiment that 'small is beautiful', the latter source of legitimacy may be significant. Following Scott, I refer to this mode of authority as 'goal-based' authority but emphasize that goals may be expressed in terms of organizational structure and processes, as well as in terms of production values.

Schools and models of authority and organization

These institutionalized models of authority and organization may offer alternative sources of legitimacy for school organization. As argued, the public schools are captive to the rational-legal or bureaucratic model. Religious private schools may be seen as captive to the traditional model. The majority are more or less directly governed by Catholic organizations with hierarchical orders representing individuals' ordainments, service and loyalty. Traditional authority is established for religious schools by this relevant model of organization, which often is enforced by governance arrangements. Further, religious doctrines and norms which prescribe lines of deference and obedience as bases of social order are likely to be legitimized and enforced within the schools' religious communities. Alternatively, non-religious private schools organize around the authority of specialized goals — whether focused on educational aims, instructional processes or alternative models of administration. Constituents seek and support a school's special purposes so long as the goals are valued and the school succeeds in symbolizing the goals by its organization and culture.

This institutional perspective on contrasts in school organization de-emphasizes the role of voluntarism in distinguishing private from public school organization, except in assuming that private schools select constituents who legitimize the authority principle around which their school is organized. It also questions the organizational importance of different external governance structures among the religious schools, since a common authority principle derives from their reliance upon commitments to religious values and obedience to formally sanctioned, or 'ordained', representatives of these values. In sum, public, religious and non-religious private schools are organizationally distinct because they gain legitimacy by being isomorphic with alternative models of authority and organization.

Expected organization contrasts

In order to test and refine the argument, I hypothesized specific organizational tendencies likely to be shown by public, religious and non-religious private schools. I considered how the alternative models of authority and organization might be expressed in educational goals, teacher recruitment standards, administrative controls over instruction, external accounting requirements, emphases on school 'climate', monitoring of clients, and decision-making structures of schools. Most of these variables are commonly discussed and analyzed in the school organization literature and are referenced in comparisons of public and private schools or in comparisons of more and less effective public schools. Expected tendencies for each school type are outlined below for each of the organization variables.

H_1: Goal emphases vary by school type. Public schools accommodate the broadest range of goals encompassing equity aims and students' preparation for academic and vocational futures; religious schools emphasize basic academic skills and value education; non-religious private schools are most specialized, emphasizing 'residual' goals such as students' self-concept and social development.

H_2: The extent of teacher selection standards varies by school type. Public schools rely upon teacher credentials; non-religious private schools rely additionally upon teachers' educational philosophy and experience; and religious schools rely additionally upon teachers' personal values and religious affiliations.

H_3: The extent of internal instructional control varies by school type. Religious schools are most, and public schools are least, likely to exercise controls on curricula, instructional methods, and student progress review and dismissal. This hypothesis assumes that (a) clear goal emphasis allows for school policy on instruction; and (b) hierarchical structures establish controls when possible.

H_4: The extent of external accounting requirements varies by school type. Public schools are subject to the most, and non-religious private schools to the least demands by external authorities for data on programs and student achievement. This hypothesis references bureaucratic emphases on standardized data and the wider participation of religious than non-religious schools in publicly funded programs and in larger organizational systems.

H$_5$:   Emphasis on school social climate varies by school type. Religious schools are most, and public schools least, concerned with teacher commitment, student morale and discipline and parent involvement. This hypothesis references the traditional models' reliance upon value commitments and loyalties and the bureaucratic models' norms against personal values and informal ties as bases of organization.

H$_6$:   Monitoring of clients varies by school type. Religious schools are most, and non-religious private schools are least, likely to use systematic data on student and parents' attitudes and individual students' accomplishments. This hypothesis follows from the two preceding hypotheses and assumes that non-religious private schools are more likely than religious schools to rely upon informal communication and feedback from students and parents.

H$_7$:   Decision structure varies by school type. Religious schools are the most hierarchically controlled, while influence is more evenly distributed across administrative, lay, and faculty groups among public and non-religious private schools. This hypothesis assumes that (a) the traditional model gives school and religious officials authority over a range of decisions (on curriculum, staff hiring and firing and school budgets); (b) the rational-legal model supports a system of checks-and-balances, as represented by lay boards of education, as well as specialized divisions of decision authority; and (c) the goal-based model supports a partnership among school heads, teachers and parents.

These hypotheses anticipate significant differences on each organizational variable between schools grouped by authority type. They imply that independent religious schools are organizationally more like the religious schools in larger systems than they are like non-religious, independent private schools. They also imply that schools can be correctly classified as public, religious or non-religious according to their reports on all of these organization variables. In other words, they suggest a syndrome of organizational tendencies based in the three alternative models of authority and organization.

Empirical evidence

School-level data from the IFG survey of San Francisco Bay Area schools allowed for an initial test of these expectations.[5] Results should be taken as tentative, given high non-response rates for segments of the private school population and very small sample sizes yielded for school types defined at the secondary school level. Further, the measures of organizational variables are crude; they rely upon official reports and most represent responses to a single-item checklist.[6]

The analysis followed three stages. First, I compared average school scores on measures of the organizational variables for four school subsamples, distinguishing parochial and diocesan from independent religious schools. This comparison was important in evaluating whether the authority principle established by religious affiliation or the governance condition established by organizational hierarchy versus autonomy was the basis of organizational differences shown for religious schools; most religious schools in the sample were parochial or diocesan Catholic schools. This and subsequent comparisons of sector means included only the primary schools, given small numbers of private secondary schools. The data showed commonality on more of the organizational variables for the two religious school subsamples than for the independent religious and non-religious school sub-samples. This observation warranted subsequent analyses addressed to the proposed distinctions among public, religious and non-religious private schools.

Second, I tested the hypotheses of particular differences across school types on each organizational variable. Expected differences were shown for the variables teacher selectivity, external accounting requirements, climate emphasis, client monitoring, and decision structure. Unexpected tendencies for the public schools were shown for the goal variable. Public schools showed substantially lower emphasis on *all* goal categories than both types of private schools (while the religious and non-religious schools showed the expected goal emphases and ordering on the range of goals represented). Perhaps the wide diversity of goals for public education and conflicts surrounding the alternative goals prompt public school officials to avoid stating goal emphases. No significant differences across school types were shown on the instructional control variable, given commonly high tendencies for schools to report policy on curricula and student progress reviews and low tendencies to report policy on teaching methods. More refined measures, including teacher supervision and evaluation practices, may have revealed greater variation among schools and school types on this variable.

Third, I assessed the organizational 'distinctness' of the three school types using multiple discriminant analysis techniques. This analysis included the organizational variables enumerated above and dummy variables representing the school types (table 2 shows correlations of the school type and organization variables for the primary and secondary school sub-samples). The data yielded homogeneous within-sector covariance matrices (chi square = .07) and fairly high rates of classification success (84 per cent of public schools, 96 per cent of the religious schools, and 93 per cent of the non-religious schools were correctly classified by values on the eight organizational indices).

Table 2: Correlations of Organizational Indices with School Type Dummy Variables, for Primary and Secondary Schools Separately*

	Primary Schools			Secondary Schools		
	Public	Religious	Non-religious private	Public	Religious	Non-religious private
Range of explicit goal emphases	−.54*	.54*	−.03	−.20	.46*	−.31*
Teacher selectivity	−.45*	.41*	.03	−.26*	.36*	−.10
Instructional control	0	−.07	.12	−.25	.15	.15
External accounting requirements	.19	.03	−.34*	.22	.08	−.40*
Climate emphasis	−.27*	.29*	−.06	−.12	.27*	−.17
Client monitoring	.09	.22*	−.22*	.12	.16	−.37*
Hierarchical control	−.50*	.58*	−.17*	−.18	.12	.10
Lay influence	.59*	−.61*	.07	.51*	−.12	−.54*
Faculty influence	−.09	−.02	.17*	−.50*	.05	.61*

* Asterisks in the table indicate correlations statistically significant at the .05 level. N = 125 for the primary school sample; N = 37 for the secondary school sample. Given high non-response rates and the small N for secondary schools, these results should be viewed as highly tentative.

Discussion

This study identified lines of organizational distinctness across public, religious, and non-religious private schools consistent with the claim that these schools embrace alternative models of authority and organization. The data support previous observations that goal conditions, selection principles, and organizational environments distinguish schools by sector and point to additional differences on these variables between types of private schools. The analysis revealed two additional organizational variables which distinguish school types and which relate to features praised in the effective schools literature: emphasis on school climate and parent involvement.

First, public school officials reported much less emphasis on constituent commitment, discipline and involvement as important to school success than did private school officials — particularly those heading religious schools. This pattern could express public schools' general failure in achieving community; but it is consistent with the view that rational-legal organizing norms discourage both attention to members' values and demands on commitment and involvement beyond contract and performance standards, while traditional organization relies upon shared values and loyalty.

Second, a breakdown of data on patterns of influence across decision areas portrayed public schools as balancing mainly lay boards' and officials' influence, religious schools as relying upon hierarchical control, and non-religious private schools as extending decision authority to their faculties.[7] Specifically in terms of parent involvement and influence in the schools, it appears that parent participation is co-opted by organized lay boards in the public sector and by officials' authority among religious schools, while non-religious private schools support a more even distribution of influence among school heads, faculties, parent boards and aggregates of parents. In theoretical terms, the rational-legal and traditional authority principles appear to inhibit parent involvement, while goal-based authority legitimizes parent involvement and influence in school affairs.

The view of school organization as following alternative institutionalized models and the available evidence that the three school types are organizationally distinct cautions against a prescription that public schools take private schools as models of organization. First, alternative and quite different organizational models seem to operate among private schools; no single model of school organization is offered by the private sector. Second, the effectiveness of particular organizational strategies may well be conditioned by norms of authority and organizational patterns established within different school types. Unfortunately, the available data do not allow for an exploration of such interaction possibilities.[8] I turn now to the question of what these organizational contrasts might mean for school effectiveness. Do the special conditions of school organization in each sector promote or inhibit school features deemed effective?

Implications for Effective Schools

The analyses of organizational differences across school sectors and types suggest a range of local consequences which relate to features associated with effective public schools. Here I summarize the analyses in terms of effective schools features, considering (a) which features are most likely to distinguish schools by sector; (b) which organizing conditions of the public sector are most constraining of effective schools features and which features are least constrained within the public sector; and (c) how the roles of strong administrative leaders might be dependent upon the special conditions of different school types.

Patterns by Sector

Table 3 presents a matrix of effective schools features by organizing conditions for the public and private sectors. I have indicated with '+' or '−' instances where sector conditions facilitate or inhibit a feature of effective schools ('±' is used in cases where wide school variation is associated with an organizing condition).[9] In general, the organizational conditions of public schools inhibit effective schools features, while conditions in the private sector facilitate them.

Rows of the matrix indicate on which school features public and private schools are likely to differ the most. Those effective-schools features facilitated by at least two private sector conditions and inhibited by at least two public sector conditions include goal clarity and convergence, school autonomy, resource and program coordination, and sense of community or discipline and order. The features commonly pertain to the integration of school programs and social systems around locally shared purposes. In this general respect, the sectors contrast substantially as a function of their respective organizing conditions. Note that the two authority models within the private sector yield one difference in comparison with the public sector: parent involvement is promoted by goal-based authority and inhibited by traditional authority.

The Public Sector

The left-hand columns of table 3 suggest which organizing conditions most constrain the public schools on the effectiveness features. The

Table 3: *Facilitating or Constraining Effects of the Sectors' Conditions of Organization on Effective Schools Features*

Effective Schools Features	Public Sector				Private Sector				
School administration and program	Compulsory selection by jurisdiction	Multiple, conflicting goals	Rational-legal authority	Complex organizational environment	Voluntarism (mutual selection)	Delimited goal domain	Traditional authority (religious sub-sector)	Goal-based authority (non-religious) sub-sector	Integrated organizational environment
Goal Clarity and Convergence/Basic Skills Emphasis	±	−		−	+	+	+	+	+
School Autonomy			−	−			+	+	
Resource/Program Co-ordination		−		−		+			+
Joint Planning by Staff/Collegiality				−				+	
Staff Development/Inservice			+	+					

Clear Principles and Guidelines for Student Behavior		−					+	
Strong Administrative Leadership				−				
Frequent Review of Student Progress								
School-wide Recognition of Student Success								
Social system								
Sense of Community/ Discipline and Order	±	−	−		+	+	+	+
High Expectations for Academic Success	±	−			+			±
Parent Involvement and Contact			−				−	+

condition of multiple and conflicting goals, and the complex organizational environments they have generated in the atmosphere of legislative and judicial action in education, appear the most consequential for schools. The complex administrative environment exacerbates constraints imposed by the goal condition (on goal coherence and program coordination) and creates new constraints (on school autonomy, staff collegiality, and administrators' roles), while the goal condition independently constrains features based on shared community values.

The other organizing conditions of the public sector also appear relevant to effective schools features. Compulsory attendance produces variation among public schools on students' academic orientations and aptitudes and on the degree of homogeneity in constituents' values, yielding extremes on the features of goal coherence, sense of community, and high expectations for students' academic success. The rational-legal authority principle enforces constraints on schools' autonomy, de-emphasizes values and a sense of community as important to school business, and discourages wide parent involvement by promoting specialized and representational structures for participation. It also supports the trends in US education which yield complex, fragmented environments of public schools.

Effective-schools features which appear unconstrained in the public sector include frequent review of student progress, school-wide recognition of student success, and staff development and in-service training (the only feature facilitated by sector organizing conditions). Those features which show relatively limited constraints include joint staff planning and collegiality, clear guidelines for student behavior, parent involvement and contact, and strong administrative leadership.

In sum, diverse and competing goals for US public education, and the organizational complexity they have generated under rational-legal norms, appear most inhibiting of effective school features. Features consistent with rational-legal organizing norms and not dependent upon local value consensus are least constrained in the public sector.

What About Administrative Leadership?

The variable of strong administrative leadership is celebrated in current analyses of school effectiveness, whether in comparisons of most and least effective public schools or in attributed sources of private schools' success. Yet, behavioral definitions of the variable are vague and diverse; and it is not possible to translate the organizing conditions of school sectors as promoting or impeding strong leadership.[10] If the school administrator's role is central to school effectiveness, then it is important to consider its meaning and potential in different school sectors.

Notions of strong leadership in the private school sector run the gamut between strict disciplinarian and symbolic leader, while strong administrators in the public sector often are portrayed as instructional leaders. What can we make of these different conceptions of effective administrative roles? Can we hope to define administrator roles that are effective in all schools and then assess their prevalence among public and private schools?

My organizational analysis of school sectors suggests that strong leadership may differ substantially across types of schools. First, if different models of authority are important in distinguishing between public, religious and non-religious private schools, we would expect different administrative roles to be effective within these schools. The student, parent and teacher populations they attract would hold different expectations for authority relations in the school and would respond differently to particular administrative structures and roles. Shared understandings about proper school administration would differ across public, religious and non-religious private schools; and school heads' leadership would build upon these understandings. Effective leadership styles and roles would thus look quite different in the public and private school sectors.

Second, the special organizational conditions of the school sectors generate different kinds of resources, responsibilities and problems for heads of public and private schools. Strong leadership may entail mobilizing resources to manage perceived instructional and social system problems in the school and to consolidate strengths. The talents and tasks of strong administrators among the public schools should differ substantially from those among the religious and non-religious private schools. As examples, public school principals may use their instructional expertise or system specialists and in-service programs to manage educational problems generated by diverse student populations, divergent goals, and specialized programs and staffs; religious school heads may use their social skills and church leaders to generate parent involvement and contact; non-religious school heads may use negotiating skills to establish educational innovations and school rituals which maintain constituents' commitments and the school's special identity.

In sum, the leadership of school administrators would be expected to differ across the sectors, enlisting different styles, talents, tasks, and standards. In this view, the potentials for strong administrative leadership are qualitatively different within the public and private school sectors. In order to assess whether the organizational conditions of private schools facilitate strong leadership among school heads, we would need first to establish clear definitions of strong leadership within each sector. The analysis of facilitating and inhibiting conditions of strong leadership would then address variation within, rather than across, school sectors.

Discussion

This chapter offers an organizational account of average sector differences in school effectiveness without assuming that private schools are run better than public schools. Basic conditions of private school organization facilitate program, administrative, and social system features viewed as desirable and educationally productive, while many of these features are constrained by conditions of public school organization. More specifically, the private sectors' specialized goals and authority types promote program and social-system integration, while competing educational goals and the rational-legal model of organization established for the public sector generate complex educational programs and administrative structures and constrain the development of school community. Against current standards of school effectiveness, the public sector is organizationally disadvantaged.

The analysis relies upon theoretical formulations of qualitative sector differences in school organizations which require further empirical testing and upon conclusions drawn from studies of more and less successful public schools. The latter line of research has received considerable criticism (cf. Rowan, Bossert and Dwyer, 1983); and additional research is needed to determine what, if any, generalizations can be drawn regarding public school features conducive to success. Further, we have yet to identify school features associated with success within the private sector. If they are not the same as those isolated for the public sector, then cross-sector comparisons on a common set of school features would not be valid. In short, the empirical grounding of this analysis is rather weak and one should be cautious in drawing conclusions. In particular, one would not conclude that organizational conditions and authority established in the private sector are educationally superior to those operating in the public sector, though they promote some desirable features of school life.

The most obvious reason for refraining from conclusions on relative educational success is that much of the recent research on academic productivity across sectors indicates comparable school effectiveness on this criterion (see note 1). We must then conclude that the effective schools research was biased toward the quality-of-life criterion of school effectiveness, on which private schools are generally superior (cf. Morgan, 1983), or that the private sector is disadvantaged on school features which are academically productive and taken for granted in the public sector. A quality-of-life bias could derive from the studies' heavy sampling of poor urban schools, where goal consensus and order might be more strongly related to academic success than among other public schools, and from biased sampling of school variables during a climate of concern with school discipline problems. The private sector's relatively uniform curricula and standardized pedagogies may represent academic disadvantages compared with the public sector's ideal of adapting schools or programs and instruction to special student needs. It is possible that some such missing part of a general equation for schools' academic productivity is facilitated in the public sector and inhibited in the private sector; this would explain the discrepancy between results of this analysis and findings of comparable academic success across the school sectors.

One should thus interpret results of the present analysis in terms of the quality-of-life criterion of school effectiveness. In brief, conditions of school organization which distinguish the sectors appear to give a substantial advantage to private schools on school-life quality, as they both facilitate desirable school features among the private schools and inhibit such features among public schools. We may assume that this advantage does not translate uniformly into academic success. We could also question whether the school-life criteria are fair and important bases for comparing public and private school effectiveness.

A common criticism of sector comparisons on academic productivity is that public schools pursue a wider range of educational goals than do private schools. This criticism may also be relevant to sector comparisons which indicate superior quality-of-life among the private schools. Specifically, when the goals of public education include preparing students for life in a culturally diverse society, for managing conflicts inherent to democratic society, for work in complex organizations, etc., then we cannot say that private schools are educationally superior because they recruit value communities and assure consensus and order in the schools. Surely, some level of dissent and tension in the social systems of public schools would be seen as productive. While private schools avoid the chaotic, destructive conditions occasionally found in the public sector, the majority may fall below a threshold of social debate productive by public education standards. Perhaps, then, it is best to view this analysis as pointing to ways in which private schools achieve social-system integration and to conditions which interfere with such integration in the public sector. Instead of emulating the traditional and goal-based authority operating in private schools as ways of improving public schools, we should consider challenges to public schools engendered by their own conditions of organization.

The current reform movement has generated various proposed correctives to perceived problems with the public schools. One strategy, expressed by *A Nation at Risk*, the report of the National Commission on Excellence in Education (1983), implicitly aims to shift both the goal framework and authority model of public education to be more like conditions of private school organization, particularly those following the traditional model. It proposes a renewed emphasis on basic academic skills (presumably aimed at generating goal consensus, program integration and higher academic achievement scores) and a leadership role for the principal which de-emphasizes the rational-legal administrative model and champions community building (NCEE, 1983, p. 32). The proposal follows prescriptions of the effective-schools literature and could, at least temporarily, more closely align the public and private school sectors organizationally. However, it signifies a retrenchment from the elaborated goal framework and rational-legal organizing norms for public education and thus may achieve only partial and temporary legitimacy within the sector.

Another strategy, signified by various local system models of choice, aims for organizational diversity in the public school system. This strategy allows for specialization among the public schools on various features of school organization, for example, in goal emphases, authority relations and instructional models, and for family choice of schools. It follows the rational-legal model of organization in establishing a differentiated structure adaptive to 'product demands' but generates what I have called 'goal-based' authority among schools in the public sector. Whether or not specific alternatives survive, the strategy accommodates diverse educational ideals and is likely to promote local school community.

The reform strategies commonly aim to generate, or reinstate, a sense of community within the public schools. Comparisons with private schools support this goal. Perhaps more important, this emphasis is legitimate in the public sector at a time when the business community has begun looking at organizational culture as a productivity factor. This chapter suggests that the public schools must meet this new standard of rational organization with administrative structures and roles quite different from those established in the private sector.

Notes

1   The subsequent analyses tend to challenge the claim that private schools are academically superior to public schools, after student selection and curricular placements are adequately taken into account (cf. GOLDBERGER and CAIN, 1982; WILLMS, 1982; ALEXANDER and PALLAS, 1983; SASSENRATH, CROCE and PENALOZA, 1984), but they support the view that private schools generally have more desirable social systems (cf. MORGAN, 1983). Thus, sector contrasts on effectiveness criteria may be limited mainly to social-system conditions not tightly linked to academic outcomes.

2   It is important to note at the outset that the same set of features may not distinguish relatively successful private schools, either because they do not vary much on a particular feature or because the feature is not associated with school success in the private sector. Research on school effectiveness within the private sector would be needed to identify common and sector-specific correlates of success.

3   My treatment of the literature is indebted especially to PURKEY and SMITH's (1983) incisive critique and synthesis. The list replicates their conclusions, except for my exclusion of 'efficient use of classroom time', 'principal's recruitment of won staff', and 'staff stability', which appear less well substantiated within this domain of research.

4   The empirical study I report in this chapter was funded by the National Institute of Education (Grant No. NIE-G-83-0003). I want to thank colleagues at the Stanford Institute for Research on Educational Finance and Governance (IFG) for their collaboration on the larger research project. I am especially grateful to Kendyll Stansbury for assistance with data analysis and to John Meyer for helpful comments on an earlier draft of this chapter. See Project Report No. 84-A10 for a more complete description of the data and findings of the study.

5   The survey included a sample of public schools and all private schools, public school districts, and Catholic diocese in six countries of the San Francisco Bay Area. Questionnaires were designed collaboratively by researchers at the Stanford Institute for Research on Educational Finance and Governance (Jay Chambers, Jody Encarnation, John Meyer W. Richard Scott, and Joan Talbert). They survey and data analyses were

supported by funds from the National Institute of Education (Grant No. NIE-G–83–0003).

6 Such 'institutional' measures are appropriate for studies concerned with external perceptions of an organization, as this was; but they clearly are less useful than survey measures for accurately representing internal organization processes.

7 The public sector also showed more specialization of decision domains across groups, a pattern consistent with norms of rational organization. The other sectors showed higher aggregate influence scores for all domains except major curriculum decisions, which appear to generate broad participation and influence in public school systems.

8 Numerous critiques of the effective-schools literature emphasize, as well, the possibility of interaction effects involving public school variables and effectiveness criteria (cf. ROWAN, BOSSERT and DWYER, 1983; Purkey and Smith, 1983). Selected studies of schools in the public sector have considered such interaction possibilities and reveal interaction effects involving: schools' SES base and administrative emphasis on discipline (BROOKOVER *et al.*, 1979); level of instructional complexity and the principal's involvement in instruction (COHEN and MILLER, 1979); and level of instructional complexity and administrative emphasis on school policies and rule enforcement (SALOMON, KING and YUEN, 1979). Such observations illustrate the importance of attending to the organizational context of school features in assessing their relationship to school effectiveness. This is particularly critical in comparing schools across sectors.

9 Some of these inferences are direct, for example, the public sectors' complex organization environments reduce school autonomy and emphasis on basic skills. Others assume indirect effects, for example, complex environments: (a) generate fragmented programs which, in turn, inhibit program coordination, staff collegiality, and orderly social systems; (b) offer support services which facilitate in-service training programs; and (c) demand administrative time and thus may inhibit strong leadership. I have attempted to stay close to the available analyses and to provide a reasonable and fairly conservative assessment of local consequences of each organizing condition.

10 However, I suggest that public schools' complex organizational environments constrain the feature, given evidence that administrators' time is consumed by work demanded by — and directed toward — parties outside the local school system. I have not coded traditional authority as facilitating strong administrative leadership because (a) school administration should be relatively routine and (b) socialization and selection of administrators should be highly standardized under this model, limiting both strong leadership and administrative failures.

PART II:
SOME DIMENSIONS OF CHOICE

8 Patterns of Compensation of Public and Private School Teachers

Jay G. Chambers

General impressions suggest that public school teachers are paid high-er salaries than private school teachers. Indeed, the evidence is consis-tent with this general impression. But why the difference? Do public school teachers have better qualifications? Are private schools better places to work, and are they able to pay lower wages for comparable teachers? Do public and private schools even operate in the same market for teaching personnel? Are those individuals who seek em-ployment in the private school sector drawn from the same popula-tion as those seeking public school employment? What part does the structure of ownership or sponsorship of the school play in the deter-mination of teacher compensation? It is the purpose of this chapter to provide some insights into these and related questions about the patterns of variation in compensation of public and private school teachers.

The findings reveal that public school teachers earn more than teachers in non-public schools and these results hold true even after controlling for certain teacher characteristics and working conditions. Teachers in parochial schools are the lowest paid, while teachers in non-sectarian private schools are the highest paid among non-public school teachers. There appear to be structural differences in the pat-terns of wage variation between the different sectors, which means that the markets for public school teachers operate to some degree independently of the markets for certain types of non-public school teachers. Relative to non-public school teachers, public school teachers possess more of those characteristics that are rewarded in the markets for teachers. Non-public school teachers give up between 10 per cent and 40 per cent of the public school teacher salary to work in the non-public sector (depending on type of school within the non-public sector), and they are aware of their sacrifice. Finally, organizational and ownership structure of the school appears to make a difference in salaries, with profit-making and parochial schools paying the lowest salaries.

Almost 90 per cent of the students in the United States attend public schools. The remaining 10 to 12 per cent of students are split between Catholic, other religious and private non-sectarian schools, with the Catholic schools accounting for approximately 60 per cent. Teachers are generally allocated in the same proportions with a slightly higher than proportional representation in the other religious and private non-sectarian schools because of the relatively lower pupil-teacher ratios in these sectors (McLaughlin and Wise, 1980).

While non-public schools are similar to public schools in the basic ways in which school services are delivered, they differ from one another in some more subtle dimensions that may affect the nature of the educational experience for their pupils. Non-public schools are generally smaller in size than public schools at any given level of instruction (for example, elementary or secondary). Non-public schools generally reveal more homogeneous student populations in background and ability than public schools in surrounding neighborhoods.[1] In order to survive or succeed in the market for educational services, non-public schools tend to specialize their services with respect to educational offerings, educational philosophies, disciplinary approaches or mixes of behavioral or educational objectives. The non-public schools can be more selective in enrolling eligible students, while public schools must be open to all school-age children living within designated attendance areas. Compared to public schools, non-public schools generally operate with somewhat more flexibility and differences in incentives in the ways they recruit, employ and utilize teacher services.

With these kinds of differences in mind, this chapter will draw upon the pertinent areas of economic theory including 'hedonic wage theory' and 'property rights theory' to explore how these differences in public and non-public schools become translated into patterns of compensation for public and private school teachers. Hedonic wage theory provides a framework for explaining variations in salaries of individuals in terms of their personal characteristics as well as the characteristics of the jobs in which they are employed. This theoretical framework is based on the assumption that individuals care both about the quality of their work environment and the monetary rewards associated with particular employment alternatives. An individual considering the choice between teaching or some other occupation within a geographic area would consider not only the differences in the rates of pay between the alternative occupations, but also the satisfactions obtained from the nature of the work itself as well as the specific environment in which the work is conducted.[2] While individuals care about the quality of their work environments as well as pay, employers also care about the types of individuals they hire. Employers are not indifferent to the personal attributes of the individuals they employ in certain positions. Using this theoretical framework, one may then employ statistical methods to break down the patterns of variation in salaries into the component parts related to the individual personal and job characteristics.

The property rights theory deals with the impact of different institutional arrangements on the incentives of decision makers and managers to reduce costs. The basic notion underlying property rights theory is that any reduction in the ability of owners and managers to obtain for themselves profits of a firm (or the excess of revenues over expenses) reduces the incentives for them to act in such a way as to minimize the costs of production. The attenuation of property rights of owners/managers associated with a shift from a for-profit to a non-profit and finally to a governmental enterprise tends to increase the incentives to seek non-pecuniary forms of compensation. Owners or managers with reduced property rights over the firm's assets will exhibit stronger preferences for employing individuals who will make their lives easier (for example, who are more cooperative and easier to get along with) whether or not they are more productive. Moreover, managers will also have reduced incentives to monitor internal operations or external markets for inputs. Both of these reasons tend to set the wage determined in the most competitive market as a lower bound and produce a tendency to pay higher wages to workers in the government and non-profit as opposed to the for-profit sector. Thus, in accordance with the degree to which property rights attenuation occurs for managers and owners, one would expect the public schools to exhibit the highest wages, followed by non-profit schools which should have higher wages than for-profit schooling organizations.

The Sample

The data for this analysis come from an intensive survey during the 1981/82 school year of public and private schools within the greater San Francisco Bay Area, including the central cities of Oakland and San Jose as well as San Francisco. This area includes six counties containing two contiguous Standard Metropolitan Statistical Areas (SMSAs): San Francisco-Oakland and the San Jose metropolitan areas.

Packets of teacher questionnaires were sent to 105 public and 168 private schools, accounting for approximately 2500 teachers in each sector. (Copies of the teacher questionnaires will be made available on request from the author.) The private sector was overrepresented relative to the public sector to ensure adequate numbers in the sample for statistical analysis. The public and private schools were sampled from among a more comprehensive list of public and private schools that were selected to receive various school questionnaires constructed for each sector.[3] Samples were stratified to achieve maximum diversity among the respondents and to ensure the adequate representation of respondents in each stratum.

The private sector was stratified by level (elementary and secondary) and according to four sub-sectors (Catholic parochial, Catholic private, other religious, and non-sectarian private). The public sector sample was designed to include the maximum number of districts represented among the teachers responding to the survey. The stratification scheme in each case was based on the number of schools and the number of teachers in those schools. Table 1 shows the stratification scheme and the response rates for the public and private school teacher samples, respectively. The sample available for analysis includes between 400 and 500 teachers in each of the public and non-public sectors.

Table 2 presents the mean values of the variables that were used for the statistical analysis. It provides an illustration of some of the basic differences between the public and non-public schools included in the sample. The gross annual salary figures indicate, as expected, that public school teachers are paid significantly higher salaries than non-public school teachers in all sub-sectors. At the elementary level, non-public school teachers earn from $9000–12,000 less than their public school counterparts, while at the secondary level this range is from $9000–15,000.

The concentrations of minorities and females tend to vary considerably by sub-sector among the non-public schools, although on average there tends to be a somewhat higher concentration of females and lower concentration of minorities in the non-public schools at both the elementary and secondary levels. Public schools report a higher proportion of teachers with masters degrees than any other sector except for the non-sectarian private schools at both the elementary and secondary level. Moreover, far greater percentages of public school teachers report having taken more than sixty hours of graduate college credit hours than in any other sector.

On average, the percentage of teachers attending colleges with

Table 1: Public School Teacher Samples and Returns

School type	Population of schools from which sample schools were selected	Number (%) of schools in teacher sample	No. (%) of schools returning at least 1 teacher quest	Estimated total no. teachers in population schools	Estimated total no. (%) teachers in sample schools	No. (%) of teachers returning survey
1 Public schools:						
High schools	153	19 (12.42%)	11 (57.89%)	8653	1003 (11.59%)	181 (18.05%)
Junior high schools	37	4 (10.81%)	4 (100.00%)	1268	158 (12.46%)	30 (18.99%)
Intermediate schools	45	7 (15.56%)	5 (71.43%)	1381	234 (16.94%)	20 (8.55%)
1–6 elem schools	135	34 (25.19%)	23 (67.65%)	2007	473 (23.57%)	94 (19.87%)
7–11 elem schools	52	15 (28.85%)	11 (73.33%)	988	289 (29.25%)	43 (14.88%)
12–20 elem schools	61	16 (26.23%)	11 (68.75%)	983	274 (27.87%)	48 (17.52%)
GT 20 elem schools	51	10 (19.61%)	7 (70.00%)	78	172 (21.91%)	50 (29.07%)
Public school totals:	563*	105 (18.65%)	72 (68.57%)	16423	2603 (15.85%)	466 (17.90%)
2 Non-public schools						
Cath par, elem	150	48 (32.00%)	36 (75.00%)	1640	638 (38.90%)	162 (25.39%)
Cath par, sec	13	9 (69.23%)	7 (77.78%)	395	373 (94.43%)	65 (17.43%)
Cath priv, elem	6	6 (100.00%)	2 (33.33%)	136	136 (100.00%)	2 (1.30%)
Cath priv, sec	23	12 (52.17%)	12 (100.00%)	806	544 (67.49%)	158 (29.04%)
Other relig, elem	62	39 (62.90%)	14 (35.90%)	738	420 (56.91%)	35 (8.33%)
Other relig, sec	8	5 (62.50%)	2 (40.00%)	135	91 (67.41%)	10 (10.99%)
Non-sectarian, elem	56	34 (60.71%)	11 (32.35%)	902	401 (44.46%)	40 (9.98%)
Non-sectarian, sec	17	15 (88.24%)	13 (86.67%)	444	275 (61.94%)	104 (37.82%)
Non-public sch totals	370	168 (45.41%)	97 (57.74%)	5688	2896 (50.91%)	576 (19.89%)

* The POPULATION from which the teacher sample was selected in the public sector consisted only of those schools that were included among the school level sample and were sent school level questionnaires as part of the overall IFG public and private school study.

average freshman SAT scores above 1000 was greater among three of the four non-public school sectors than in the public sector at the elementary level, while being roughly comparable among secondary teachers.

Public school teachers tended to remain longer in their jobs than non-public teachers and exhibited a considerably higher overall level of teaching experience. The average class sizes tended to be largest among Catholic schools, followed by public schools; other non-sectarian private schools show the smallest classes. The public schools included in this sample were larger than non-public schools by one-and-a-half to almost three times at the elementary level and one-and-a-half to almost four times at the secondary levels, and they exhibited greater school discipline problems related to drugs, vandalism and violence among students (as reported by the teachers) than their non-public school counterparts.

Private school teachers in general also answered yes in larger proportions than their public school counterparts when asked, 'Do you feel a strong sense of commitment and loyalty to your school?' Among public school teachers, 84 and 72 per cent answered yes at the elementary and secondary levels, while 90 and 86 per cent of the non-sectarian private elementary and secondary teachers answered yes to this question. Somewhat similar patterns, though smaller percentages, were also observed among other non-public school sectors.

But how do all of these differences in characteristics of teachers and schools translate into differences in salaries? What impact do these various factors have on patterns of salary variation? The next section explores these issues.

The Empirical Results

Ordinary least squares regression was used to obtain parameter estimates for the teacher earnings functions. An earnings function is a statistical attempt to explain variations in earnings or salaries attributable to personal and job characteristics. Initially, an earnings function for public school teachers was estimated in order to decide on an appropriate set of independent variables for the remainder of the analysis. The reason for this was that the public schools represent far and away the largest sector (in terms of relative numbers of teachers) and are likely to dominate the patterns of variations observed in teacher salaries. It is also the sector that has been analyzed the most and for which we have some benchmarks in terms of which variables

		Classification of school type				
Item	*Public*	*Catholic parochial or diocesan*	*Catholic Private*	*Other Religious*	*Non- sectarian*	*Overall mean*
ELEMENTARY TEACHERS:						
Gross annual salary	$ 23,789	$ 11,713	$ 12,611	$ 12,325	$ 14,016	18,244
Race/Sex:						
% White female	65.53	77.66	100.00	76.67	90.32	72.40
% White male	22.03	9.12	0.00	20.00	6.45	16.43
% Minority female	10.47	13.19	0.00	0.00	3.23	9.87
% Minority male	1.97	0.03	0.00	3.33	0.00	1.30
% Salaries paid to religious org	0.00	7.44	0.00	0.00	0.00	2.34
% With health problems that limit work	7.00	2.95	0.00	0.00	0,00	4.58
Highest degree:						
% No BA degree	0.50	1.65	0.00	0.00	3.23	1.04
% Community college degree	0.00	0.00	0.00	3.33	0.00	0.26
% BA degree	52.26	77.69	50.00	73.33	64.52	62.92
% Masters degree	35.18	12.40	50.00	13.33	29.03	25.85
% 6 yr certificate	10.05	8.26	0.00	6.67	3.23	8.62
% Doctorate in educ	1.01	0.00	0.00	0.00	0.00	0.52
% Other doctorate	1.01	0.00	0.00	3.33	0.00	0.78
Graduate hours						
% With < 14 hours	7.50	30.58	0.00	53.33	38.71	20.83
% 15–29 hours	2.00	11.57	0.00	10.00	6.45	5.99
% 30–44 hours	7.00	29.75	100.00	20.00	22.58	16.93
% 45–59 hours	8.50·	14.05	0.00	6.67	9.68	10.16
% >=60 hours	75.00	14.05	0.00	10.00	22.58	46.09
% California teaching certificate	93.50	81.67	100.00	44.83	58.06	83.14
% With teaching certificate-out of state	26.90	16.81	0.00	41.38	41.94	25.93
% Attended community college	21.61	33.33	0.00	26.67	12.90	24.88
% Teachers from undergrad colleges with freshman S.A.T. scores:						
<=799	1.50	0.00	0.00	0.00	0.00	0.78
800–999	19.00	14.05	50.00	10.00	16.13	16.67
1000–1199	63.50	79.34	50.00	80.00	64.52	69.79
1200–1399	15.50	5.79	0.00	6.67	16.13	11.72
>=1400	0.50	0.83	0.00	3.33	3.23	1.04
Years employed present school/district	13.36	4.55	2.00	3.10	4.58	9.02
Total years experience in education	16.69	9.60	4.00	7.53	9.81	13.12
% Full time	98.25	98.43	100.00	96.67	95.97	98.01
% Time teaching outside area of trng	8.77	14.09	27.50	12.37	14.71	11.31
% Expressing strong commitment to school	82.50	92.56	100.00	90.00	93.55	87.24
Average class size	26.91	33.49	22.50	22.63	19.03	27.99
% Employed in sch w/ accelerated curr	66.62	14.05	0.00	40.00	61.29	47.20
% Employed in sch w/ discipline problems related to drugs, vandelism and violence among students	8.92	1.65	50.00	0.00	0.00	5.43
Average school enrollments	467.76	340.99	263.50	179.13	179.29	380.91
% Employed in schools by organizational and ownership structure:						
Parochial schools	0.00	100.00	0.00	80.77	0.00	37.37
Catholic diocesan high school	0.00	0.00	0.00	0.00	0.00	0.00
Catholic private schools	0.00	0.00	100.00	0.00	0.00	0.53
School owned by central relig assoc	0.00	0.00	0.00	3.85	0.00	0.26
Other non-profit schools	0.00	0.00	0.00	0.00	70.97	5.79
Proprietary schools	0.00	0.00	0.00	15.38	19.35	2.63

		Classification of school type				
Item	Public	Catholic parochial or diocesan	Catholic Private	Other Religious	Non-sectarian	Overall mean

Item	Public	Catholic parochial or diocesan	Catholic Private	Other Religious	Non-sectarian	Overall mean
SECONDARY TEACHERS:						
Gross annual salary	$ 25,941	$ 16,104	$ 16,453	$ 10,931	$ 16,812	20,352
Race/sex:						
% White female	35.23	34.69	60.41	50.00	55.56	45.73
% White male	53.98	61.22	27.36	50.00	39.51	45.24
% Minority female	3.97	0.00	8.33	0.00	2.42	4.23
% Minority male	6.81	4.08	3.90	0.00	2.52	4.80
% Salaries paid to religious org	0.00	12.24	10.38	0.00	0.00	4.05
% With health problems that limit work	5.68	6.12	3.77	0.00	2.47	4.52
Highest degree:						
% NO BA degree	0.00	0.00	1.89	14.29	0.00	0.72
% Community college degree	0.00	0.00	0.00	0.00	0.00	0.00
% BA degree	43.18	46.94	47.17	42.86	30.86	42.24
% Masters degree	48.86	40.82	43.40	42.86	54.32	47.49
% 6 yr certificate	7.39	10.20	5.66	0.00	6.17	6.92
% Doctorate in educ	0.57	0.00	0.00	0.00	1.23	0.48
% Other doctorate	0.00	2.04	1.89	0.00	7.41	2.15
Graduate hours						
% With < 14 hours	3.41	6.12	15.09	62.50	30.86	13.10
% 15–29 hours	1.70	2.04	7.55	0.00	7.41	4.29
% 30–44 hours	8.52	24.49	29.25	12.50	22.22	18.33
% 45–59 hours	10.23	16.33	18.87	12.50	12.35	13.57
% >=60 hours	76.14	51.02	29.25	12.50	27.16	50.71
% California teaching certificate	93.71	77.55	79.25	12.50	52.50	78.68
% With teaching certificate-out of state	18.71	20.41	22.55	37.50	16.67	19.84
% Attended community college	36.78	18.37	13.46	12.50	8.75	22.88
% Teachers from undergrad colleges with freshman S.A.T. scores:						
<= 799	0.00	0.00	0.00	0.00	0.00	0.00
800–999	12.50	8.16	16.04	25.00	12.35	13.10
1000–1199	68.18	77.55	66.98	75.00	62.96	68.10
1200–1399	15.91	14.29	12.26	0.00	17.28	14.76
>= 1400	3.41	0.00	4.72	0.00	7.41	4.05
Years employed present school/district	14.08	7.92	5.76	2.38	5.38	9.36
Total years experience in education	16.62	12.45	10.68	2.75	9.89	13.07
% Full time	98.86	99.08	95.38	91.00	96.80	97.46
% Time teaching outside area of trng	11.54	14.51	7.82	3.75	14.00	11.28
% Expressing strong commitment to school	75.01	80.67	86.11	75.00	85.22	80.44
Average class size	27.84	29.14	29.92	22.25	14.89	25.91
% Employed in sch w/ accelerated curr	76.22	63.27	64.15	0.00	74.07	69.79
% Employed in sch w/ discipline problems related to drugs, vandelism and violence among students	15.31	17.35	10.38	12.50	8.24	12.89
Average school enrollments	1511.55	813.69	963.31	497.00	274.48	33.87
% Employed in schools by organizational and ownership structure:						
Parochial schools	0.00	22.45	0.00	100.00	0.00	4.59
Catholic diocesan high school	0.00	77.55	0.00	0.00	0.00	9.18
Catholic private schools	0.00	0.00	100.00	0.00	0.00	25.60
School owned by central relig assoc	0.00	0.00	0.00	0.00	0.00	0.00
Other non-profit schools	0.00	0.00	0.00	0.00	100.00	18.12
Proprietary schools	0.00	0.00	0.00	0.00	0.00	0.00

are likely to be significant.[4] Similar earnings functions were also estimated for sub-sectors among the non-public school teachers within the sample. Of particular interest is how structures for schools and teachers in the nonpublic sector differ from those of the public sector.[5]

To say that there are structural differences between sectors means that the relationships between teacher earnings and the teacher and job characteristics differ between sectors. Statistically, it means that the coefficients on the independent variables that reflect the patterns of wage variation across schools differ according to the type of school in which the teacher is employed. Conceptually, this structural difference means that there are essentially some other factors besides those which we have included in the analysis which are causing differences in salaries. These unmeasured factors could be unobservable differences in the quality of teachers or systematic differences in the preferences of those individuals who offer their services in the two sectors.[6] They could involve everything from systematic characteristics of student populations to the interpersonal relationships between principals and teachers within the school. The estimated salary differentials between sectors would, therefore, reflect variations both in preferences and in the associated sector-specific characteristics.

In general, the results of the statistical analysis suggest that such structural differences do exist. The patterns of salary differences are different for public school teachers than they are for teachers in the non-public sector. Catholic private schools exhibit patterns of variation similar to the non-sectarian private schools. Catholic parochial schools reveal patterns of variation similar to other religious schools. And each of these two groups of schools exhibit patterns of variation that are different from public schools and from one another. For the remainder of the analysis, the earnings equations have been combined in accordance with these structural similarities.

Table 3 presents three separate earning equations: one for the public sector, one for the Catholic parochial and other religious schools combined (subsequently referred to simply as parochial schools), and one for the Catholic private and non-sectarian private combined (subsequently referred to as the private schools). For each sector, the coefficient and corresponding t-ratio is presented for each variable. The differences between individual coefficients as well as between the overall vectors of common coefficients were tested using t-tests and F-tests, respectively. Those individual coefficients in the two non-public school equations that were statistically different from the public school coefficient are marked by asterisks: a single asterisk (★) designates a 10 per cent level of significance, a double asterisk (★★)

designates a 5 per cent level of significance, and a triple asterisk (★★★) indicates the 1 per cent level of significance. Equations for the Catholic parochial and Catholic private schools were also estimated and will be made available on request from the author. These results are discussed further below.

It is important to recognize that even though public schools generally operate with lockstep salary schedules that are dependent only upon the longevity and training of teachers, other factors must be taken into account in examining the patterns of salary variation. In the long run, teachers with better options (for example, with higher perceived qualifications) can go to districts that are higher paying or are more attractive places to work. The earnings functions estimated in this analysis are an attempt to capture some of the measurable factors that reflect these alternative employment opportunities for different individuals. Thus, all of the teacher and job characteristics represent factors that might have effects on the teacher reward structure and need to be included in our statistical analysis.

Salary Variations for Public School Teachers

Virtually all of the variables included in the public sector regression have the expected sign on the coefficients, although some are not statistically significant at even the 10 per cent level. The dummy variables designating the county in which the school is located are intended to control for variations in the labor market conditions, cost of living and other amenities and drawbacks associated with these particular counties. No attempt is made here to unravel all of the possible factors underlying these regional variations as they do not represent the focus of the analysis.

Despite the single salary schedule system commonly employed in the public school districts, males appear to earn more than females and whites appear to earn more than racial minorities in the labor market.[7] White males earn a wage premium of about 2 per cent over white females, while minority males enjoy about a 7 per cent wage differential over their female counterparts. Stated another way, these results suggest that, on average, a given wage offer will attract better qualified females than males. Schools pay more per unit of 'real teaching services' for males than for females. A similar statement can be made with respect to racial minorities. Whether or not discrimination occurs in the education labor market, this result would hold as long as discrimination existed in the larger labor market for professionals in

Table 3: Parameter Estimates for Unweighted Teacher Salary Equations (Dependent Variable = Natural Log of Gross Annual Salary)

Variable name	Variable label	Coefficient[1] (t-ratios)		
		Public school teachers (1)	Parochial school teachers (2)	Private school teachers (3)
INTERCEP	INTERCEPT	8.402766 (63.19)	7.589854 (21.83)	6.622372 (27.91)
WH_FEM	=1 if white female	—	—	—
WH_MALE	=1 if white male	0.022131 (1.40)	0.089345 (2.12)	0.096011** (2.76)
MIN_FEM	=1 if minority female	-0.075644 (-3.08)	-0.011829 (-0.22)	0.009504 (0.14)
MIN_MALE	=1 if minority male	-0.008917 (-0.27)	0.255469** (2.06)	0.159287 (1.84)
SALREL	School pays salary to relig organz	—	-0.871168 (-15.05)	-0.317331 (-4.13)
HLTHLIM	Has health problems that limit work	-0.063945 (-2.57)	-0.055845 (-0.66)	0.343403*** (3.66)
DEG_NOBA	=1 if has no BA degree	0.036743 (0.30)	-0.184453 (-1.47)	-0.413717** (-3.41)
DEG_BA	=1 if highest degree is BA	—	—	—
DEG_AA	=1 if highest degree is assoc degree		-0.455339 (-2.02)	—
DEG_MA	=1 if highest degree is masters	0.055079 (4.12)	0.048869 (1.24)	0.049802 (1.47)
DEG_EDSP	=1 if highest degr-ed spec-6yr cert	0.051721 (2.25)	0.076258 (1.44)	-0.028876 (-0.44)
DEG_EDD	=1 if highest degree is Ed.D.	0.113373 (1.67)		0.185667 (0.92)
DEG_DOC	=1 if highest degree is other doc	0.101520 (1.17)	-0.063706 (-0.42)	0.025287 (0.92)
GHRS0014	=1 if grad hrs < -14	-0.021925 (-0.78)	0.017768 (0.37)	-0.025758 (-0.52)
GHRS1529	=1 if grad hrs = 15-29	-0.173813 (-3.51)	-0.119168 (-1.95)	-0.115990 (-1.78)
GHRS3044	=1 if grad hrs = 30-44	-0.115220 (-4.51)	-0.048000 (-1.12)	-0.109954 (-2.52)
GHRS4559	=1 if grad hrs = 45-59	-0.060490 (-2.70)	-0.037370 (-0.75)	-0.045474 (-0.98)
GHRSGT60	=1 if grad hrs > -60	—	—	—
CERT_CA	Has permanent calif tchg certification	0.129850 (4.58)	0.080364 (2.08)	0.043285* (1.25)
CERT_OTH	Has tchg certificate outside calif	0.003747 (0.24)	-0.009203 (-0.24)	-0.043200 (-1.10)
COMCOL	Attended community college 1 yr or more	-0.032369 (-2.14)	0.045323** (1.38)	0.078250** (1.68)
SAT_600	1=mean undrgrd col S.A.T = 600-799	-0.147069 (-2.00)		
SAT_800	1=mean undrgrd col S.A.T = 800-999	0.033010 (1.90)	-0.018286 (-0.43)	0.021627 (0.54)
SAT_1000	1=mean undrgrd col S.A.T = 1000-1199			

Variable	Description	(1)	(2)	(3)
PYRS	...urs employed in present job or...	(7.00)	(2.06)	(2.83)
PYRS2	PYRS squared	-0.000628 (-4.94)	-0.000349 (-0.90)	-0.000622 (-1.08)
TYRS_ED	Total yrs exper in education	0.010849 (2.50)	0.014452 (2.36)	0.022652 (3.24)
TYRS_ED2	TYRS_ED squared	-0.000205 (-1.82)	-0.000232 (-1.40)	-0.000360 (-2.01)
PFULLTIM	Percent of full time	0.013060 (16.94)	0.015785 (9.52)	0.015948** (14.39)
LEVEL_SE	=1 if employed in secondary school	0.084183 (3.43)	-0.075262 (-1.34)	-0.042055 (-0.83)
POUTTRNG	% time tchg outside area of training	-0.000238 (-1.06)	0.000037 (0.08)	0.000892** (1.66)
COMMIT	Strong comitment to school	0.026022 (1.68)	-0.026277 (-0.55)	0.075958 (1.72)
LCLSZ	Nat log, average class size	0.004942 (0.38)	-0.068215 (-1.15)	0.105904* (2.25)
ACADVCUR	School has accelerated or advanced curr	0.020870 (1.50)	0.049698 (1.30)	0.073799 (2.28)
DIS_PROB	Sch discpl probs-drugs, vandlsm, violence	0.011122 (0.61)	0.003395 (0.06)	0.067001 (1.25)
LENR	Nat log of total school enrollment	-0.016833 (-0.94)	0.060842* (1.50)	0.102249*** (3.15)
STYP_NPR	=1 if employed in nonsectrn private sch	—	—	0.123340 (2.60)
STYP_ORE	=1 if employed in non-cath relig sch	—	0.028567 (0.55)	—
CO_SC	=1 if in Santa Clara county	-0.098060 (-5.15)	-0.115581 (-2.40)	-0.080323 (-1.68)
CO_AL	=1 if in Alameda county			
CO_CC	=1 if in Contra Costa county	-0.058055 (-2.18)	-0.022497 (-0.43)	-0.184541** (-3.50)
CO_MA	=1 if in Marin county	-0.077194 (-1.80)		0.036174 (0.64)
CO_SF	=1 if in San Francisco county	-0.155151 (-7.13)	-0.143891 (-2.77)	-0.073730* (-1.60)
CO_SM	=1 if in San Mateo county	-0.077507 (-4.16)	0.075776 (0.29)	0.014157* (0.29)
Sample size =		374	206	219
R-square =		0.8106	0.7963	0.7904
ADJ R-SQ =		0.7898	0.7516	0.7464
F-test =		38.973	17.850	17.964
(PROB>F) =		0.0001	0.0001	0.0001
F-test for differences in slope coefficients from public sector equation:		—	4.0622	12.0906
Degrees of freedom:		—	(37,688)	(35,688)

[1] The asterisks that appear in the parochial and private school teacher equations designate statistically significant differences from those reported in the public school teacher equation:
* = 10% level of significance.
** = 5% level of significance.
*** = 1% level of significance.

which the education labor market is contained. If males and white workers have better opportunities in the labor market at large, it will require higher salaries to attract them into teaching than for females. It may be that the observed wage differentials are actually lower in the education labor market because of conscious policies against discrimination, but the results reveal nevertheless that some wage differential remains. These results are not isolated to this study. This author and others have observed similar patterns in studies using data from other states and at other points in time.[8]

The results indicate that, all else being equal, secondary teachers in the public sector appear to earn about 8 per cent more than elementary teachers. Teachers with higher degrees and more graduate hours beyond the BA degree earn more than those without this additional education. Teachers without the BA degree do not exhibit lower wages, although there are only two teachers in this cell, raising issues of reliability of this result. These may be vocational education teachers who often have other better opportunities in the labor market. Teachers with a masters degree or doctorate in education earn about 5.5 per cent and 10 per cent more, respectively, than teachers with only a BA degree.

Teachers who attended a community college for part of their college education earn about 3 per cent less than teachers who did not attend such institutions. It was hypothesized that teachers who attended a community college were likely not to have done sufficiently well in high school to attend a four-year institution immediately after high school graduation, an indicator of lower ability. Hence, lower salaries might be expected for these individuals, all else being equal.

The results show an inverted U-shaped relationship between the quality of undergraduate college attended and earnings. Quality of the undergraduate college was measured by the mean Scholastic Aptitude Test score (SAT variables) of freshmen who attended that college during the 1960s, the decade during which most of our sample attended college. That is, there is a premium for having attended an institution in the middle ranges of quality over those at either extreme. This is consistent with an unpublished result of a previous analysis by this author of the relationship of Florida public school teacher earnings and verbal ability (as measured by the verbal score on the Graduate Record Examination), although in the Florida study the results were statistically stronger than those reported here.

Having a California teaching certificate appears to be associated with a salary differential of about 13 per cent, while a certificate from out of state contributes nothing. Based on the coefficient of the variable per cent full-time, a half-time teacher would earn about 52 per cent of what a full-time teacher would earn, *ceteris paribus.*[9]

Both specific experience in a district as well as general experience in teaching contribute positively to salaries up to some point. The positive contribution of specific experience (i.e., years in the present district) appear to be more significant statistically than general experience in teaching. However, this positive contribution of specific experience peaks out at about 23 years, while the positive contribution of general experience reaches its maximum at almost 26 years. Taken together, these two experience variables would reveal an age earnings profile for teachers that reaches a maximum at about 46 years of age assuming job entry occurred at age 23 after completion of a BA degree and an additional year required for a California teaching certificate.

One might expect that a strong positive attitude about teaching or the teaching environment would contribute positively to success and ultimately to compensation even if only indirectly. This appears to be the case, with those who indicate a strong commitment and loyalty to their school receiving about 2.5 per cent higher salaries. Teachers in schools with an accelerated or advanced curriculum show a 2 per cent salary differential. This could be interpreted in a number of ways. On the one hand, one might expect that such a school would be a preferred place to teach, and that teachers would be willing to give up wages to work in a school with advanced placement students. On the other hand, such a school would likely be a more challenging place to teach and require a great deal more responsibility and perhaps 'better quality' teachers. If both of these factors are indeed operating, then the results suggest that the latter factor outweighs in importance the first, since the observed wage differential is positive.

The results reveal that teachers who spend larger proportions of time teaching outside areas for which they were trained receive lower wages. A teacher spending about 10 per cent of the time teaching outside of his or her area of training would earn about one-quarter of one per cent less than a teacher spending no time teaching outside the area of training. One could view this variable from both the supply and demand sides. Presumably teachers would prefer to teach in the areas for which they were trained and would require inducements to do otherwise. At the same time, one would expect that these teachers would be less productive teaching in areas outisde of their areas of preparation and would receive lower wages, *certeris paribus*. Moreover, placement of teachers in a position teaching in areas outside of their training may perhaps be a tactic of district administrators who are trying to encourage less preferred teachers to quit the system. It may be more difficult to find principals willing to take less preferred teachers into their schools and so these teachers may often end up in less preferred positions and performing less productively in areas or subjects beyond their training. Although this coefficient is not statistically significant for the public sector equation, it is significant and positive for the private school teacher equation.

Teachers who have had health problems that have limited their work received about 6 per cent less than other teachers, all else equal. This presumably reflects the perceived relatively lower productivity of these teachers in providing educational services.

Teachers in schools where the school-wide disciplinary problems are best characterized by drug abuse, theft and vandalism, fighting among students or violent acts committed against faculty appear to receive a salary differential of about 1 per cent and it is not even close to be statistically significant at the 10 per cent level. A 10 per cent increase in class sizes leads to about a 0.5 per cent increase in salaries, although the coefficient of the class size variable is not statistically significantly different from zero at even the 10 per cent level. The reason for its inclusion in the analysis is that class size has long been considered a significant working condition and one that teachers would be willing to trade off wages to improve. The results here at least raise some questions as to just how willing teachers really are to trade off wages for lower class sizes. Of course, the range in class sizes observed in the public sector is fairly narrow with the vast majority (approximately 70 per cent) of teachers having classes in the range 26 to 35. Finally, school size appears to contribute nothing to the variations in wages. The results in the public sector equation show virtually no statistically significant relationship between school size and salary. Inclusion of this variable was based on the hypothesis that holding level of instruction constant (i.e., elementary vs. secondary), teachers would prefer to teach in smaller schools where levels of coordination would be greater and the level of personal interactions among colleagues would be enhanced. This result was not observed in the public sector.

Teacher Salary Differences Between Public and Non-public Schools

Although most of the analysis of public and non-public school teacher salary differences was done using the equations in table 3, a single earnings function was also estimated for all sectors combined. This earnings function was estimated under the assumption of no structural differences. Using this earnings function (not presented here), one can observe a salary differential of about 20–30 per cent between public and parochial schools and an 11 per cent differential between public and private (Catholic private and non-sectarian) schools. In both cases these differences hold other teacher and job-related characteristics constant. These salary differentials reflect substantially smaller values than those differences in actual salaries between these sectors presented in table 2. Thus, we have been able to account for some of the differences between public and non-public school teachers' salaries with teacher and job-related characteristics.

One interesting aspect to explore is the differences in the way teacher education and experience are compensated in the public and non-public schools. Even though public school teacher salary equations find variables other than experience and education important in the determination of patterns of variation, the formal teacher salary schedules that are common in the public sector are based almost exclusively on longevity within the district and educational qualifications. While California State teacher certification appears to make a difference in the public and parochial school sectors, it does not appear to make a difference in the private school sector. At the same time, an out-of-state teaching certificate does appear to affect salaries in the private school sector.

With respect to educational preparation, non-public schools tend to compensate teachers less for additional educational attainment than public schools. The lower salaries for teachers without a BA degree tend to be more pronounced in non-public schools. Also the number of teachers employed in the non-public sector without a BA degree is larger than in the public sector (i.e., about 1.4 per cent of the non-public teacher samples in comparison to about 0.25 per cent in the public sector). Compensation for a master's degree is about 6 per cent in both the public and private sector, while it is only about 5 per cent in the parochial sector. Only in the public sector does a doctorate in education make a difference (about a 10 per cent salary differential), while neither an EdD nor a PhD makes any difference in salaries in any part of the non-public sector. Additional graduate hours also appear to make a difference in the public sector, but do not necessarily show the same consistent and strong effects on salaries in the non-public sector, either parochial or private.

Compensation for experience shows some differences between the three sectors. In the public sector, the variable PYRS refers to years in the present district, while in the non-public sector this variable refers to years in the present school. The reason for this difference is that the public school teachers are hired at the district level, while non-public school teachers are hired by individual schools. In all three sectors, years in the present school or system tend to be more important than overall years of experience in causing salary differences among teachers. This finding is consistent with the hypothesis that specific knowledge of school operations is more important than general teaching skills. The earnings profile peaks out at about 52 years of age in the parochial sector and about 51 years of age in the private school sector, in contrast to about 46 years in the public sector.

Both the parochial and private school teachers show about a 35 per cent larger coefficient on per cent of full-time. Thus, while a half-time teacher in the public sector earns about 52 per cent of full-time pay, a half-time teacher in the non-public schools earns about 45 per cent of full-time pay, and this difference is statistically significant at about the 1 per cent level for the private school sector.

Larger class sizes, which traditionally have been assumed to be disdained by teachers, show a positive and statistically significant effect on salaries only in the private sector. Class size carries a positive coefficient in the public sector and a negative coefficient in the parochial sector though in neither case is the coefficient significant. Strong commitment to the school shows a positive and statistically significant effect on salaries among teachers in both the public and private sectors, but no significant impact in the parochial schools.

Teaching outside one's area of training shows negative salary effects (presumably due to lower perceived productivity) in only the public sector, while showing no statistically significant effects in the parochial and a positive, statistically significant effect (10 per cent level) in private schools. Interestingly, placement of teachers in positions outside their areas of training appears to occur only marginally less frequently in the non-public secondary schools and somewhat more frequently among non-public elementary schools than in their public school counterparts. The positive coefficient in the private sector could reflect a reward for a teacher's flexibility in an uncertain market where future course needs may change.

Salary differences with respect to sex and race show an interesting pattern of differences. While the public sector reveals about a 2 per cent differential favoring white males over white females, the non-public schools show a 9 per cent and 10 per cent male-female salary differential for whites in parochial and private schools, respectively. Male-female wage differentials among minorities are about 7 per cent in the public sector and are between 15 per cent to 25 per cent in the non-public schools. Only the private school differential is statistically different from that of the public sector differential. It is also interesting to note that, holding level of instruction constant, the public school teacher sample included a larger proportion of male teachers at both the elementary and secondary levels than did their non-public school counterparts in all but one case, namely, the Catholic parochial secondary schools.

One would expect that health problems that limit work activity would have negative effects on productivity and ultimately on compensation. As indicated earlier, such a negative relationship is observed in the public and parochial sectors and is significant in the public sector. However, a very strong and statistically significant positive coefficient (amounting to about 41 per cent) is observed in the private school sector. There is no obvious explanation for this very strong, positive relationship other than the possibility of it simply being an artifact of small cell size. Less than 10 per cent of the samples reported health problems in each sector including a total of nineteen teachers in the private schools (fifteen teachers in the Catholic private and four in the non-sectarian private schools).

School size tends to show a strong and statistically significant positive effect on salaries in the private school sector. The elasticity of salaries with respect to school size was not significantly different from zero in the public sector, while it was significant with values of .0608 and .1023 in the parochial and private sectors, respectively. This effect is also independent of level of instruction (elementary versus secondary). Larger schools may be more impersonal places in which to teach, more bureaucratic, and offer a different product to the consumer of educational services.[10] If larger schools are indeed less preferable to teachers, then one would anticipate a positive salary differential. Indeed, some of the differences in compensation between public and non-public schools may well be attributed to the fact that public schools are, on average, relatively larger, holding constant level of instruction. Using the estimates of the salary elasticities obtained in these salary equations, anywhere from 2 to 12 per cent of the salary differential between public and non-public elementary schools can be explained by differences in school size, while this range of difference is about 4 to 8 per cent at the secondary level.

As noted earlier in the discussion of the public sector salary equation, teacher salaries show an inverted U-shaped relationship with the quality of the undergraduate college attended by the teacher. In the non-public schools, no particularly strong pattern emerges, although the coefficient of the highest level of college quality is at least positive in the non-public school teacher equations.

Some scholars (for example, Lindsay, 1976) predict a lower reliance by non-public relative to public schools on visible and measurable attributes like teacher's degree level and years of education and a somewhat greater reliance on less visible attributes like the quality of the college attended. Non-public schools have to be more sensitive to market pressures than public schools. Long-term survival depends on their ability to satisfy clientele. For these reasons non-public schools will pay more attention to factors that actually make a difference in productivity rather than factors (such as additional training and educational qualifications) which the public at large has come to believe are correlated with productivity.[11] The results reported above do not provide much support for this hypothesis. More direct measures of teacher 'quality' (for example, direct measures of verbal ability) would be necessary to confirm such hypotheses.

Another way of comparing the compensation and employment patterns of public and private school teachers is to estimate what the average teacher in one sector would be making if he or she taught in one of the other sectors. For example, how much would the average teacher working in the non-sectarian private school sector earn if he or she would teach in the public sector?

The results of these comparisons across all sectors for elementary and secondary teachers separately are reported in table 4. These simulations were carried out by using the equation reported in table 3. The locational variables (those designating the counties in which the school is located) are held constant at their mean values so the simulated salaries do not reflect differences in the location of the school which might reflect differences in cost of living or the attractiveness of regions as places to live and work. The simulated salaries for each sector are based on the mean school characteristics for the corresponding sector, the actual teacher characteristics in each sector, and the parameter estimates as they apply to the sector in question. Thus, to estimate what a public school teacher would make in the non-sectarian private sector, we would use the equation based on the private schools (non-sectarian and Catholic private combined as reported above) and substitute the values of the characteristics of the non-sectarian private schools for the corresponding school variables (the sector specific dummy variables plus ACADVCUR, DIS_PROB, SALREL, LCLSZ, and LENR) and the values of the teacher characteristics of the public school teacher.

Each row of table 4 represents the average simulated salaries for teachers from the sector indicated in the corresponding column. The number of teachers included in each average is indicated immediately below the salary value. Salary figures in table 4 do not include the value of the fringe benefit package as existing data are not adequate to make this determination.

The actual average salaries for each sector are reported in the first row. On average, the public school teachers earn the highest salaries. Actual public elementary teachers' salaries average $23,789, while public secondary salaries average $25,941. In contrast, actual private elementary salaries range from $11,713 in the Catholic parochial schools to $14,360 in the non-sectarian private sector, while private secondary teachers' salaries range from $10,931 in the other religious sector to $16,922 in the non-sectarian private sector.

Comparisons of salaries across the rows of table 4 reveal the differences in salaries across sectors associated with differences in teacher characteristics holding the school characteristics and structure of the earnings function constant. Using the simulated public sector elementary teacher salaries as an example (row 2 of the elementary portion of table 4), public elementary teachers have simulated salaries of $23,705 in the public sector, while the 'typical' Catholic private elementary school teacher would earn $16,917 in the public sector and the 'typical' non-sectarian elementary school teacher would earn $18,718 in the public sector.

Comparisons of salaries down the columns of table 4 reflect differences in structure and differences in school characteristics, holding teacher characteristics constant. Reading down the first column for public school teachers, the simulated salary of the 'typical' public elementary school teacher in this sample is $23,705. This same public school teacher would earn $14,924 in the Catholic parochial school sector, $19,011 in the Catholic private schools sector, $16,304 in the other religious schools, and $20,540 in private non-sectarian schools.

In general, the results of these simulations reveal that public school teachers would be the highest paid regardless of the sector in which they worked. This result implies that, on average, within our sample, public school teachers possess greater levels of those characteristics which are compensated in the market for school teachers than

Table 4: Actual and Simulated Salaries for Public and Private School Teachers

	Sector in which teacher is employed (Teacher characteristics are held constant within each column)					
	Public	Catholic parochial or diocesan	Catholic private	Other religious	Non-sectarian	Overall mean
Elementary teachers:						
Actual avg gross annual salary	$ 23,789	$ 11,713	$ 12,611	$ 12,325	$ 14,360	$ 18,244
Number of teachers	199	121	2	30	32	384
Simulated salary by sector (School characteristics and structure are held constant within each row):						
Public sector	$ 23,705	$ 18,247	$ 16,917	$ 17,070	$ 18,718	$ 21,009
Number of teachers	198	121	2	30	32	383
Catholic parochial sch sector	$ 14,924	$ 11,867	$ 10,655	$ 11,327	$ 11,929	$ 13,404
Number of teachers	198	121	2	30	32	383
Catholic private sch sector	$ 19,011	$ 13,508	$ 10,840	$ 12,670	$ 13,581	$ 16,280
Number of teachers	198	121	2	30	32	383
Other religious sch sector	$ 16,304	$ 12,964	$ 11,640	$ 12,375	$ 13,032	$ 14,643
Number of teachers	198	121	2	30	32	383
Private non-sectarian sector	$ 20,540	$ 14,595	$ 11,712	$ 13,690	$ 14,674	$ 17,589
Number of teachers	198	121	2	30	32	383

Avg estimate by public (private) sch Tchrs of salary if employed in the Private (public) sector	$ 15,737	$ 18,771	$ 13,000	$ 18,583	$ 21,103	$ 17,528
Number of teachers	141	103	1	24	29	298
Secondary teachers:						
Actual avg gross annual salary	$ 25,941	$ 16,104	$ 16,453	$ 10,931	$ 16,922	$ 20,352
Number of teachers	174	49	106	8	82	420
Simulated salary by sector (School characteristics and structure are held constant within each row):						
Public sector	$ 25,677	$ 22,085	$ 20,737	$ 17,637	$ 20,411	$ 22,842
Number of teachers	175	49	106	7	82	419
Catholic parochial sch sector	$ 17,948	$ 15,595	$ 14,244	$ 11,875	$ 14,160	$ 15,893
Number of teachers	175	49	106	7	82	419
Catholic private sch sector	$ 23,902	$ 19,511	$ 17,191	$ 13,123	$ 17,201	$ 20,199
Number of teachers	175	49	106	7	82	419
Other religious sch sector	$ 19,907	$ 17,297	$ 15,799	$ 13,171	$ 15,707	$ 17,628
Number of teachers	175	49	106	7	82	419
Private nonsectarian sch sector	$ 23,357	$ 19,066	$ 16,799	$ 12,823	$ 16,808	$ 19,739
Number of teachers	175	49	106	7	82	419
Avg estimate by public (private) sch Tchrs of salary if employed in the Private (public) sector	$ 18,668	$ 23,603	$ 20,415	$ 19,429	$ 21,104	$ 20,201
Number of teachers	147	42	95	7	75	366

teachers in other sectors. Other religious secondary school teachers exhibit the lowest simulated secondary salaries, while Catholic private elementary school teachers tend to show the lowest simulated elementary salaries (although ther are only two Catholic private elementary school teachers in the sample). Non-sectarian private elementary school teachers exhibit the highest simulated elementary salaries, while Catholic parochial secondary teachers show the highest simulated secondary salaries with non-sectarian and Catholic private close behind.

What do these teachers give up to work in the sector in which they are presently employed? Salary comparisons down the columns reveal what the averge teacher would earn in each sector. Public school teachers would have to give up somewhere between approximately $2000 and $9000 to teach in non-public schools depending on the sector and the level. The amount that would have to be given up at the secondary level tends to be somewhat smaller than at the elementary level. The range of absolute differences between the public sector salaries and the salaries that teachers would earn in the non-public sectors is somewhat smaller than that observed for public school teachers, although the proportionate differences are of the same order of magnitude. In all cases, the sacrifice for teaching in the non-public sector as opposed to the public sector is significant, amounting to about 40 per cent. This figure includes the compensating differential which presumably reflects the somewhat better working conditions that exist in the private sector. Part of this compensating differential is measured by differential school characteristics included in the empirical analysis. However, some of the compensating differential may be reflected in the unmeasured school characteristics and are contained in the coefficients on the sector dummy variables.

Although there are no usable time series data on salary differences between public and private school teachers, the perception that these differences exist in the fashion demonstrated above has persisted for a long time. Whether the magnitudes of the relative differences have changed significantly is unknown. But it would seem that the apparent long term existence of a public-private teacher wage differential could not be dismissed as a disequilibrium phenomenon. The teachers in our sample of the non-public schools were aware of the magnitude of their financial sacrifice for working in the non-public as opposed to the public sector. The last row of table 4 reports the estimate of what teachers in each sector thought their salaries would be in the other sector. Public school teachers were asked what they thought they would earn in the non-public sector, and private school teachers were asked what they thought they would earn in the public sector. On average, the non-public school teachers were able to estimate what they would have earned had they taught in the public sector within 5 per cent.

The differential that exists between public and non-public school teachers appears to be fairly substantial and the evidence seems to suggest that there is a compensating differential associated with working in the public sector beyond that which we can account for with our school characteristics. The differential appears to exist for reasons beyond the present specification of the model. The teachers are aware of the sacrifice and in general are satisfied with their career choices.

Organizational Factors

There has been considerable discussion of what might happen to educational costs under alternative arrangements for the financing of schools or under arrangements which offer greater school choice. As part of the present analysis, one final earnings equation was estimated to explore the effects of the organizational and ownership structure of the school on teachers' salaries holding constant other explanatory factors. For the purposes of this analysis, schools were classified according to the following organizational/ownership categories:

- public schools;
- parochial schools (regardless of religious affiliation);
- Catholic Diocesan high schools which are centrally run by the local Catholic Diocese;
- Catholic private schools which are schools generally owned and operated by religious orders within the Catholic Church and run independently of the local Diocese;
- schools owned by a central religious association at the regional or national level;
- other non-profit schools; and
- proprietary (or for-profit) schools.

The results of this analysis are presented in table 5.

The patterns of the salary differences are largely what one would expect based on the property rights theory of the firm: lower wages will be found, *ceteris paribus,* in firms where the property rights of managers and owners are greatest and where survival is dependent on market performance. First, we have already observed that non-public schools pay lower teachers' salaries. Now, the results of table 5 indicate that holding other factors constant, the proprietary schools pay almost 22 per cent lower wages than the public schools, and only one other group of schools (the parochial) pays lower salaries (almost 27 per cent). Diocesan high schools are 19 per cent lower, while the remaining categories of school types range from about 7 per cent to 12 per cent lower salaries than public schools. It might be argued that the strong religious orientation of the parochial schools could tend to be a factor explaining the relatively low salaries and in particular the fact that the differential was lower than for proprietary schools. It should be noted, however, that the equation included a variable (SAL-REL) which indicates whether the school pays the individual salary to a religious organization. This variable is intended to control for the existence of 'religious personnel', who are often paid substantially lower salaries (often subsistence level) than lay teachers, in the school.[12] However, this variable may not have fully captured some of the differences in pay rates that may be related specifically to the religious orientation of the school. A strong commitment to further-ing religious values among lay professionals could also account for this differential. However, the results are clear that at least among the sample of non-religiously affiliated schools, the for-profit organiza-tions are lower paying than the non-profit or public schools.

Table 5: *Teachers' salary differences associated with differences in the organizational and ownership structure of schools*

Organizational/ownership class	Percent salary difference relative to public schools
Public schools	0.0
Parochial schools	−26.9%*
Catholic Diocesan high schools	−19.1%*
Catholic private schools	−9.7%*
School owned by central religious assoc	−7.7%
Other non-profit school	−11.8%*
Proprietary (for-profit) school	−21.9%*

Based on this analysis one could conclude that a free open market for educational services as might arise under a voucher type arrange-ment would probably lead to lower salaries for public school teachers. On the other hand, the infusion of public funds into non-public schools and the potential for restrictions on expenditure of those funds that would be likely to accompany their utilization may well lead to an increase in the salaries paid non-public school teachers. At the same time, the public schools would then be subject to competition for public funds with non-public schools and might tend to seek greater efficiencies in staffing and compensation. Thus, salaries for teachers in the public and non-public schools are likely to move closer together. Private teacher salaries would be likely to rise as public funds raised demand for such teachers and created additional requirements for them. At the same time, the survival instincts of private school managers would tend to decrease, while these instincts would increase somewhat among public schools. By making public and non-public schools more alike in their sources of funding, the prospect of teacher unionization might also have to be considered among non-public schools. Finally, if one can argue that at least some of the existing public school salary premium may be attributed to the greater demands for public outputs and the requirement of serving relatively more diverse student populations in public schools, then private schools participating in a voucher system with a non-discriminatory admissions policy will tend to have to pay higher teachers' salaries. More diverse student populations will increase the difficulty of teaching and hence potentially the pay required to induce teachers into jobs.

Concluding Remarks

Ultimately, this research is expected to contribute to an increased understanding of the patterns of resource allocation in different types of schooling organizations. This will eventually reveal how different organizational arrangements for schools might affect the patterns of resource allocation. How might increased parental choice affect patterns of employment of school personnel? What role does competition play? To what extent does the market survival mechanism operate to create differences in these patterns? The objective of this research is not to suggest which of these kinds of policy alternatives is preferred, but rather to reveal what their ultimate effects on the patterns of resource allocation might be. This kind of information should help to inform the process of determining policies regarding alterations in the structure of schooling organizations or the public funding of private schools.

The findings reveal that public schools pay higher salaries than non-public schools, with parochial schools paying the lowest salaries and non-sectarian private schools paying the highest salaries among non-public schools. We observed some structural differences in the patterns of wage variation between the public and private sectors as well as among different segments of the private sector. Public school teachers appear to possess greater 'qualifications' at least in terms of those personal characteristics included in this analysis. Moreover, the differences in salaries between the two sectors were not entirely explained in terms of the personal and school characteristics included in the analysis. Non-public school teachers give up anywhere from $2000 to $9000 (depending on sub-sector among non-public schools) and are well aware of their sacrifice to teach in that sector. Finally, we observed that organizational and ownership structures made a difference, holding other personal and school characteristics constant. Only parochial schools paid lower salaries than profit-making schools. Diocesan high schools were somewhat higher than profit-making schools, with higher salaries yet being paid in non-profit schools, Catholic private schools, and schools owned by a central religious association, respectively.

Future work should be directed toward examining these issues in larger samples, particularly from those components of the sample which were inadequately represented. Additional information on teacher qualifications, such as verbal ability or GRE test scores or other ability measures, would also prove valuable in addressing some of the other critical elements likely to distinguish public and non-public schools.

Acknowledgements

I would like to acknowledge the efforts of Charles Bethel Fox, Suzanne Lajoie, Craig Richards, and Bill Blanford, all of whom played a role in the development of the databases used for IFG study of public and private schools. I would also thank Professor Ed Haertel for his diligence in the conduct of the often tedious task of constructing the sample weighting structure used in the statistical analyses. I would like to express my gratitude for the helpful comments and support provided by Henry M. Levin throughout this project. Thanks are also due for the helpful comments of the two referees who reviewed this chapter and to Richard Murnane for his comments which were helpful in clarifying the interpretation of some of the results. Finally, I am thankful to my secretary, Claudette Sprague, for her unceasing attention to detail in preparation of some of the tables prepared for this manuscript, and I am grateful to Michelle Greer, the administrative assistant at AEFP, Inc., who has reviewed and prepared this manuscript through a number of drafts.

Notes

1 Some have suggested that Catholic schools tend to reveal higher proportions of minority pupils than public schools, but this appears to be because they are predominantly located in urban centers where there are higher proportions of minority pupils than in the average population.

However, when these Catholic schools are compared with similar public schools in the neighborhoods which they serve, this racial difference tends to disappear.

2 For a more formal and complete discussion of hedonic price theory applied to labor markets for school personnel, see CHAMBERS (1981a and 1981b).

3 These teacher data used for this chapter were part of a large data collection effort on public school districts, public and private schools, and school principals/heads conducted by the IFG. For further details on the nature of the IFG study and the database development the reader is referred to BALLANTYNE, CHAMBERS and LAJOIE (1984).

4 See, for example ANTOS and ROSEN (1975); AUGENBLICK and ADAMS (1979); CHAMBERS (1980); and WENDLING (1979).

5 Both weighted and unweighted statistical analyses were carried out on the samples. The weighting factor used was designed to reflect representation of specific categories of schools in the population from which the sample was drawn. Since the results of these analyses are substantially the same, only the unweighted results are reported below.

6 Self-selection of teachers into the public and non-public sectors may be a potential source of bias in the analysis presented in this chapter. This issue is beyond the scope of this initial investigation, but it is being considered as an extension of the present analysis.

7 The lockstep salary schedules commonly found in local public school systems base salary payments to teachers solely on longevity in the system and educational preparation (i.e., credits earned and/or degree level and certification).

8 See CHAMBERS' studies of ILLINOIS (1982), FLORIDA (1981) (with Phillip E. Vincent), CALIFORNIA (1978 and 1980), and studies by AUGENBLICK and ADAMS (1979), WENDLING (1979) and ANTOS and ROSEN (1975).

9 Given a coefficient of 0.013 for the variable per cent full-time, the determination of what a half-time teacher would earn is carried out as follows:

$$\ln \text{SAL(H)} - \ln \text{SAL(F)} = 0.013 \times (50 - 100)$$

where SAL(H) = salary of a half-time teacher and SAL(F) = salary of a full-time teacher, all else being equal. The final percentage then is determined by the expression:

$$100 \times [\text{SAL(H)}/\text{SAL(F)}] = \text{EXP} [0.013 \times (-50)].$$
$$= 0.52205$$

10 See CHAMBERS (1981b) on the effects of a voucher system on school size and BARKER and GUMP (1964) on the effects of school size on the affective outcomes of schooling.

11 See LINDSAY (1976).

12 Religious personnel includes those individuals whose salaries are paid to religious associations or organizations which in turn provide support for the individual.

9 Teaching in Public and Private Schools: The Significance of Race

Craig E. Richards and Dennis J. Encarnation

Looking back over the past two decades, few social policy analysts would contest the conclusion that federal and state anti-poverty programs generally failed to meet their ambitious economic objectives. At the same time, the expansion of the welfare state generated new employment opportunities in professional service occupations. According to some researchers, federal and state equal employment legislation and subsequent judicial interventions in pursuit of affirmative action established a new economic niche in the public sector for a growing minority middle class (for a summary see Wallace, 1977).

In the first round of research on the employment impact of affirmative action policies, no distinction was drawn between public and private sector employment gains, especially for professional occupations. Subsequent research indicated that the gains in minority professional employment were attributable not so much to growth in the private sector but to the direct creation of publicly funded jobs in government agencies (Carnoy, Girling and Rumberger, 1976; Freeman, 1973). Moreover, increases in minority employment were greatest among government agencies that implemented federal and state social welfare and education programs designed to serve low-income clientele (Brown and Erie, 1981; Newman, 1976). At the state and local levels, where most of this new public employment took place, *public education* accounted for two-thirds of the increase in minority professional employment (Brown and Erie, 1981). The contribution of education to increases in the employment of minority professionals is the subject of this study.

Most of the research comparing staffing patterns in public and private sectors has focused on black employment gains.[1] The consensus is that blacks took a rising share of new government positions during the period of accelerated state and federal involvement in social

218

policy. So important were these gains that by 1976 more than five out of every ten black professionals were employed by government agencies — federal, state, and especially local. The ratio for Anglos was less than three out of every ten (*ibid*).

Trends in California — in the state civil service as well as in local public agencies — have been consistent with national trends. In the early eighties, blacks held nearly twice as many professional positions in public institutions as they did in the private sector (Richards 1983; Richards and Encarnation, 1982). Although the evidence is less compelling for Hispanics, earlier employment data at least partially support this conclusion in California: a larger percentage of Hispanic professionals were employed in the state civil service and, to a lesser extent, in public schools, than were employed in the private sector (Richards, 1983; Richards and Encarnation, 1982). Equally important, these comparisons further suggest that the employment experience of minorities, while different from Anglos, also varied between blacks and Hispanics in California.

Differences in the employment experiences of black and Hispanic teachers in public and private schools could be the result of a number of influences. For example, lower average salaries for teachers in private schools could discourage minority teachers, who are in relatively short supply, from entering the private school market; or, employment discrimination in the form of preferences for white teachers could be evident in private schools whose students were predominately white. Moreover, teachers themselves might prefer to work in schools where a significant proportion of the students were of similar racial and ethnic backgrounds. And finally, because fiscal and regulatory monitoring by government is more prevalent, public schools could be more responsive to affirmative action mandates than are private schools.

While our data are drawn from California, the theoretical and policy implications of our findings are more far reaching. In the past, state and federal fiscal and regulatory interventions were justified, both philosophically and politically, on the presumption of the efficacy of the welfare state. The current restructuring of government under the Reagan administration is predicated upon the philosophical and political presumption that the private sector can do better than the state. As before, the social impact of this 'new' restructuring of the social contract is the subject of controversy, as well as our own speculation below.

While discussing theoretical and policy issues, it will become very difficult to isolate the independent effects of supply and demand. For example, we have been unable to determine the extent to which minority teachers might prefer schools with large minority enrollments. We believe, based on conversations with school administrators, that large urban districts, where most minority teachers are employed, assign teachers to specific schools. New teachers apply to district personnel offices in large school systems; the district then determines how to allocate them to the various school sites. Thus, if minority teachers are poorly represented in predominantly white schools in urban districts it is reasonable to view the outcome as a result of the assignment process, rather than self-selection. By contrast, in smaller suburban districts, self-selection could be more prevalent. There, minorities may not even apply for teaching jobs because they presume that those districts will not hire them, because they feel uncomfortable in those settings, or because they prefer to teach minority students.

State and Federal Programs as Determinants of Employment

Minority employment gains have been most notable in those state and local agencies that have actively implemented federal and state social programs. Between 1964 and 1975, the federal government created over thirty major educational and related manpower training programs (H. Levin, 1977). Non-public schools (through the entitlements of their students) were eligible for funding or 'in kind' services under a number of federal programs (Encarnation, 1983; Manno, 1978); and as Coleman, Hoffer and Kilgore (1982a) reported, participation was far more selective than in the public sector (see table 1). Each federal program, in turn, was matched by an even broader array of state categorical aid programs whose funding often surpassed federal levels, especially in states like California. By 1979, for example, no fewer than forty-five state and federal categorical aid programs could be identified in California (Kirst, 1982). Nationally, almost one-half of all government financial aid for non-public education could be attributed to direct state and federal expenditures channeled through such categorical programs (Encarnation, 1983).

These state and federal categorical aid programs were generally of two types: incentive grants and targeted grants (see table 1). Incentive grants allocated funds to educational providers, both public and non-public, for broadly defined purposes. Such programs were designed to strengthen the content and process of instruction for all students in the recipient school, and usually granted local administrators wide discretion in the use of funds. In addition to the absence of federal control over the use of funding, participation was facilitated by the ease of application (NCEA, 1980a). As a result, the federal program that funded the purchase of library materials is as much a Catholic school program as a public school program. By contrast, non-public school participation in vocational education programs is more limited given the greater difficulties of applying created by the 'excessive entanglement' provision of the First Amendment (Reutter and Hamilton, 1976), and the lower frequency of students demanding such an education.

The wide discretion granted to local administrators in allocating program resources distinguished library and vocational programs from a second class of categorical aid. Whether these other categorical programs required local application (for example, federal bilingual education) or were funded as an entitlement (for example, California state bilingual education), they severely restricted local discretion in the internal allocation of program-funded resources. According to table 1, participation rates varied considerably across sectors and across programs. For example, the proclivity of public school students to participate in bilingual education programs was not matched by participation rates in non-public schools. By contrast, compensatory education affected a sizeable number of Catholic school students, albeit at lower rates of participation than in the public sector.

Table 1: Public and Catholic Schools Compared or Selected Federal Indicators (United States, 1980)

Federal Categorical Aid Programs	Public Schools	Catholic Schools
Incentive Grants for Board Purposes		
• Library materials	86	99
• Vocational education (basic program)	67	5
Targeted Aid for Selected Students		
• Compensatory education	69	24
• Bilingual education	12	0

Source: Coleman et al., 1982, tables 3-3 and 3-4, p. 35.
Values given are percentages of schools participating.

Bilingual education, compensatory education, and other such targeted categorical grants merit closer scrutiny because, as noted above, social welfare programs designed to serve low-income clientele were a major source of minority employment gains. To illustrate, the Emergency School Aid Act required as a condition for funding that school facilities had to be racially balanced; so did many school desegregation and affirmative action decisions. Other programs like compensatory education and Head Start have been linked to black employment gains as a result of their specific focus on the needs of low income, inner city students (Brown and Erie, 1981). Still other programs introduced special certification and training mechanisms, and stipulated that new teachers with these credentials must be hired if the school district is to satisfy program mandates. In the case of one such program, bilingual education, ethnic identity and professional specialization appear to overlap. Since bilingual proficiency is a condition of employment, Richards (1985) demonstrated that Hispanics and other language minorities have an edge in this expanding sector of the teacher labor market. For example, Hispanics comprised almost 40 per cent of all bilingual education teachers in California during 1980, yet they were less than 6 per cent of the entire teaching force (Richards, 1985; Richards and Encarnation, 1982).

In short, categorical aid programs designed to serve targeted students restructured the labor market for school personnel by creating a selective demand for personnel needed to address the special educational needs of low income and minority students.[2] To the extent that this restructuring created new opportunities for blacks and Hispanics, minority employment patterns in the educational labor market should be a function of certain kinds of state and federal categorical programs. That is, as the number of students participating in targeted aid programs increased, the number of minority teachers employed in that school increases. By the same logic, the relationship between incentive grants earmarked for broad purposes and minority staffing patterns should be negligible. The direction of these effects should hold irrespective of the educational sector within which the school operates. This direct relationship between sector and minority employment may be mitigated, however, by the relationship between targeted aid and minority employment. As table 1 suggests, the programmatic involvement of a school may itself be influenced by the school's sectoral affiliation, and equally important, by the racial and socioeconomic background of the students in that school.

Client Demand for Minority Teachers

Institutional sources of employer demand — internal to each sector or as the result of external regulatory interventions by state and federal agencies — do not alone explain variation in staffing patterns across public, Catholic, and private schools. Other sources of variation can be explained by the different demands schools confront from their own clients, the students, and the parents of students, who attend schools. While these demands may be institutionalized — witness the emergence of parent-teacher associations and school site councils — more often than not they are reflected in the characteristics of the students who attend schools. Existing research identifies two broad sets of student (client) characteristics that have an effect on school (provider) operations generally, and staffing patterns specifically. While the linkages between client and provider may be direct, they may also interact with institutional factors.

The Characteristics of Clients

Indeed, federal and state categorical aid programs alter the relationship between client and provider. The racial, ethnic, and socioeconomic composition of students, along with their age distribution, total number, and community location, determine the eligibility of the school or its students for categorical funding or 'in kind' services. They also determine the extent of state and federal regulatory oversight. Compensatory education and bilingual education programs are illustrative. The absence of large concentrations of minority, poor, or other 'educationally disadvantaged' students of elementary school age precludes eligibility for many of these programs, and exempts public and nonpublic schools from the regulation and oversight tied to program funding. Since such 'educationally disadvantaged' students are principally located in urban areas, the community location of students may prompt funding, as in California's Urban Impact Aid.

Of course, client-provider relations may be more direct and not mediated by institutional factors. For example, a growing body of research on teacher supply and demand draws direct linkages between staffing patterns across schools and the racial segregration of students in those schools. On the demand side, three sets of interrelated variables have been identified. First, research suggests that minority teachers are important learning and role models for minority students (Dworkin, 1980; Naboa, 1980; Haney, 1978). Second, for reasons of social control within schools, the Safe School Study recommended that more minority teachers be assigned to predominantly minority schools to reduce violence against teachers (Department of Health, Education and Welfare, 1978). Third, minority employment gains may be a response to political demands emanating from both the larger polity and the local school site. The hiring of minority faculty in public schools figured prominently in the demands of civil rights leaders and community groups who had been protesting and litigating for decades (Peterson, 1983; Kirp, 1982). Likewise, the absence of minority faculty figured among the demands of student militants in public schools (Richards, 1983). However, there is little indication that comparable sets of demands, from the larger polity or the local school site, affected the employment practices of Catholic and other private schools.

There is limited evidence to suggest, moreover, that client influence on minority employment may vary between public and non-public schools. To the extent that political influence is related to representation in the institution, schools with few minority students (and parents) are less likely to pressure the school to increase their employment of minority teachers. As we see in table 2 Coleman and his colleagues (1982) have discerned important racial and ethnic differences between public and non-public school enrollments. For example, the average Catholic school, when compared to its public counterpart, enrolls a relatively larger number of wealthy, usually Anglo (except in the west) students who attend more Anglo-segregated schools, often in suburban communities.

Research on post-secondary education also supports the conclusion that client characteristics vary considerably according to the sector in which the service provider operates; with a corresponding impact on the personnel employed. The Carnegie Council (1976) has rank-ordered such providers, beginning with private prestigious universities at the top and state-supported colleges at the bottom. Not only does minority enrollment in general increase as one moves down this scale, but minority employment likewise increases — although the pattern is not necessarily monotonic. This research provides one of the few indications that minority enrollment and minority employment are at least correlated, if not causally related, in educational institutions.

Such variation across sectors among the clients of educational providers — be they K-12 or post-secondary — may ultimately shape the incentive structures of educational managers. A growing body of research concerning theories of agency and government enterprise predicts that public and private managers producing the same general set of services will, nevertheless, exhibit differences in behavior, differences that arise from systematic variation in the incentive structures operating in the two sectors (for a summary, see Mueller, 1979). Much of this research has focused on the non-educational service sector. In one study, Lindsay (1976) found that a relatively smaller

Table 2: Percent Black and Hispanic Enrollments in Public and Catholic Schools (United States, 1980)

Schools with four levels of black or Hispanic enrollment	Percentage total black students		Percentage total Hispanic students	
	Public schools	Catholic schools	Public schools	Catholic schools
0 to 19%	19.4	54.6	59.7	58.8
20 to 49%	35.4	24.0	18.4	21.0
50 to 79%	21.8	8.5	16.7	14.4
80 to 100%	23.4	12.9	5.3	5.8

Source: Coleman, Hoffer and Kilgore, 1982: tables 3–3 and 4–4, p. 35.

proportion of minority physicians were employed by private hospitals, as compared to Veterans Administration hospitals. As an explanation, Lindsay pointed to client demands on private hospitals: since managers perceive that 'patients prefer to be treated by white physicians, . . . the attribute "white race" . . . command[s] a positive premium in the market for physicians' (p. 1071). It is possible that a similar client/provider relationship operates in schools.

That non-public managers, at least in the educational sector, may find it relatively easy to satisfy their demand for Anglo teachers is indicated by research concerning the supply side of the labor market. Looking at occupational preferences, recent empirical analyses of hedonic price theory have reconfirmed what has long been known about the sociology of work: job characteristics and working conditions figure prominently in an individual's choice among alternative employment opportunities. To attract an employee to a job less preferred by a potential applicant, these labor market studies show that an employer must pay a higher wage, holding other determinants of employment constant. For example, in several studies of teacher employment in California and Florida public schools, Chambers (1979) found that school districts must pay higher wages to Anglo teachers in order to attract them to schools with one or more of the following characteristics: a minority-segregated student body, high levels of violence, and location in an inner city. Employment in such schools is not preferred by Anglo teachers, leaving open an avenue for minority employment. Correlatively, Anglo teachers will accept lower wages to work in public schools (and, by inference, private schools as well) that have low levels of violence, are located in pleasant suburban surroundings, have large proportions of Anglo students, operate a well-maintained physical plant, and so on. In these schools, managers who prefer to employ Anglo teachers have ample supply to do so. Since the existing supply of minority teachers is relatively small in the total educational labor force, the high demand for minority teachers in urban (largely public) schools may absorb available supply. Private and public managers outside of these urban schools may thus have little choice but to hire Anglo teachers, independent of any preference for the race of the teacher they employ. This research also points to wide variation among public institutions in their employment of minorities, a variation that is not limited to education. Borjas (1982), for example, shows that federal social service agencies employ greater proportions of minority professionals than do other public agencies providing different services (for example, agriculture agencies). Borjas points to the impact of consumer demands on government agencies:

these agencies must rely on different constituencies for political and other resources and, in turn, respond to constituency demands through the policies they advocate and the personnel they employ. Public education institutions may be more sensitive to such pressures than private schools when they serve minority clients.

The Changing Composition of Clients

In addition to the existing configuration of client characteristics discussed above, dynamic elements may alter the employment pattens of minority teachers in public, Catholic and private schools. For example, most federal and state categorical aid programs originated during a period of relative growth in the total population served by public schools, and in the fiscal capacity of local school districts. Since the size of the educational labor force is a positive function of the size of student populations and of budgetary expenditures, such growth resulted in expanded hirings of all teachers — Anglo, black, and Hispanic. In short, we hypothesize that growth has had a positive effect on the employment of minority teachers.

Over the last two decades, however, there have been dramatic changes in the student populations served by public and non-public schools, as well as changes in the fiscal capacity of local public school districts. As the total number of children attending public schools declined sharply over the last decade, total enrollments in all private schools increased. Yet, despite an overall decline in public enrollments, the number of students classified as disadvantaged for reasons of race, language, income, or physical disabilities has risen in public schools in absolute and relative terms (Encarnation and Richards, 1981). To a lesser extent, cursory evidence suggests that the same may be said for Catholic and other private schools.

In California for example, public school enrollments declined by over 350,000 between 1967 and 1979, while students identified as ethnic minorities and educationally disadvantaged increased their numbers absolutely and relatively. This precipitous decline in total enrollments was due to a 26 per cent decline over the twelve year period in Anglo students who, by 1979, constituted no more than 60 per cent of all public school students. The remainder were minorities, of which Hispanics constituted the largest single group in public schools. Having grown by over 50 per cent during the last decade, Hispanics by 1979 comprised over one-quarter of all public school students in California. By comparison, the black growth rate over the same period mirrored the proportion of black students in California's public schools during 1979: 10 per cent (California State Department of Education, 1979).

Declining total enrollments precipitated a fiscal crisis in California's public schools, a crisis worsened by Proposition 13, by an economic recession, and by a corresponding reduction in state revenues. Thus, many districts were financially unable to reduce class sizes as a way to cushion teachers from layoffs caused by declining enrollments. Since the level of state funding was linked by formula to student enrollments, little short-term relief from the state was available to districts with declining enrollments. Because teacher salaries and fringe benefits accounted for over 80 per cent of district budgets, the standard solution to budgetary deficits was to reduce the teaching staff. The seniority and tenure provisions secured over the last two decades by teacher unions determined the sequence of reduction-in-force decisions. The first teachers dismissed were, by state law, those with the least seniority. Since the employment gains of black and especially Hispanic teachers were of recent origin, these two minority groups were most vulnerable to dismissal (Richards and Encarnation, 1983). In this way, demographic declines and fiscal constraints interacted to erode previous minority employment gains. Accordingly, we hypothesize that fewer minority teachers are employed in schools that experienced sharp employment declines.

Summary of Hypotheses

At least nine testable propositions were identified in the preceding discussion. We will summarize them now. The number of minority teachers employed in a given school will increase if:

H_1: the school is in the public sector;
H_2: the proportion of students participating in targeted aid programs increases;
H_4: the proportion of minority students increases;
H_5: the number or proportion of poor students increases;
H_6: the school is located in an urban area;
H_7: the school serves elementary school-age students;
H_8: the number of teachers employed by the schools increased over the last few years.

The numbers of minority teachers employed are predicted to be unaffected if:

H_3:   the number or proportion of students participating in state and federal incentive grant programs increases.

The numbers of minority teachers employed are predicted to decline if:

H_1:   the school is located in the non-public sector;

H_9:   the number of teachers employed in a school declined over the last few years.

Data and Methodology

In summary, our review of extisting research has identified several determinants of the employment of minority teachers in public, Catholic and private schools. Much of this previous research comparing public-private labor markets suffers from aggregation problems. With a few exceptions (for example, Lindsay, 1976), racial employment comparisons are based on summary statistics for the nation as a whole; and on comparisons among dissimiliar occupations. This study overcomes these objections by being both geographically and occupationally specific: we examine patterns of employment for elementary and secondary teachers in public, Catholic and private (non-Catholic) schools operating in the six counties surrounding San Francisco Bay.

Data required for the analysis of this model were collected during the spring of 1982 by Stanford University's Institute for Research on Educational Finance and Governance (IFG), under a research grant from the National Institute of Education. Through school and district questionnaires, local K-12 educational institutions in the public, Catholic and private sectors were asked to report on their operations during the 1980/81 and 1981/82 academic years. These survey data were supplemented by data from other sources: (i) for public schools only, the 1982 California Basic Educational Data System (CBEDS) supplied by the California State Department of Education (CDOE); (ii) for all non-public schools, the 1982 California Private School Directory also supplied by CDOE; and (iii) for Catholic schools only, detailed financial reports generously supplied by Catholic dioceses in the areas surveyed.

The samples of schools and school districts come from the six counties that comprise the San Francisco Bay area: Alameda, Contra Costa, Marin, San Francisco, San Mateo and Santa Clara.[3] The schools sampled in these six counties exhibited wide variation in the variables of interest to this study, while at the same time operating in close proximity to one another. For example, the sampling region encompasses three central cities (Oakland, San Francisco and San Jose) and numerous suburban towns with wide diversity and different rates of change in the racial, ethnic, and socioeconomic composition of their inhabitants. Moreover, the type and frequency of K-12 educational institutions vary widely across the six counties. Such wide diversity among the clients (students) and providers (schools) of educational services is a precondition for wide diversity in state and federal regulation and finance of education. Yet, because of geographic proximity, the labor market for teachers overlaps considerably, thereby reducing the number of confounding factors that would otherwise be present in a nationwide sample of schools.

From these data we were able to operationalize the variables identified in figure 1 using the indicators identified in table 3. Figure 1 depicts the relationship among the several hypotheses and their corresponding variables as identified above. In order to isolate the contributions of these several independent variables in estimating minority employment, ordinary least-squares procedures were employed using a step-wise inclusion criterion designed to maximize R^2. Given the fact that the response rates from the stratified sampling design varied by both school sector and location, the regression model was weight-

Table 3:   An Operationalization of the Model

Variable	*School-level measures and indicators*
Minority employment	The number of minority teachers employed
Public	A dummy variable for school sector, where 1 = public and 0 = non-public
Catholic	A dummy variable for school sector, where 1 = Catholic and 0 = non-Catholic
Library materials	A dummy variable for school participation in former ESEA Title IV-B, where '1' indicates that the school receives federal funds and '0' indicates non-participation
Compensatory education	The proportion of students enrolled in federally funded compensatory education programs (former ESEA Title I)
Bilingual education	The proportion of students enrolled in state or federally funded bilingual education programs (former ESEA Title VII)
Minority enrollment	The proportion of minority students in the school
Student wealth	The proportion of low SES students enrolled in the school
Urban community	A dummy variable for inner-city location, where '1' indicates that the students enrolled live largely within the city limits of Oakland, San Francisco and San Jose, and '0' indicates all other locations
Elementary school age	A dummy variable for students enrolled in grades K-8 schools, where 1 = elementary and 0 = secondary
Employment growth	The number of teachers with five or less years of seniority
Employment decline	The number of teachers laid off during the two-year period 1979–1981
School size (K-12)	The total enrollment of K-12 students
School size (pre-school)	The total pre-school enrollment

Figure 1: A Model of Minority Employment

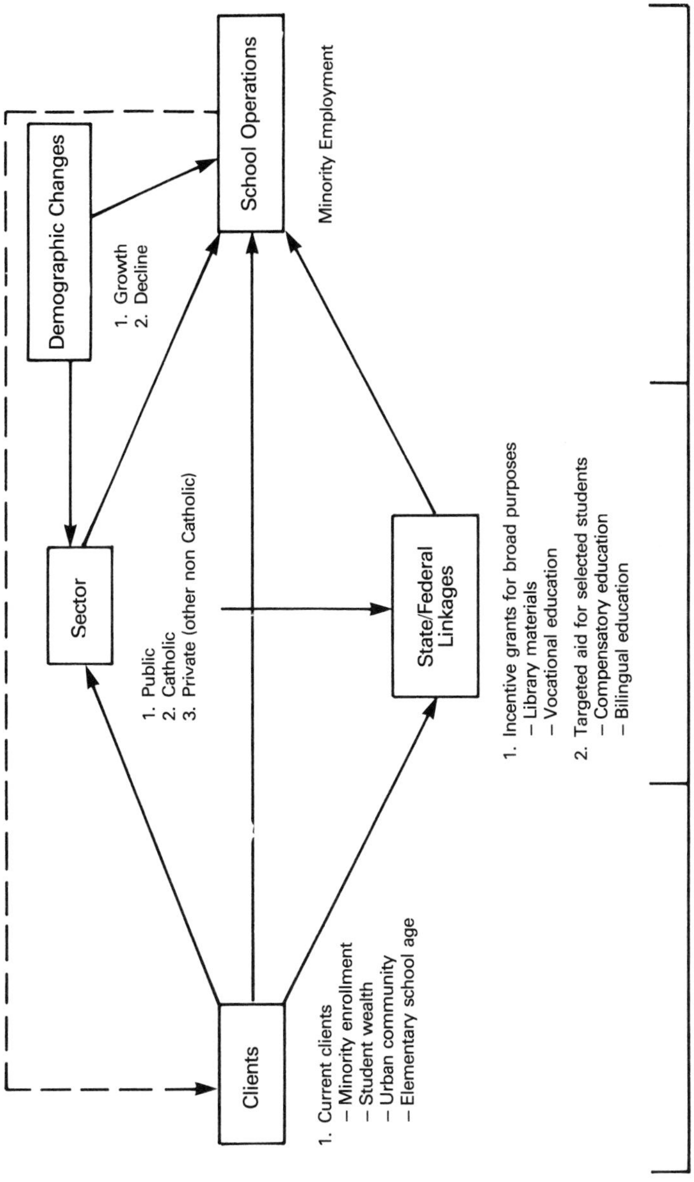

ed to reflect the population of schools by sector and by urban or suburban location.

Findings

Table 4 summarizes the results for our weighted linear regression model. The R^2 for the model was 0.72. Note that none of the hypothesized relations were reversed, including all statistically significant coefficients. Also note that the estimated variance in the employment of minority teachers can be explained by a small subset of variables: the proportion of minority students enrolled in the school, the proportion of low socioeconomic students enrolled, the proportion of students receiving compensatory aid enrolled, the size of the school, and growth in faculty size. These five variables were positively and strongly related to minority employment. In addition, Catholic and private schools were significantly and negatively associated with minority employment.

Table 4: Hypothesized Relations and Empirical Findings: Determinants of Minority Employment (includes interaction terms)

Independent variables	Hypothesized relationship[a]	Linear Model ($R^2 = .72$)	
		B Value	Significance
Institutional factors			
Sector			
Public	+	−1.656	.059
Incentive grants			
Library materials	0	−0.568	.042
Targeted aid			
Compensatory education	+	3.004	.0004
Bilingual education	+	1.027	N.S.
Teacher growth and decline:			
Growth	+	0.080	.002
Decline	−	−0.086	N.S.
Client characteristics			
Minority race	+	−0.918	N.S.
Low SES	+	.872	N.S.
Urban community	+	0.992	.007
Elementary school age	0	0.209	N.S.
Size (K-12)	0	.000	N.S.
Interaction terms			
Public X Minority	+	5.604	.000
Public X Size (K-12)	+	0.004	.028

Notes: [a] Key: (+) or (−) indicate a positive or negative relationship, respectively; (0) indicates no predicated relationship.

The Contribution of Student Characteristics

The number of minority teachers employed in the schools in our sample can best be explained by the proportion of minority students in the school and the total school size. The model predicts that we would find approximately one more minority teacher if the proportion of minority students increased by 24 per cent (from 10 to 34 per cent).

Less important, but still significant, is whether the school has been increasing the size of its teacher labor force. Because we were unable to measure student growth and decline directly, growth is proxied by the number of teachers in the school with less than five years of seniority and decreases are proxied by the number of layoffs in the two-year period 1979–1981. The results indicate that increases were positively associated with minority employment and decreases were statistically insignificant. For every twenty additional teachers with less than five years seniority the model predicts less than one will be a minority.

Institutional Effects

While client characteristics dominate the model, two sets of institutional factors are also important determinants of minority employment, sector and government aid. The Catholic sector emerges as a significantly negative factor in the employment of minority teachers, even after controlling for the effects of client characteristics and state and federal programs. A school's inclusion in the Catholic sector was the fourth most important in terms of its contribution to the model's fit. The model predicts that a Catholic school would reduce the number of minority teachers employed by one, everything else held equal. In the case of government programs, after controlling for other environmental influences, general aid grants that permit wide local discretion (our example was library materials aid) had, as predicted, a negligible impact on minority employment. Consistent with Coleman's findings (see table 1), we found that library materials aid was as much a Catholic school program as a public school program. In sharp contrast to such broadly defined grants, more tightly regulated programs targeted for selected students had a positive effect on minority employment, even after controlling for other determinants of minority employment. For example, the proportion of students receiving compensatory aid was strongly associated with the increased employment of minority teachers: a 43 per cent increase in the proportion of students receiving aid is predicted to increase the number of minority faculty by one. By comparison, the b value for bilingual education was large, but statistically insignificant.

For public schools in the State of California as a whole, Hispanic employment has shown to be significantly related to the percentage of Hispanic students enrolled (Richards, 1985), but not to the proportion of students enrolled in bilingual education.

Inconsistencies

While the above findings were generally consistent with the model, there were a few surprises. In particular, we were surprised to find that whether the school was public or private, by itself, did not predict the proportion of minority teachers in the school. We expected the public/private (dichotomous) variable to be an effective proxy for the substantial wage differential for the two sectors. Instead we found that the most powerful predictor of the number of minority teachers was the proportion of minority students in the school — and that was true irrespective of sector.

Upon reflection, there are at least three possible shortcomings with our specification of the model. First, we aggregated black and Hispanic teachers, assuming that the model predicted equally well for both groups. Yet, the history of black and Hispanic employment experiences in California are not similar; Hispanic teachers entered the system in larger numbers nearly a decade after black teachers. Second, we failed to examine within-sector variations. That failure was, of course, based on our belief that 'publicness' would be the most significant predictor of the number of minority teachers in the district. Dichotomizing schools into public and private may, however, fail to account for significant variation in minority employment within sectors, variation attributable to school clients. For example, Catholic inner city schools may be very much like public inner city schools in terms of the students they enroll. Third, the first model may have been under-specified. Perhaps we failed to examine potentially important interaction effects among independent variables. These deficiencies and further reflections provided the impetus for a reanalysis of the data.

Retesting A Model

Our previous findings suggest that 'sector' as we originally defined it — public vs. private schools — does not capture the complex variation in patterns of minority employment among public and private schools. Our own empirical findings combined with limited outside evidence give reason to hypothesize significant variation among and between private and public schools in their employmet of Anglo, black and Hispanic teachers.

Among public schools, for example, we predict that the highest number of minority teachers will be found when minority enrollments are large and growing, and when enrollment in categorical programs is similarly large. However, we further hypothesize, that a private school with high scores on each of three dimensions — large minority enrollment, high employment growth, sizeable categorical programs — should look much like a public school with similar characteristics, particularly in its employment practices. (We have depicted our elaborated model in figure 2). In other words, one can imagine a continuum of 'publicness' in which selected private schools begin to look more and more like public schools depending upon the clients they serve and the federal/state programs in which they participate. With regard to the employment of minorities, this continuum would run from Quadrant I to Quadrant IV in figure 2, from the highest probability of minority employment to the lowest.

To test for interaction effects, we restricted the sample to public and Catholic schools. The original twelve variables (minus the Catholic dummy variable) were entered into a regression equation and then the interaction variables were allowed to enter into the equation using a stepwise inclusion criterion. Two interaction terms were statistically significant (see table 4). The analysis was restricted to a public-Catholic school comparison because of the low number of minority students in private (non-Catholic) schools and their low levels of participation in state and federal categorical programs.

To test whether or not our model was equally predictive of the number of both black and Hispanic teachers employed, we made two further changes. First, we ran separate regressions for *black teachers* and *Hispanic teachers*, rather than for minority teachers as a whole. Second, we altered the independent variables so that they reflected the proportions of black and Hispanic students rather than the proportions of minority students, our earlier variable. Thus, for example, in our new regression, the dependent variable became the number of black teachers employed and our corresponding student enrollment

Figure 2: HYPOTHESIZED RELATIONSHIPS:
Factors Shaping the Probability of Minority Employment

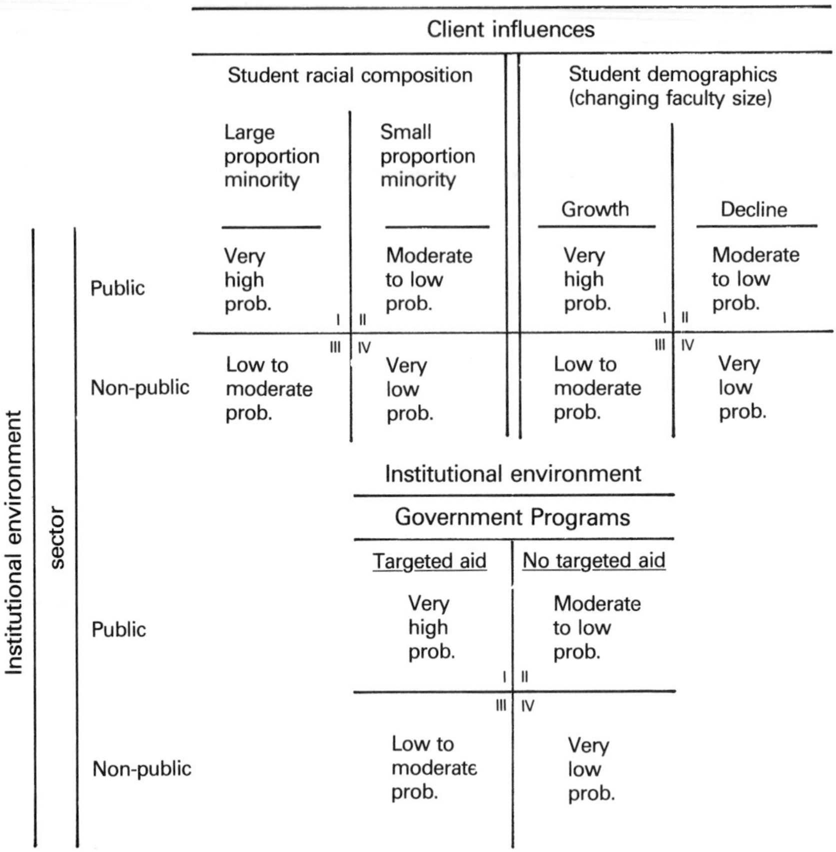

Client influences				

		Student racial composition		Student demographics (changing faculty size)	
		Large proportion minority	Small proportion minority	Growth	Decline
	Public	Very high prob. I	Moderate to low prob. II	Very high prob. I	Moderate to low prob. II
	Non-public	Low to moderate prob. III	Very low prob. IV	Low to moderate prob. III	Very low prob. IV

Institutional environment		
Government Programs		
	Targeted aid	No targeted aid
Public	Very high prob. I	Moderate to low prob. II
Non-public	Low to moderate prob. III	Very low prob. IV

(Left margin labels: Institutional environment — sector)

variable became the proportion of black students enrolled. The next regression (with the number of Hispanic teachers employed as the dependent variable) utilized a parallel modification for Hispanic students. Tables 5 and 6 describe the fit of the model for black and Hispanic teachers, respectively.

Public and Private School Differences

Our first objective was to determine if sector and the various predictors in our model interact. That is, for example, whether minority enrollments have the same impact on the employment of minority teachers in public and Catholic schools. Statistically significant interaction terms provide positive evidence of different within-sector slopes for the corresponding predictor. The logic of this procedure is similar to that for the Chow test. The results are reported at the bottom of tables 5 and 6. Of the several interaction terms introduced into the new model, only two were significant: the proportion of minority students enrolled and school size. Both variables were significant at the .05 level. These results indicate that the proportion of minority students enrolled and school size are more strongly related to minority empolyment in public schools than in Catholic schools.

Black and Hispanic Teacher Employment

As stated previously, we were also concerned whether our model would predict equally well for black and Hispanic teachers in separate regressions. There is reason to believe that black and Hispanic teacher employment patterns might be differentially affected by the predictors in our model.

Based on earlier research (Richards and Encarnation, 1982) we found that in California, black teachers on average had more years of teaching experience than Hispanic teachers, suggesting they entered the labor force in the 1960s and 1970s. This was a time when overall school enrollments were expanding; it was prior to the era of fiscal constraint engendered by Proposition 13; and, it was at the apex of the civil rights and school desegregation movements. This confluence of demographic, fiscal and social forces may have generated historically unique empolyment opportunities for black teachers. Hispanic teachers, on the other hand, began entering the teacher labor force in California in the mid-to-late 1970s, at a time when overall enrollments were dramatically declining; fiscal constraints were a serious impediment to expanded teacher employment; and the momentum of the civil rights movement had slowed considerably. Thus, one might expect our model to fit better for black teachers and not as well for Hispanic teachers. The regression for black and Hispanic teachers are reported in tables 5 and 6 respectively. With respect to these issues we found:

1 A significant interaction between 'publicness' and the racial composition of the school in predicting both black and Hispanic teacher employment. The result suggests that client (student) characteristics influence the employment of black and Hispanic teachers more strongly in public schools than in Catholic schools. This effect is cancelled out when blacks and

Table 5: *Hypothesized Relations and Empirical Findings: Determinants of Black Teacher Employment*

Independent variables	Hypothesized relationship[a]	Linear Model (R² = .79) B Value	Significance
Institutional factors			
Sector (Public)	+	−0.039	N.S.
Incentive Grant			
(Library materials)	+	−0.367	.050
Targeted aid			
(Compensatory education)	+	0.516	N.S.
(Bilingual education)	+	3.477	.022
Teacher labor force			
(Growth)	+	0.023	N.S.
(Decline)	−	−0.037	N.S.
Client characteristics			
Proportion black students	+	2.111	.053
Low SES	+	1.246	.069
Urban community	+	0.523	.027
Elementary school age	0	−0.188	N.S.
Size (K-12)	0	0.001	.0004
Interaction terms			
Public X black Students	+	7.886	.0001

Notes: [a] Key: (+) or (−) indicate a positive or negative relationship respectively; (0) indicates no predicted relationship.

Table 6: *Hypothesized Relations and Empirical Findings: Determinants of Hispanic Teacher Employment*

Independent variables	Hypothesized relationship[b]	Linear Model (R² = .57) B Value	Significance
Institutional factors			
Sector (Public)	+	−1.491	.007
Incentive Grant			
(Library materials)	0	0.092	N.S.
Targeted aid			
(Compensatory education)	+	−0.067	N.S.
(Bilingual education)	+	0.212	N.S.
Teacher labor force			
(Growth)	+	0.060	.0005
(Decline)	−	0.002	N.S.
Client characteristics			
Proportion hispanic students	+	0.954	N.S.
Low SES	+	−1.072	.066
Urban community	+	0.117	N.S.
Elementary school age	0	−0.053	N.S.
Size (K-12)	0	−0.001	N.S.
Interaction terms			
Public X Hispanic students	+	3.270	.036
Public X size (K-12)	0	0.003	.004

Notes: [b] Key: (+) or (−) indicate a positive or negative relationship, respectively; (0) indicates no predicted relationship.

Hispanics are aggregated as 'minorities'. Only one other interaction term was significant in our study. Public sector and school size interacted to predict increased employment of Hispanic teachers.

2   We found important differences in the fit of our two models, as indicated by the R^2, when we decomposed the original model into separate regressions for black and Hispanic teachers. The fit *increased* for black teachers, and sharply *decreased* for Hispanic teachers. These new findings support our concern that generalizing about 'minorities' underestimates the complexity of a school's environment and its impact on employment in education. One further point emerges: cross-section model, such as ours, only permit speculation about historical influences as they are reflected in the data.

Conclusions

Despite some modifications to our original model, our re-analysis supports the significance of race in the client-provider relationship. The race of the client is the most significant predictor of minority teacher employment. Within the public schools in our sample, this was particularly strong, and the finding held for both black and Hispanic teachers. In Catholic schools, the relationship was significantly weaker. An explanation for the observed relationship consistent with previous research, is that public schools, in contrast to private and Catholic schools, are more sensitive to what Hans Weiler (1983) has termed the 'compensatory legitimacy' claims placed by clients on state-sponsored institutions. Weiler uses the term legitimacy in the general sense — the state engages in activities designed to sustain its credibility and acceptability to its citizens. Legitimacy is compensatory when the state undertakes actions designed to protect subgroups, minorities, or other societal factions that are challenging the right of the state to govern.[4] Thus, it is argued, the combination of fiscal, regulatory, and judicial mandates of the previous decade emerged in response to a 'crisis of legitimacy' attending the civil rights protests and student rebellions of the 1960s. One social by-product of state intervention was the increased employment of minorities in schools with high proportions of minority clientele.

By this logic, neither private nor public schools with few minority students would need to respond to these legitimacy claims. It is not in the nature of a 'compensatory' response to alter the total structure of education. All that is necessary is to respond to such pressures at their point of origin. Thus, minority segregated schools become the focus of employment reform, not white segregated schools. By implication, client political pressure generates the regulatory and judicial mandates that are expressed in current affirmative action or equal employment opportunity legislation. Presumably the state's enthusiasm for enforcement will wax and wane in response to its perceptions of the public's sense that the mandates are indeed legitimate.

Generalizations about the leadership role of public schools in increasing minority professional employment are not warranted by available evidence. The response of public schools to minority demands for more minority teachers has been directly related to the presence of minority students in the school. Only those public schools with large minority constituencies have responded by increasing their employment of minority teachers, and even that response is qualified by complex demographic, fiscal and regulatory factors. Similarly, Catholic schools with large minority constituencies have also responded by hiring more minority teachers, though somewhat less vigorously.

Certainly it is the case that government political, fiscal and judicial interventions have served to increase the number of minority teachers employed. In fact, we argue that the weaker response of Catholic and private schools with similar client profiles can partially be explained by the less extensive nature of state political, fiscal and judicial intrusion. Nonetheless, our evidence leads us to conclude that the government's contribution to the employment of minority teachers, at least in the counties we studied, was a compensatory response.

Perhaps most interesting, however, is our growing conviction that the public/private dichotomy is false. We believe that our findings are consistent with the conclusion that, in the case of education, 'publicness' and 'privateness' are as much determined by clients and by fiscal and regulatory entanglements, as by ownership. This has certainly been the case with respect to the employment of minority teachers.

Two important policy implications emerge from this study. First, there is cause for concern, particularly in the case of public schools, but also for the general education labor market, that most employment gains for minority teachers have been limited to public schools with high proportions of minority students. The prevailing economic climate for education in combination with the continous decline in student enrollment in suburban schools suggests that the employment of minority teachers is likely to drop below the peak percentages established in the 1970s. Futhermore, all of our evidence suggests that general aid has no minority employment impact, and that categorical aid has modestly contributed to increased minority employment only in urban, segregated public schools. The present trend away from categorical aid and toward block grants is likely to erode the positive employment effects in urban schools of previous categorical funding.

Finally, the current preoccupation with the 'technical' and 'efficiency' aspects of teacher selection and training, as voiced by a score of recent national commissions, is likely to ignore the legitimacy of the relationship between teacher and student. Available evidence shows that urban schools are more segregated today than in 1967 (Orfield, 1983) and that minority interest in education as a profession has sharply dropped. Urban schools may be confronted with yet another 'crisis of legitimacy' in the near future as parents and students once again challenge a model of education where minority children in urban segregated schools are taught by non-minority teachers.

Acknowledgements

The larger study from which this chapter was taken was supported by the National Institute of Education through the Institute for Research on Educational Finance and Governance at Stanford University. The authors, and not the Institute, are responsible for the views expressed herein. We wish to thank Thomas James and Henry M. Levin for their careful editorial assistance and anonymous reviewers for unusually helpful criticisms and suggestions on earlier drafts of this chapter.

Notes

1   The racial classification of teachers and students as either Anglo, black, or Hispanic is at best imprecise. Blacks, for example, may be of Ibero-American (Hispanic) origin. Moreover, the consistent use of the term 'race' as a substitute for the cumbersome phrase 'race and ethnicity' is not meant to obfuscate the point that many Hispanics share a common Caucasion racial history with Anglos.

2   Note that the sharply increased demand for all teachers engendered by targeted categorical programs often resulted in an undersupply of qualified teachers. This was especially true in the case of bilingual certification.

3   For a discussion of the sampling procedures, response patterns, and biases introduced by these, see: GILLILAND, EM and RADLE, J (1984) *Characteris-*

tics of Public and Private Schools in the San Francisco Bay Area: A Descriptive Report, Institute for Research on Educational Finance and Governance, Stanford, CA. We are particularly indebted to Edward Haertel for his technical assistance in the statistical analyses and for devising the weighting design used in the regression analyses. Details of the design are available from the Institute for Research on Educational Finance and Governance, Stanford University.

4 For an interesting series of discussions on the concept of legitimacy, see HABERMAS, J (1973) 'What does a crisis mean today? Legitimation problems in late capitalism', *Social Research*, 40, 4. OFFE, C (1983) 'Political legitimation through majority rule?', *Social Research*, 50, 1. and WISMAN, J (1979), 'Ideology-critique, and economics', *Social Research*, 46, 2.

10 Public Policy and Private Choice: The Case of Minnesota

Linda Darling-Hammond and Sheila Nataraj Kirby

The debate over public funding of private education has had several dimensions. The issue of church/state separation has occupied the courts for two decades, while advocates and opponents of public support for private schools have argued about the fairness of various approaches to encouraging 'choice'. Debate also centers on the potential long-range consequences of public funding for the independence of private schools and the institutional viability of public schools. Proponents argue that subsidies to parents for private school costs (in the form of tuition tax credits, deductions or vouchers) will enhance educational equity and quality by providing options to poor and middle-income parents that would otherwise be available only to the rich, and by encouraging competition among schools. Opponents counter that poorer parents will be constrained in using the subsidies. The availability of subsidies to more affluent parents will encourage flight from the public schools, undermining public support and leaving them with a more racially and socioeconomically stratified population.

These arguments have necessarily been conducted on largely theoretical gounds because direct subsidies to parents for private school costs have, until recently, been overturned by the courts before their effects could be assessed. Data have not been available to answer two questions central to the debate: (i) What influence does the presence of a tuition subsidy have on school choice?; and (ii) What parents will be able to use subsidies for private education? That is, who will know about, have access to, and actually use both the subsidy and private school alternatives?

This chapter examines the effects of a tax deduction for educational expenses on parents' school choices in the state of Minnesota. Minnesota's tax deduction (upheld by the Supreme Court in 1983) is the first state policy subsidizing private school tuition costs to pass judicial review through all levels of the court system. The deduction allows parents of both public and private school children to deduct educational expenses of up to $650 per elementary school child and $1000 per secondary school child from their income when figuring their state income tax liability. Eligible expenses include tuition, cost of secular textbooks, transportation costs, costs of school supplies and fees for such things as athletic equipment.

Both public and private school parents may claim the deduction; however, most public school parents do not incur such expenses, and those they do face are generally much smaller than the tuition costs faced by private school parents. Thus, the deduction operates primarily as a tax subsidy for private educational costs and might be expected to influence parents' choice of public or private school.

It is important to note, however, that this educational subsidy is a deduction, not a tax credit. As such, its real value to a household depends both on the eligibility of the household (only those who itemize expenses on the tax return are eligible to use the deduction) and on the marginal tax rate facing them. The actual price faced by eligible households is then $(1 - t)P$, where P is total private school costs and t is the marginal tax rate. Marginal tax rates in Minnesota vary between 1.6 and 16 per cent of taxable income, but most households pay at least 10 per cent. The table below illustrates clearly that (a) the effect of the deduction in lowering the price of schooling is actually rather small and (b) for a given tuition level, the value of the deduction increases with the marginal tax rate (and, therefore, with income).

Marginal tax rate *t*	Price of schooling *P*	Reduction in price due to deduction $(P - (1 - t)P)$
10 per cent	$500	50
13 per cent	$500	65
16 per cent	$500	80

If the price faced by households is greater than the maximum deduction allowed, then the proportionate reduction in price may be considerably smaller than that implied by the marginal tax rate. For example, with a 10 per cent marginal tax rate, a family that paid $1000 in tuition costs when the maximum allowable deduction was $500 would still save only $50 in taxes; which amounts to only a 5 per cent decrease in price.[1]

This tax deduction, in existence at a lower level since 1955, is supplemented by a number of other state policies providing support for non-public schools and children. Other state aid includes free student transportation to non-public schools; direct aid to private schools for books, health services, and counseling and testing services; and provision of certain other educational services to non-public school children through shared-time arrangements in the public schools. These other forms of aid operate like the tax subsidy to lower the price parents would otherwise have to pay for a given quantity or quality of private school services. Thus, Minnesota provides a unique test case of how parents make school choices in an environment where private school choice is actively encouraged.

The analysis is based on a telephone survey of 476 Minnesota parents of public and private school children conducted during the summer of 1984. The sampling area, a seven-county area surrounding and including the Minneapolis-St. Paul SMSA, includes 48 per cent of all school-age children in the state and 58 per cent of the state's non-public school children. The region includes urban, suburban and rural communities. A random digit-dial telephone sample of parents was supplemented with a choice-based sample of private school parents residing within the Minneapolis school district.[2] The final combined sample consists of 339 parents of public school children and 137 parents of non-public school children.[3]

Note that, because of our choice-based sample, the proportion of survey parents sending their children to private schools is much larger than the national average (28.7 per cent as compared to about 10 per cent). Table 1 presents an economic and demographic profile of the survey sample; similar statistics on the general US family population are also presented, for comparison purposes. The two groups are not strictly comparable. The Minnesota sample is limited to households of families with school-aged children. The US population data include all families and, in the case of residential location, households. US education data are for all persons aged 25 to 44.

Even allowing for these differences, it is clear that the generalizability of our analytic results is fairly limited. The Minnesota sample is predominantly white, fairly affluent, largely Protestant (but with a substantial proportion of Catholics), married and living with their spouses, predominantly suburban, and highly educated. The sample significantly underrepresents minorities (especially black families), low income families, and rural households. The Minnesota respon-

Table 1: Selected Sample Characteristics

| | Survey respondents[a] | | US families[b] |
	Number	Per cent	Per cent
Race			
White	436	91.6	87.3
Black	12	2.5	10.5
Native American	12	2.5	—
Other	11	2.3	2.2
Income[c]			
<$15,000	61	12.8	29.0
$15,000–24,999	99	20.8	24.4
$25,000–49,999	210	44.1	35.5
$50,000+	86	18.1	10.9
Religious affiliation			
Protestant	230	48.3	
Catholic	191	40.1	No comparable
Other	18	3.8	data available
None	28	5.9	
Marital status			
Married, living with spouse	388	81.7	80.5
Not married	84	17.7	19.5
Residential location[d]			
Urban	182	38.2	29.5
Suburban/medium city	249	52.3	38.6
Small city/rural	43	9.0	31.9
Respondent's education[e]			
Less than high school	21	4.4	16.6
High school degree	180	37.9	40.9
Some college	132	27.8	19.5
College degree	139	29.3	23.0

[a] Total number of survey respondents was 476. Where percentages do not total to 100, remainder reflects respondents who did not answer specific question.
[b] Population data are drawn from US Dept. of Commerce, Bureau of the Census, *Statistical Abstract of the United States, 1984* (104th edition). All data are for families from the 1980 population census, unless otherwise noted.
[c] National family income data are for 1982.
[d] US population figures are for households. Urban and suburban represent metropolitan area 'in central city' and 'outside central city', respectively.
[e] US population data are for persons aged 25 to 44 years in 1982.

dents also appear to be much more highly educated than the general population aged 25 to 44. However, our analysis is applicable to particular sub-groups and does provide information about the differential behavior of these sub-populations.

The chapter is divided into four sections. The first analyzes choice-making behavior and models the determinants of choice. The second examines the level of knowledge and extent of use of the income tax deduction among the survey respondents and presents some evidence on the importance of the deduction in making school-

In the third section, we model the propensity of public
to switch to private schools at an increased level of tax
`st summarizes the main conclusions.

,oice-Making Behavior

∠nt choice of schools can occur in at least two stages: the decision
∠o search actively for school options and the actual selection of a
particular school for attendance. However, the latter may actually be a
non-decision if the parent does not perceive school selection as a
choice among alternatives. Public policies designed to encourage
'choice' among schools are likely to have their greatest effect on the
school selection of those who perceive that schooling decisions are a
matter for conscious deliberation. In order to understand how and
why parents select private schools over no-cost public alternatives (or
public schools when financial subsidies exist to offset private school
costs), it is also necessary to understand when it is that parents
perceive school selection as an active choice.

Search Behavior

Previous studies of parental choice have found that a substantial number of public school parents give little thought to schooling options
and passively opt for the public school closest to them. These parents
tend to be less well-educated, obviously less well-informed about
alternatives, to have lower incomes, and to have attended public
schools themselves (Cogan, 1979; Bridge and Blackman, 1978; Kamin
and Erickson, 1981; Nault and Uchitelle, 1982; Williams, Hancher and
Hutner, 1983). For public school parents, location (convenience and
distance) is particularly important in schooling choices (Kamin and
Erickson, 1981; Bridge and Blackman, 1978; Cogan, 1979).

It has generally been assumed that private school parents make
more active choices about where they want their children to attend
school. In the Minnesota sample, however, public school parents
were actually more likely to be 'active choosers' than private school
parents.

We defined search behavior to include (a) consideration of other
schools at the time of the current schooling choice; and (b) consideration of public schools in the residential location decision. Thus broadly defined, we found that 62 per cent of public school parents reported

Table 2: Extent of Search by Current School Choice

	Public school parents	Private school parents
Percent who considered:		
1 Other schools	25.7	34.3
2 Public schools in residential choice	53.1	35.0
3 Neither 1 nor 2	37.8	46.7
(N)	(339)	(137)

being 'active choosers' as compared to only 53 per cent of private school parents (table 2). Although less likely than private school parents to have considered other schools at the time of current school choice (26 per cent as opposed to 34 per cent of private school parents), most of them had considered public school quality as an important factor in determining residential location.

Table 3 presents a profile of active school choosers, active home choosers, and non-choosers, broken down by public versus private school choice. The first two categories are not mutually exclusive. Interpreting the evidence on the relationships between 'search' behavior and the various socio-economic variables is made complex by the fact that local school quality, socioeconomic status, and knowledge or taste for alternatives may be jointly distributed. Active consideration of alternatives probably depends on what might be termed as 'push' and 'pull' factors along with ability to pay. 'Push' factors might consist of having poor neighborhood schools (an encouragement to seek other options), while 'pull' factors might be the attraction of good alternatives and subsidies like the tax deduction, free transportation, or scholarship support.

In general, active consideration of alternatives increases with income because higher income parents have more options available to them at each stage of the search process: they can purchase high-priced homes in 'good' school districts, and they can purchase private education. The greater propensity of lower income public school parents (those in the bottom two income ranges) to consider actively other schools at the time of school enrollment may be the result of 'push' factors if they face relatively poor public schools in their neighborhoods. For those in the $15,000–25,000 group who chose private schools, consideration of other options is much lower than for other groups since, using this reasoning, they may not consider the poor public schools in their neighborhoods as viable alternatives. Public school parents in the $25,000–50,000 income range are less likely than others to consider other schools at the time of enrollment (though

248

Table 3: Consideration of Schooling Alternatives by Current School Choice (%)

	Public				Private			
	Other schools (1)	Public school in residence choice (2)	Neither 1 nor 2	(N)	Other schools (1)	Public school in residence choice (2)	Neither 1 nor 2	(N)
All Respondents	25.7	53.1	37.8	(339)	34.3	35.0	46.7	(137)
Income								
Less than $15,000	29.6	40.9	45.4	(44)	35.3	23.5	52.9	(17)
$15,000–25,000	34.2	53.9	35.5	(76)	21.7	8.7	73.9	(23)
$25,000–50,000	19.3	54.3	39.3	(140)	34.3	37.1	44.3	(70)
$50,000+	28.6	58.7	31.7	(63)	43.5	60.9	21.7	(23)
Mother's education								
Non-high school graduate	26.9	30.8	53.8	(25)	33.3	16.7	50.0	(6)
High school graduate	19.7	46.9	45.6	(147)	30.8	26.9	51.9	(52)
Some college	34.1	52.7	33.0	(91)	21.5	39.5	52.6	(38)
College graduate	26.3	72.4	23.7	(76)	51.2	43.9	34.1	(41)
Father's education								
Non-high school graduate	32.5	47.5	40.0	(79)	33.3	25.0	50.0	(24)
High school graduate	20.0	43.3	46.7	(90)	31.0	37.9	44.8	(29)
Some college	26.1	49.3	39.1	(69)	22.2	18.5	63.0	(27)
College graduate	24.7	68.3	27.7	(101)	42.1	45.6	38.6	(57)
Mother's schooling								
Public school only	24.4	55.0	37.1	(229)	33.3	42.4	42.4	(66)
Private school only	34.3	45.7	42.9	(35)	40.0	23.3	53.3	(30)
Both public and private schools	27.9	55.7	32.8	(61)	30.8	33.3	48.7	(39)
Religion								
Protestant	27.4	60.3	31.8	(179)	33.3	41.2	41.2	(51)
Catholic	24.8	47.0	42.7	(117)	29.7	31.1	52.7	(74)
All others	25.0	44.4	41.7	(36)	80.0	40.0	20.0	(10)
Residential location								
Urban	40.6	58.3	29.2	(96)	36.1	32.6	46.5	(86)
Suburban/medium city	19.7	53.7	37.9	(203)	32.6	41.3	45.7	(46)
Small city/rural	20.0	37.5	57.5	(40)	20.0	20.0	60.0	(5)

they consider public schools in their residential choice), perhaps because they have good public schools available to them.

Non-choosing behavior is inversely related to income and parents' (especially mother's) education level among public school parents. The relationship is not as clearcut among private school parents.

Rural parents have few alternatives available to them; hence, they are least likely to exhibit active choice-making behavior. Parents who had themselves attended only private schools are less likely than others to consider public school quality in their residential choice, but are more likely to consider several schools at the time of enrollment. Not unexpectedly, among private school parents, Catholics were most likely to be non-choosers.

Active school choosers were much more likely to stress school quality factors as being most important in determining their current school choices than non-active school choosers (table 4). Non-active school choosers tended to cite situational and convenience factors (public school parents) and moral/religious instruction (private school parents) far more frequently than active choosers. Among active choosers who considered more than one school at the time of enrollment, both public and private school parents cited the quality of teaching staff, discipline and academic standards as very important factors in their choice of schools. Public school parents were far more likely to cite the courses offered by the school and parent involvement

Table 4: *Most Important Reasons for Current School Choice (% of Responses)*

	Active school choosers			Non-active school choosers		
	Public	*Private*	*Total*	*Public*	*Private*	*Total*
Financial factors	11.5	0.0	7.5	20.3	0.0	15.1
Convenience/proximity of school	5.8	0.0	3.8	21.4	3.2	16.7
Situational circumstances	0.0	0.0	0.0	26.6	3.2	20.6
Belief/support of education type	0.0	0.0	0.0	1.3	3.2	1.8
Quality of school/education/program	59.8	43.5	54.1	21.4	35.7	25.1
Moral/religious factors	0.0	17.4	6.0	0.0	30.1	7.7
Disciplinary standards	1.2	15.2	6.0	0.5	13.5	3.9
Student composition	3.4	2.2	3.0	0.8	0.0	0.6
Family factors	5.7	4.3	5.3	7.4	11.1	8.3
Other	12.6	17.4	14.3	0.3	0.0	0.2
(N)*	(87)	(46)	(133)	(365)	(126)	(491)

* Represents total number of responses, not number of respondents. Although asked for the most important reason for current school choice, respondents frequently cited two or more factors. We have, therefore, included all responses rather than introduce bias by arbitrarily selecting one answer.

as very important factors, while private school choosers were more likely than their active public school counterparts to stress moral values and religious instruction as very important factors (table 5).

Table 5: *Factors Cited by Active Searchers as Very Important in Influencing Current School Choice*

	% of respondents	
	Public school parents (n = 86)	Private school parents (n = 47)
Teaching staff	87.2	85.1
Discipline in school	80.2	74.5
Academic standards	77.9	80.9
Courses offered	75.6	48.9
Individual attention	72.1	76.6
Parent involvement	60.5	46.8
Moral values	51.2	63.8
Size of school	47.7	40.4
Financial costs	43.5	17.0
Location of school	43.0	23.4
Child's desire to attend	43.0	38.3
Socio-economic background of students	27.9	21.3
Desegregation policy/student body composition	21.2	17.0
Religious instruction	14.1	40.4

Overall, the picture that emerges of choice-making behavior shows a modest relationship between income and parents' educational levels and the propensity to actively seek out school options. Higher income and education definitely increase the likelihood that parents will have considered public school quality in their residential choice, but these factors have a much less clearcut relationship to whether parents considered more than one school at the time of enrollment. Given the possibility that household income and public school quality may be jointly distributed, it is not entirely surprising that lower income parents — who cannot afford to buy homes in the 'priciest' neighborhoods — are most active in considering school options at the time of enrollment. More affluent parents apparently first 'vote with their feet' when thinking about school alternatives by moving to locations where public schools better meet their expectations.

Surprisingly, nearly half (47 per cent) of private school parents did not actively consider school alternatives either in residential choice or school selection. This finding brings into question the assumption that the selection of a private school is generally the result of comparing schools and choosing the most 'competitive' option. Just as many public school parents automatically send their child to the nearest public school, a large number of private school parents — especially those who attended private schools themselves — seemingly 'automatically' send their child to a particular private school.

Public and private school choosers share a common concern for school academic quality in making their decisions, but they weigh other factors — location, costs, and type of educational program — differently in the choice-making process. Below we examine the determinants of public/private school choice in more detail.

Current School Choice

Previous studies have found that households choosing private schools tend to be white, to have higher incomes, to live in metropolitan areas, and to reside in the north east or north central regions of the country. They also tend to have attended private schools themselves (Kamin and Erikson, 1981; Williams, Hancher and Hutner, 1983). Gemello and Osman (1984), using data on unified school districts in California and census tracts within the San Francisco Bay Area, found that income, taste-related variables (measured by education and type of occupation) and racial/ethnic composition of the district/tract all appeared to have significant effects on private school attendance.

Current school choice and the determinants of such choice form the major focus of our analysis. Several variables were examined in an effort to determine the direction and significance of their effect on school choice. Tables 7, 8 and 9 illustrate these bivariate relationships. Note that the proportions reported in the first three tables can be interpreted as the propensity of households within a given sub-group to make the particular school choice. As noted earlier, our sample deliberately included a larger proportion of private school parents than would have occurred in a totally random sample of households. Somewhat surprisingly, non-white respondents were slightly more likely than white parents to choose non-public schools. However, there was very little variation in the racial and marital status of the sample households: over 92 per cent of the household are white and well over 80 per cent are married. Catholics have, as expected, a much higher propensity to enroll in private schools, as do households with larger numbers of school-aged children. This latter result may at first be surprising unless one considers that these households may tend to be predominantly Catholic and, secondly, that tuition reductions are frequently offered for multiple children from the same family.

Two-parent (i.e., married couple) households and households with children in elementary schools have a much higher propensity to

Variable	Public schools	Private schools	(N)
	Proportion within sub-group choosing:		
All Respondents	71.3	28.7	(476)
Race			
White	71.1	28.9	(436)
Non-white	68.6	31.4	(35)
Religion			
Protestant	77.8	22.2	(230)
Catholic	61.3	38.7	(191)
All others	78.3	21.7	(46)
Number of school-aged children			
1 child	74.0	26.0	(196)
2 children	72.9	27.1	(181)
3+ children	62.6	37.4	(99)
Marital status			
Married	70.1	29.9	(388)
Not married	75.0	25.0	(84)
Grade			
Elementary	66.1	33.9	(218)
Secondary	75.7	24.3	(259)
Residential location			
Urban	52.7	47.3	(182)
Suburban/medium city	81.5	18.5	(249)
Small city/rural	88.4	11.6	(43)
School search behavior			
Did not consider other schools	73.8	26.2	(343)
Considered other schools	64.9	35.1	(134)

choose private schools. The greater enrollment of elementary students in private schools may be partly a result of greater availability (there are more than twice as many elementary than secondary private schools in the sampling area, as is true in the state as a whole), and partly the result of lower costs for private school education at the elementary level. Additionally, parents of elementary-age children may have a greater concern for individual attention or religious education at this age than for older students.

Urban households also appear to have a much higher propensity to enroll in private schools. However, our supplemental choice-based sample of private school parents was drawn entirely from the urban area. Thus, the differential enrollment rates are largely an artifact of our sampling method. Some of the remaining difference between urban/suburban households may be explained in terms of differences in public school quality in these locations and the differential accessibility of private schools.

Active searchers — parents who considered other schools before enrolling their child in the current school — were more likely to choose private schools than those who did not compare schools at the time of enrollment.

Table 7 examines the relationships between income and school choice. Middle income families ($25,000–50,000) appear to have markedly higher propensities to choose private schools. Higher income families presumably live in areas with the best public schools; lower income families may be restricted in their ability to pay for private schooling.

Table 7:   Family Income and Current School Choices

Variable	Public schools	Private schools	(N)
	Proportion within sub-group choosing:		
Family Income			
Less than $15,000	72.1	27.9	(61)
$15,000–25,000	76.8	23.2	(99)
$25,000–50,000	66.7	33.3	(210)
$50,000+	73.3	26.7	(86)

Parents' schooling and level of education have frequently been found to be important in defining the 'taste' variable. We find this to be true in the Minnesota case as well, as table 8 makes evident. Level of education displays a monotonically increasing relationship with the propensity to enroll in private schools. Parents who have private school backgrounds tend to have a strong 'taste' for private schools for their children.

To test the significance of the observed differences in the distribution of the variables across schooling choices, we used the chi-square (χ^2) test. The null hypothesis was one of no difference between public school and private school parents across any of the selected variables. Table 9 presents the results of the chi-square tests. Somewhat surprisingly, we cannot reject the null hypothesis for race, income, level of education, or active search behavior. That is, these four variables appear to be unrelated to schooling choices. Household characteristics significantly related to the choice of private schooling include religion (Catholics), residential location (urban), parents' own attendance at private schools, number of school-aged children (three or more), two-parent households, and child's grade level (elementary).

The foremost reasons for their choices cited by public school parents were school quality factors (29 per cent), financial factors (19

Table 8:   Parents' Schooling, Level of Education and Current School Choice

	Proportion within sub-group choosing:		
Variable	*Public schools*	*Private schools*	*(N)*
Mother's education			
Non-high school graduate	76.5	23.5	(17)
High school graduate	73.9	26.1	(199)
Some college	70.5	29.5	(129)
College graduate	64.3	35.7	(115)
Mother's schooling			
Public school only	77.6	22.4	(295)
Private school only	53.8	46.2	(65)
Both public and private schools	51.0	39.0	(100)
Father's education			
Non-high school graduate	82.1	17.9	(28)
High school graduate	75.6	24.4	(119)
Some college	71.9	28.1	(96)
College graduate	64.1	35.9	(156)
Father's schooling			
Public school only	76.2	23.8	(273)
Private school only	51.0	49.0	(49)
Both public and private schools	62.3	37.7	(77)

Table 9:   Results of Chi-Square Test Comparing Public School and Private School Parents

Variable	
Race	3.74
Religion	18.67*
Number of school-aged children	16.42*
Marital status	11.15*
Grade level of child (elementary/secondary)	5.35*
Residential location	52.92*
Family income	5.11
Mother's education	9.17
Father's education	13.54
Mother's schooling	27.38*
Father's schooling	19.01*
School search behavior	3.67

*Note: *indicates that the computed chi-square statistic is greater than $X^2_{.05}$ with the appropriate degrees of freedom.*

per cent), and convenience or proximity of the school (18 per cent). Private school parents most often cited school quality factors (38 per cent), moral and religious instruction (27 per cent), and school discipline standards (14 per cent). Financial factors played a role in some parents' school choice decisions. The costs of non-public school were cited by 29 per cent of public school parents as a reason for not considering other school alternatives and by 42 per cent of the much smaller number (n = 77) who had considered a private school but decided against it. Of those relatively few parents who had transferred children from private to public schools (n = 42), 17 per cent cited costs as the reason for the switch.

A Multivariate Model of Current School Choice

In modelling current school choice, we start with the traditional assumption that individuals are utility maximizers. Each household selects among the given discrete alternatives (private school, public school) based upon a choice index which depends upon the measurable attributes of the alternatives, measurable attributes of the decision-makers and a random component reflecting unobserved or unmeasured factors or consumer idiosyncrasies. The decision-maker chooses the alternative which maximizes utility; the probability of choosing a particular alternative can, under certain assumptions, be estimated using a logit or probit specification. These are more appropriate choices for the functional form than the linear probability model, since they restrict the value of the dependent variable to between zero and one.

Empirically, the choice variable is defined as:

Y_i = 0, if individual i chose public school
= 1, if individual i chose private school

The model relates the current school choice of the ith individual to a vector of characteristics for the individual and perceived attributes of the alternatives. The assumed relationship is:

$$Y_i = P(x_i) + \varepsilon$$

$$\text{where} \quad P(x_i) = \frac{1}{1 + \exp\left[-\left(a + \sum_{j=1}^{k} b_j x_{ij}\right)\right]}$$

The parameters of the model were estimated using the discriminant function method. The estimated coefficients reported in table 10 are derived by re-scaling the least squares coefficients relating Y and X. These estimates have been shown to satisfy the conditional logit functional form given above (Chow and Polich, 1980; Haggstrom, 1983; Halperin, Blackwelder and Vorter, 1971).

The estimation procedure is modified to correct for the fact that the sample of households in the data base was partially formed on the basis of choice, the result of combining the random digit dial and the choice-based samples. Manski and Lerman (1977) and Hosek (1979) have shown that unweighted parameter estimates of the conditional logit model derived from choice-based sample data are consistent except for the intercept, which can be adjusted *ex post* by adding $\ln k_1/k_0$ to its estimate where

$k_0 = \dfrac{\text{share of the population choosing outcome '0'}}{\text{share of the sample choosing '0'}}$

and

$k_1 = \dfrac{\text{share of the population choosing outcome '1'}}{\text{share of the sample choosing '1'}}$

The constant term reported in table 10 is adjusted using this weight.

Table 10:   Regression Results on the Current School Choice Model

Independent Variables	Dependent variable: current school choice 0 = public school; 1 = private school Coefficient (t - statistic)
Constant	−3.68
Family income < $15,000	0.56 (1.25)
$25,000 < Family income < $50,000	0.63 (1.87)*
Family income > $50,000	0.29 (0.67)
Mother attended private schools	0.69 (2.48)*
Father college graduate	0.81 (2.71)*
Child in grades K-6	0.55 (2.09)*
Location of school important	−1.27 (3.86)*
Religious/moral instruction important	4.13 (11.20)*
Cost of school important	−1.28 (4.04)*
Considered other schools	0.18 (0.45)
Considered public schools in choosing residence	−0.79 (2.93)*

* Significant at .05 level.
Note: The table presents actual regression coefficients, not probabilities. Conditional probabilities are calculated by substituting these coefficients into the following equation:

$$P(x_i) = \frac{1}{1 + \exp\left[-\left(a + \sum_{j=1}^{k} b_j x_{ij}\right)\right]}$$

These probabilities will be between 0 and 1.

Several versions of the model were estimated using different sets of variables and different transformations of the variables identified earlier as important in determining school choices. The level of education of fathers and mothers appeared to be highly correlated with each other, as did the type of schooling received by each. We selected the two (mother's schooling, father's education) that appeared to have greater explanatory power in the model. Residential location was not included because of the bias introduced in the variable because of the choice-based sample. Race was not included because of the lack of variation in the sample. Number of children neither added to the model nor changed the magnitude and significance of the other co-efficients. It was, therefore, excluded from the final version. Most of the variables are self-explanatory. The attitudinal variables are derived from a number of questions, both specific and open-ended, on factors considered important when making current school choice.

Of the dummy variables representing income, only one (family income between $25,000–50,000) proved significant (using a one-tail test) and positively related to private school choice. Relative to the omitted category (income between $15,000–25,000), both low and high income households also have slightly higher propensities to choose private education, although neither proved significant. One could speculate that tuition assistance might account for this slightly higher representation of low income families in private schools, but this does not appear to be the case in our sample. Only nineteen families reported receiving any kind of tuition reduction, and only two of these were in the lowest range, while most were in the groups earning $25,000 or more. It is more likely that the relatively high enrollment of low income students is due to the 'push' factors discussed earlier and to the low cost of the schools they attended. (One-third of low income parents paid less than $500 in annual tuition.)

The effects of the other variables are as one would expect: private school background and higher level of father's education both lead to a greater proclivity for choosing private schools, as does having elementary school-aged children. This latter finding may be explained by the several factors mentioned earlier: tuitions are generally lower for elementary schools, perceived differences in quality between private and public school may be greater at this level, and/or a solid *early* grounding in religious education may be considered essential and sufficient by those who value this feature of education. The attitudinal variables behave as expected: if location or cost are important considerations in making school choices, then evidently there is a smaller probability of choosing private schools; quite the opposite is true of those who consider religious instruction important. Two variables were introduced to capture search behavior; only one proved significant. Households who 'voted with their feet' by moving to locations where the public schools better met their expectations (Tiebout effect) are far less likely to choose private schools.

The next section of the chapter looks more closely at respondents' knowledge and use of the Minnesota tax deduction and its effects on their school choices.

Knowledge, Use and Effects of the Income Tax Deduction

A few previous studies have attempted to examine the effect of tax subsidies on schooling choices and the extent to which such a proposal would induce shifts in enrollment. These studies have, necessarily, been based on parent choice behavior in the absence of tuition aid. Coleman *et al.* (1981) claim that tuition tax credits would encourage poor and minority families to participate in the private sector. Catterall and Levin (1982) dispute this assertion by pointing out that poor families are generally more constrained in their ability to participate in such a program because of their inability to meet the cash requirements of enrollment and the uncovered portion of the expenses as well as the outright ineligibility of families with no tax liability. Gemello and Osman (1983) report that adopting public policies that increase family income through tax cuts or educational vouchers would increase private school enrollment rates by about two-thirds of one percent for every one percent increase in family income. Noell and Myers (1982) also report similar findings with respect to income elasticity, and they report small price elasticities of -0.42 for parochial schools and approximately zero for non-parochial schools.

This study presents the first experiential evidence on knowledge, use and effect of a tax subsidy on households' schooling choices. Minnesota's income tax deduction for dependents' educational expenses was enacted in 1955 as an amendment to a larger Educational Omnibus bill. Declared constitutional by the US Supreme Court in 1983, the Minnesota statute is the first such tax subsidy to pass judicial muster. At the time this study was begun, the deduction allowed both public and private school parents to deduct up to $500 per child in tuition and other school expenses (books, transportation, school supplies, etc.) for children in elementary school and $700 per child for secondary school expenses from their gross income for state income tax computations. Since then, the maximum levels have been raised to $650 per elementary school child and $1000 per secondary school child.

Obviously, only households itemizing deductions are eligible to use the deduction. Persuasive evidence exists to show that the deduction appears to benefit mostly higher income households. For example, we have shown elsewhere that the proportions of households who claimed the deduction in 1980 rise sharply with income, as does the size of the average deduction claimed (Darling-Hammond and Kirby, 1985).

Table 11 provides a convenient summary of the level of knowledge and use of the income tax deduction among the households in our sample. Although nearly two-thirds of our respondents had heard of the deduction, only 28 per cent had ever claimed it. Both knowledge and use are much higher for private school parents than for public school parents. Knowledge and use of the deduction also differ significantly by family income, while knowledge appears to vary by mother's level of education. Households who knew of the deduction and did not use it most frequently said they thought it did not apply to public school children.

Table 11: Knowledge and Use of Income Tax Deduction

	Percentage of respondents who:		
	Had heard of deduction	Ever claimed deduction	N
All Respondents	63.0	28.2	476
School choice			
Public	55.3	14.7	339
Private	81.8	61.3	137
(χ^2)	(29.3)*	(105.0*)	
Family income			
Less than $15,000	42.6	9.8	61
$15,000–25,000	60.6	20.2	99
$25,000–50,000	70.0	36.7	210
$50,000 or more	65.1	31.4	86
(χ^2)	(16.7*)	(21.4*)	
Mother's education			
Non-high school graduate	46.9	18.7	32
High school graduate	51.8	23.6	199
Some college	75.2	32.6	129
College graduate	72.7	33.3	117
(χ^2)	(27.2*)	(6.2)	

Note: *indicates that the computed chi-square statistic is greater than $\chi^2_{0.05}$ with the appropriate degrees of freedom.

When asked how important the availability of the deduction was in their choice of a private school, only 10 per cent of private school users said the deduction was very important; another 26 per cent said it was somewhat important. Fully 98 per cent of these parents said they would still have sent their child to private school if the deduction had not been available. By contrast, 40 per cent of those who received free bus transportation to private schools said the availability of this service was very important, and another 26 per cent said it was somewhat important. Twenty-two per cent of the parents who said free bus service was important in their choice also said they would not have sent their child to that school if the service was not available.

The importance of the income tax deduction in schooling choice is one of the central questions of our study. To answer this question, we need to allow for the effect of such knowledge in our choice model. One could assume a fully recursive system and introduce knowledge of the deduction as an exogenous variable in the choice model. However, if, as seems plausible, the two variables (knowledge and choice) are indeed simultaneously determined,[4] then such a procedure would mean that knowledge is really endogenous in this system of equations. As such, we used an instrumental variables approach, first modelling knowledge as a function of income, level of education and religious affiliation. The predicted level of knowledge is then entered as an explanatory variable in the schooling choice model.

The estimation results are reported in table 12. As can be seen, the major determinants of school choice did not change from what they had been in the basic choice model, although the coefficients are somewhat smaller. The income variable, previously significant, is not significant in this model. Predicted knowledge did not appear to have a significant effect on choice, although its coefficient is considerably larger in magnitude than most of the other variables.

The relative unimportance of the tax deduction is not surprising for at least two reasons. First, the actual value of the deduction is much smaller than its face value, since it is a deduction rather than a credit. Parents must assume direct, immediate costs for private schooling before some of them (those who itemize and pay taxes) can recoup a small portion of those expenses through the deduction. Second, while costs of private schooling are a factor in school choice decisions, other factors like parents own prior schooling experiences, concern for religious instruction and logistical considerations bear stronger relationships to school choices.

Table 12: *Instrumental Variable Approach: Regression Results on the Current School Choice Model, with Predicted Level of Knowledge*

Independent variables	Dependent variable: current school choice 0 = public school; 1 = private school Coefficient (t - statistic)
Constant	−4.70
Family income < $15,000	0.69
	(1.49)
$25,000 < Family income < $50,000	0.53
	(1.53)
Family income > $50,000	0.07
	(0.14)
Mother attended private schools	0.63
	(2.23)*
Father college graduate	0.70
	(2.25)*
Child in grades K-6	0.55
	(2.07)*
Location of school important	−1.28
	(3.87)*
Religious/moral instruction important	4.12
	(11.14)*
Cost of school important	−1.28
	(4.02)*
Considered other schools	0.17
	(0.41)
Considered public schools in choosing residence	−0.83
	(3.05)*
Knowledge of tax deduction (predicted value)	1.84
	(1.45)

*Significant at .05 level.

A Model of Switching Behavior

The recent NIE Private School Study asked several questions regarding the likelihood of switching to private schools in the face of different levels of tuition tax credit. Williams, Hancher and Hutner (1983) reported that low income and minority group respondents expressed the greatest interest in using tax credits to subsidize a shift to private schooling. Their expressed desire to take advantage of a tax credit was significantly higher than that of other groups even at the lowest credit levels.

We asked similar questions of the public school respondents. Surprisingly, when asked about the likelihood of transferring to private schools if offered a deduction *at the then current level* ($500 for elementary school children and $700 for secondary school children), 23 per cent reported that they were 'very likely' or 'somewhat likely'

Table 13: Likelihood of Transferring to Private School by level of Income Tax Deduction

	If level of deduction were:	
	$500/$700 *(1)*	*$850/$1200* *(1)*
Very likely	9.4	16.4
Somewhat likely	13.6	13.3
Somewhat unlikely	13.9	13.3
Very unlikely	59.7	53.6
Don't know	3.3	3.3
Total	100.0	100.0

Note: (1) The two numbers indicate maximum level of deduction for elementary and secondary school children, respectively.

to transfer (table 13). Since that level of deduction was already in effect, and had been for many years, we must assume that these parents either did not know about the deduction or did not understand how the deduction operates. At slightly higher levels of tax deduction ($850 and $1200, respectively) then proposed in the state legislature, the proportion of parents saying they would be likely to switch to private schools increased to 30 per cent. More than 50 per cent said they would be *very* unlikely to transfer at either level.

Reports of possible future behavior based on a policy whose actual benefits and operation may be poorly understood by respondents must obviously be viewed with some skepticism. However, these answers suggest which types of respondents have a desire to switch to private schools. In an attempt to identify the parents at the choice margin, we modelled the propensity to switch, based on the answers to the higher level of deduction. The dependent variable is again a dichotomous choice variable: 0, if the household reported that it would be unlikely to transfer to a private school even given the increased deduction, 1 otherwise. The estimation results are reported in table 14.

The model is dominated by three variables. Parents who are dissatisfied with the current school appear most likely to switch given a large deduction, as are households with children in grades K-6.

The third variable, a knowledge index, was introduced to control for the actual level of knowledge characterizing each household. Our hypothesis was that households who understood the ramifications and the actual workings of the deduction (as opposed to, say, a tax credit) would be much less likely to transfer. The index was simply an additive one where responses to a series of nine questions relating to the tax deduction were used to score the respondent's knowledge level, with the respondent being given a '1' for every correct answer.

Table 14: *Regression Results on the Model of the Propensity of Public School Parents to Transfer to Private School*

Independent variables	Dependent Variable: Current school choice 0 = public school; 1 = private school
	Coefficient (t - statistic)
Constant	−1.53
Family Income < $15,000	0.49
	(1.07)
$25,000 < Family income < $50,000	0.27
	(0.77)
Family income > $50,000	−0.62
	(1.40)
Mother attended private schools	0.43
	(1.45)
Father college graduate	−0.24
	(0.73)
Child in grades K-6	0.72
	(2.27)*
Location of school important	−0.01
	(0.02)
Cost of school important	0.37
	(1.22)
Considered other schools	0.19
	(0.51)
Dissatisfied with current school residence	1.54 (3.55)*
Level of knowledge of tax deduction	−1.12
	(2.16)*

*Significant at .05 level.

The index is strongly and negatively related to the propensity to transfer.

Somewhat surprisingly, we find no income effects. None of the coefficients is significant, although low income and medium income households have slightly higher and high income households a slightly lower propensity to transfer. The level of education of parents (father being a college graduate) has a small, negative effect on the probability of transfer. The negative effects of high income and education levels may be because these families had made careful choices of their current schools (through residential location or active school search) and were pleased with the quality of public schooling they were able to obtain. It may also reflect the fact that more highly educated parents better understand the tax subsidy, and realize that the actual benefit of a tax deduction is far smaller than its face value.

Other 'taste' and attitudinal variables, though not significant, have the expected signs. Slightly greater propensities to transfer are shown by families where the mother had attended private school, where other schools had been actively considered at the time of enrollment, and where the higher costs of alternatives were an important reason for the current school choice.[5] Those who considered school location to be important were slightly less likely to say they would transfer because of a tax deduction.

Conclusions

We have analyzed data collected during a telephone survey of 476 Minnesota households with school-aged children conducted in August 1984. The final sample was a combination of a choice-based sample of public and private school parents in the Minneapolis School District and a random digit-dial sample of parents in the surrounding seven-county area. Minnesota was chosen as it offers a unique opportunity to study the experimental effects of an income tax deduction for dependents' educational expenses.

We focused on three issues: current school choice and the determinants of such choice; knowledge and use of the income tax deduction; and the propensity of public school parents to transfer to private schools if offered larger tax deductions.

Contrary to what most other parent choice studies have found, race and income do not show significant bivariate relationships to schooling choices in this sample. With respect to race, there are at least two possible reasons for this finding: it may be due to more equitable access to private schooling than found in other areas; alternatively, it may be that we have little variation in the sample, as over 92 per cent are white. With respect to income, again, there may be fewer obstacles to private school attendance for low and moderate income parents (and these parents may have more incentives to look for private school alternatives); on the other hand, our income ranges may be too aggregated to show a relationship.

Income exerts only a modest influence on school choice in our model. Three dummy variables were included in a logit model of school choice to capture the effect of different income levels. Only one, households with family income between $25,000–50,000, proved significant and positive. Relative to the omitted group ($15,000 < income < $25,000), low income households (income less than $15,000) had a slightly higher, and higher income households (over $50,000) a slightly lower propensity to choose private schools.

Attitudinal variables (importance of location, cost, and religious instruction) and 'taste' for private schools, as captured by the type of schooling received by parents and level of educational attainment, dominate the model. The Tiebout effect was apparent in the model: households that 'voted with their feet' had a lower propensity of choosing private schools, having selected the community that best fit their needs.

In an effort to determine the importance of the tax deduction on schooling choice, we introduced knowledge of the deduction into the school choice model, using an instrumental variables approach which allowed for the endogeneity of this variable. It did not appear to be significant. Furthermore, private school parents overwhelmingly reported that their school choices would remain unchanged in the absence of the deduction. While exerting little effect on parental choice, the deduction disproportionately benefits private school parents and higher income and higher educated households.

Other non-public school aid policies, such as free bus transportation, appear to have much greater effect on parental choice. A supplemental survey of ninety-eight non-public schools in the same region of Minnesota suggests that state aid to non-public schools in the form of books and instructional equipment, guidance and counseling services, health services, and special education services may also increase access by keeping tuition costs at levels lower than they would have been in the absence of such aid.

Minnesota recently increased the level of the income tax deduction from $500 to $650 for elementary school children and from $700 to $1000 for secondary school children. Public school parents were asked about their propensity to switch to private schools when faced with higher deduction levels.[6] Thirty per cent of them reported that they were 'very' or 'somewhat likely' to switch. A model of switching behavior based on their responses showed no significant patterns except that parents that were dissatisfied with the current school and those who had children in grades K-6 appeared the most likely to switch. Households that understood the actual workings of the deduction (as captured by a knowledge index) were far less likely to say they would transfer.

Whether these households would transfer to the private sector in reality is debatable. First, in order to take advantage of the deduction, households must itemize and pay taxes. Second, they must be willing to assume direct costs for the tuition and other expenses before they can recoup a small portion of these expenses at a much later date. Third, there may be some confusion as regards the exact magnitude of the tax deduction on the part of these households. The fact that this is a deduction, not a tax credit, and as such, the actual value will vary across households facing different marginal tax rates may not have been fully understood by households reporting high probabilities of switching. This is supported to some extent by the fairly large proportion of households (approximately 20 per cent) who claimed that they were likely to transfer if offered deduction levels of $500 and $700, levels that have been in place for some time now. For those parents at the margin, it seems that policies which directly increase access to school alternatives (through lower immediate costs and increased convenience) are more likely to affect actual school choices than an indirect tax subsidy.

Notes

1 Of course, the amount saved on the overall tax bill would be substantially greater if use of the deduction moves the taxpayer to a lower tax bracket. For example, a family with taxable income of $37,000 in 1983 could reduce its marginal tax rate from 16 per cent to 15 per cent by taking a $500 deduction for educational expenses. The resulting decrease in the family's tax bill would be $445.00. This effect operates only for households near the bottom of a given tax bracket, and is most powerful for those in the upper income ranges. Although it is unlikely that the exact effect would be known at the time schooling choices are made, households in some income ranges might actively consider the effects of the various deductions offered in making schooling and non-schooling decisions.

2 The choice-based sampling approach samples the population conditional on the choices it has made; it thus ensures that sufficient observations are obtained for each choice (public school; private school) to allow empirical analyses of choice. It also has the decided advantage of being less expensive than purely random sampling in generating a suitably large sample.

3 The sample was limited to parents of children in grades K–12 whose schooling choices for the current school year were already made. Although we might have sampled parents of pre-school children to ascertain their sensitivity to the deduction and other factors *prior* to making a choice, we would have had no way of determining whether in fact their actual (later) choices conformed with their expected plans.

4 This simultaneity is likely, given that 35 per cent of private school parents reported that they learned about the deduction from their child's school.

5 The variable 'cost of school important' in table 14 reflects, for public school parents, whether costs of alternatives were an important factor in parents' choice of current school. It is equal to 1 if parents said that costs were a 'very' or 'somewhat' important factor, and 0 otherwise.

6 The hypothetical levels were those proposed in the state legislature at that time — $850 and $1200 — somewhat higher than the ceilings ultimately enacted.

PART III
MINORITY GROUPS IN PUBLIC
AND PRIVATE SCHOOLS

11 Private Schools and Black-White Segregation: Evidence from Two Big Cities

Robert L. Crain

The public controversy surrounding recent proposals to support private schools through tuition tax credits has prompted an interest in the impact of private schooling on racial segregation in education. Coleman, Hoffer and Kilgore's report (1981) and book (1982) divide this issue into four questions:

1 Do private schools enroll more or fewer minority students than do public schools?

2 Are the minorities presently attending private schools more racially segregated or integrated than minorities attending public schools?

3 Has the presence of private schools competing with public schools created more or less segregation?

4 If some form of private school subsidy were enacted, would the accelerated transfer of whites and minorities to private schools increase or decrease segregation in education?

Using the 1980 data from the High School and Beyond survey of high school sophomores and seniors, they concluded that although minorities are underrepresented in private schools (question 1) they are also highly desegregated there (question 2). Using a simple accounting model, they conclude that the presence of private schools in the United States has not increased the segregation of black students in American education (question 3). Question 4 requires an exercise in predictive modeling, and is hence the most difficult; their answer is equivocal.

This chapter addresses the middle two of these questions. National data on segregation of private school blacks and Hispanics from private school whites and Anglos (question 2) is unavailable, but the first section of this chapter reports the degree of black-white and Hispanic-Anglo segregation in the two private systems where we have data, the Catholic schools of two large metropolitan areas. In both communities, the elementary schools are highly segregated — as segregated as the public schools ever were. The Catholic high schools are less segregated than the public high schools were when traditional nearest-school student assignments were used.

The second part of the chapter critically analyzes the accounting model used by Coleman, Hoffer and Kilgore to answer question 3. We conclude that the accounting model used to measure the segregative impact of private schools on the combined public and private system of schools is in error. It appears that Catholic schools, which are the majority of private schools in the US, have contributed to racial segregation in American education. But the chapter argues that the issue is complex and that the presence of private schools simultaneously increases and decreases segregation in schools.

The last section of the chapter discusses the educational effect of desegregated private schools for minority students. It is very difficult to predict how a subsidy for parents sending their children to private schools would affect racial segregation (question 4); this question is discussed briefly in the conclusions.

Racial Segregation in Private Schools

Coleman, Hoffer and Kilgore used data for eighty-four randomly sampled Catholic high schools and twenty-seven randomly sampled non-Catholic high schools to compute indices of segregation. They find that segregation of blacks from (non-Hispanic) whites is lower in either group of private schools than it is in public schools. (In this chapter, 'whites' always means 'non-Hispanic whites.') For Hispanics, the pattern is muddier; they seem less segregated in Catholic schools, more segregated in other private schools.

The Coleman, Kilgore, Hoffer Analysis

The statistical index that Coleman, Kilgore and Hoffer used is often called the 'exposure' index, E, and is simply the mean, computed across all students of one race, of the proportion of opposite-race students in their school. If there were no internal segregation within high schools, the mean proportion of students who are black in the average white student's high school could be thought of as the probability that the student sitting next to any white student is black (with a parallel interpretation for the exposure of black students to whites). The index ranges from a low of 0 to a maximum of the proportion of students of the opposite race in the set of schools as a whole. (Under conditions of perfect racial integration, a school district which was 30 per cent black would have each of its schools 30 per cent black, and E_{wb}, the mean percentage of black students in the high schools attended by white students, would be .30. If the district were perfectly segregated, each white would be in a school with no blacks, and the mean per cent black of the schools attended by whites would be 0.)

The indices can be used to measure the segregation of any group from any other — whites from non-whites, non-whites from whites, blacks from Hispanics, blacks from Anglos, etc. E_{bw}, the percentage white of the average black's school, is not the same as E_{bw}, the percentage black of the average white's school, but when the index is 'standardized'[1] the indices of segregation of whites from blacks and of blacks from whites are identical: $S_{bw} = S_{wb}$.

Using the standardized exposure index, Coleman, Hoffer and Kilgore found that private high schools were less segregated than public high schools.

The unstandardized indices show that whites in private schools attend schools with a smaller proportion of black students than do whites in public schools; 7 per cent of the average public school white student's classmates are black, compared to 4 per cent for a white in a Catholic school and 2 per cent for a white in another private school, simply because there are fewer blacks in private schools: 14 per cent of the students in public school are black, compared to 6 per cent in Catholic schools and 3 per cent in other private schools.

Standardization controls for this, and Coleman, Kilgore and Hoffer's standardized indices indicate that those blacks who are present in private schools are more evenly distributed across the schools than are the more numerous blacks in public schools. The standardized indices measuring segregation of blacks from whites were public schools .49, Catholic schools .31, and other private schools .21.[2]

One criticism (Page and Keith, 1981) argued for an index which took the small number of blacks in private schools into consideration, and standardized the indices of white exposure to blacks, E_{bw}, of both public and private schools by using the percentage black of all US high schools, both public and private. Since the percentage black is lower in private schools, private schools appear more segregated than public schools when this standardized index is used.

Whether one agrees with the criticism is a matter of values. There is no particularly compelling reason for using either standardized index; standardized indices are commonly used, but only because they are appropriate for evaluating the degree to which a school district deviates from a norm of all schools having identical racial composition, a measure that is useful in assessing the success of school desegregation plans, or for analyzing factors associated with segregation in particular school districts. In these cases the number of students of each race is taken as given; but a private school system's minority enrollment is not fixed by exogenous factors. It can recruit more or accept fewer minorities if it wishes. How should one evaluate a private school system which desegregates its minority students, but has very few? Using the unstandardized index, we find whites in private schools have fewer black schoolmates, and are in that sense more segregated. Blacks have more white schoolmates in private schools and are in that sense less segregated there. Which way to look at the problem is mostly a matter of taste.

Since many Hispanics are Catholic, it is not surprising that the Catholic schools in the Coleman, Kilgore and Hoffer sample had as many Hispanics as the public schools: both sectors were 7.1 per cent Hispanic, while the non-Catholic private schools were 4.4 per cent Hispanic. Hispanics are less segregated than blacks in both the public and Catholic sectors, where the average white non-Hispanic is in a school which is 5 per cent Hispanic (public sector) or 5.3 per cent Hispanic (Catholic sector). Non-Catholic private schools were more segregated (non-Hispanic whites' schools average 2.0 per cent Hispanic). The standardized indices were public .30, Catholic .25, and other private .55.

Sampling error is never an issue in single district segregation studies, since the entire school district is used, rather than a sample. But it is an issue in a national sample containing only eighty-four Catholic and twenty-seven non-Catholic private schools. In the report version Coleman, Hoffer and Kilgore (1981) suggest that the high index of segregation for Hispanics in non-Catholic schools may be due to sampling error, and note that 64 per cent of the Hispanics in their non-Catholic private schools are in one school. It may be that a larger sample would show something different. But this is also possible for the sample of blacks in non-Catholic schools or the samples of blacks and Hispanics in Catholic schools.

Sampling-error statistics do not exist for the segregation indices, so it is impossible to say what the confidence interval around each of these figures is. However, it may well be very high. If the sample of

Catholic schools had contained two all-black schools instead of the one apparently in the sample, the standardized index of segregation for Catholic schools would increase by approximately .10. Sampling error affects not only the segregation indices but estimates of the number of minority students in private schools. If it is a sampling fluke that caused 64 per cent of all the Hispanic students in non-Catholic private schools to be in a single predominantly Hispanic school, then that same sampling fluke would have given us an extremely high mis-estimate of the total number of Hispanics located in non-Catholic private schools.

Segregation in Catholic Schools in Two Big Cities

Coleman, Hoffer and Kilgore's indices of school segregation are unusual in that they are computed for the entire nation rather than for particular school districts. In all previous research, segregation indices have been computed separately for individual school districts and not for very large units, such as the entire United States. One problem with a national segregation index is that it is impossible to separate the index into that amount contributed by segregative policies and practices in individual school systems and the amount of segregation which arises because blacks and whites are distributed differently across regions and city types. If many blacks live in New York City and very few live in the Pacific Northwest, a high segregation index will arise regardless of local public school desegregation policies. Similarly, if private schools tend to be concentrated in areas which range widely in their racial mix, the index would have a very large value even if the private schools in each area worked hard to desegregate. Conversely, if the areas where private high schools are located tend to be more homogeneous in racial mix than the United States as a whole, then it would be possible for a lower segregation index to exist without private schools exerting much effort to desegregate.

The segregation of private schools in individual communities is of scholarly interest because private schools normally use a different geographic attendance rule than do public schools. Public schools almost always assign students on the basis of geography; a student at a certain address must attend a certain school. Normally a school draws all its students from a single geographic zone surrounding the school. This is sometimes called 'nearest school' or 'neighborhood school' assignment, even though attendance zones are normally drawn to accommodate school needs and student safety, not to conform to natural urban neighborhoods, and do not send all students to their nearest school. In desegregated school districts, schools also have a geographic assignment policy, but often with two non-adjacent geographic zones, one in a minority neighborhood and the other in a majority neighborhood, sending students to the same school. Recently school districts have begun experimenting with voluntary desegregation plans in which students are allowed to choose schools without geographic restriction. Catholic elementary schools often use parish boundaries, while Catholic high schools almost always have no geographic restrictions. What impact does this have on racial segregation?

We are unlikely to soon find the definitive answer to the question 'Are private school systems more or less segregated than public systems?'. No doubt the degree of racial segregation in private school systems will vary with the size and the racial and religious mix of the community being served, the school assignment policies used by the private school systems, and the school assignment policy used by the public schools with which the private schools compete for students.

While data on the racial composition of some private schools are available, they are not assembled into a single compendium as is the case with data on public schools in the United States.[3] However, data have been obtained from two large Northern metropolitan places: Chicago and Cuyahoga County (Cleveland).[4] Table 1 presents data for these school districts. For comparison purposes, data have also included segregation for the public schools. Table 1 analyzes segregation of blacks from non-Hispanic whites. Hispanics and other minority students are removed from the computations entirely; a school with two blacks, three whites and 100 members of other minority groups is treated as a school whose total enrollment is only five students. This is the simplest way to compare segregation of whites from blacks, since other minority groups often serve as a kind of buffer group which is more integrated with both blacks and whites than blacks and whites are with each other. Thus the more non-black minorities are present the higher the apparent amount of integration of (non-Hispanic) whites with others and the higher the integration of blacks with non-blacks, even though whites and blacks may remain highly segregated from each other (see Farley, 1981).

We used 1968 data for the public schools to be certain that we were calculating indices for public schools when they adhered to a strict 'nearest-school' policy. Beginning in the early 1970s both Chica-

Table 1:   *Segregation in Public and Private School Systems in Two Large Metropolitan Areas*

	Chicago		Cleveland	
	Public	Catholic	Public	Catholic
Elementary:	1968	1981	1968	1981
Total Enrollment	437,343	81,988	119,119	41,966
% black	55.3	27.9	58.2	10
% other minority	10.1	19.9	1.6	3.8
B-W dissimilarity index, d	94	94	90	90
% black of average whites' school, E_{wb}	6.0	3.9	8.6	2.1
Standardized index, S_{bw}	.90	.92	.86	.79
% of all blacks who are in schools with more whites than blacks	2.3	4.9	0.8	16.8
% of all whites who are in schools with more blacks than whites	4.4	1.5	5.5	0.6
High school				
Total Enrollment	136,719	33,880	35,627	—
% black	46.0	16.9	47.0	9.1
% other minority	7.2	13.4	1.7	2.4
B-W dissimilarity index, d	80	73	87	65
% black of average whites' school: E_{wb}	14.0	7.2	9.1	7.4
Standardized index, S_{bw}	.72	.63	.81	.19
% of all blacks who are in schools with more whites than blacks	9.5	31.0	7.6	100
% of all whites who are in schools with more blacks than whites	9.2	1.9	5.0	0

go and Cleveland allowed at least small amounts of desegregation to occur, and Cleveland now has an extensive desegregation plan. The Cleveland public schools cover the city of Cleveland; the Catholic Diocese covers the whole metropolitan area, and the data in table 1 are for the whole of Cuyahoga County, which covers some of Cleveland's suburbs along with the central city.

Table 1 uses three indices of desegregation: the exposure index E_{bw} (the percentage black of the average white's school), the standardized index, S_{bw}, and the other commonly-used index, the index of dissimilarity, which is based upon the sum across all schools of the absolute difference between the proportion of the district's whites and the proportion of the district's blacks found in each school building.[5]

The dissimilarity index ranges from 0 (perfect desegregation) to 100 (perfect segregation). The dissimilarity index can be interpreted as the percentage of students of either race who would have to be relocated in order that every school in the district have the same racial mix. Both indices are calculated using only the whites and blacks.

Table 1 shows that the two Catholic school systems differ from their counterpart public systems and also from each other. Both systems are smaller than the public schools, and have proportionately fewer blacks but more non-black minorities. The elementary schools in both cities are highly segregated, as segregated as the public schools in 1968. The Chicago public schools in 1968 were as highly segregated as any system in the north. It and other highly segregated public schools have all desegregated to at least a small degree; this means that the Chicago Archdiocese may be the most segregated elementary school system, public or private, in the US.

The exposure indices show the same pattern. In Chicago Catholic schools, the average white child is in an elementary school which is only 3.9 per cent black; for Cleveland the figure is 2.1 per cent. The standardized index for Cleveland is only .79 because the Cleveland Catholic schools are only 10 per cent black.[6]

The last two rows of the top panel indicate the extent of segregation in another way; they show that in Chicago Catholic elementary schools, only 4.9 per cent of black students are in predominantly white schools and only 1.5 per cent of whites are in predominantly black schools. In 1968 the Chicago public schools had fewer blacks in predominantly white schools (2.3 per cent) and more whites in predominantly black schools (4.4 per cent). This is for two reasons: the public schools had fewer predominantly white schools and more predominantly black ones; and public schools had a rigid geographic school assignment policy. Black students were not allowed to transfer to predominantly white schools but white students were also not allowed to flee from predominantly black schools. We suspect that in the Catholic schools it is easier for white children to transfer out of their predominantly black parish school.

The pattern in Cleveland's public schools in 1968 and Catholic schools today is the same but more pronounced; many more blacks were in predominantly white schools in the Catholic system, but very few whites were in predominantly black schools. In Catholic schools 83.2 per cent of blacks but only 0.6 per cent of whites are in schools where whites are in the minority.

Catholic high schools are less segregated than public schools were in 1968. Both the dissimilarity and exposure indices show this. The last two lines of the lower panel of the table show why this is true. In Chicago, 31 per cent of all blacks in Catholic high schools are in predominantly white schools. Older than elementary school students, black high school students are apparently more willing to embark on long bus rides to schools in white areas. Whites use the open-enrollment policies of Catholic high schools to avoid black schools. Only 1.9 per cent of whites in Chicago Catholic schools go to predominantly black high schools. The data for Cleveland are more striking because all eighteen Catholic high schools in Cuyohoga County are predominantly white. This yields an extraordinarily low standardized exposure index. The dissimilarity index is rather high, because this index is sensitive to a maldistribution of blacks within these schools; blacks are concentrated in nine of the eighteen schools, although there are not enough blacks to make a majority in any of these schools.[7]

The Effect of School System Size on Segregation

One would have expected the Catholic elementary schools to show less segregation than the public schools because the absolute number of black students enrolled is smaller. In cities with a high level of residential segregation, the amount of desegregation which occurs under a neighborhood school policy is basically a function of the relative size of the boundary zone between black and white areas (where integrated neighborhood schools might appear) compared to the size of the black residential area. At one extreme, if the black population is too small to fill one public elementary school, the public school serving this area under a neighborhood school policy would necessarily have an attendance zone large enough to include some whites and result in the school being integrated. At the other extreme where there are very large black residential areas, as is the case of these cities, the number of black students living on the boundary of the black residential area and thus likely to attend integrated schools with whites under a neighborhood school policy is small relative to the total black school age population.

If Catholic schools serve a small black population, they can only do so by providing elementary schools which serve extremely large areas; even with a large black residential area, if attendance in Catholic schools occurs with relatively low density, the black areas served by each Catholic elementary school might be very large and could easily go outside the black residential area to include whites as well.

Figure 1 shows the data for a number of public school systems, supporting the hypothesis that districts with small black populations are less segregated. In that figure we have plotted the 1968 exposure indices (for elementary and secondary schools combined) for the seventy-two largest northern public school districts, plotted against the (natural log of) total black enrollment in the school districts. Generally, the fewer blacks in a district, the lower the level of seg-regation in 1968, when nearly all these public school systems used a simple neighborhood school policy. We have shown this by fitting an s-shaped cubic equation to the 1968 data. An s-curve is appropriate since there are both floor and ceiling effects in the standardized exposure index.

We have identified the Chicago and Cleveland public schools in figure 1; they both show very high levels of segregation. We have also shown, in the upper center and upper right, the data points for the combined Catholic elementary and high schools of Chicago and Cleveland. The Catholic systems, with smaller black enrollments should be less segregated. Chicago is not; Cleveland is, but this is because of its lower high school segregation. We have already seen that its elementary schools are as segregated as the public schools. Perhaps this model of segregation as a function of black enrollment is not applicable to private school systems, but it does intuitively seem that school systems with colorblind school assignment policies will have less segregation if they have fewer minorities.

It looks like these Catholic systems have as much segregation as would appear in a typical public school system using a neighborhood school policy. Such a neighborhood school assignment policy has been judged illegal in nearly every city. Taeuber and James (1982) show Boston's Catholic schools to be much more segregated than the court-desegregated Boston public schools. We also see in figure 1 that public districts are likely to have reduced their level of segregation in the decade from 1968 to 1978. A second curve has been drawn to show the relationship of black population size to the 1978 standardized exposure index, and this curve is much lower. The 1978 curve is furthest below the 1968 curve in the middle of the figure; districts in the left region would benefit little from desegregation since their indexes were already low in 1968, while districts with very large black populations were unlikely to desegregate.

The Effects of Open-Enrollment Policies

One explanation for the high level of elementary school segregation in these Catholic elementary schools and the much lower level of segregation at the high school level is that both Catholic school districts do not use a strictly enforced neighborhood attendance boundary system. Most public schools in the era before desegregation assigned students to their nearest school under a strict geographic rule — exceptions were made on a case-by-case basis but generally discouraged. Catholic elementary schools typically do not strictly enforce

Figure 1: Level of Segregation By Number of Black Students
In District, for 72 Cities Using Nearest-School Assignment
(1968 data)

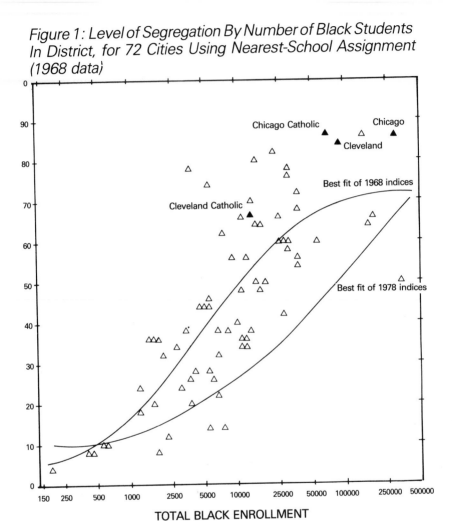

TOTAL BLACK ENROLLMENT

their parish boundary rules, and Catholic high schools usually have no attendance zones. At the high school level this results in an increase in segregation to the extent that black students are willing to travel (sometimes long) distances in order to attend predominantly white high schools. For example, in Chicago there are twelve Catholic high schools where blacks outnumber whites; but 1746 blacks chose not to attend them, instead traveling to one of thirty predominantly white high schools; there are only two high schools within the Chicago city limits which do not enroll any blacks at all.

However, an unrestricted free choice system works to further segregation in an important way. Just as blacks are free to travel to predominantly white schools, so are whites free to avoid predominantly black schools. In Chicago, only 1.9 per cent of all white non-Hispanics are in high schools where blacks outnumber them, and even this overstates the case, since 90 per cent of these students are in schools which are predominately Hispanic or in one nearly racially balanced school. Only 0.2 per cent of whites are in schools where blacks are 51 per cent or more of the total enrollment (including Hispanics).

At the elementary school level, parents are much less willing to have their children travel long distances, and this is reflected in a much higher level of segregation. In Chicago there are ninety-five Catholic elementary schools which are predominantly white and enroll fewer than ten black students — most of them having none. At the same time, freedom of choice does mean that whites are free to avoid predominantly black schools, and they do. Only 226 of Cuyahoga County's 36,000 non-Hispanic white elementary parochial school students attend predominantly black schools. By comparison, there were nearly 7000 whites in predominantly black public elementary schools.

Thus, the open enrollment policy of the Catholic schools probably creates less segregation at the high school level than a strict 'neighborhood school' student assignment policy. But at the same time there appears to be more segregation in Catholic elementary schools than would result from a 'neighborhood school' policy. These same conclusions would probably also apply to a public school system with an open enrollment policy.

Private schools are not permitted to discriminate in their pupil-assignment policy, but there has never been an effort to require parochial school systems to adhere to the desegregation policies normally required of public school systems. Certainly no public school system as large as either of these private school systems and with as small a number of black students could expect to avoid being required to desegregate by a court.

Segregation of Hispanics from Non-Hispanic Whites

Table 2 shows the degree of segregation of Hispanics from non-Hispanic whites in Chicago and Cleveland. Table 2 has the same format as table 1, but does not show 1968 public school data for comparison, since much migration of Hispanics to these cities occurred after 1968. The segregation levels in both cities are high at the elementary level, lower for high schools. For comparison, Farley (1981) computes for Chicago a combined elementary and high school Hispanic versus non-Hispanic white dissimilarity index of 65 and a standardized exposure index of 50 for 1978.

Table 2: Hispanic Segregation in Chicago and Cuyahoga County Caholic Schools

	Chicago	Cuyahoga county
Elementary schools		
Dissimilarity index	68%	60%
%Hispanic of schools attended by average non-Hispanic whites	11.9%	2.3%
Standardized exposure index	49	14
% of Hispanics in schools with more non-Hispanic whites than Hispanics	43.7%	100%
% of non-Hispanic whites in schools with more Hispanics than non-Hispanic whites	3.9%	0%
High schools		
Dissimilarity index	44	38
% Hispanic of schools attended by average non-Hispanic whites	11.1	1.6
Standardized exposure index	26	3
% Hispanics in schools with more non-Hispanic whites than Hispanics	72.0%	100
% non-Hispanic whites in schools with more Hispanics than non-Hispanic whites	1.3%	0

Segregation in Other Cities

The degree of segregation by race in private schools can vary greatly from one city to another across the United States. We see that in the difference between Cleveland and Chicago. Cleveland, for whatever reason, does not have a predominantly black high school. Consequently, its level of segregation in its high schools is much lower. By extension, we should expect to find a large number of cities where the public schools have predominantly black public schools and there is no predominantly black parochial elementary or high school. This leads us to predict that there are certain cities in the US where the Catholic elementary schools may be less segregated than the public schools. This might occur in some cities which have relatively small total pupil enrollments and large proportions of black students in the public schools. East Chicago, Gary, Oakland, Trenton, Newark and Hartford are examples of cities which might fit this description. All are relatively small but have such a large black proportion of the schools that their schools are highly segregated, and it may be that one or more of these cities has parochial schools which are less segregated than the public schools.

White Flight: The Effect of Private Schools on Public School Segregation

Private schools can also affect the amount of racial segregation in education by providing havens for whites fleeing from desegregated schools. If whites transfer from schools which have larger numbers of blacks to schools with fewer blacks, the amount of segregation will increase.

Discussions of white flight to private schools have usually been concerned with flight from newly desegregated public school systems. There seems to be a general consensus that white flight does occur in many cases when public schools are desegregated. White flight is especially likely to occur when whites are reassigned from their own neighborhood school, and when the schools that they are assigned to have large black populations or are in black neighborhoods, (Rossell, 1983). In one analysis of the Boston school desegregation plan, Rossell and Ross (1979) concluded that over half of the flight from public schools by whites after desegregation was to private schools. The appendix of their report lists a number of parochial and other private schools whose enrollment increased markedly after desegregation; the types of schools range widely, seeming to include all types of private schools. In a second analysis of Boston, Taylor and Stinchecombe (1977) found that the families who moved from Boston were more tolerant of school desegregation than the white families who remained behind, suggesting that most of the families who moved to the suburbs were the young, well educated, upwardly mobile families who would have still moved to the suburbs if there had been no desegregation plan. This supports the idea that in Boston much racially motivated change in enrollment came about because of movement to private schools, not residential relocation.

Orfield (1978) draws the same conclusion in analyzing the early stages of the Los Angeles desegregation plan — he found no softening of the central city housing market but a considerable effort under way to establish new private schools.

Another case which provides evidence that private schools are used to escape desegregation comes from Jacksonville where Giles (1977) finds a drop in white enrollment for those particular grades where white students are reassigned to schools in black neighborhoods. In the Jacksonville plan this only occurs in certain middle school grades. For those grades the white enrollment is considerably lower than it is for the grades before and after that. This again suggests that private schools are used, since families who moved out of the school district would be lost permanently and there would be no increase in public school attendance among whites in the upper grades (the school district in this case covers the entire quite large Duval County; it would be quite inconvenient for families who work in the Jacksonville area to move beyond the county boundaries to escape desegregation).

None of these studies provides us with a reasonable estimate of how much movement to private schools has occurred because of desegregation nationally. Boston is probably not typical of other cities; nearly a third of Boston's whites attended private schools before desegregation began; less than a dozen large cities in the Unites States had a higher proportion of their white population in private school (Becker, 1978). Boston schools also experienced more controversy and violence than nearly any other city involved in desegregation. In other cities, white flight may have been lower; in Cleveland, only 3 per cent of the Catholic school enrollment is non-Catholic whites, suggesting that white non-Catholics are not using it as a haven (Dobos, 1984). Thus, it seems safe to conclude that there is a considerable amount of flight from newly desegregated public schools to private schools in a number of different school districts, but not in all; but there is no data to permit us to establish what proportion of all white flight is to private schools or the total number of students who moved from public to private schools because of desegregation.

There is also racially motivated white flight from segregated school systems. If, as Rossell argues, whites flee the public schools to avoid having their children attend predominantly black schools, then many cities with segregated schools will have flight from the schools in changing neighborhoods where the public school is predominantly black under a neighborhood school policy. Becker (1978) analyzes growth in private school enrollment in the largest cities in the US for the decade of the 1960s, when there was little desegregation in southern school districts and even less in the north. He found that the larger the black enrollment in the public schools, the larger the growth of the private schools serving that city. This is, in fact, the single best predictor in his multiple regression equation estimating growth in private school enrollment from a number of demographic factors. Of the fifty-two cities studied the city with the largest increase in the percentage of white students in private school was Washington, DC: 37 per cent of its whites were in private school in 1959 and 46 per cent in 1969.

The Coleman, Hoffer and Kilgore Model of Flight to Private Schools

Coleman, Hoffer and Kilgore construct an accounting model which leads them to conclude that the existence of private schools does not increase racial segregation in American education. However, their model is based on an erroneous assumption and it seems likely that the conclusion of the model is wrong.

They argue that one can analyze the role of private schools by asking a question, 'What would happen if all private schools were closed and the students presently enrolled in them were returned to public schools?'. If private schools have had a segregating influence in America, then closing them and reassigning all the students to public schools should result in a lower index of segregation. They conduct a 'thought experiment' which does exactly this, and conclude that if private schools were closed the public schools would be no more racially integrated than the present mix of public and private schools are — hence the private schools do not have a segregating influence.

Unfortunately, there is a serious error in their hypothetical model.[8] They assume that when private schools are closed, the white and black students in them will be dispersed into the existing public school system, with each public school gaining an increase in white and black enrollment proportional to its present white and black enrollment. Each school would increase its tenth grade white enrollment by 7.6 per cent of its present white enrollment, and increase its black enrollment by 2.6 per cent of its present black enrollment.)

Such a model may seem reasonable at first glance, but a hypothetical example using Chicago's 1968 public high school data, shown in table 3, immediately reveals the problem. The students should be returned to the schools that they would attend if the private schools did not exist. Yet this model assumes that each public school across the nation would gain a number of whites equal to 7.6 per cent of its present white enrollment, implying that students left all these public schools or chose not to attend them equally, in a manner uncorrelated with the racial composition of the schools. This means, first, that since there are only 63,936 whites in the Chicago public schools, the thought experiment would add only 4859 whites to the Chicago public schools, even though there were 23,634 whites enrolled in Chicago Catholic schools in 1980. Second, it means that nearly all whites in Catholic schools are assumed to live in areas served by predominantly white schools; for example, that only twenty-one Catholic school whites lived in areas served by Chicago's twenty-three high schools which were 95 per cent or more black. This runs exactly contrary to all the research on white flight, which indicates that whites are more likely to withdraw to attend private schools if they are assigned to schools with large numbers of black students.

Table 3: Application of the Coleman-Hoffer-Kilgore Accounting Model to the Chicago Public High Schools

Percent racial mix* % high school	Before closing Catholic schools			After closing Catholic schools	
	Number of schools	Number of whites	Number of blacks	Increase in number of whites (7.6%)	Increase in number of blacks (2.6%)
0–5% black	20	31380	306	2385	8
5–20% black	12	19050	2472	1448	64
20–50% black	7	6602	3233	502	84
50–80% black	10	6624	11917	503	310
80–95% black	0	0	0	0	0
95–100% black	23	280	45007	21	1170
TOTAL	72	63936	63005	4859	1636
white + black total		126,941		6495	

* Non-black minorities excluded

In other words, this model assumes that there was no white flight from public schools to private schools because of race. Of course, if there were no white flight for racial reasons, then there is no reason to assume that the movement from public schools to private schools created segregation.

We do not know the extent of white flight. Perhaps in the larger scheme of things the white flight in Boston, Los Angeles and Jacksonville is negligible and the Coleman, Hoffer and Kilgore model is a sensible approximation of the real world. But we do not know this and there is certainly no reason to assume something which runs directly contrary to the little existing evidence.

The other problem with the model is that it is based exclusively on high school data. If Cleveland and Chicago are representative of other cities, there is a good deal more segregation at the elementary level in private schools than at the high school level. Much of the movement in those cities from public schools to private schools consisted of blacks leaving segregated public elementary schools to attend segregated private schools, and whites leaving a mixture of segregated and integrated elementary schools to attend schools which are overwhelmingly white.

The Other Side of the Argument: What Private Schools May Be Doing to Help Desegregation

The role of private schools in racial segregation in American education is not simply one-sided. There are three ways in which private schools may work to help integrate American schools or at least help integrate the neighborhoods these schools serve. First, Rossell (1983) has shown that the white flight which occurs after desegregation tends to be of limited duration. By approximately the fourth year of a desegregation plan the rate of white loss is, according to some models, actually less than would have occurred had there been no desegregation. We suspect that one of the reasons for this is that many families withdraw their children not by moving to the suburbs but by entering them in private schools while remaining in the city. These families are likely to return their children to public schools after a few years of desegregation. Had there been no private schools at least some of these families would have moved to the suburbs, and in doing so would have made it impossible for their children to later return to the desegregated public schools of the central city. If whites flee from desegregation, it is preferable (from a desegregationist's point of view) for them to remain in the city sending their children to private schools than for them to move to the suburbs. (At the same time, we should note that many families would leave their children in the public school and not move to the suburbs if no private schools existed.)

The same argument applies to white flight from segregated systems. In segregated school systems it is often the case that a changing neighborhood is served by an all-black public elementary school long before the neighborhood itself loses its last white family. This is not because Blacks have larger families than whites, but because the whites in older changing neighborhoods are often themselves older, with children who have finished school. Thus, a number of homes occupied by whites will have relatively few children of school age, and some of those will have always attended parochial schools for non-racial reasons. In contrast, black families moving into the area often move there in order to locate a good public school for their children. For this reason a neighborhood may be racially mixed but have a school which is overwhelmingly black and hence unacceptable to many white families. In this situation a private school alternative may enable some families to remain living in their integrated neighborhood rather than moving out and hurrying the process of 'tipping'.

It is, however, possible for public schools to provide the same sort of opportunity. In some urban areas, racially balanced magnet schools serve as alternatives to the neighborhood school for white families in integrated neighborhoods where the local school is overwhelmingly black. Of course, a segregated school system can stabilize integrated neighborhoods by adopting a full-blown desegregation plan which guarantees residents of neighborhoods in transition an integrated public school for the indefinite future. Cities whose public school systems are desegregated do find their integrated neighborhoods considerably more stable and are experiencing a growth in residential integration as a result (see Pearce, Crain, Farley and Taeuber, 1984; Pearce, 1980). But, in the absence of public school desegregation, a private school system may serve to slow neighborhood change by providing a 'haven' for white school children whose parents would move out otherwise.

A predominately white private school system sometimes provides an opportunity for voluntary integration for some black students. In cities like Chicago and Cleveland, the Catholic school system serves as a last resort for minority families fearful of low quality of education and serious discipline problems in inner city public schools. If there were no private schools there would be more whites in the public schools in Chicago, but the Chicago public schools still might not be racially desegregated. Many black students would be trapped in inner city public schools without a reasonable alternative.

Whether the transfer of minority students from public schools to private schools creates desegregation for them or not depends, of course, on whether the private school systems are segregated. In the two large cities we have studied, there is not much chance that a minority student enrolling in a Catholic elementary school will receive a desegregated education. But at the high school level in Cleveland, where there are no predominantly black or predominantly Hispanic high schools, minorities will be desegregated. For cities like Hartford, whose public schools are segregated but which have no predominantly black Catholic elementary school, the presence of parochial schools can play either a segregating or a desegregating role, depending on whether the number of blacks entering the private school system outweighs the number of whites using the private school system to escape attending integrated schools.

The public schools in large metropolitan areas with large black school enrollments could themselves provide an alternative to segregated education for these students. In the St. Louis metropolitan area a large number of black students assigned to segregated schools in St. Louis City are taking advantage of the opportunity to transfer to white suburban public schools under a federal court order. Milwaukee and Indianapolis are two other cities where inner city black students are permitted to attend suburban public schools. In Cleveland and Chicago a very large number of segregated black students could be desegregated if they were allowed to attend suburban public school systems. Unfortunately these cities do not permit transfer across district lines. Thus, in some cities a private school system or the suburban public schools provides an opportunity for desegregation and improved education which is not otherwise available. Even this can be viewed as a two-edged sword, however, because it amounts to a kind of tracking in which the children from highly motivated families are allowed to segregate themselves into schools which in many cases are selective, excluding students with academic or behavior problems. The public schools thus become a bottom track, and evidence from studies of tracked schools indicate that students in the lower tracks learn less than they would if they were in heterogeneously grouped rooms. Thus the operation of two school systems may function to make inner city low-income schools worse than they would otherwise be. (For a discussion of the public-private schools as a 'tracked' educational system, see McPartland and McDill, 1982.)

Private schools are a two-edged sword, encouraging racial integration of the public schools and of central city neighborhoods (and providing desegregated education for some black students) at the same time that they serve as havens for white flight which destabilizes both segregated and desegregated central city school systems and creates segregated public schools. We do not have all of the data necessary to make a balancing of these competing processes.

The Educational Effects of Attending Desegregated Private Schools

Coleman, Hoffer and Kilgore and also Greeley (1982) talk about the educational benefits of parochial schools to minority students. Both refer to the idea that the parochial school is a 'common school', better able to serve the needs of a wide range of students than is the public school system. Greeley makes this argument explicit, saying that the Catholic schools have had a tradition of educating immigrants entering the United States and therefore are almost instinctively oriented toward providing avenues for upward mobility of persons not yet in the mainstream of the society.

It is clearly the case that the black students in private schools in the High School and Beyond sample score much higher on standard achievement tests than do blacks attending public school. There is no way, however, to be sure that the common school hypothesis is correct. There are two alternative arguments. First is that private schools are highly selective and only admit brighter minority students; the second argument is that private schools are educationally superior to public schools for minority students because, having fewer blacks, they are in many cases racially integrated. Research on public schools has indicated that black students attending desegregated public schools score higher on achievement tests as a result of that desegregation. In Cleveland and Chicago, black students who transfer from public schools to private schools are not very likely to receive a desegregated education, at least at the elementary school level, so we don't think that there is much chance of an educational benefit being derived because of desegregation in these cities. But there must be a large number of smaller cities where black students can leave segregated inner city schools to attend predominantly white Catholic schools, and here there would be good reason to expect their education to improve because of desegregation.

A recent review of the literature on desegregation and minority achievement seems to yield convincing evidence that minority students in desegregated schools score higher on standard achievement tests than they would if they were in segregated schools. Previous research had been inconclusive on this, but the latest review (Crain and Mahard, 1983) identifies a factor which explains reasonably well why previous research often found conflicting results. Most studies of desegregation analyze the test scores of black students who attended segregated schools through second or third grade and then transferred to desegregated schools and were tested shortly thereafter. In fact, this is an unrepresentative situation, since nearly all desegregation plans in the United States begin in kindergarten and first grade, and nearly all desegregated students attend desegregated schools throughout their educational career. (The reason why there are so many studies done of students who have transferred from segregated to desegregated schools is because so many studies are done during the first year or two of desegregation, and researchers do not attempt to study the achievement of students in first and second grade because tests administered to students in the upper elementary grades are more reliable.)

The Crain and Mahard review identified twenty-three studies that compared black students who had been desegregated from first grade to blacks in segregated schools or in the same grade in the same school district before desegregation. The authors of these studies analyzed forty-five samples of students involved in nineteen desegregation plans. Of the forty-five studies, forty show positive effects and for those for which a size of effect could be estimated, desegregation appeared to raise achievement by a quarter of a standard deviation — the equivalent of 25 points on the SAT verbal or quantitative score.[9]

Will Private School Subsidies Lead to Desegregation?

The last question asked by Coleman, Kilgore and Hoffer is whether any sort of subsidy to private schools would increase or decrease segregation. They use a simple model in which they liken a subsidy to a general increase in affluence, and conclude that the students on the margin, those most likely to shift, will include enough minorities so that the differences in racial mix between public and private schools will decline. The model has been severely criticized by several analysts (see Crain and Hawley, 1982, for a review) and we will not do so again here, except to note that their model shows the most segregated and deprived sector of the population, low-income blacks, *least* likely to transfer to private schools.

In fact, it is very unlikely that all subsidy plans will have the same effect on segregation; they will depend on the specifics of the plan. The voucher plan proposed in California has strict controls designed to encourage desegregation and participation of low-income families; a tuition tax credit would clearly not encourage low-income families to transfer. It is also likely that specific requirements for desegregation of private schools might be either imposed or required by the Constitution. For example, subsidy legislation (or a court order) might require that transportation be provided to enable minority students to attend desegregated private schools. Certainly one can easily imagine a private school subsidy plan which would enable more low-income minority students to gain a desegregated education. But it is useless to speculate on the abstract, since so much depends on the specifics of any legislation.

Conclusions

The optimistic conclusions drawn by Coleman, Hoffer and Kilgore do not seem to be supported by the data from the two large metropolitan areas studied here. From these data there is little reason to believe that the impact of private schools is simply benign. At the same time not enough data are available to draw the more complicated conclusion which is probably the correct one: private schools further the segregation of schools under certain conditions and encourage racial integration of either schools or residential neighborhoods in others.

Notes

1   The index can be standardized by dividing by the percentage of the entire universe of students which is of the opposite race, and subtracting this from 1.0. This yields an index which ranges from 0 when schools all have the same racial compositions to 1.00 when they are totally segregated. The formula for the indices are

$$\text{unstandardized: } E_{wb} = \frac{\sum_{i=1}^{n} W_i b_i}{\sum_{1=1}^{n} W_i}$$

$$\text{standardized: } \quad S_{bw} = S_{wb} = 1 - \frac{E_{wb}}{b}$$

where W_i = number of whites in the ith school, b_i the percentage black of the ith school, and b the percentage black of the entire sample of schools (usually a whole single school district but in Coleman, Kilgore and Hoffer's case a national sample of schools.)

2 TAEUBER and JAMES (1982) note that of several indices available, this index, which they call the variance ratio index and we call the standardized exposure index, is most sensitive to the racial mix of the schools. A group of schools with fewer blacks will appear less segregated than a group with more blacks. They compute a dissimilarity index (discussed below) and find segregation levels of public and private schools to be more similar: public .70, private .63.

3 Since 1967, the United States government has published on computer files and bound volumes the racial composition of all schools in all but the smallest school districts. The first of these was *Directory of Public Schools in the United States with Enrollment and Staff by Race, 1967*, National Center for Education Statistics, US Government Printing Office, 1969. Volumes are readily available only for even numbered years after that.

4 The data for Chicago was provided by Joe T. Darden, Urban Affairs Program, Michigan State University: the data for Cleveland was provided by Richard Obermanns of the Cuyohoga Plan of Cleveland, a group concerned with housing segregation issues.

5 Specifically the formula for computing the dissimilarity index is

$$d = 100 \, \frac{\sum_{i=1}^{n} \left| \frac{B_i}{B} - \frac{W_i}{W} \right|}{2}$$

Where B_i and W_i are the number of blacks and whites in the ith school and B and W the number of blacks and whites in the total district.

6 DOBOS (1984) reanalyzed the data using only the Catholic elementary schools in the city of Cleveland. These schools are 23 per cent black and have a dissimilarity index of 90.

7 DOBOS (1984) finds the dissimilarity index for the high schools in Cleveland proper to be only 50.

8 This argument has also been presented by TAEUBER and JAMES (1982) and CRAIN (1981).

9 In 1982, the National Institute of Education organized a panel of mainly conservative experts to rebut this review. The panelists concluded that desegregation did raise achievement but that the effects were much smaller than those found by Crain and Mahard. None of the panelists elected to test the hypothesis that the effects would be stronger for studies of students desegregated in Kindergarten or first grade on the grounds that it is methodologically too difficult to study students who are desegregated in kindergarten or first grade and that twenty-one of the twenty-three studies analyzed by Crain and Mahard were methodologically too weak to be evaluated (COOK *et al.*, 1984).

12 Educational Choice for Blacks in Urban Private Elementary Schools

Barbara L. Schneider and Diana T. Slaughter

Even though enrollments in private schools across the nation essentially remained constant or declined between 1970 and 1980, as did those of public schools, the number of black students enrolled in private schools nearly doubled in this same ten-year period (National Center for Education Statistics, 1981). If it were not for the presence of minority students in private schools, many of these schools would have experienced declining enrollments. In Chicago-area Catholic schools, black students represented 17 per cent of the total population of elementary school students in 1970. Within a ten-year period, the percentage of black students in the school population increased to 30 per cent. Catholic schools are not the only type of private schools that have shown increases in black enrollments. Headmasters of small, private independent schools also report increases in Black enrollments (Private School Report, 1981).

Several speculations have been made to explain the growth in black enrollments. Usually, authors emphasize that black families choosing private schools are seeking to improve their child's academic performance, socialize their child in an educational setting that closely complements their own beliefs and aspirations, and exert greater influence and authority over school policies (Abramowitz and Stackhouse, 1981; Coleman, Hoffer and Kilgore, 1981; Blum, 1985). In addition to these explanations, Slaughter and Schneider (1986) have suggested that this nationwide phenomenon could be the result of growing black dissaffection with the quality of education offered in neighborhood public schools, rising affordability of private education among black middle-class families, changing admission and recruitment policies in urban private schools to expand the racial and ethnic population of the potential student applicant pool, and a changing 'zeitgeist' in America since the 1954 Supreme Court decision in the *Brown* case.

After reviewing black enrollment trends, the limited empirical research on school choice, and the lack of information on school life in private elementary schools, we conducted an ethnographic study, to learn why black parents are sending their children to private schools and what black children are experiencing in these schools (Slaughter and Schneider, 1986). Assuming that the most appropriate way to answer these questions was to gain a holistic understanding of how black children are socialized in their school cultures, we decided to use ethnographic data collection techniques which included open-ended and informal interviews with school administrators, teachers and parents, narrative school observations, reviews of school records and publications, and analyses of achievement tests and personality inventories administered by teachers to the students. This ethnographic approach revealed new information about why black families, who for the most part attended public schools in the past, are now selecting private schools in increasing numbers. While limitations of ethnographic research prevent generalizing the findings of this study to the entire black population achieving access to private schools, the data provide insights into black educational values, particularly the expectations that influence their views of what constitutes quality schooling for black children.

To gain a fuller understanding of the significance of changes in black school preferences, this chapter describes the types of private schools blacks are currently attending, reviews the ethnographic data collected regarding educational goals of black parents, and interprets how these findings contribute to our understanding of educational choice.

Types of Private Schools Black Students are Attending

Private schools are typically categorized into two major groups, sectarian and non-sectarian. Approximately 85 per cent of all private schools are religiously affiliated, and of that group over three-fourths are Roman Catholic (Erickson, Nault and Cooper, 1978). Other types of sectarian schools include Baptist, Episcopal, Friends, Greek Orthodox, Jewish, Lutheran, Methodist, National Union of Christian Schools, Presbyterian, Protestant and Seventh Day Adventist (Illinois State Board of Education, 1981). The non-sectarian category includes the following school types: (i) independent schools, often referred to as elite schools, which are highly selective in entrance requirements and offer a college-bound curriculum; and (ii) alternative schools, often established as an 'alternative' to public education and sometimes referred to as street academies, free schools or neighborhood community schools. Usually considered part of this latter group are schools such as Montessori schools which follow a specific educational philosophy, and parent-operated schools which are exclusively managed by parent groups. Many of these alternative schools, like elite schools, also provide a college preparatory curriculum.

Increases in black enrollments in these various types of private schools have been extremely difficult to document. For example, the Illinois State Board of Education, not unlike other state education agencies, does not tabulate minority enrollments in private schools. Part of the state's difficulty in attempting to estimate the private school population is that some schools choose not to publicly release any type of enrollment information. Student data recorded by the state of Illinois for every 'recognized private school' has been limited to numbers of boys and girls, and number of students who report family incomes below poverty level (*ibid*).

Associations such as the National Association for Independent Schools, to which elite schools tend to belong, or Alternative School Networks, to which some alternative schools belong, typically do not disseminate information on specific minority enrollments at various levels, such as the number of black students in elementary schools. Moreover, the National Center on Educational Statistics does not record minority enrollments by school type or level (Private School Survey, 1980). However, the US Census Bureau does tabulate enrollments in church-related and other private schools by racial and ethnic groups and family income (US Bureau of the Census, Detailed Population Characteristics, 1984).

Even though the majority of black students attend public schools, the number of black low and middle income families attending private school is not an inconsequential group (US Census Detailed Population Characteristics, 1984). Private school enrollments at the elementary level among the black community is occurring among low, middle and high income families (see table 1).

The number of black families below the poverty level who are selecting private schools is surprising. Nearly 25 per cent of those black families choosing to send their children to private elementary schools have reported incomes below $9999. Many parents in these economic circumstances are faced with having to make significant financial sacrifices to send their children to private schools particularly if scholarship aid is not available.

The black private school population consists not only of poor

Table 1: *Private Elementary School Enrollments and Black Family Income*

School type	Family Income								Totals
	Less than $5000	$5000 to 9999	$10,000 to 14,999	$15,000 to 19,999	$20,000 to 24,999	$25,000 to 34,999	$35,000 to 49,999	50,000 or more	
Children age 6–13 enrolled in public school	816,254 22%	829,047 22%	621,713 17%	477,507 13%	358,378 9.6%	393,161 10.6%	164,937 4%	46,976 1%	3,707,972 99%*
Children age 6–13 enrolled in church-related schools	22,863 11%	27,315 13%	29,891 14%	28,020 13.5%	27,129 13%	39,964 19%	24,933 12%	7,379 3.5%	207,494 99%
Children age 6–13 enrolled in other private schools	4,887 12%	5,383 13%	5,593 14%	4,880 12%	4,709 11.8%	6,630 16.5%	5,267 13%	2,663 6.7%	40,012 99%

* Percentages are rounded to nearest hundredth.
Source: US Bureau of the Census, Detailed Population Characteristics, PC80-1-D1-A. March 1984, Washington, DC, US Government Printing Office.

families selecting religious schools. Census data at the elementary level reveal that the greatest proportion of those black families selecting private education are in the middle income range (see table 1). Black middle income families choosing private schools are disproportionately represented in comparison to the numbers of all black children in public elementary school in these same income categories (see table 1).

Although it is difficult to determine in what type of private schools blacks have been matriculating, interviews with various school personnel and a small study of Chicago private schools indicate some interesting trends for Chicago (Schneider and Slaughter, 1984). The largest proportion of black families enroll their children in church-related schools which for the most part are Catholic. However, it cannot be assumed that all of these black families are Catholic. In a recent nationwide study of inner-city Catholic schools serving low income families, survey data reveal that the majority of black families (55 per cent) sending their children to Catholic schools are not Catholic (Cibulka, O'Brien and Zewe, 1982). Many of these families are not necessarily supporting private schools because of religious values and convictions, but because they believe that the Catholic schools provide a better education for their children. Similar values were found among black families in an ethnographic study of non-Catholic black families in Catholic schools (Hickey and Cooper, 1983).

Support for Catholic education within the black community has been a fairly established tradition particularly in certain geographical regions, such as the south. The recent change with respect to the black Catholic school population is that some blacks are now attending Catholic schools which were exclusively white. Prior to the 1960s, Catholic schools for the most part were segregated in much the same way as public schools. The student body in most Catholic schools prior to the 1960s was drawn from neighborhood parishes, which in most major metropolitan areas were racially segregated. Assuming that blacks had the educational values and resources, the only real option they had for selecting private education prior to the 1960s was in segregated Catholic schools. Today the racial and ethnic populations of some Catholic schools are quite diverse; however, in those schools which draw their students from segregated neighborhood parishes, the student body in these schools reflects the racial and ethnic composition of the communities in which the schools are located. All black Catholic schools are still very much the norm in neighborhoods which are predominately black (Schneider and Slaughter, 1984).

Increases in the numbers of black students in previously all white Catholic schools may be reflecting shifts in neighborhood composition rather than a commitment on the part of the schools or parents to desegregate. For example, Schneider and Slaughter (1984) found among a randomly sampled group of elementary Catholic schools in Chicago that in 1970, fifty-one out of seventy-one Catholic schools were less than 20 per cent black. By 1981 there were forty-one schools that were less than 20 per cent black. While it would seem that the schools were becoming more desegregated, the number of schools that had become all black during this same time controverts this assumption. In 1970, fourteen of the sampled Catholic schools were over 80 per cent black; by 1980, twenty-five schools had become nearly entirely black. It would seem that the desire for a desegregated education for these Chicago black families is not a convincing explanation for Catholic school choice.

Although their numbers are relatively small, blacks are also matriculating in other types of religious schools, including Lutheran, National Union of Christian Schools, Seventh-Day Adventist and Black Muslim schools all of which have distinctively different ideological philosophies (Carper and Hunt, 1984). It could be inferred, as other researchers have found with respect to Catholic schools (Bauch, Blum, Taylor and Valli, 1985; Cusick, 1984; Erickson, 1983), that black families are selecting these schools primarily because of the emphasis on religious values. However, there is no empirical research on blacks in these institutions to validate or refute such conclusions.

Because of the ways in which data are tabulated, it is difficult to estimate the proportion of the black population choosing these private schools. The National Catholic Education Association estimates that in 1979 approximately 200,300 students in Catholic elementary schools were black (NCEA, 1980). Since the total black elementary enrollment in church-related schools for 1980 is estimated at 207,494 students (US Census, 1984) it is reasonable to conclude that the numbers of black students in these other religious schools are comparatively small. Schneider and Slaughter (1984) indicate that in Chicago, these non-Catholic religious schools have not experienced any significant proportional increases in black enrollments.

Assessing increases in black enrollments among independent schools is as difficult as it is in the religious sector. Diversity of independent school types and lack of standardized record keeping procedures make it nearly impossible to estimate changes in black enrollments. One organization of independent schools which has openly acknowledged the relatively small number of black students is the National Association of Independent Schools (NAIS). Total enrollment for NAIS elementary and secondary schools is 342,403, approximately 4.2 per cent (14,355) of whom are black (NAIS, 1986). The majority of black students are enrolled in NAIS secondary schools.

Established to provide an education for the wealthy elite of American society, many of the schools which belong to NAIS pride themselves on their rich histories and reputations. Emphasizing traditional college preparatory programs, these schools are widely recognized for their high academic quality and commitment to preparing students for leadership positions in American businesses and government (Baird, 1977; Lightfoot, 1983; Cookson and Purcell, 1986). Families that support these schools tend to have higher family incomes than the national average (Kraushaar, 1972). High family income is a basic component for entrance in many of these schools, where the average elementary school tuition can be as high as $5000 per year.

Prior to the 1960s NAIS schools were not desegregated for the most part. In a study of elite boarding secondary schools, Baird (1977) described some of the socialization problems that the first adolescent black students encountered when they entered these predominantly white environments. Slaughter and Schneider (1986) addressed similar issues in their study of black elementary school students in recently desegregated elite schools. Black students in these elite schools may find that they are the only black student in their grade. This can present serious problems particularly to adolescents who are interested in dating. Most of these schools have very few black faculty members, so that black students do not have role models with whom they can identify. And finally, many of these schools in their efforts to be equitable de-emphasize racial or ethnic differences. This lack of attention and appreciation of racial and ethnic differences has the potential among black students to negate their black identity (Slaughter and Schneider, 1986).

Recognizing some of the problems that black and other minority students are encountering in NAIS schools, the association has embarked on a major effort to increase minority enrollments in its member schools and among their faculty members (Reed and Dandridge, 1979). Several organizations are attempting to increase black enrollments in NAIS schools. One such organization is A Better Chance (ABC), whose primary mission is to increase minority enrollments in private schools. Founded in 1963 by a group of headmasters from twenty-three private secondary schools, ABC has recruited over

5000 eighth and ninth grade minority students from public schools into their programs (Griffin, 1984). An organization similar to ABC is the Black Student Fund, whose purpose is to encourage black enrollment in private schools in the Washington, DC area. Started in 1964, it has awarded over 1806 scholarships to black students to enter private schools. At the elementary level, several organizations such as the Independent School Alliance for Minority Affairs, Channels for Educational Choices, and the Bay Area Coalition for Minority Affairs, are working to increase support, resources and minority enrollments in NAIS schools.

Since 1981/82, black enrollments in NAIS elementary and secondary schools have increased from 12,649 in 1981/82 to 14,355 in 1986 (NAIS, 1981/82; NAIS, 1986). However, when considering total enrollments of NAIS schools from 1981/82 (300,981) to 1986 (342,403) the proportion of black students has remained constant.

In addition to these elite private schools, there are a number of alternative schools which also recruit black students. Although much smaller in number than the schools that belong to NAIS, these alternative schools with their considerably lower tuition rates in comparison to elite schools provide black parents with another schooling option. Many of these schools were created in the 1960s during the alternative school movement and consonant with their liberal ideologies openly encourage ethnic and racial diversity among their students (Deal and Nolan, 1978; Graubard, 1974). Before the initiation of the Slaughter and Schneider study in 1983 (1986), studies had not examined life for black students in these private alternative schools at either the elementary or secondary level. School life of black students in alternative public school education has, however, been examined in some detail (see Duke, 1978).

Another type of private school attended by blacks are those alternative schools specifically established for minority students. Many of these schools belong to the National Center for Neighborhood Enterprise, which has identified over 250 such schools throughout the United States (Brookins, 1986; Ratteray, 1984). Preliminary estimates indicate that the range of enrollment in these schools is from twenty-two to 800 students (Ratteray, 1984). The US Census estimates that 40,012 blacks are enrolled in private non-church related elementary schools (US Census Detailed Population Characteristics, 1984). Given that NAIS estimates its total black elementary school enrollment below 7000 students (NAIS, 1986), it appears that black enrollments in these alternative schools account for a sizable proportion of the black population in private non-church related elementary schools. Precise enrollment figures for these schools are currently being determined (Ratteray, 1986).

Most of these schools have an open door admissions policy and charge tuition rates from $800 to $2500 (Ratteray, 1984). Although reported to be diverse in terms of philosophy, these schools are designed to provide their students with an educational alternative that will improve their achievement and provide them with an understanding of their cultural heritage. In a small exploratory study of ten independent black schools that are members of the Council of Independent Black Institutions, which functions as an umbrella organization for some of these type of independent schools, Brookins (1986) found that these schools provide three interrelated types of educational experiences: academic, cultural and political. The degree of intensity with which each of these goals was pursued varied among the schools and was directly related to the schools' ability to attract students and funds. Furthermore, active parental involvement was characteristic of all the schools. Preliminary findings of an ethnographic study of black private schools that included one such school indicate that the cultural and political values are as important as the academic ones (Johnson, 1985).

These studies of black alternative schools challenge some conventional explanations regarding black school choice. Black families choosing these types of schools are not necessarily selecting them on the sole basis of reinforcing black identity in their children. Nor are they opting for schools that promote a separatist ideology. Rather, these parents, many of them with limited financial resources, are selecting private schools that will provide their children with a strong academic background. The interests of black parents in securing a quality education for their children, an education that results in the acquisition of knowledge and skills and that leads to occupational and social mobility, were clearly identified in the *Newcomer* study (Slaughter and Schneider, 1986).

Black parents with middle and low incomes are choosing different types of private schools. Research on why they are making these decisions is very limited. Scholars interested in issues of choice have tended to focus on (i) what the government's interest should be in guaranteeing parent rights to choose private education (Coons and Sugarman 1978; Burt, 1982; Frey, 1982); and (ii) what the economic and social consequences would be for families of low, middle and high incomes if there were greater financial support for private school choice (Catterall and Levin, 1982; Vitullo-Martin, 1982; West, 1982).

In contrast to these approaches, the *Newcomer* study examined through in-depth interviews the question of parental perception of private school choice and how families went about making their decision. Findings of the *Newcomer* study reveal that school choice is directly tied to the views that black parents hold about the aims of education for their children, views that are more complex than popular notions have suggested.

Choosing Schools: An Issue of Educational Goals and Expectations

To learn about school choice for the *Newcomer* study, parent interviews were conducted with 131 families, both black and non-black, who sent their children to any one of four distinctively different private elementary schools in Chicago. With respect to specific school choices a decision was made to select uniquely different types of private schools, i.e., elite, alternative and sectarian. By selecting different types of schools there would be greater opportunities to examine a fuller range of black perspectives concerning the reasons and decision-making process the black families used when choosing to enroll their children in private schools. Specific school selections were based on the school's reputation for academic excellence, key organizational characteristics such as school size, adult-child ratios, grade levels served, and size of teaching staff, and demographic characteristics such as an increase in black enrollment over the past ten years and racial composition of the student body of which 10 per cent are black Americans. (One elite school that did not meet the sample criteria asked to be included in the study. Although we already identified a school which ideologically represented the elite group, we decided to include this school because of its outstanding academic reputation and its willingness to participate which thereby facilitated our access into other schools. For further explanation of the sample selection procedures see Slaughter and Schneider, 1986.)

The family interviews, which lasted approximately three hours and were usually conducted with mothers, included information on family background characteristics, family educational goals, parent participation and involvement in school activities and the family's view of the child's socialization experiences at school and home. It was assumed that by obtaining comprehensive background data on the family it would be possible to gain a fuller understanding of the goals and expectations the family had for the child, and how these goals and expectations were related to the type of social and educational experiences they desired and constructed for the child both in and out of school. Interviews were administered to 74 black and 57 non-black parents (about 10 per cent were Asian or Hispanic), most of whom had children in fifth through eighth grades. Black parents were selected randomly from lists provided by the schools, while non-black parents were selected from lists constructed by teachers indicating families who were perceived as friendly to black children. The intent was to construct two similar groups of parents, so that any differences in responses that occurred among the groups would be less likely to be the result of racial or ethnic prejudices and would be able to provide additional insights into the educational goals of black parents.

Interview questions designed to explore school choice included an assessment of prior family elementary and secondary educational experiences. Parents were also asked how they received information about this school and other schools, and what led to the family decision of private schooling for their child. Parents were specifically asked how they chose a particular private school and other school experiences such as those at the pre-school level. Interviewers queried parents on the differences between the teacher's job and the parent's job in helping children to learn, the essential elements of a quality education, and educational and social qualities the parents would like the school to develop in their child. Parents were also asked about the educational and occupational aspirations and expectations they had for their child.

Based on this approach, the results indicated that parents had distinctive views of education and were likely to select particular educational environments for their child that complemented their own predilections. For example, some of the parents felt that educational experiences should occur in settings that are pleasant, joyful and relatively non-competitive. Consequently, they wanted their child in an educational environment that exemplified these qualities. Other parents believed that the primary purpose of schooling was the development of the child's social and moral character. These parents were likely to participate in a school environment for their child where these social and moral goals were likely to be met.

Six different family goal types (i.e., authoritative, deliberate, humanistic, moral, practical and traditional) were identified. Key constructs which distinguished goal categories among family responses included (i) role and authority of the family versus the school in the child's education; (ii) family norms regarding the essential elements of a quality education for their child; (iii) the importance that the family attaches to the school's reputation; and (iv) the family's view of the relationship between the school's curriculum and their expectations for future educational attainment levels and occupational choices of their child. Although more than one family goal type appeared in each school, there was a strong relationship between family goal categories and type of school (i.e., alternative, Catholic and elite). Similarily, family goal types also differed significantly by race. (For a comprehensive discussion on coding procedures, reliability and validity of the ratings, and statistical analyses of the data see Slaughter and Schneider, 1986.) Each goal category contained several distinguishing characteristics with respect to the four key constructs, only the most salient of which are discussed in the following paragraphs.

Parents whose response patterns were classified as authoritative see themselves as having the primary responsibility for their child's education and feel it is their obligation to be actively involved in their child's education both in and out of school. The overwhelming majority of these parents indicate that they reached their decision to send their child to this particular school after a systematic assessment of alternative options. Black parent responses were more likely than non-black parents to be classified in this category. An example of an authoritative response to the question regarding the difference between the teacher's and parent's job in helping children to learn is the father who responded: 'Children learn from parents. Teachers are to supplement that learning with more particular goals in a more structured sense. The federal government says you have to have schooling, it's not left up to a particular municipality to decide that . . . but I don't feel that the teachers are responsible for education . . . They're the catalyst — the parents are responsible to see to it that their kids are educated.'

Parent responses classified as deliberate were more likely to place greater confidence in the ability of the teachers and school than themselves in helping their child acquire a quality education. These parents tended to believe that good teachers are absolutely essential for children to learn and the mark of a good school is excellent teaching. Black parent responses were more likely than non-black parent responses to be classified as deliberate. Following is an example of a deliberate parental response to the same question above: 'They both should play a part in helping the child to learn. There are some things the teacher should be responsible for and some things the parent should be responsible for. The actual fundamentals should be the teacher's function to set the groundwork for learning. It is also the parent's part to reiterate what the teacher is doing so that when a child comes home you can carry on what they learned in school in terms of helping them with their homework even doing other things not related to homework but will help them learn. It's two-fold. It tends to overlap.'

Parents whose educational philosophies exemplify the humanistic goal category seek educational environments for their children that are pleasant, child-centered and non-competitive. The child's learning and development result from a partnership between the parents and the child's teachers, and the school's role is perceived as an extension of the family. Non-black parent responses were more likely to be classified as either humanistic or traditional. Following is an example of a humanistic response to the question, what are the essential elements of a quality education: 'High motivation; an environment where he feels happy; challenging work, the ability to compete with himself, and excitement for learning. . . That's my main criteria. I am not as concerned about competition. The excitment for learning should carry over after school hours.'

Parent educational philosophies representative of the moral response pattern indicate that the primary focus of education should be the development of the child's moral and social character in a disciplined learning environment. In comparison to parent responses in the humanistic category, which consistently state feeling comfortable with an open and flexible approach to learning, parent responses in the moral category reveal a desire for a highly structured curriculum. Children are expected to behave in accordance with school and teacher standards and expectations. In one example of a moral response to the question of what the child needs to know in order to get along in this world, the parent replied: 'To be good in everything. But I don't know what will happen in the future. Every day I tell my kid, listen to teacher and parent, to be good; don't play too much. To be a boss, supervisor . . . many things [are involved]. . . If you want to be a nun, sister o.k. Don't play around on the street and don't smoke.'

Parent responses classified into the practical category view the world as unstable and tend to select their present school because it is the only viable educational alternative which can protect their child from a threatening external environment. The school serves as a sanctuary where the child can be safe and thus learn in a protected environment. Their private school choice is the most 'practical' alternative given their life styles and family resources. Of utmost importance to parents who give the practical response pattern is that the teacher must demonstrate care and concern for the academic and emotional needs of the child. Often based on their own reported past or present experiences and observations, these parents believe that any unfairness, insolence or rudeness by the school to themselves or their children is intolerable. An example of a parent giving a practical response to the question of what led to the family's decision to find a new school for the child? 'It was chosen because on account of one of my friends who told me about St. August one day in the grocery store. I told her that I started calling the Board of Education to see why M school was out of the district. Sara (her child) had to pass six taverns and bums on the street to get to G (a public school in the district). I would keep her out a year if I had to. I told her [i.e., the friend] of my distress. She told me to call St. August. It was right by my house. I didn't know it existed. It was hidden. I was pleased. When I walked into the school and saw how the kids were walking the halls and behaving, I said, "Oh yes! I would pay a million dollars if it takes it to get her into a good school".' In the study, moral and practical response patterns were more typical of lower income parents.

The last category of parent response patterns is the traditional one. Parent responses that typify the traditional response pattern are committed to the belief that the best training for the high achievement goals they have for their children is to be found in private schools. In contrast to other parent responses, in the view of these parents the teachers per se are not perceived as having special status; they are expected to be competent in the subject matter so that they can contribute to the development of the child's intellectual potential. Almost as important as teachers is the school social environment. After school, peer group contacts are encouraged among schoolmates, and many parents may devise elaborate ways of ensuring that their children interact with socially accepted peers. Asked how far in school the child should go, one parent responded, 'He says he wants to be a surgeon.' When asked what type of occupation would be most un-satisfactory, the same parent answered, 'a male nurse'. Typical career expectations for their children among these parents are medicine and law. As another parent commented, 'Medicine or law ... we don't want her in education. Education is such a dead issue.'

With respect to school types, at one elite school, parent responses tended to be deliberate and humanistic; at the other elite school the responses were primarily traditional with smaller groups indicating humanistic or deliberate goals. At the Catholic school the patterns were practical and moral and at the alternative school the choices were humanistic and authoritative. Although there were differences among the response patterns, these parents shared some common views on certain issues. For example, they all had high educational aspirations for their children, valued pre-school education, and expected the schools to provide a solid foundation in language, arts and mathematics. These parents were not opposed to public education, but they felt that the quality of education in their neighborhood schools was inferior. Overall they were satisfied with the quality of education their children were currently receiving. Black parents were more likely to emphasize the importance of a desegregated education and to stress that education should provide children with an opportunity to learn about other people's cultures. Consequently, they were more likely to link educational quality with social diversity in the schools.

The *Newcomer* findings demonstrate that black and non-black parents have educational goals that can be differentiated. Often intuitive, these goals spring from educational perspectives that guide parental selections of private schools. These perspectives reflect the parents' own prior elementary and secondary educational experiences, and continue to be shaped by their ongoing assessment of how their particular school choice fulfills their vision of what an appropriate educational experience should be for their child. This assessment begins during the admissions process and is reinforced while the child remains in school. These results, which emphasize the criteria that parents use to choose schools, have important implications for our understanding of educational school choice in general.

Understanding School Choice

Many black parents from middle and low family income backgrounds make private school choices. These black families are breaking with the traditional rejection of support for private education by the black community (Slaughter and Schneider, 1986). This rejection has been based on the assumption that such support would further segregate the schools and would ultimately result in fewer resources for the poor and minorities who would eventually constitute the public school population. One explanation for the change is the disaffection expressed by some black families with the education that black children are receiving in public schools (Slaughter and Schneider, 1986). Evidence of this disaffection can be seen in the results of national polls, which indicate that non-whites rate the public schools less favorably than whites (Gallup Poll, 1985). Fewer non-whites are likely to give grades of 'A' to the performance of public schools, and more non-whites are likely to give failing grades to the performance of public schools.

Black support for private education should not be viewed as a rejection of public education in general. Rather, it is a statement that some black parents are making about the ability of urban public schools to provide opportunities for blacks to acquire the knowledge and skills which lead to occupational and social mobility in American society. Results from the *Newcomer* study indicate that black and non-black parents alike are interested in having their children achieve access to schools that will ensure their child's chances for future academic and occupational success. The concerns that these black parents have with the abilities of urban public schools to fulfill these expectations for their own children are more pragmatic than some who believe that urban public schools in time with certain resources and changes in policy can become effective academic institutions for all black children (Edmonds, 1979; Sizemore, 1984).

The quality of urban public schools which draw predominately minority students has been under close scrutiny in the educational research community and policy arena. One indicator that seems to signify that many of these schools are not providing a strong college preparatory program is evidenced by the number of colleges who are tending to recruit black students who graduate from prep schools and suburban public schools rather than inner city public schools (Staples, 1986). If colleges are not recruiting black students from urban public schools, certainly black parents with resources are going to place their children in the schools from which college entrance is likely to be assured. The inability of urban public schools to provide opportunities for social mobility for black children may be the major reason that private schools are emerging as a significant competitor to public education for black students.

With respect to school choice, results from the *Newcomer* study demonstrate that parents, both black and non-black, have distinctive educational philosophies which guide their selections of, and participation in specific private schools. Parents in the *Newcomer* study did not shop for a specific educational program or teaching style. Their concerns centered more on the type of schooling environment that best suited their own educational philosophies and the needs of their child. These philosophies were not necessarily well articulated nor were they always firmly established. Parents in the *Newcomer* study were keenly aware of the link between educational quality and social mobility. Although some parents preferred that their child be educated in a more structured environment, and others preferred that it occur in a more open child-centered one, they all recognized the value of a quality education and how it would enhance their child's future success.

Findings of the *Newcomer* study can help us to understand issues of family school choice in general. To these parents, aspirations and expectations for a quality education for their child took preference over specific educational programs and instructional techniques. Black parents choosing private schools are seeking environments that complement their philosophies and maximize their child's academic potential and social development. Thus, it may be that the primary consideration for parents both black and non-black in selecting a school whether it be public or private, is one that will enhance their child's academic and social development in an environment that is consistent with their own intuitive philosophy of what constitutes a quality education.

Bibliography

ABRAMOWITZ, S. and STACKHOUSE, E. A. (1981). *Private High School Today*. Washington, DC: National Institute of Education.

ABRAMOWITZ, S. and TENENBAUM, E. (1978). *High School '77: A Survey of Public Secondary School Principals*. Washington, DC: National Institute of Education.

ALEXANDER, K. L. and PALLAS, A. M. (1983). Private schools and public policy: New evidence on cognitive achievement in public and private schools. *Sociology of Education, 56*, 170–82.

ANTOS, J. R. and ROSEN, S. (1975). Discrimination in the market for public school teachers. *Journal of Econometrics, 3*, 123–50.

ARIZONA REV. STAT. ANN. sec. 15–310 (Supp. 1983).

ARMOR, D., CONREY-OSEGUERA, P., COX, M., KING, N., McDONNELL, L., PASCOE, A., PAULY, E. and ZELLMAN, G. (1976). *Analysis of the School Preferred Reading Program in Selected Los Angeles Minority Schools*. Santa Monica, CA: Rand Corporation.

AUGENBLICK, J., and ADAMS, K. (1979). *An Analysis of the Impact of Changes in the Funding of Elementary/Secondary Education in Texas: 1974/75 to 1977/78*. Denver, CO: Education Commission of the States.

AUSTIN, G. R. (1979). 'An analysis of outlier exemplary schools and their distinguishing characteristics', paper presented at the annual meeting of the American Educational Research Association, San Francisco, CA, April.

BAILEY, S. (1981). Political coalitions for public education. *Daedalus, 110*, 27–44.

BAILYN, B. (1972). *Education in the Forming of American society*. New York, NY: W. W. Norton.

BAIRD, L. (1971). *The Elite Schools: A Profile of Prestigious Independent Schools*. Lexington, MA: Lexington Books.

BALLANTYNE, M., CHAMBERS, J. G. and LAJOIE, S. (1984). IFG comparative study of public and private schools in the San Francisco Bay Area: Descriptive Report of the data set. Report No. 84-A17. Stanford, CA: Institute for Research on Educational Finance and Governance, Stanford University.

BANKSTON, M. (1982). Organizational reporting in a school district: State and federal programs. Report No. 82-A10. Stanford, CA: Institute for Research on Educational Finance and Governance, Stanford University.

BARKER, R. G. and GUMP, P. V. (1964). *Big School, Small School — High School Size and Student Behavior.* Stanford, CA: Stanford University Press.

BARON, J. N. and BIELBY, W. T. (1980). Bringing the firms back in: Stratification, segmentation, and the organization of work. *American Sociological Review, 45,* 737–65.

BASCOMB ASSOCIATES (1975). *State and Federal Laws Relating to Non-public Schools.* Washington, DC: US Office of Education.

BAUCH, P., BLUM, I., TAYLOR, N. and VALLI, L. (1985). Themes and findings from the five schools: Final report. Washington, DC: the Catholic University of America Center for the Study of Youth Development.

BECK, W. M. (1963). *Lutheran Elementary Schools in the United States.* St. Louis, MO: Concordia Publishing House.

BECKER, H. J. (1978). The impact of racial composition and public school desegregation on changes in non-public school enrollment. Report 252. Baltimore, MD: Center for Social Organization of Schools, Johns Hopkins University.

BENDER V. WILLIAMSPORT AREA SCHOOL DIST., 563 F. Supp. 697 (M.D. Pa. 1983).

BERKE, J. S. and KIRST, M. W. (1975). The federal role in American school finance: A fiscal and administrative analysis, in WIRT, F. M. (Ed.), *The Polity of the School.* Lexington, MA: Lexington Books, 15–232.

BERMAN, P., et al. (1981). *Improving School Improvement: A Policy Evaluation of the California School Improvement Program.* Berkeley, CA: Manifest International.

BERMAN, P. and McLAUGHLIN, M. W. (1977). *Federal Programs Supporting Educational Change: Factors Affecting Implementation and Continuation.* Vol. 7. Santa Monica, CA: Rand Corporation.

BIDWELL, C. (1965). The school as a formal organization, in MARCH, J. G. (Ed.), *Handbook of Organizations.* Chicago, IL: Rand McNally.

BLAU, P. M. (1970). A formal theory of differentiation in organizations. *American Sociological Review, 35,* 201–18.

BLUM, V. (1985). Private elementary education in the inner city. *Phi Delta Kappan, 66,* 643–6.

BOARD OF PARISH EDUCATION (1983). *Statistical Report.* Department of Elementary and Secondary Schools. Lutheran Church.

Book of the General Laws of the Inhabitants of New Plymouth. (1685).

Book of the General Laws and Liberties Concerning the Inhabitants of the Massachusetts, Collected out of the Records of the General Court for the Several Years Wherein they were Made and Established. (1648). Cambridge, MA.

BORJAS, G. (1982). The politics of employment discrimination in the federal bureaucracy. *Journal of Law and Economics, 25,* 271–99.

BORJAS, G. J., FRECH III, H. E. and GINSBURG, P. B. (1983). Property rights and wages: The case of nursing homes. *Journal of Human Resources, 18,* 231–46.

BOYER, E. L. (1983). *High School: A Report on Secondary Education in America.*

Washington, DC: Carnegie Foundation for the Advancement of Teaching.

BRANDON V. BOARD OF EDUCATION, 635 F.2d 971 (2d Cir. 1980), *cert. denied*, 454 US 1123 (1981).

BRIDGE, R. G. and BLACKMAN, J. (1978). *A Study of Alternatives in American Education: Family Choice in Schooling*. Washington, DC: Rand Corporation.

BRIDGES, E. M. (1982). Research on the school administrator: The state of the art, 1967–1980. *Educational Administration Quarterly, 18*, summer, 12–33.

BROOKINS, C. (1986). 'Exploring independent black schools', paper presented at the annual meeting of the American Educational Research Association, San Francisco, CA, April.

BROOKOVER, W. P., BEADY, C., FLOOD, P., SCHWEITZER, J. and WISENBAKER, J. (1979). *School Social Systems and Student Achievement: Schools Can Make a Difference*. New York, NY: Praeger.

BROOKOVER, W. P. and LEZOTTE, L. W. (1979). Changes in school characteristics coincident with changes in student achievement. East Lansing, MI: Institute for Research on Teaching, Michigan State University.

BROWN, M. and ERIE, S. P. (1981). Blacks and the legacy of the great society: The economic and political impact of social policy. *Public Policy, 29*, 299–330.

BRUCE, G. M. (1928). *Luther as an Educator*. Minneapolis, MN: Augsburg Publishing House.

BUETOW, H. A. (1970). *Of Singular Benefit: The Story of US Catholic Education*. New York, NY: Macmillan.

BURNS, J. A. and KOHLBRENNER, B. J. (1937). *A History of Catholic Education in the United States*. New York, NY: Bensinger Brothers.

BURT, W. (1982). The new campaign for tax credits: 'Parochaid' misses the point, in MANLEY-CASIMIR, M. (Ed.), *Family Choice in Schooling: Issues and Dilemmas*. Lexington, MA: DC Heath.

BUSHNELL, H. (1853). *Common Schools: A Discourse on the Modifications Demanded by the Roman Catholics*. Hartford, CT: Case, Tiffany & Co.

BUTTS, R. F. (1955). Say nothing of my religion. *School and Society, 81*, 182–8.

BUTTS, R. F. and CREMIN, L. A. (1953). *A History of Education in American Culture*. New York, NY: Henry Holt.

CALIFORNIA STATE DEPARTMENT OF EDUCATION (1980). *Report on the Special Studies of Selected ECE Schools with Increasing and Decreasing Reading Scores*. Sacramento, CA: Office of Program Evaluation and Research.

CALIFORNIA STATE DEPARTMENT OF EDUCATION. *School Statistics*. Sacramento, selected years.

CARNEGIE COUNCIL ON POLICY STUDIES IN HIGHER EDUCATION. (1976). *A Classification of Institutions of Higher Education*. (rev. edn). Berkeley, CA: Carnegie Council.

CARNOY, M., GIRLING, R. and RUMBERGER, R. (1976). Education and public sector employment. Palo Alto, CA: Center for Economic Studies.

CARPER, J. C. (1983). The Christian day school movement. *The Educational Forum, 47*, 135–49.

CARPER, J. C. and HUNT, T. C. (1984). *Religious Education in America*. Birmingham, AL: Religious Education Press.
CATTERALL, J. S. (1983a). *Tuition Tax Credits: Fact and Fiction*. Bloomington, IN: Phi Delta Kappa Educational Foundation.
CATTERALL, J. S. (1983b). Tuition tax credits: Issues of equity, in JAMES, T. and LEVIN, H. M. (Eds.), *Public Dollars for Private Schools*. Philadelphia, PA: Temple University Press.
CATTERALL, J. S. (1984). Politics and aid to private schools. *Educational Evaluation and Policy Analysis, 6*, 435–40.
CATTERALL, J. S. and LEVIN, H. M. (1982). Public and private schools: Evidence on tuition tax credits. *Sociology of Education, 55*, 144–51.
CHAMBERS, J. G. (1979). Educational cost differentials and the allocation of state aid for elementary/secondary education. *Journal of Human Resources, 13*, 459–81.
CHAMBERS, J. G. (1980). The development of a cost of education index: Some empirical estimates and policy issues. *Journal of Education Finance, 5*, 262–81.
CHAMBERS, J. G. (1981a). The hedonic wage technique as a tool for estimating the costs of school personnel: A theoretical exposition with implications for empirical analysis. *Journal of Education Finance, 6*, 330–54.
CHAMBERS, J. G. (1981b). An analysis of school size under a voucher system. *Educational Evaluation and Policy Analysis, 3*(2), 29–40.
CHAMBERS, J. G. and LAJOIE, S. (1983). A comparative study of private and public schooling organizations: A descriptive summary. A report to the National Institute of Education. Stanford, CA: Institute for Research on Educational Finance and Governance, Stanford University.
CHAMBERS, J. G. and PARRISH, T. B. (1983). Adequacy and equity in state school finance and planning: A resource cost model approach. Stanford, CA: Institute for Research on Educational Finance and Governance, Stanford University.
CHAMBERS, J. G. and VINCENT, P. E. (1981). Analysis and development of a cost-of-education index for use in the Florida education finance program. Volume I — Summary and recommendations. Volume II — Technical report. Reports prepared under subcontract with SRI International for the Florida Department of Education.
Charters and General Laws of the Colony and Province of Massachusetts Bay. (1644).
CHOW, W. K. and POLICH, J. M. (1980). Models of the first-term reenlistment decision. Report R-2468-MRAL. Santa Monica, CA: Rand Corporation.
CIBULKA, J., O'BRIEN, T. and ZEWE, C. (1982). *Inner-city Private Elementary Schools: A study*. Milwaukee, WI: Marquette University Press.
COGAN, S. (1979). 'Determinants of parental choice in schooling: The Coquitlam experience', paper presented at the annual meeting of the American Educational Research Association, San Francisco, CA, April.
COHEN, D. K. and NEUFELD, B. (1981). The failure of high schools and the progress of education. *Daedalus*, summer, 110.
COHEN, E. G. and MILLER, R. H. (1980). Coordination and control of instruction in schools. *Pacific Sociological Review, 23*, 446–73.

COLEMAN, J. S., HOFFER, T. and KILGORE, S. (1981). *Public and Private Schools*. Chicago, IL: National Opinion Research Center and University of Chicago.

COLEMAN, J. S., HOFFER, T. and KILGORE, S. (1982a). *High School Achievement: Public, Catholic, and Private Schools Compared*. New York, NY: Basic Books.

COLEMAN, J., HOFFER, T. and KILGORE, S. (1982b). Various reports based on the High School and Beyond study. Chicago, IL: National Opinion Research Center.

COLLEGE BOARD. (1983). *Academic preparation for College: What Students Need to Know and be Able to Do*. New York, NY: College Board Publications.

COLLINS V. CHANDLER UNIFIED SCHOOL DISTRICT, 644 F.2d 759 (9th Cir. 1981), *cert. denied*, 454 US 863 (1981).

COMMONWEALTH V. RENFREW, 332 Mass. 492, 126 NE 2d 109 (1955).

COOK, T., ARMOR, D., CRAIN, R., MILLER, N., STEPHAN, W., WALBERG, H. and WORTMAN, P. (1984). School desegregation and black achievement. Washington, DC: National Institute of Education.

COOKSON, P. and PURCELL, C. (1986). *Preparing for Power: America's Elite Boarding Schools*. New York, NY: Basic Books.

COONS, J. and SUGARMAN, S. (1978). *Education by Choice: The Case for Family Control*. Berkeley, CA: University of California Press.

COOPER, B. S. (1969). *Free and Freedom Schools*. Washington, DC: President's Commission on School Finance.

COOPER, B. S. (1973). Organizational survival: A comparative case of seven American 'free schools'. *Education and Urban Society*, 5, 487–508.

COOPER, B. S. (1985). The changing universe of US private schools. Report P/NP-12. Stanford, CA: Institute for Research on Educational Finance and Governance, Stanford University.

COOPER, B. S., MCLAUGHLIN, D. H. and MANNO, B. V. (1983). The latest word on private school growth. *Teachers College Record*, 85, 88–98.

COSTANZO, J. F. (1959). Thomas Jefferson, religious education and public law. *Journal of Public Law*, 8, 81–108.

COUNCIL FOR AMERICAN PRIVATE EDUCATION (1983). CAPE Outlook (No. 85).

CRAIN, R. L. (1981). 'Initial comments' in school research forum. Coleman report on public and private schools. Arlington, VA: Educational Research Service.

CRAIN, R. L. and HAWLEY, W. D. (1982). Standards of research. *Society*, 19(2), 14–21.

CRAIN, R. L. and MAHARD, R. E. (1981). Minority achievement: Policy implications of the research, in HAWLEY, W. D. (Ed.), *Effective School Desegregation: Equity, Quality and Feasibility*. Beverly Hills, CA: Sage Publications.

CRAIN, R. L. and MAHARD, R. E. (1983). The effects of research methodology on desegregation-achievement studies: A meta-analysis. *American Journal of Sociology*, 88, 839–54.

CREMIN, L. A. (1951). *The American Common School: An Historic Conception*. New York, NY: Teachers College Press, Columbia University.

CREMIN, L. A. (Ed.) (1957). *The Republic and the School: Horace Mann on the*

Education of Free Men. New York, NY: Teachers College Press, Columbia University.

CREMIN, L. A. (1964). *The Transformation of the School: Progressivism in American Education, 1876–1957.* New York, NY: Vintage Books.

CREMIN, L. A. (1980). *American Education: The National Experience, 1783–1876.* New York, NY: Harper & Row.

CUBBERLEY, E. P. (1920). *The History of Education.* Boston, MA: Houghton-Mifflin.

CUSICK, P. (1984). 'A study of inner city parochial secondary schools', paper presented at the annual meeting of the American Educational Research Association, New Orleans, LA, April.

DARLING-HAMMOND, L. and KIRBY, S. N. (1985). *Tuition Tax Deductions and Parent School Choice: A Case Study of Minnesota.* Santa Monica, CA: Rand Corporation.

DAVIS, M., DEAL, T. E., MEYER, J. W., ROWAN, B., SCOTT, W. R. and STACKHOUSE, E. A. (1977). The structure of educational systems: Explorations in the theory of loosely-coupled organizations. Stanford, CA: Stanford Center for Research and Development in Teaching, Stanford University.

DAVIS, T. N. (1955). Footnote on church-state. *School and Society, 81,* 180.

DEAL, T. and NOLAN, R. (Eds.). (1978). *Alternative Schools: Ideologies, Realities, Guidelines.* Chicago, IL: Nelson-Hall.

DEWEY, J. (1965). *The School and Society* (21st impression). New York, NY: Alfred A. Knopf.

DILL, W. R. (1958). Environment as an influence on managerial autonomy. *Administrative Science Quarterly, 2,* 409–43.

DIMAGGIO, P. J. and POWELL, W. W. (1983). The iron cage revisited; Institutional isomorphism and collective rationality in organizational fields. *American Sociological Review, 48,* 147–60.

DOBOS, F. (1984). A response to the Crain study. Archdiocese of Cleveland School System, Cleveland, MO, December.

DOLAN, J. P. (1975). *The Immigrant Church.* Baltimore, MD: Johns Hopkins University Press.

DOLBEARE, K. M. and HAMMOND, P. E. (1971). *The School Prayer Decisions.* Chicago, IL: University of Chicago Press.

DUKE, D. (1978). *The Retransformation of the School: The Emergence of Contemporary Alternative Schools in the US.* Chicago, IL: Nelson-Hall.

DWORKIN, G. (1980). The changing demography of public school teachers: Some implications of faculty turnover in urban areas. *Sociology of Education, 53,* 54–66.

EDMONDS, R. R. (1979). Effective schools for the urban poor. *Educational Leadership, 13,* 15–24.

EDMONDS, R. R. (1981). Making public schools effective. *Social Policy 12,* 56–60.

EDUCATIONAL MANAGEMENT and EVALUATION COMMISSION (California) (1982). California school governance: An analysis and call for papers. Report to the California State School Board, unpublished, December.

EDWARDS, N. (1941). The evolution of American educational, ideals in

EDWARDS, N. (Ed.), *Education in a Democracy*. Chicago, IL: University of Chicago Press.

EDWARDS, N. and RICHEY, H. G. (1974). *The School in the American Social Order*. Boston, MA: Houghton Mifflin.

EDWARDS, S. and RICHARDSON, W. (1981). A survey of MCPS withdrawals to attend private school. Rockville, MD: Montgomery County Public Schools.

ENCARNATION, D. J. (1983). Public finance and regulation of non-public education: Retrospect and prospect, in JAMES, T. and LEVIN, H. M. (Eds.), *Public Dollars for Private Schools*. Philadelphia, PA: Temple University Press, 175–95.

ENCARNATION, D. J. and MITCHELL, D. E. (1983). Critical tensions in the governance of California public education. Stanford, CA: Institute for Research on Educational Finance and Governance, Stanford University.

ENCARNATION, D. J. and MITCHELL, D. E. (1984). Alternative state policy mechanisms for influencing school performance. *Educational Researcher, 13*(5), 4–11.

ENCARNATION, D. J. and RICHARDS, C. (1981). Labor unions and categorical programs. *IFG Policy Notes*. Stanford, CA: Institute for Research on Educational Finance and Governance, Stanford University.

ENCARNATION, D. J. and RICHARDS, C. (1984). Government social policy and minority employment in public, Catholic and private schools. Stanford, CA: Institute for Research on Educational Finance and Governance, Stanford University.

ENGEL V. VITALE, 370 US 421 (1962).

ERICKSON, D. A. (Ed.). (1969). *Public Controls for Non-public Schools*. Chicago, IL: University of Chicago Press.

ERICKSON, D. (1983). Private schools in contemporary perspective. Report No. TTC-14. Stanford, CA: Institute for Research on Educational Finance and Governance, Stanford University.

ERICKSON, D. A. (1986). Choice and private schools: Dynamics of supply and demand, in LEVY, D. (Ed.), *Private Education: Studies in Choice and Public Policy*. New York: Oxford University Press, 82–109.

ERICKSON, D. A. and MADAUS, G. F. (1972). *Issues of Aid to Non-public Schools. Vol. 3: Public Assistance Programs for non-public Schools*. Washington, DC: President's Commission on School Finance.

ERICKSON, D. A., NAULT, R. L., COOPER B. S. and LAMBORN, R. (1976). *Recent Enrollment Trends in US Non-public Schools*. Washington, DC: National Institute of Education.

ERICKSON, D. A., NAULT, R. L. and COOPER, B. S. (1978). Recent enrollment trends in US non-public schools, in ABRAMOWITZ, S. and ROSENFELD, S. (Eds.), *Declining Enrollment: The Challenge of the Coming Decade*, pp. 81–127. Washington, DC: National Institute of Education.

EUCHNER, C. (1983). Private school officials fear reforms may infringe upon their autonomy. *Education Week, 3*, 21 December, 21, 1.

FARLEY, R. (1981). Final report, NIE Grant G–79–0151. Population Studies Center, University of Michigan, Ann Arbor, Mich.

FARRAR, E., NEUFELD, B. and MILES, M. B. (1983). Effective schools programs in high schools: Implications for policy, practice and research. National Commission on Excellence in Education, January.

FARRINGTON V. TOKUSHIGA, 273 US 284 (1927).

FIRESTONE, W. A. and HERRIOTT, R. E. (1982). Effective schools: Do elementary prescriptions fit secondary schools? *Educational Leadership,* *40*, 51, December.

FISCHER, D. H. (1964). The myth of the Essex Junto. *William & Mary Quarterly, 21*, 191–235.

FLOREY V. SIOUX FALLS SCHOOL DIST., 619 F.2d 1311 (8th Cir.), *cert. denied* 101 S. Ct. 409 (1980).

FREEMAN, J. H. and KRONENFELD, J. E. (1974). Problems of definitional dependency: The case of administrative intensity. *Social Forces, 52*, 108–21.

FREEMAN, R. B. (1973). Changes in the labor market for black Americans, 1948–1972, in *Brookings Papers on Economic Activity* 1, 67–120.

FREY, D. (1982). The tuition tax credit: Uncertain directions in public policy, in MANLEY-CASIMIR, M. (Ed.), *Family Choice in Schooling: Issues and Dilemmas.* Lexington, MA: D.C. Heath, 135–48.

FREY, D. (1983). *Tuition Tax Credits for Private Education.* Ames, IA: Iowa State Press.

FURUBOTN, E. and PEJOVICH, S. (1972). Property rights and economic theory: A survey of recent literature. *Journal of Economic Literature, 10*, 1137–1162.

GAFFNEY, E. M., JR. (Ed.). (1981). *Private Schools and the Public Good.* Notre Dame, IN: Notre Dame University Press.

GALBRAITH, J. (1973). *Designing Complex Organizations.* Reading, MA: Addison-Wesley.

GALLUP POLL (1985). The 17th annual Gallup Poll of the public's attitudes toward the public schools. *Phi Delta Kappan, 67*, 35–47.

GARMS, W., GUTHRIE, J. and PIERCE, L. (1978). *School Finance: The Economics and Politics of Education.* Englewood Cliffs, NJ: Prentice-Hall.

GEIGER, R. (1984). *Private Sectors in Higher Education: Structure, Function and Change in Eight Countries.* Ann Arbor, MI: University of Michigan Press.

GEMELLO, M. and OSMAN, W. (1983). The choice for public and private education: An economist's view, in JAMES, T. and LEVIN, H. M. (Eds.), *Public Dollars for Private Schools.* Philadelphia, PA: Temple University Press, 196–210.

GEMELLO, J. M. and OSMAN, J. W. (1984). Estimating the demand for private school enrollment. *American Journal of Education, 92*, 262–79.

GILES, M. W. (1977). Racial stability and urban school desegregation. *Urban Affairs Quarterly, 12*, 499–510.

GILLILAND, E. M. and RADLE, J. (1984). Characteristics of public and private schools in the San Francisco Bay Area: A descriptive report. Stanford, CA: Institute for Research on Educational Finance and Governance, Stanford University.

GITLOW V. STATE OF NEW YORK, 168 US 652 (1925).

GLENN, B. C. (1981). What works: An examination of effective schools for poor black children. Cambridge, MA: Center for Law and Education, Harvard University.

GLENN, C. (1984). Can we stop fighting over religion and public education? manuscript based on talk at the Second Annual Berkshire Prayer Breakfast, Pittsfield, MA, 2 February.

GOETTEL, R. J. (1976). Federal assistance to national target groups: The ESEA Title 1 experience, in TIMPANE, M. (Ed.), *The Federal Interest in Financing Schooling*. Cambridge, MA: Ballinger, 173–208.

GOLDBERGER, A. S. (1964). *Econometric Theory*. New York, NY: John Wiley & Sons.

GOLDBERGER, A. S. and CAIN, G. G. (1982). The causal analysis of outcomes in the Coleman, Hoffer and Kilgore report. *Sociology of Education, 55,* 103–22.

GOODLAD, J. I. (1984). *A Place Called School: Prospects for the Future*. New York, NY: McGraw-Hill.

GOVERNOR'S CHRISTIAN SCHOOL ISSUE PANEL (1984). *Report*. Office of the Governor, State of Nebraska, 26 January.

GRATIOT, M. H. (1979). Why parents choose non-public schools: Comparative attitudes and characteristics of public and private school consumers. Ph.D. dissertation, Stanford University.

GRAUBARD, A. (1972). *Free the Children: Radical Reform and the Free School Movement*. New York, NY: Pantheon.

GREELEY, A. M. (1977). *The American Catholic*. New York, NY: Basic Books.

GREELEY, A. M. (1982). *Catholic High Schools and Minority Students*. New Brunswick, NJ: Transaction Books.

GREELEY, A. M., McCREADY, W. C. and McCOURT, K. (1976). *Catholic Schools in a Declining Church*. Kansas City, MO: Sheed & Ward.

GREELEY, A. M. and ROSSI, P. H. (1966). *The Education of Catholic Americans*. Chicago, IL: Aldine Press.

GRIFFIN, J. (1984). '*A Better Chance, Inc. Investing in Excellence*', paper presented at the annual meeting of the National Black Child Development Institute, Chicago, IL.

GRODZINS, M. (1966). *The American System*. Chicago, IL: Rand McNally.

HABERMAS, J. (1973). What does a crisis mean today? Legitimation problems in late capitalism. *Social Research, 40*(4), 40–64.

HAERTEL, E. H., JAMES, T. and LEVIN, H. M. (Eds.). (1987). *Comparing Public and Private Schools: Volume 2: School Achievement*. Philadelphia, Falmer Press.

HAGGSTROM, G. W. (1983). Logistic regression and discriminant analysis by ordinary least squares. *Journal of Business and Economic Statistics, 1,* 229–38.

HALPERIN, M., BLACKWELDER, W. C. and VORTER, J. I. (1971). Estimation of the multivariate logistic risk function: A comparison of the discriminant function and maximum likelihood approaches. *Journal of Chronic Diseases, 24,* 125–58.

HALVORSEN, R. and PALMQUIST, R. (1980). The interpretation of dummy variables in semilogarithmic equations. *American Economic Review, 70,* 474–5.

HANEY, J. E. (1978). The effects of the Brown decision on black educators. *Journal of Negro Education, 78,* 88–95.

HANNAWAY, J. and SPROULL, L. S. (1978–79). Who's running the show?

Coordination and control in educational organizations. *Administrator's Notebook,* 27(9), 1–4.

HANUSHEK, E. A. (1979). Conceptual and empirical issues in the estimation of educational production functions. *Journal of Human Resources, 14,* 351–88.

HARGROVE, E., GRAHAM, S. G., WARD, L. E., ABERNETHY, V., GUNNING-HAM, J. and VAUGHN, W. K. (1981). School systems and regulatory mandates: A case study of the implementation of the Education for all Handicapped Children Act, in BACHARACH S. B. (Ed.), *Organizational Behavior in Schools and School Districts.* New York, NY: Praeger, 97–123.

HARTMAN, W. (Ed.) (1981). Education for the handicapped: What is the appropriate federal role? (Policy Notes Series). Stanford, CA: Institute for Research on Educational Finance and Governance, Stanford University, Winter.

HICKEY, C. and COOPER, B. S. (1983). 'The challenge of non-Catholic children in Catholic schools', paper presented at the annual meeting of the American Educational Research Association, Montreal, Canada, April.

HILL v. STATE, 381 So. 2d 91 (Ala. Crim., App. 1979).

HILL v. STATE, 410 So. 2d 431 (Ala. Crim., App. 1981).

HOFFER, T., GREELEY, A and COLEMAN, J. (1984). *Achievement Growth in Public and Catholic High Schools.* Chicago, IL: National Opinion Research Center and University of Chicago.

HOSEK, J. R. (1979). An introduction to estimation with choice-based sample data. P-6361. Santa Monica, CA: Rand Corporation.

HUNTER, M. G. (1979). Final report of the Michigan cost-effectiveness study. East Lansing, MI: Michigan Department of Education.

ILLINOIS STATE BOARD OF EDUCATION (1981). 1981 Non-public registration, enrollment and staff report. Raw data file. (Available from Illinois State Board of Education, Springfield, IL).

IOWA v. MOORHEAD, 308 N.W. 2d 60 (Iowa 1981).

JACOBS, M. (1980). Tuition tax credits for elementary and secondary education: Some new evidence on who would benefit. *Journal of Education Finance, 5,* 233–45.

JAFFREE v. WALLACE, 705 F. 2nd 1526 (11th Cir. 1983).

JAMES, E. (1982). The private provision of public services: A comparison of Holland and Sweden. PONPO Working Paper No. 60. New Haven, CT: Institution for Social and Policy Studies, Yale University.

JAMES, E. (1984). Benefits and costs of privatized public services: Lessons from the Dutch educational system. *Comparative Education Review, 28,* 605–624; expanded varsion reprinted in *Private Education: Studies in Choice and Public Policy,* ed. D. Levy (New York: Oxford University Press, 1986).

JAMES, E. (1986). 'The private non-profit provision of education: A theoretical model and application to Japan', *Journal of comparative Economics* 10: 255–276.

JAMES, E. 1986. 'Differences in the Role of the Private Educational Sector in developing Countries.' Presented at the International Conference on the Economics of Education, Dijon and available as PONPO Working Paper No. 112 (New Haven, Yale University, ISPS).

JAMES, E. (1987). The non-profit sector in comparative perspective, in POWELL, W. (Ed.), *The Non-profit Sector: A Handbook for Research*. New Haven, CT: Yale University Press.

JAMES, E. 1987. 'Public Policies Toward Private Education.' World Bank Discussion Paper.

JAMES, E. and BENJAMIN, G. (1988, in press). *Public Policy and private education in Japan*. London: Macurillan.

JAMES, E., and Benjamin, G. 1988. 'Educational Distribution and Redistribution Through Education in Japan.' *Journal of Human Resources* (forthcoming).

JAMES, T. (1982). Public versus non-public education in historical perspective. Report TTT-6. Stanford, CA: Institute for Research on Educational Finance and Governance, Stanford University.

JAMES, T., and LEVIN, H. M. (Eds.) (1983). *Public Dollars for Private Schools: The Case of Tuition Tax Credits*. Philadelphia, PA: Temple University Press.

JERNEGAN, M. W. (1918). Compulsory education in the American colonies. *School Review, 26*, 731–749; and 1919, *27*, 24–43.

JERNEGAN, M. W. (1931). *Laboring and Dependent Classes in Colonial America. 1607–1783*. Chicago, IL: University of Chicago Press.

JOHNSON, D. (1985). Identity formation and racial coping strategies of black children and their parents: A stress and coping paradigm, unpublished paper. Northwestern University, Evanston, IL.

KAMIN, J., and ERICKSON, D. (1981). 'Parental choice of schooling in British Columbia: Preliminary findings', paper presented at the annual meeting of the American Educational Research Association, Los Angeles, CA, April.

KARPIK, L. (Ed.) (1978). *Organization and Environment: Theory, Issues and Reality*. Beverly Hills, CA: Sage Publications.

KATX, D., and KAHN, R. L. (1966). *The Social Psychology of Organizations*. New York, NY: John Wiley & Sons.

KATZ, M. (1975). *Class, Bureaucracy and Schools: The Illusion of Educational Change in America* (2nd edn). New York, NY: Praeger.

KIRP, D. E. (1982). *Just Schools*. Berkeley, CA: University of California Press.

KIRP, D. L. and JENSEN, D. N. (1986). *School Days, Rule Days: The Legalization and Regulation of Public Education*. Philadelphia, Falmer Press.

KIRST, M. W. (1980). A tale of two networks. *Taxing and Spending 3*, 43–9.

KIRST, M. W. (1982). Teaching policy and federal categorical programs. Stanford, CA: Institute for Research on Educational Finance and Governance, Stanford University.

KOTIN, L. and AIKMAN, W. F. (1980). *Legal Foundations of Compulsory School Attendance*. Port Washington, NY: Kennikat Press.

KRALLBILL, D. B. (1978). *Mennonite Education: Issues, Facts, and Changes*. Scottsdale, PA: Herald Press.

KRAUSHAAR, O. F. (1972). *American Non-public Schools: Patterns of Diversity*. Baltimore, MD: Johns Hopkins University Press.

LANOUETTE, W. J. (1977). The fourth R is religion. *National Observer*, 15 January, 1 and 18.

LAUBACH, J. H. (1969). *School Progress, Congress, the Court and the Public.* Washington, DC: Public Affairs Press.

LAWRENCE, P. R. and LORSCH, J. W. (1967). *Organization and Environment.* Boston: Graduate School of Business Administration, Harvard University.

Laws of the Province of Pennsylvania. (1683).

Laws of Virginia, 1642–43, Act 43.

Laws of Virginia, 1646, Act 27.

LEE, J. M. (1967). Catholic education in the United States, in LEE, J. M. (Ed.), *Catholic Education in the Western World.* Notre Dame, IN: University of Notre Dame Press.

LEVIN, B. (1977). *The Courts as Educational Policymakers and their Impact on Federal Programs.* Santa Monica, CA: Rand Corporation.

LEVIN, H. M. (1977). A decade of policy developments in improving education and training for low-income populations, in HAVEMAN, R. H. (Ed.), *A Decade of Federal Antipoverty Programs.* New York, NY: Academic Press, 123–88.

LEVINE, D. U. and STARK, J. (1981). Extended summary and conclusions: Institutional and organizational arrangements and processes for improving academic achievement at inner city elementary schools. Kansas City, MO: Center for the study of Metropolitan Problems in Education, University of Missouri, August.

LEVY, D. C. (1984). *The State and Higher Education in Latin America: Comparing Public to Private Sectors.* Chicago, IL: University of Chicago Press.

LEVY, D. C. (1986a). *Higher Education and the State in Latin America: Private Challenge to Public Dominance.* Chicago, IL: University of Chicago Press.

LEVY, D. C. (1986b). *Private Education: Studies in Choice and Public Policy.* New York: Oxford University Press.

LIGHTFOOT, S. (1983). *The Good High School.* New York, NY: Basic Books.

LINDSAY, COTTON, M. (1976). A theory of government enterprise. *Journal of Political Economy, 84,* 1061–77.

LINES, P. (1983). Private education alternatives and state regulation. *Journal of Law and Education, 12,* 189–234.

LINES P. (1987). An Overview of Home Instruction *Ph: Delta Kappan, 68,* 510–517.

LOWRIE, R. W., JR. (1971). Christian school growing pains. *Eternity,* January, 19–21.

LUBBOCK CIVIL LIBERTIES UNION V. LUBBOCK IND. SCHOOL DISTRICT, 669 F. 2d 1038 (5th Cir. 1982).

LUCAS, R. E. B. (1972). Working conditions, wage-rates and human capital: A hedonic study. Ph.D. dissertation, Massachusetts Institute of Technology.

LUTHER, M. (1963). Letters to the mayors and councilmen of all German cities in behalf of Christian schools, 1524, in STILLHORN, A. C. *Schools of the Lutheran Church, Missouri Synod.* St. Louis, MO: Concordia Publishing House.

McCLUSKEY, N. G. (1967). The new secularity and the requirements of pluralism, in SIZER T. R. (Ed.), *Religion and Public Education.* Boston, MA: Houghton Mifflin.

McCluskey, N. G. (1969). *Catholic Education Faces its Future*. Garden City, NY: Doubleday.

McDonnell, L. M. and McLaughlin, M. W. (1982). *Education Policy and the Role of the States*. Santa Monica, CA: Rand Corporation.

McLaughlin, D. L. (1983). Non-public school pupils: A validation check of NCES surveys. SAGE Technical Report No. 20. Palo Alto, CA: American Institutes for Research.

McLaughlin, D. L. and Bakke, T. W. (1981). *Non-public School Pupils, How Many Are There, Really?* Palo Alto, CA: American Institutes for Research.

McLaughlin, D. H. and Wise, L. L. (1980). Non-public education of the nation's children. SAGE Technical Report No. #9. Palo Alto, CA: Statistical Analysis Group in Education, American Institutes for Research.

McPartland, J. M. and McDill, E. L. (1982). Control and differentiation in the structure of American education. *Sociology of Education, 55*, 77–88.

Manno, B. (1978). *How to Service Students with Federal Education Program Benefits*. Washington, DC: National Catholic Education Association.

Manno, B. V. and Cooper, B. S. (1983). 'The State of Catholic Education', Paper presented to the American Education Research Association, Special Interest Group; Associates for Research on Private Education, Montreal, Canada, April.

Manski, C. F. and Lerman, S. R. (1977). The estimation of choice probabilities from choice-based samples. *Econometrica, 45*, 1977–88.

May v. Cooperman, 572 F. Supp. 1561 (D.N.J. 1983).

Meyer, J. (1981). Organizational factors affecting legalization in education. Program Report No. 81-B10. Stanford, CA: Institute for Research on Educational Finance and Governance, Stanford University.

Meyer v. Nebraska, 262 US 390 (1923).

Meyer, J. (1983a). Centralization of funding and control in educational governance, in Meyer, J. W. and Scott, W. R., *Organizational Environments: Ritual and Rationality*. Beverly Hills, CA: Sage Publications, 179–97.

Meyer, J. (1983b). Conclusion: Institutionalization and the rationality of formal organizational structure, in Meyer, J. W. and Scott, W. R., *Organizational Environments: Ritual and Rationality*. Beverly Hills, CA: Sage Publications, 261–82.

Meyer, J. (1983c). Organizational factors affecting legalization in education, in Meyer, J. W. and Scott, W. R., *Organizational Environments: Ritual and Rationality*. Beverly Hills, CA: Sage Publications, 217–32.

Meyer, J. W. and Rowan, B. (1977). Institutionalized organizations: Formal structure as myth and ceremony. *American Journal of Sociology, 83*, 340–63.

Meyer, J. W. and Scott, W. R. (1983a). Centralization and the legitimacy problems of local government. In J. W. Meyer and W. R. Scott, *Organizational Environments: Ritual and Rationality*. Beverly Hills, CA: Sage Publications, 199–215.

Meyer, J. W. and Scott, W. R. (1983b). *Organizational Environments: Ritual and Rationality*. Beverly Hills, CA: Sage Publications.

MEYER, M. and ASSOCIATES (Eds.) (1978). *Environments and Organizations.* San Francisco, CA: Jossey-Bass.

MITCHELL, D. E. (1981). *Shaping Legislative Decision: Education Policy and the Social Sciences.* Lexington, MA: DC Heath.

MORGAN, W. R. (1983). Learning and student life quality of public and private school youth. *Sociology of Education, 55,* 187–202.

MORRIS, V. C., CROWSON, R. L., HURWITZ, E., JR., and PORTER-GEHRIE, C. (1981). *The Urban Principal: Discretionary Decision-making in a Large Educational Organization.* Chicago, IL: College of Education, University of Illinois at Chicago Circle.

MUELLER, D. C. (1979). *Public Choice.* Cambridge; Cambridge University Press.

MUELLER V. ALLEN, 103 US 3062, 3066 (1983).

MURNANE, R. J. (1975). *The Impact of School Resources on the Learning of Inner-city School Children.* Cambridge, MA: Ballinger.

MURNANE, R. J. (1983). Comparisons of public and private schools: Lessons from the uproar, unpublished paper. Harvard Graduate School of Education, Cambridge, MA.

MURPHY, J. T. (Ed.) (1980). *State Leadership in Education: On Being a Chief State School Officer.* Washington, DC: Institute for Educational Leadership.

MURPHY, J. T. (1981). The paradox of state government reform. *The Public Interest,* No. 64, 124–39.

NABOA, A. (1980). Hispanics and desegregation: Summary of Aspira's study on Hispanic segregation trends in US school districts. *Metas, 1*(3), 1–24.

NATIONAL ASSOCIATION OF INDEPENDENT SCHOOLS (1982). *Spring Statistics, 1982–82.* Boston, MA: National Association of Independent Schools.

NATIONAL ASSOCIATION OF INDEPENDENT SCHOOLS (1986). *Spring Statistics, 1986.* Boston, MA: National Association of Independent Schools.

NATIONAL CATHOLIC EDUCATION ASSOCIATION (1980a). *How to Service Students with Federal Education Program Benefits.* Washington, DC: National Catholic Education Association.

NATIONAL CATHOLIC EDUCATION ASSOCIATION (1980b). Raw data file. (Available from National Catholic Education Association, Washington, DC).

NATIONAL CENTER FOR EDUCATION STATISTICS (1981, 1982, 1983). *The Condition of Education.* Washington, DC: US Government Printing Office.

NATIONAL COMMISSION ON EXCELLENCE IN EDUCATION (1983). *A Nation at Risk: The Imperative for Educational Reform.* Washington, DC: US Government Printing Office.

NAULT, R. L., ERICKSON, D. A. and COOPER, B. S. (1977). Hard times for non-public schools. *National Elementary Principal, 56*(6), 16–21.

NAULT, R. and UCHITELLE, S. (1982). School choice in the public sector: A case study of parental decision making, in MANLEY, M. and CASIMIR, S. (Eds.), *Family Choice in Schooling: Issues and Dilemmas.* Lexington, MA: Lexington Books.

NEUFIELD, B., FARRAR, E. and MILES, M. B. (1983). A review of effective schools research: The message for secondary schools. Report to the National Commission on Excellence in Education. Cambridge, MA: The Huron Institute, January.

NEWMAN, D., *et al.* (1976). *Protests, Politics, and Prosperity.* New York, NY: Pantheon.

NOELL, J. (1982). Public and Catholic schools: A reanalysis of public and private schools. *Sociology of Education, 55,* 123–32.

NOELL, J. (1984). 'Recent patterns of private school enrollment and tuition', paper presented at the annual meeting of the American Educational Research Association, New Orleans, LA, April.

NOELL, J. and MYERS, D. (1982). 'The demand for private schooling: A preliminary analysis', paper presented at the Annual Meeting of the American Education Finance Association, Philadelphia, PA.

NORDIN, V. D. and TURNER, W. L. (1980). More than segregationist academies: The growing Protestant fundamentalist schools. *Phi Delta Kappan, 61,* 391–4.

NORTH DAKOTA v. REVINUIS, 328 N.W. 2d 220 (N.D. 1982).

ODDEN, A. and DOUGHERTY, V. (1982). *State Programs of School Improvement: A 50-state Survey.* Denver, CO: Education Commission of the States.

OFFE, C. (1983). Political legitimation through majority rule? *Social Research, 50,* 710–56.

O'MALLEY, C. J. (1981). Governance of private schools. *Private School Quarterly,* 12–5, summer.

ORFIELD, G. (1978). Report to the Superior Court of the State of California for the County of Los Angeles, Mary Ellen Crawford *et al.,* v. Board of Education of the City of Los Angeles.

ORFIELD, G. (1983). *School Desegregation Patterns in the States, Large Cities and Metropolitan Areas.* Washington, DC: Joint Center for Political Studies.

OSTLING, R. (1977). Why Protestant schools are booming. Christian Herald. July–August, 44–7.

OUCHI, W. G. (1980). Markets, bureaucracies and clans. *Administrative Sciences Quarterly, 25,* 129–41.

PADOVER, S. K. (Ed.) (1943). *The Complete Jefferson.* Freeport, NY: Books for Libraries Press.

PAGE, E. and KEITH, T., (1981). Effects of US private schools: A technical analysis of two recent claims. *Educational Researcher, 10,* 7–17, August.

PEARCE, D. (1980). Breaking down barriers: The effect of metropolitan school desegregation on housing patterns, unpublished paper, Catholic University Law School.

PEARCE, D., CRAIN, R. L., FARLEY, R. and TAEUBER, K. (1984). Lessons not lost: The effects of school segregation on housing segregation, unpublished paper, Center for the Social Organization of Schools, Johns Hopkins University.

PETERSON, P. (1983). *Making the Grade: Report of the Twentieth Century Fund Task Force on Federal Elementary and Secondary Education Policy.* New York, NY: Twentieth Century Fund.

PFEFFER, J. and SALANCIK, G. (1978). *The External Control of Organizations.* New York, NY: Harper & Row.

PHI DELTA KAPPA (1980). *Why Do Some Urban Schools Succeed?* Bloomington, IN: Phi Delta Kappa.

PIERCE v. SOCIETY OF SISTERS, 268 US 510 (1925).

PLISKO, V. (Ed.) (1984). *The Condition of Education: 1984.* Washington, DC: National Center for Education Statistics.

PRESIDENT'S COMMISSION ON SCHOOL FINANCE (1971). *Public Aid to Non-public Education.* Washington, DC: The Commission.

PRIVATE SCHOOL REPORT (1981). *A Report of the Private Schools Committee.* (Available from Dr. Robert Church, School of Education, Northwestern University, Evanston, IL.), September.

PRIVATE SCHOOL SURVEY (1980). Raw data file. (Available from US Department of Education, National Center for Educational Statistics, Washington, DC.)

Public Records of the Colony of Connecticut to 1655.

PURKEY, S. C. and SMITH, M. S. (1983). Effective schools: A review. *Elementary School Journal, 83,* 427–52.

RATTERAY, J. (1984). One system is not enough: A free market alternative for the education of minorities. *Lincoln Review, 4*(4), 25–31.

RATTERAY, J. (1986). Personal communication, Barbara L. Schneider, Northwestern University, Evanston, IL.

Records of the Colony and Jurisdiction of New Haven, 1653–1665 (1858).

Records of the Governor and Company of Massachusetts in New England, 1642 (14 June), 6–9.

REED, B. and DANDRIDGE, W. (1979). *Recruiting Minority Students.* Boston, MA: National Association of Independent Schools.

REUTTER, E. and HAMILTON, R. (1976). *The Law of Public Education.* Minola, NY: Foundation Press.

RICE, In re. 204 Neb. 732, 285 N.W. 2d 223 (1979).

RICHARDS, C. E. (1983). Race and educational employment: The political economy of teacher labor markets. Ph.D. dissertation, Stanford University.

RICHARDS, C. E. (1985). Bilingualism and Hispanic employment: School reform or social control, in GARCIA, E. E. and PADILLA, R. V. (Eds.), *Advances in Bilingual Education Research.* Tucson, AZ: University of Arizona Press.

RICHARDS, C. E. (1986). Race and demographic trends: The employment of minority teachers in California public schools. *Economics of Education Review, 11,* 57–64.

RICHARDS, C. E. and ENCARNATION, D. J. (1982). *Race and educational employment.* Stanford, CA: Institute for Research on Educational Finance and Governance, Stanford University.

ROGERS, D. and WHETTEN, D. (Eds.) (1981). *Interorganizational Coordination.* Ames, IA: Iowa State University Press.

ROSEN, S. (1974). Hedonic prices and implicit markets: Product differentiation in pure competition. *Journal of Political Economy, 82,* 34–55.

ROSSELL, C. H. (1983). Desegregation plans, racial isolation, white flight, and community response, in ROSSELL, C. H. and HAWLEY, W. D. (Eds.), *The Consequences of School Desegregation.* Philadelphia, PA: Temple University Press.

ROSSELL, C. H. and ROSS, J. M. (1979). *The long-term effect of court ordered desegregation on student enrollment in Central City school systems: The case of Boston 1974–1979.* Boston, MA: Sociology Department, Boston University.

Rossi, P.H. and Wright, J. D. (1982). Best schools — better discipline or better students? A review of high school achievement. *American Journal of Education, 91,* 79–89.

Rothbard, M. N. (1974). Historical origins, in Rickenbacker W. F. (Ed.), *The Twelve-year Sentence.* LaSalle, IL: Open Court Publishing.

Rothschild-Whitt, J. (1979). The collectivist organization: An alternative to rational bureaucratic models. *American Sociological Review, 44,* 509–527.

Rowan, B. (1981). The effects of institutionalized rules on administrators, in Bacharach, S. B. (Ed.), *Organizational Behavior in Schools and School Districts.* New York, NY: Praeger, 47–75.

Rowan, B. (1982). Instructional management in historical perspective: Evidence on differentiation in school districts. *Educational Administration Quarterly, 18,* 43–59, winter.

Rowan, B., Bossert, S. T. and Dwyer, D. C. (1983). Research on effective schools: A cautionary note. *Educational Researcher, 12,* 24–31.

Rowan, B., Dwyer, D. C. and Bossert, S. T. (1982). 'Methodological considerations in studies of effective principals', paper presented at the meeting of the American Educational Research Association, New York, NY, April.

Rumberger, R. (1983). Social mobility and public sector employment. Stanford, CA: Institute for Research on Educational Finance and Governance, Stanford University.

Rutter, M., Maughan, B., Mortimore, P., Ouston, J. and Smith, A. (1979). *Fifteen Thousand Hours: Secondary Schools and their Effects on Children.* Cambridge, MA: Harvard University Press.

Salganik, L. H. and Karweit, N. (1982). Voluntarism and governance in education. *Sociology of Education,* 55, 152–61.

Salomon, G., King, D. and Yuen, S. (1979). School governance and sociological correlates: Summary of secondary analyses of the environment for teaching data. Stanford, CA: Institute for Research on Educational Finance and Governance, Stanford University.

Sanders, J. W. (1976). *The Education of an Urban Minority: Catholics in Chicago: 1833–1965.* New York: Oxford University Press.

Santa Fe Community School v. New Mexico Board of Education, 85 N.M. 783, 518 P. 2d 272 (N.M. 1974).

Sassenrath, J., Croce, M. and Penaloza, M. (1984). Private and public school students: Longitudinal achievement differences? *American Educational Research Journal, 21,* 557–63.

Satow, R. L. (1975). Value-rational authority and professional organizations: Weber's missing type. *Administrative Science Quarterly, 20,* 526–31.

Schiff, A. I. (1966). *The Jewish Day School in America.* New York: Jewish Education Committee Press.

Schneider, B. and Slaughter, D. (1984, October). 'Assessing educational choices: Blacks in private urban elementary schools', paper prepared for the Conference Comparing Public and Private Schools. Institute for Research on Educational Finance and Governance, Stanford University.

School District of Abington Township v. Schempp, 374 US 203 (1963).

School Research Forum (1981). Educational Research Service, April.

Scott, W. R. (1981). *Organizations: Rational, Natural and Open Systems.* Englewood Cliffs, NJ: Prentice-Hall.

SCOTT, W. R. (1983). The organization of environments: Network, cultural and historical elements, in MEYER, J. W. and SCOTT, W. R. *Organizational Environments: Ritual and Rationality*. Beverly Hills, CA: Sage Publications, 155–75.

SCOTT, W. R. and MEYER, J. W. (1983). The organization of societal sectors, in MEYER, J. W. and SCOTT, W. R. (Eds.) *Organizational Environments: Ritual and Rationality*. Beverly Hills, CA: Sage Publications, 127–53.

SCOTT, W. R. and MEYER, J. (1984). Environmental linkages and organizational complexity: Public and private schools. Project Report No. 84-A16. Stanford, CA: Institute for Research on Educational Finance and Governance, Stanford University.

SERGIOVANNI, T. J., BURLINGAME, M., COOMBS, F. D. and THURSTON, P. (1980). *Educational Governance and Administration*. Englewood Cliffs, NJ: Prentice-Hall.

SEVENTH DAY ADVENTIST CHURCH (1965). *Church Manual on Family Life*. Washington, DC: Seventh Day Adventist Church.

SIZEMORE, B. (1984). An abasing anomaly: The high achieving predominately black elementary school. *Point of View*, Washington, DC: Congressional Black Caucus Foundation, 4–5, spring.

SLAUGHTER, D. and SCHNEIDER, B. (1986). *Newcomers: Blacks in Private Schools*. (Contract No. NIE-G-82-0040, Project No. 2-0450). Washington, DC: National Institute of Education. ERIC Document Reproduction Service nos: ED 274 268 and ED 274 269.

SMITH, P. and JACOBS, C. M. (1913). *Luther's Correspondence and Other Contemporary Letters*. Philadelphia, PA: Lutheran Publications Society.

SONSTELIE, J. (1979). Public school quality and private school enrollments. *National Tax Journal, 32*, 343–51.

SOUTH DAKOTA CODIFIED LAWS ANN. sec. 13–27–3 (Supp. 1983).

SPANN, R. M. (1974). Collective consumption of private goods. *Public Choice, 20*, 63–82.

STACKHOUSE, A. (1982). The effects of state centralization on administrative and macrotechnical structure in contemporary secondary schools. Project Report No. 82-A24. Stanford, CA: Institute for Research on Educational Finance and Governance, Stanford University.

STAPLES, B. (1986). The dwindling black presence on campus. *New York Times*. Sunday, April 20.

STATE OF NEBRASKA. (1984). *Report of the Governor's Christian School Issue Panel*.

STATE v. FAITH BAPTIST CHURCH, 107 Neb. 802, 301 N.W. 2ds 571 (1981), 102 S. Ct. 75 (1981).

STATE v. KASUBOSKI, 87 Wis. 2d 407, 275 N.W. 2d 101 (Wis. App. 1978).

STATE v. LABURGE, 134, Vt. 276, 357 A. 2d 121 (1976).

STATE v. NOBEL, Nos. S 791-0114-A & S 791-0115-A (Mich. Dist. Ct., Allegon County, Dec. 12, 1979).

STATE v. RIDDLE, 285 S.E. 2d 359 (W. Va., 1981).

STATE v. SHAVER, 294 N.W. 2d 833 (N.D., 1980).

STATE v. WHISNER, 47 Ohio St. 2d 181, 351 N.E. 2d 750 (1976).

STEIN v. OSHINSKY, 348 F 2d 999 (2d Cir. 1965).

STONE v. GRAHAM, 101 S. Ct. 192 (1980).

SULLIVAN, D. J. (1974). *Public Aid to Non-public Schools.* Lexington, MA: Lexington Books.

SWANSON, G. E. (1980). A basis of authority and identity in post-industrial society, in HOLZNER, B. & ROBERTSON, R. (Eds.), *Authority and Identity.* Oxford, England: Blackwells.

SWIDLER, A. (1979). *Organization Without Authority: Dilemmas of Social Control in Free Schools.* Cambridge, MA: Harvard University Press.

SYME, D. (1983). Reform Judaism and day schools. The great Historical dilemma. *Religious Education, 78*(2), 153–81.

TAEUBER, K. E. and JAMES, D. R. (1982). Racial segregation among public and private schools. *Sociology of Education, 55,* 133–43.

TALBERT, J. E. (1984). Toward an institutional-contingency view of school organization. Project Report No. 84-A10. Stanford, CA: Institute for Research on Educational Finance and Governance, Stanford University.

TAYLOR, D. G. and STINCHECOMBE, A. L. (1977). The Boston school desegregation controversy. Chicago, IL: National Opinion Research Center.

THOMPSON, J. D. (1967). *Organizations in Action.* New York, NY: McGraw-Hill.

TIEBOUT, C. (1956). A pure theory of local expenditures. *Journal of Political Economy, 64,* 416–24.

TOMLINSON, T. M. (1980). 'Student ability, student background and student achievement: Another look at life in effective schools', paper presented at the Educational Testing Service Conference on Effective Schools, New York, NY, May.

TREEN v. KAREN B., 102 W.S. 1267 (1982).

TRISMAN, D. A., WALLER, M. I. and WILDER, C. A. (1976). A descriptive and analytic study of compensatory reading programs: Final report. Vol. 2 (PR 75–26). Princeton, NJ: Educational Testing Service.

TYACK, D. and HANSOT, E. (1982). *Managers of Virtue: Public School Leadership in America, 1820–1980.* New York, NY: Basic Books.

US BUREAU OF THE CENSUS (1984, March). *United States Census Detailed Population Characteristics,* PC80-1-D1-A. Washington, DC: US Bureau of the Census.

US BUREAU OF EDUCATION (1918). *Cardinal Principles of Secondary Education* (Bulletin No. 35). Washington, DC: US Bureau of Education.

US DEPARTMENT OF HEALTH, EDUCATION AND WELFARE. National Institute of Education. (1978). Violent schools — safe schools: The safe school study report to the US Congress, Vol. 1. Washington, DC: US Government Printing Office.

UMBECH, N. (1960). *State Legislation on School Attendance and Related Matters.* (Office of Education Circular No. 615). Washington, DC: US Office of Education.

VITULLO-MARTIN, T. (1978). Federal policies and private schools, in WILLIAMS' M. F. (Ed.), *Government in the Classroom.* Proceedings of the Academy of Political Science, *33*(2), 124–35.

VITULLO-MARTIN, T. (1982). The impact of taxation policy on public and private schools, in EVERHART, R. E. (Ed.), *The Public School Monopoly.* Cambridge, MA: Ballinger, 369–91.

WALLACE v. JAFFREE, 105 S. Ct. 2479 (1985).

WALLACE, P. A. (1977). A decade of policy developments in equal opportunities in employment and housing, in HAVEMAN, R. H. (Ed.), *A Decade of Federal Antipoverty Programs.* New York, NY: Academic Press, 329–59.
WEATHERLEY, R. A. (1979). *Reforming Special Education: Policy Implementation from State Level to Street Level.* Cambridge MA: MIT Press.
WEAVER, N., NEGRI, R. A. and WALLACE, B. (1980). Home tutorials vs. the public school in Los Angeles. *Phi Delta Kappan, 62,* 251–5.
WEBER, G. (1971). Inner-city children can be taught to read: Four successful schools. Washington, DC: Council for Basic Education.
WEBER, M. (1924). *The Theory of Social and Economic Organization.* HENDERSON, A. H. & PARSONS, T. (Eds.). Glencoe, IL: Free Press (1947 tr.).
WEICK, K. E. (1976). Educational organizations as loosely coupled systems. *Administrative Science Quarterly, 21,* 1–19.
WEILER, H. (1982). The politics of educational reform: Notes on the comparative study of innovations in education. Report No. 82-A22. Stanford, CA: Institute for Research on Educational Finance and Governance, Stanford University.
WEILER, H. (1983). Knowledge and legitimation: The national and international politics of educational research, unpublished manuscript, Stanford University.
WEISBERGER, B. A. (1970). *The American Heritage History of the American People.* New York, NY: American Heritage Publishing Co.
WEISBROD, B. A. (1975). Toward a theory of the voluntary non-profit sector in a three-sector economy, in PHELPS, E. (Ed.), *Altruism, Morality and Economic Theory.* New York, NY: Russell Sage Foundation.
WEISBROD, B. A. (1977). *The Voluntary Non-profit Sector.* Lexington, MA: Lexington Books.
WEISBROD, B. A. (1983). Non-profit and proprietary sector behavior: Wage differentials among lawyers. *Journal of Labor Economics, 1,* 246–63.
WELLISCH, J. B., McQUEEN, A. H., CARRIERE, R. A. and DUCK, G. A. (1978). School management and organization in successful schools. *Sociology of Education, 51,* 211–26.
WENDLING, W. (1979). Cost-of-education indices for New York state school districts. Denver, CO: Education Commission of the States.
WEST, E. (1982). The prospects for educational vouchers: An economic analysis, in EVERHART, R. E. (Ed.), *The Public School Monopoly.* Cambridge, MA: Ballinger, 369–91.
WESTERHOFF, J. H. III. (1978). *McGuffey and his Readers.* Nashville, TN: Abington Press.
WIDMAR v. VINCENT, 454 US 263 (1981).
WILEY, D. (1983). *State Boards of Education: Quality Leadership.* Alexandria, VA: National Association of State Boards of Education.
WILLIAMS, M. F., HANCHER, K. S. and HUTNER. A. (1983). Parents and school choice: A household survey. School Finance Project Working Paper, US Department of Education, December.
WILLMS, D. (1982). Achievement outcomes in public and private schools: A closer look at the 'High School and Beyond' data. Stanford, CA: Institute for Research on Educational Finance and Governance, Stanford University.

WINTER, N. H. (1966). *Jewish Education in a Pluralist Society.* New York, NY: New York University Press.

WISE, A. (1979). *Legislated Learning.* Berkeley, CA: University of California Press.

WISEMAN, J. (1979). Ideology-critique, and economics. *Social Research, 46,* 291–320.

WOLCOTT, H. F. (1973). *The Man in the Principal's Office.* New York, NY: Holt, Rinehart and Winston.

WYNNE, E. A. (1980). *Looking at Schools: Good, Bad, and Indifferent.* Lexington, MA: Heath.

ZELLNER, A. and LEE, T. H. (1965). Joint estimation of relationships involving discrete random variables. *Econometrica, 33,* 382–94.

Notes on Contributors

Thomas James is Assistant Professor of Education and Public Policy at Brown University. He has written about the history of the public-private distinction in education and democratic reasoning underlying arguments about the public good in schooling institutions. His publications include *Exile Within: The Schooling of Japanese Americans, 1942–1945* (Harvard University Press, 1987) and, with David Tyack and Aaron Benavot, *Law and the Shapig of Public Education 178701954* (University of Wisconsin Press, 1987).

Henry M. Levin is Professor of Education, Affiliated Professor of Economics, and the Director of the Center for Educational Research at Stanford (CERAS). He is a specialist in the economics of education and the economics of human resources. He is the co-author of *Schooling and Work in the Democratic State* (Stanford University Press, 1975).

Bruce S. Cooper is Associate Professor of Educational Administration at Fordham University. His recent research on federal policies and private schooling includes *The Separation of Church and Child*, an analysis of the impact of the courts on provision of equitable services to children attending private and parochial schools (written with Thomas Vitullo-Martin).

James C. Catterall is Assistant Professor of Educational Administration and Policy at the Graduate School of Education, University of California at Los Angeles. His specialties include the political economy of education and education policy analysis. His current research focuses on youth who drop out of school. He is the editor of *Economic Evaluation of Public Programs* (Jossey-Bass, 1985).

Patricia M. Lines is an attorney and senior policy analyst at the US Department of Education. At the time she prepared this chapter, she was director of the Law and Education Center at the Education Commission of the States. This chapter presents her views and not those of USDE or ECS. Her published work includes several articles on private schools, home instruction and choice within public schools.

Estelle James is a Professor of Economics at the State University of New York at Stoney Brook. She has written many papers on the economics of education and nonprofit organizations, and is the co-author of *The Nonprofit Enterprise in the Market Economies*. (Harwood Academic Publishers, 1986) and *Public Policy and Private Education in Japan* (Mamillan, 1988).

W. Richard Scott is Professor in the Department of Sociology with courtesy appointments in the Schools of Education, Business and Medicine at Stanford University. He is the Director of Research Training Programs on Organizations and Mental Health and on Organizations and Aging at Stanford. His most recent books are *Organizational Environments: Ritual and Rationality* (Sage, 1983) coauthored with John W. Meyer, and *Organizations: Rational, Natural and Open Systems*, 2nd ed., 1987.

John W. Meyer is Professor of Sociology (and, by courtesy, Education) at Stanford. He has worked on (a) the origins and expansion of modern educational systems, (b) their organizational structure, and (c) institutional models of their effects. His work on educational organization has recently appeared in a book co-authored with W. R. Scott on *Organizational Environments: Ritual and Rationality* (Sage, 1983).

Joan E. Talbert is Assistant Professor of Education and, by courtesy, Sociology at Stanford University. She is a specialist in social stratification and organizational sociology and has published articles on wage inequalities and careers in selected occupations. Her current research analyzes gender-education-work patterns across selected industrialized nations.

Jay G. Chambers is President and Senior Economist for the Associates for Education Finance and Planning (AEFP), Inc. His general fields of interest are economics of education and human resources. His primary publications have focused on school finance, program cost differences in education, and markets for school personnel. His current efforts are directed toward the development and implementation of planning models for state and local educational agencies.

Craig E. Richards is Assistant Professor in the Graduate School of Education, Department of Educational Theory, Policy and Administration at Rutgers University. He is also a Research Fellow at the Center for Policy Research in Education located at the Eagleton Institute of Politics at Rutgers University where is conducting a national study of the monitoring of school reform.

Dennis J. Encarnation is Associate Professor of Management at the Graduate School of Business Administration, Harvard University. He specializes in the political economy of regulation, both in the United States and abroad. He is author of *Bargaining in the Uneasy Triangle: Multinationals, the State and Local Enterprises in India* (Princeton University Press, forthcoming, 1987).

Linda Darling-Hammond is a Senior Social Scientist and Director of the Education and Human Resources Program at the RAND Corporation. Her research center on effects of educational policies on state and local education agencies and on teaching. Her recent work has included studies of teacher evaluation and selection practices, teacher supply and demand, the development of educational indicators, and teacher competency testing policies. She is the author of 'Beyond the Commission Reports: The coming crisis in teaching'.

Sheila Nataraj Kirby is an Economist with the RAND Corporation and an Associate Professional Lecturer at George Washington University. Her present research focuses on enlistment and attrition in the military reserve forces, recruitment of mathematics and science teachers from nontraditional sources, and the market for intellectual property.

Robert L. Crain, Professor of Sociology and Education at Teachers College, Columbia University, has done considerable research on race and schools. He was formerly at the Center for Social Organization of Schools, Johns Hopkins University, where he wrote several papers on achievement in private schools and on the effects of school desegregation.

Barbara L. Schneider is Assistant Professor of Education, in the School of Education and Social Policy, Northwestern University. Her area of specialization is school organizations, and she has written several chapters and articles on private education. Her most recent chapter 'Schooling for minority children: An equity perspective' is forthcoming in *Private Schools and Public Policy: International Perspectives*, edited by William Lowe Boyd and James Cibulka, Falmer Press.

Diana T. Slaughter is Associate Professor of Education and Social Policy, Human Development and Social Policy Program, Northwestern University. Her research areas include: family influences on academic achievement, black education, and early intervention studies. She recently guest co-edited (with Edgar G. Epps of the University of Chicago) a special issue of *The Journal of Negro Education* (Winter, 1987) devoted to the black child's home environment and student achievement. She is currently co-editing a volume under contract (Greenwood Press) entitled *Visible Now: Blacks in Private Schools*.

Index

THE DEADLIEST

HURRICANES THEN AND NOW

BY
DEBORAH HOPKINSON

SCHOLASTIC
FOCUS

NEW YORK

Library of Congress Cataloging-in-Publication Data available

ISBN 978-1-338-36017-2

10 9 8 7 6 5 4 3 2 1   22 23 24 25 26

Printed in the U.S.A.   113
First edition, January 2022

Book design by Abby Dening

Illustration, previous page: Galveston's awful calamity.
This 1900 illustration depicts the horror of the hurricane
that devastated Galveston, Texas, on September 8, 1900.

For Bonnie and Jamie in Texas

(and all the dogs)

Contents

Harry Maxson struggled through flooded streets in Galveston on September 8, 1900, much like this scene in Providence, Rhode Island, during a 1938 hurricane.

PROLOGUE
Harry Runs for Home

Galveston, Texas

Saturday, September 8, 1900

Four o'clock in the afternoon

The storm had burst by the time Harry Maxson started for home. Rain fell in torrents, slashing his skin. Gusts of wind beat against his face. He had twenty-two blocks to go.

Harry was just fourteen, but he was big for his age and strong. His father worked for the railroad and had helped

Harry Maxson

Harry land his first part-time job, hauling freight at the railroad yard for sixteen cents an hour. On Saturday, even as the storm grew worse, Harry and the grown men kept working until finally the boss said they could go.

By then, the water was already so deep that in some places Harry had to wade. But when he reached a street with only two inches of water, he began to run.

"I saw a roof being lifted off of a house. Believe me I sprinted as fast as I could as some shingles came toward me," said Harry. "I threw up my hand to guard my head and a nail in one of the shingles struck me and cut the back of my hand. At that minute—the wind, the water—dodging the shingles, I finally slipped and fell."

Harry's face hit the water and he licked his lips. Wait! What was this? He could taste salt. All this water? It wasn't from the torrential rain. No, this was the Gulf of Mexico itself surging over the city streets.

Harry struggled to his feet. The wind kept blowing. The water kept rising. His house was on M Street,

close to the beach on the Gulf side. By the time he arrived around five o'clock, water in the yard was nearly a foot deep.

Saturday afternoon was just the beginning. The deadliest hurricane in American history had Galveston in its grip.

Not a soul was ready.

BEFORE YOU GO ON

This book tells the story of a terrible disaster, through the words of survivors. Their accounts help us understand what it was like to experience the Great Galveston hurricane. And that's possible because ordinary people took the time to share their stories in letters, oral histories, interviews, and journals.

Telling our stories is so important—even more than you might imagine. I wanted the accounts here to reflect various points of view and life experiences from both white and Black survivors. Yet, as I began my research, I mostly found accounts from white people. The voices of African Americans were missing. Luckily, I discovered a book entitled *Island of Color: Where Juneteenth Started* by Izola Collins (1929–2017). A Galveston teacher for many years, Ms. Collins was part of a family who

had lived in Galveston for five generations. She was inspired to publish a history of African Americans in her city by seeing her grandfather Ralph Albert Scull (1860–1949) write in his own journal.

"I remember passing his bedroom late evenings, and seeing Papa (as we girls called him, since this is what my mother called her father) sitting at his little desk, writing in the green composition tablet," she recalled. He spent years recording his observations and experiences as an educator and pastor in the African American community.

Thanks to Ralph Albert Scull and Izola Collins, we can read the story of Annie Smizer McCullough, Izola's great-aunt, who was in her nineties when she shared her memories of the storm. We have insights and details that would otherwise be lost to historians, writers, and readers like you and me.

In addition to personal stories about the Galveston hurricane itself, throughout this book you'll find special sections with facts about weather science and

hurricanes. And in the back, along with other resources, I've included instructions for doing an oral history interview with a relative or friend. I hope you'll be a history detective too!

We're all part of history. Your story matters. I hope you will tell it.

—*Deborah Hopkinson*

PEOPLE IN THIS BOOK

» *Clara Barton*

Clara Barton (1821–1912) founded the American Red Cross in 1881, following her heroic efforts to aid battlefield soldiers during the Civil War. She created awareness of the Galveston hurricane disaster and traveled to Galveston to help organize relief efforts.

» *Mary Louise Bristol (Hopkins)*

Mary Louise (1893–1987), who went by her middle name, Louise, was seven when the storm struck. Her father had died when she was a baby. Louise lived in Galveston with her mother, two older brothers, and older sister. Her mother took in boarders to make ends meet. When she grew up, Louise worked for the Santa Fe Railroad and married Oscar Hopkins.

She later visited schools to share her memories of the hurricane with young people. She died in 1987 at the age of ninety-four.

» The Cline Brothers: Isaac and Joseph

The Cline brothers were two of seven children originally from Tennessee. Isaac (1861–1955) moved to Galveston in 1893 to head the weather station. He lived with his wife and three children in a house near the beach. Joseph (1870–1955) worked for his brother as a weather observer and lived with the family.

After the tragedy in Galveston, the brothers continued in the weather service. While in later years they did not keep in touch, they passed away almost within a week of each other. Isaac died in New Orleans on August 3, 1955, at age ninety-three. Joseph died in Dallas, on August 11, 1955, at the age of eighty-four.

People in This Book

» Milton Elford

Milton (1872–1930) was a young man living in Galveston with his parents, John and Fanny Elford, and his five-year-old nephew, Dwight. During the hurricane, they took shelter in a neighbor's house. He shared the terror of that night in a letter to his brothers.

» Harry Maxson

Harry I. Maxson (1885–1967) was fourteen in 1900. He lived in Galveston with his parents and younger sister. He had his first job, making sixteen cents an hour, at the railroad depot. His father worked for the railroad, and neighbors came to their house to wait out the hurricane. Harry's gripping account was discovered among his papers after his death.

» Annie Smizer McCullough

Izola Collins recorded an oral history interview with Annie, her great-aunt, in 1972. Born in 1878, Annie

died on February 14, 1974, just before her ninety-sixth birthday. She was twenty-two when the storm struck.

» *Thomas Monagan*

Thomas worked for an insurance company in Dallas and was among the first people from the outside world to arrive in Galveston following the disaster.

» *Ralph Albert Scull*

Reverend Ralph Albert Scull (1860–1949) came to Galveston in 1865 at the age of five. A pastor and educator, he taught for more than fifty years in Galveston public schools, inspiring his daughter Viola and granddaughter Izola to follow in his footsteps. His papers, including *Black Galveston: A Personal View of Community History in Many Categories of Life*, are preserved in the Rosenberg Library in Galveston.

People in This Book

» *Katherine Vedder (Pauls)*

Katherine Vedder (1894–1975) lived with her parents and older brother. She wasn't quite six years old when the storm struck. She and her family survived. Katherine (sometimes spelled Katharine) married Peter Corlis Pauls in 1916 and stayed in Galveston.

» *Arnold R. Wolfram*

Arnold Wolfram (1858–1946) lived in Galveston with his wife and four children. As he made his way home during the hurricane, Arnold struggled to rescue a ten-year-old messenger boy who lived in his neighborhood.

This is a NOAA (National Oceanic and Atmospheric Administration) weather satellite image of Hurricane Maria over Puerto Rico on September 20, 2017. In 1900, weather forecasters could look up, but not down, on storms and clouds.

Part One
BEFORE

Galveston, Texas
Early September 1900

CHAPTER 1
Path of Confusion

"The hurricane which visited Galveston Island on Saturday, September 9, 1900, was no doubt one of the most important meteorological events in the world's history."

—ISAAC M. CLINE,
GALVESTON
WEATHER BUREAU

J ust twenty-four hours before Harry struggled home, the sun shone on Galveston, Texas. There were few signs a monster storm was on the way.

Katherine Vedder, almost six, lived in the city with her parents and her older brother and sister. Her father had heard rumors about bad weather approaching. Yet when Katherine looked out the window at five o'clock on Friday, she saw no sign of trouble. "It was a

perfect late summer afternoon, the day clear blue and cloudless."

Isaac Monroe Cline, Galveston's chief weather observer, was also scanning the sky about that time. In fact, he'd been staring at the waves and the skies all week. He was hoping to make sense of the pattern, the way you look at pieces in a jigsaw puzzle and try to figure out where they fit.

But so far, the picture wasn't clear.

Isaac Cline was thirty-nine. He and his wife, Cora, had three children, with a new baby on the way. Isaac was a rising star in **meteorology**, the study of the atmosphere and weather. Since being appointed head of the Galveston weather station seven years earlier, he'd become a valued member of the community. Isaac had a lot in common with his adopted city. Both were ambitious and optimistic.

Today, just as in 1900, the city of Galveston sits on Galveston Island, a long finger of land, twenty-seven miles long and no more than three miles wide, that

lies just off the coast of Texas. The brackish waters of Galveston Bay, an estuary, are to the north, and the Gulf of Mexico is to the south. Houston is about fifty miles inland; a railroad trestle across the bay was completed in 1860. (Today, a highway bridge connects Galveston with the Texas mainland.)

Founded in the 1800s, Galveston was a busy entry point for immigrants from Germany, Scotland, and Eastern Europe. Some called it the Ellis Island or New York City of the West. With its population of European immigrants, Latinos, and African Americans, Galveston was a multicultual port city. The city boasted a bustling waterfront. Trains brought cotton, wheat, and corn from inland farms to be shipped around the globe.

Grand mansions lined Broadway, Galveston's main thoroughfare. The city boasted a host of activities for residents and visitors alike. People flocked to restaurants, concert halls, and hotels, including the beautiful five-story brick Tremont Hotel. Surrounded

by sparkling water and festooned with white oyster shells, Galveston was a glittering symbol of success, poised for the new century ahead.

Galveston's leaders had established a streetcar system and electricity services. They'd also built new houses. Isaac and Cora Cline lived in one of them, at 2511 Avenue Q, just three blocks north of the Gulf.

Not everyone lived in a new or sturdy home. As the population grew during the late 1800s, small structures sprang up on both the front streets and back alleys of the city. Some of these "alley houses" became rental housing for itinerant laborers who came to Galveston for short periods of time to work. Many became home to African American families and were built after the Civil War by Black carpenters, including Horace Scull, Ralph Albert Scull's father.

Hoping for new opportunities, Horace Scull had brought his family to Galveston in 1865, when Ralph was just five. In June of that year, a momentous event took place.

Major General Gordon Granger of the Union Army arrived in Galveston bringing official word to Texas that the Civil War was over and formerly enslaved people were free. President Abraham Lincoln's 1863 Emancipation Proclamation (which had freed any enslaved persons in Confederate states) had never been enforced in Texas.

Today, Juneteenth is celebrated on June 19 to commemorate emancipation. Juneteenth has been an official state holiday in Texas since 1980. In 2016, at the age of eighty-nine, activist Opal Lee, known as "Grandmother of Juneteenth," first walked from her home in Texas to Washington, DC, in an effort to get Juneteenth recognized as a national holiday. And on June 17, 2021, the ninety-four-year old Lee was able to celebrate. On that day, President Joe Biden signed legislation making Juneteenth a federal holiday.

In the decades after the Civil War ended in 1865, formerly enslaved people faced prejudice and huge obstacles when trying to get an education, a good job,

or to own a home. Horace Scull worked building alley houses on leased ground, meaning the landowner usually rented out the house. In 1867, Horace built a house for his own family too. But he was forced to move the house twice because the landowner either changed his mind or refused to sell the land under it to Horace because he was Black.

The small, simply built structures available to Black families weren't as big or sturdy as the houses many white families were able to afford. These homes would not be able to withstand tremendously strong floods and winds like those of America's deadliest hurricane.

Around 1900, African Americans made up about one-fifth of the city's population of nearly 38,000. In addition to working in construction, some African Americans had jobs on the docks, thanks to Norris Wright Cuney, one of the most important Black leaders of his time. He served on the Galveston city council and helped create more job opportunities for African American workers on the waterfront. In 1889, he was appointed

the United States Collector of Customs, making him the highest-ranking appointed Black federal official in the country.

Other African Americans began their own small businesses. Robert "Bob" McGuire ran a busy taxi service with a horse and buggy. He earned enough money to buy land near the shore, and built a bathhouse there that Black residents could use. He also served as a police officer.

The children of these early Black entrepreneurs went on to make a mark in their community. Horace Scull's son, Ralph, became a teacher. In the same way, Jessie McGuire Dent, daughter of Bob and Alberta McGuire, attended Howard University and then returned to Galveston to teach.

In 1943, while teaching in the Galveston schools, Jessie realized that Black teachers were paid less than whites. She fought and won a case in federal court to require equal pay for African American public school teachers. To honor this family's contributions to Galveston, educator and author Izola Collins became

the driving force in establishing the McGuire-Dent Recreation Center in Galveston.

Before 1900, other Black-owned shops and businesses grew up in the area around Bob McGuire's bathhouse between Twenty-Seventh and Twenty-Ninth Streets. In segregated Galveston, Black families often didn't feel welcome elsewhere. Izola Collins wrote, "White owners of businesses on the sand did not want their patrons to be turned off by the presence of former slaves in the water with them. Such owners, and sometimes even police, told them to move on, that they were not allowed to swim in those areas."

Despite facing many obstacles, Galveston's African American community grew to include thriving churches as well as popular restaurants and clubs. Galveston's Central High was the first African American high school in Texas, founded in 1885. However, there were separate sections for Black residents in theaters, on the beaches, and on the trolleys. Galveston was still a segregated city.

HOW HURRICANES FORM

Hurricanes form over warm ocean waters in the tropics. The **tropics** are the regions of the Earth around the equator. These areas receive a lot of direct sunlight and are hot and wet, often with ocean temperatures of 80 degrees Fahrenheit or more.

Many times, hurricanes that affect the United States begin as a weather disturbance that scientists call a **tropical wave**, or an **easterly wave**. This is a special term for an area of clouds and thunderstorms that moves from east to west. If you hold your finger in front of your face and move it from right to left, this is how a tropical wave moves. (These waves are also known as **African easterly waves**. As you can see from the chart, hot winds blowing easterly from the Sahara Desert hitting the Atlantic Ocean help to create this weather pattern.)

How Do Hurricanes Form?

NOAA

1
Hurricanes form in tropical regions where the ocean is at least 80 degrees Fahrenheit. These waters evaporate, creating warm, moist air—which acts as fuel for the storm.

The Tropics

Equator

80°F

2
Many hurricanes in the U.S. are caused by winds blowing across the Atlantic Ocean from Africa, which cause more water to evaporate into the atmosphere.

3
The warm, moist air rises high into the atmosphere where it begins to cool. Water vapor condenses back into liquid droplets and forms big, stormy anvil-shaped clouds.

1,000 Miles

10 Miles

4
As warm air rises, the winds begin blowing in a circle. The spiraling winds gather a cluster of clouds.

5
Once the spinning winds reach 74 miles per hour, the storm has officially become a hurricane. These storms can be 10 miles high and over 1000 miles across!

Thankfully, the GOES-R series of weather satellites take a scan of the U.S. every five minutes, keeping an eye on conditions that might cause a hurricane. This helps meteorologists deliver early warnings and keep people safe.

6
If a hurricane hits land, it runs out of warm, moist air and begins to slow down, but it can still cause lots of damage (especially from flooding).

SciJinks

Find out more about Earth's weather at scijinks.gov

A NOAA graphic shows how hurricanes form.
https://scijinks.gov/hurricane

How Hurricanes Form

As a tropical wave moves along, warm, moist air rises up from the ocean and is replaced by cooler air, which rushes in below. As it rises and cools, the water in the air forms clouds of water droplets, bringing rain and thunderstorms. The winds begin blowing in a circle in a counterclockwise direction. The cluster of clouds gets bigger and bigger.

This warm, moist air fuels the storm's engine. Because the air is moving up and away from the surface of the ocean, it causes an area of lower pressure below. The swirling storm keeps gathering heat and energy, spinning and growing around a center. Once its constant, or sustained, winds hit 74 mph (miles per hour), the storm is a **hurricane**.

In the center of a hurricane is an area of low air pressure, with clear skies and calm winds. It's called the **eye**. The eye is surrounded by the **eyewall**, with towering clouds and fierce winds. A clearly defined eye and eyewall are the mark of an especially intense storm.

A hurricane gets energy from the ocean's heat and

the water evaporating from the ocean's surface. That's why, once a storm hits cooler water farther north or goes over land, it begins to weaken and break apart.

Many hurricanes that hit the mainland United States travel up the Atlantic Coast. Some, like the Galveston hurricane of 1900, travel southwest of Florida into the Gulf of Mexico and may impact the Gulf Coast states of Florida, Alabama, Mississippi, Louisiana, and Texas.

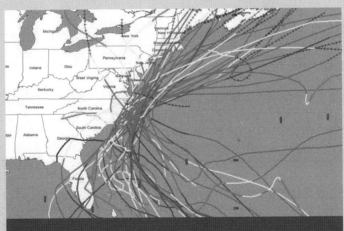

Many hurricanes that threaten the U.S. go north along the Atlantic Coast and then eventually weaken to become rainstorms. This graphic from NOAA's Historical Hurricane Tracks tool shows all hurricanes passing within sixty-five nautical miles of Cape Hatteras, North Carolina, between 1900 and 2010.

How Hurricanes Form

In the early 1800s, weather observers first proposed the notion of hurricanes as giant whirlwinds. In fact, these great churning wind circles can reach heights of ten or eleven feet. The word *hurricane* most likely comes from Spanish explorers in the Caribbean and Central America, who heard of a Mayan god of wind and storm called Hurácan or Jurakan.

In the United States, hurricane information and tracking is housed within **NOAA**, the National Oceanic and Atmospheric Administration, a federal agency dedicated to science, service, and stewardship. The National Weather Service, which includes the National Hurricane Center, is part of NOAA. Through these agencies, government scientists use sophisticated tools including aircraft, radar, satellites, and computers to predict and track hurricanes. NOAA's most advanced satellites are the **Geostationary Operational Environmental Satellite** (**GOES**)—R Series. To learn more about these amazing satellites and see pictures of Earth from above, visit: https://www.goes-r.gov.

A Hurricane Hunter in action.

Hurricane forecasting has come a long way since 1900. NOAA's "Hurricane Hunters" are specially designed aircraft that serve as "flying weather stations" and help forecasters and researchers make better predictions and learn more about dangerous storms.

In the photo, a NOAA P-3 aircraft flies in the eye of Hurricane Caroline. The circular hurricane eye is visible as a dark space in the clouds. This picture was taken on December 10, 2018.

Learn more at: https://www.omao.noaa.gov/learn /aircraft-operations/about/hurricane-hunters.

CHAPTER 2
Friday: A Change in Direction

Isaac Cline had set up his weather instruments on the roof of the E. S. Levy Building, located in the city's commercial district closer to the bay side of the island. He took his observation duties seriously. Ship captains and cotton merchants all knew Isaac and Joseph, his younger brother, who worked at the weather station and boarded in the Cline household. The dedicated Galveston team also included assistant weather observer John D. Blagdon.

Galveston was a deepwater port, which meant large cargo ships were able to dock there. This helped to make it a busy, profitable trade center. Because of that, the business community relied heavily on the station's storm forecasts. After all, there was a lot at stake: These ships carried valuable cargo across the Gulf of Mexico

and beyond, to faraway places around the globe.

People in the area trusted Isaac. Just a few months earlier, his predictions of river flooding along the Texas coast had helped save lives. He certainly never wanted to let his city down. Yet in one way, he already had.

Galveston had improved its Gulf-facing waterfront. But even though Galveston was low and flat, in many places only five feet above sea level, the city had decided against spending money to build a thick concrete barrier along the shore, called a **seawall**. A seawall would help stop high waves from rushing in to cause flooding and damage to buildings.

Galveston's leaders must have felt more comfortable with their decision not to undertake this project when, in July of 1891, their chief weatherman weighed in on the need for a seawall. "It would be impossible," Isaac wrote in the local newspaper, "for any cyclone to create a storm wave which could materially injure the city."

Isaac couldn't have been more wrong.

Weather forecasters today rely on **weather satellites**,

radar, aircraft, and sophisticated equipment and computer models to track storms. Not so in 1900. Back then, observers in different spots relayed information by telegram to the main U.S. Weather Bureau office in Washington, DC. With roots dating back to 1870, the Weather Bureau was established within the U.S. Department of Agriculture in 1890. It became the National Weather Service in 1970, when it was placed within NOAA.

In 1895, Willis Moore was appointed chief of the U.S. Weather Bureau in Washington, DC. There, in the days leading up to September 8, 1900, Moore and his team were keeping their eyes on a developing tropical storm in the Caribbean.

For most of the first week of September, Isaac Cline had no reason to worry. The cables he got from the main weather office in Washington all seemed to tell the same story: This storm was headed north along the Atlantic Coast of the United States.

As far as Isaac could tell, this storm was not a

danger. It wasn't heading into the Gulf of Mexico. It wasn't a threat to Galveston, sitting just off the coast of Texas.

Except, of course, that it was. So why was Isaac getting such wrong information?

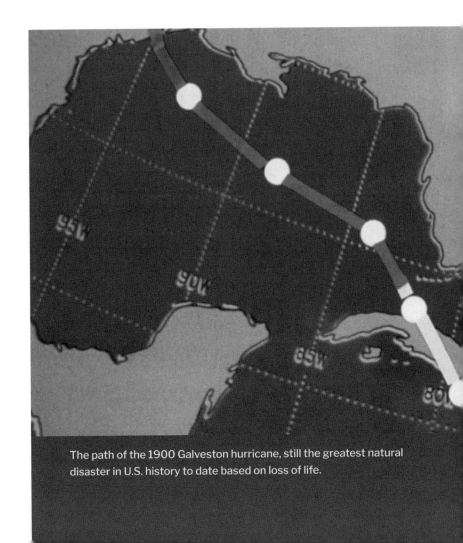

The path of the 1900 Galveston hurricane, still the greatest natural disaster in U.S. history to date based on loss of life.

Friday: A Change in Direction

The reason is a fascinating story all on its own. First, without sophisticated equipment, weather observers in 1900 relied mostly on rain gauges, cloud patterns, simple instruments to clock wind speed, and **barometers**, which measure air pressure. Since forecasters didn't

SEPT. 1–10, 1900

have a way to see storms from above, they relied on their skills and their experience of past storms. After taking readings, observers usually cabled their reports to the U.S. Weather Bureau in Washington via telegraph.

Humans did the observing; humans made the mistakes. In September of 1900, Weather Bureau chief Willis Moore and his team, including William Stockman, who ran the U.S. bureau in Havana, Cuba, made some assumptions and errors that had terrible consequences, ultimately costing thousands of lives.

The island of Cuba is in the northern Caribbean, only about a hundred miles from Florida, and had long been a colony of Spain. With the Spanish-American War in 1898, Cuba came under the control of the United States until 1902, when it became independent.

Both Willis Moore and William Stockman considered Cuba a backward place. They looked down on Cubans and didn't respect the Cuban weather observers. Moreover, they wanted to exert control. The United States was in charge now, and they expected the Cuban

forecasters to fall in line. Moore and Stockman had even managed to ban Cuban forecasters from sending reports to other weather stations in the United States. Everything had to filter through Moore.

But Cuba boasted skilled hurricane forecasters, including meteorologist Julio Jover and a Jesuit priest named Father Lorenzo Gangoite, who directed the Belen Observatory in Havana. Father Gangoite had learned his trade from the legendary Father Benito Viñes (1837–1893), known as "the Hurricane Priest," who had built a network of weather stations across Cuba. This unsung hero was a pioneer in creating some of the hurricane warning systems used today. He was also famous for his ability to use clouds to predict hurricanes and his efforts to teach people about the weather.

The Cuban forecasters had been keeping watch on this particular storm system since the end of August. On Wednesday, when the storm passed just north of Cuba, Willis Moore and William Stockman assumed it would follow a more common pattern and keep heading

northward up the Atlantic Coast. In fact, they expected it to be in New England by Friday. And they certainly weren't calling it a hurricane.

Meanwhile, the Cuban weather experts were drawing different conclusions. On Wednesday morning, September 5, Julio Jover published a report in a Havana newspaper daring to use the forbidden word: "'We are today near the center of the low pressure area of the hurricane.'"

Father Gangoite's observations of the skies Wednesday night and Thursday morning also convinced him the storm was growing stronger—and heading not north but west across the Gulf of Mexico, straight for Texas.

But because of the telegraph ban, he wasn't allowed to send a warning to weather stations in New Orleans—or to Isaac Cline in Galveston.

As longtime television weather forecaster Al Roker has written, "If Gangoite's predictions had been heard in the United States, there would have been time to give

the people of Galveston and the Texas mainland a fairly long-range warning of the impending destruction."

While throughout that week, Isaac had no reason to believe a storm was on its way, on Friday morning, September 7, he received a surprising update.

The U.S. Weather Bureau was now reporting that the tropical storm wasn't heading north up the Atlantic Coast after all. Willis Moore had gotten no reports of wind or strong rains from states on the Atlantic Coast. What had happened to the storm?

Willis Moore had to conclude that since leaving Cuba on Wednesday, the storm had veered westerly and was somewhere in the Gulf of Mexico—just as Father Gangoite had predicted. So on Friday, Moore gave Isaac orders to hoist a red-and-black storm warning flag. Moore had to accept the Cuban forecasters' conclusion about the storm's direction.

However, since most hurricanes didn't travel in this pattern, Moore still didn't believe the Cubans were correct about the storm's severity. He didn't believe that it

was a hurricane. He thought it was a heavy storm with high winds, no more than that. And so the word *hurricane* wasn't mentioned in the storm warning Moore sent to Isaac.

Heavy rains were common in early September, so Isaac wasn't terribly alarmed. Besides, he later wrote, "The usual signs which herald the approach of hurricanes were not present in this case. The brick-dust sky was not in evidence to the smallest degree."

When Isaac hoisted the storm warning flag on Friday, the sky was mostly a clear bright blue.

HURRICANE, CYCLONE, OR TYPHOON?

There are several different words used in various parts of the world to describe deadly storms.

Tropical cyclone is the general term meteorologists use for storms that begin in warm tropical oceans and have strong circulating winds that rotate around a center of low pressure. This term is also used for severe storms of hurricane force (winds more than 74 mph) when they occur in the South Pacific and Indian Oceans.

A severe tropical cyclone with constant wind speeds of 74 mph or more is called a **typhoon** or hurricane, depending on where it occurs. In the North Atlantic and northeast Pacific Ocean east of the International Date Line (IDL), and the South Pacific Ocean east of 160 degrees, it's called a hurricane. It's called a typhoon

if it occurs in the northwest Pacific Ocean west of the International Date Line.

One thing is different within the storm itself, depending on where it occurs. North of the equator, in the Northern Hemisphere, the winds rotate

Artist's rendition of the eye of a hurricane.

in a counterclockwise direction. In the Southern Hemisphere, winds rotate clockwise. This difference is due to Earth's rotation on its axis.

What about storms that are less severe? Scientists use special terms to distinguish storms of lower intensity. A tropical cyclone with maximum sustained surface winds of at least 39 mph but less than 74 mph is called a **tropical storm**. If the winds are less than 39 mph, we call it a **tropical depression**. Weather forecasters watch these areas carefully to see if they will develop into more ferocious storms.

CHAPTER 3
Saturday Morning

J oseph Cline, like Isaac, was fascinated by weather. The brothers had grown up on a farm in Tennessee, part of a large family of four boys and three girls.

Joseph and Isaac were hardworking, smart, and ambitious. "On the dark, cold winter mornings, my brothers and I would start the day early by eating breakfast, feeding the livestock, and being off to the fields by daylight," Joseph remembered.

Isaac had gone to medical school. Joseph had been a teacher and worked for the railroad before accepting his brother's offer to become an assistant weather observer. Joseph was determined to do well and learned all he could about weather science. "I applied myself to my new job with all the diligence at my command. I

studied night and day, absorbing all the current text-book material on meteorology."

Even before he woke up on Saturday, Joseph had a premonition something was wrong. Sure enough, he discovered water in their yard washing in from the Gulf beach a few blocks away. He woke Isaac and the brothers conferred. Isaac decided to investigate.

Although they were close enough to walk to the beach, Isaac wanted to cover as much ground as possible. So he hitched up his horse and wagon and drove along the shoreline, timing and measuring the swells. A wave forms when wind blows over the surface of the water. A **swell** is the term for a series of waves. These waves have formed farther away and traveled across the water. Stronger-than-usual swells are a signal that a storm system with high winds is approaching.

Isaac watched carefully for swells gaining in size and frequency. And that's exactly what he saw. The swells were rolling in about one to five minutes apart,

and growing larger all the time. That worried Isaac, because even though the wind was blowing from the shore *against* the waves, they kept getting bigger. The swells were pushing seawater farther and farther up the beach. That explained the water in their yard.

Isaac sent a telegram to the Weather Bureau office in Washington, DC, to report what he was observing: "Unusually heavy swells from the southeast, intervals

An example of a storm surge. This photo depicts sixteen feet of storm surge striking the Florida Panhandle during Hurricane Eloise in September of 1975. In coastal communities, higher-than-usual swells and the rising sea level caused by an approaching storm can wreak considerable damage. Large waves are fascinating but dangerous.

one to five minutes, overflowing low places south portion of city three to four blocks from beach. Such high water with opposing winds never observed previously."

Even then, Isaac still underestimated the strength of the approaching storm. He expected flooding and warned some shopkeepers and merchants. He suggested they move their goods at least three feet off the floor. That would not be nearly enough.

And while Isaac warned some people, since only the main U.S. Weather Bureau in Washington could issue hurricane warnings, the weather report in Saturday's *Galveston News* didn't alarm anyone. Buried on page ten was this note: "'The weather bureau officials did not anticipate any dangerous disturbance.'"

Families in Galveston had no reason to prepare or panic. They simply went about their usual Saturday routines. Later, a young woman named Sarah Hawley wrote her mother, "Friday evening the wind was very strong and Saturday morning it was even stronger, the sky dark, but otherwise there was nothing unusual."

Nothing unusual.

That changed as the day went on and weather conditions worsened by the hour. The wind picked up. It began to rain. Isaac and Joseph kept up their observations. Isaac patrolled the beach, urging people to take shelter. By three thirty on Saturday afternoon, the wind had become ferocious; the waves grew into monsters. Water poured onto the city streets.

Isaac asked Joseph to send a telegram to Washington: "Gulf rising, water covers streets of about half the city."

Wading through knee-deep water, Joseph reached the Western Union office. He was told the wires were down and nothing could go out. He tried another telegraph office with the same result. Joseph returned to his office and was finally able to make a long-distance call and get the report through. It would be the last message from Galveston before the disaster.

Joseph left the office and made a sweep of the beach area, trying to warn as many people as he could to

move inland. Then he headed to Isaac's house. John Blagdon, another assistant, stayed in the office to monitor the weather instruments, especially the barometer. The rain gauge on the roof blew away around six o'clock on Saturday night, but Blagdon bravely stayed at his post and continued to take barometer readings.

At five o'clock, the barometer read 29.05. At ten past eight, it had dropped to 28.53. These readings, Isaac later noted, "indicate the great intensity of the hurricane."

WHAT DOES A BAROMETER MEASURE?

Earth's atmosphere has weight and pushes down on anything below. Weather forecasters can measure this **air pressure**, or **atmospheric pressure**, using an instrument called a barometer.

Back in the 1600s, the noted Italian astronomer Galileo Galilei performed early experiments to show that although it is invisible, air has weight. In 1646, an Italian scientist named Evangelista Torricelli designed an instrument, later called a *barometer*, to measure air pressure using a glass tube and mercury. (The word *barometer* comes from the Greek *baros*, meaning "weight.")

By 1900, weather forecasters routinely used barometers and knew that high pressure signaled fair weather and falling barometric pressure heralded bad

weather. Remember, in hurricanes, warm, moist air rises up from the surface of the ocean. As the winds lift the air, the warm air rises higher. There is less air near the surface, making this an area of lower air pressure.

The normal air pressure at sea level is 29.92126 inches. According to Guinness World Records, the lowest air pressure ever recorded was 25.69 inches in 1979 about three hundred miles west of Guam in the eye of Typhoon Tip.

NOAA photograph of the eyewall of a hurricane taken by aircraft.

Part Two
DURING

Saturday Afternoon–Sunday Dawn

"The wreck of Galveston was brought about by a tempest so terrible that no words can adequately describe its intensity, and by a flood which turned the city into a raging sea."

—RICHARD SPILLANE,
NEW YORK TIMES,
SEPTEMBER 11, 1900

CHAPTER 4

The Cline Brothers:
Like a Lighthouse on a Rock

On Saturday afternoon, Joseph Cline had barely managed to send Galveston's last message to the outside world. After that, he walked up and down for a mile on the beach, warning everyone he saw. When he arrived at Isaac's house in the early evening, the family and neighbors had already gathered.

At first, Joseph thought they'd be safe there, although they were very close to the beach. Surely, Isaac's two-story house, built only four years before, could take a beating. The house, Joseph later wrote, was "like a lighthouse built upon a rock."

Meanwhile, Isaac continued to make weather observations from his doorstep; he invited more neighbors

in from smaller houses nearby. About fifty frightened people crowded inside.

As day turned to evening and the wind and rain grew fiercer, Joseph began to wonder if even this sturdy structure could stand. He called Isaac outside to discuss his fears. Joseph thought they should make an attempt to move toward the center of town, on the other side of the island.

"At this time, however, the roofs of houses and timbers were flying through the streets as though they were paper," Isaac wrote later. Isaac believed it would be too dangerous to move, especially since Cora, his wife, was unwell.

As the brothers stood talking, they witnessed the **storm surge**: an abnormal rise in sea level from an intense storm or hurricane. Isaac and Joseph could only watch, helpless, as the water was pushed onto shore, powered by the hurricane's fierce winds as it hit land after traveling hundreds of miles unimpeded across the Gulf of Mexico.

Isaac later reported, "The water rose at a steady rate from 3 p.m. until about 7:30 p.m., when there was a sudden rise of about four feet in as many seconds. I was standing at my front door, which was partly open, watching the water which was flowing with great rapidity from east to west. The water at this time was about eight inches deep in my residence, and the sudden rise of 4 feet brought it above my waist before I could change my position.

"The water had now reached a stage 10 feet above the ground at Rosenberg Avenue (Twenty-fifth Street) and Q Street, where my residence stood. The ground was 5.2 feet elevation, which made the tide 15.2 feet. The tide rose the next hour, between 7:30 and 8:30 p.m., nearly five feet additional, making a total tide in that locality of about twenty feet."

Isaac and Joseph rushed back inside and herded everyone upstairs. Before dark, the house stood in fifteen feet of water.

Their chance of escape was gone.

DANGEROUS STORM SURGES

According to NOAA, the storm surge of a hurricane poses the greatest threat to people and property along the coast.

When combined with the normal tides of the sea, a storm surge often increases the water level by fifteen feet or even more. This can cause severe flooding and damage, especially in places where the coastline is not far above sea level and there are many buildings and houses near the beach. Nowadays, the National Weather Service will issue storm surge warnings so people can be prepared for these life-threatening events.

But there was no warning back in 1900, when the hurricane struck Galveston straight on, creating a devastating storm surge of at least fifteen feet or

higher in some places. This brought massive destruction and flooding along with high winds, which experts estimate may have reached 140 mph.

This U.S. Navy photo illustrates how storm surges push water ashore, posing a danger to structures on land. In the same way, the storm surge of the Galveston hurricane threatened Isaac Cline's house.

CHAPTER 5

The Kitten and the Baby

Katherine Vedder's house was about half a mile from the Gulf beach and two miles west of Isaac Cline's house. Late Saturday morning, her older brother, Jacob, and her cousin Allen began racing back and forth to the beach to look at the big waves crashing in.

At first, it seemed exciting—until the boys returned with frightening news. "About half past three, Jacob and Allen came running, shouting excitedly that the Gulf looked like a great gray wall about fifty feet high and moving slowly toward the island," Katherine said.

Katherine's father worried their house wouldn't survive. He told his family that if the house began to break apart, they should tie themselves together and try to make their way to the home of their neighbor, Richard

This historic photo shows storm damage on the New Jersey shore around 1914. As global climate change makes oceans warmer, coastal areas worldwide face severe threats. In Galveston, Katherine Vedder and her family lived about a half mile from the beach. Most of the homes near theirs were totally destroyed.

Peek. He believed the Peeks' house could withstand any storm. For now, though, the Vedder family would stay put.

It turned out to be the wisest decision they made.

As fierce winds rattled the windows, neighbors who lived in small cottages and alley houses drifted in to join the Vedder family. Some soldiers from nearby Fort Crockett arrived too.

Peopled huddled on the stairs to the second floor. Katherine's father took down two inside doors and nailed them crosswise to reinforce the front door. Katherine and friends, Francesca Mason and her brother, Kearny, played with Katherine's kitten. Before it grew dark, Katherine could see the water outside covering four-foot fences. Water was seeping into the house by now, slowly rising. Everyone hoped the next gust of wind wouldn't blow off the roof.

Suddenly, Katherine felt a tremendous jolt. Next came a strange sensation, like a boat going over a big wave. Only they weren't supposed to be in a boat, they were supposed to be on land! Except they weren't. Katherine said, "The house rose, floated from its six-foot foundation and with a terrific jolt, settled on the ground."

Without its sturdy foundation, the house was now

sitting dangerously lower in the flood. Inside, the water level instantly rose about five feet, covering the children completely. The soldiers groped frantically and managed to fish all three out. The soldiers then "handed us, gasping and dripping, to our mothers, who had fled higher up the stairs," Katherine remembered.

But what about the kitten? All at once, Katherine spied it. "I called out, 'Papa, there's my kitten.' He pulled a soaking, clawing bit of fur from the water and tossed it up the stairs.

"Mrs. Mason caught it and shrieking, 'It's a rat,' tossed it back into the water. It was sometime before the kitten was safe in my arms."

The tiny kitten survived. It would have a vital role to play that night.

The family's house had been torn from its foundation, but it was still standing. A long and frightening night stretched before everyone inside. The wind ripped away the roof from over two upstairs bedrooms, so people crowded into a bathroom that still offered

Although the Vedder family home survived the hurricane, thousands of others in Galveston were destroyed.

protection from the pouring rain. Katherine's mother wrapped Katherine and her friend Francesca in a bedspread and put the girls into the tub for safety.

Downstairs, Katherine's father realized the struggle had just begun. Their house was near the new barracks at Fort Crockett, which had been constructed of large beams, twelve inches around and twenty feet long. Some of those very beams were now floating through the floodwaters, acting like massive battering rams.

Katherine's father was especially worried about the

front door, the weakest part of the house. When the house settled, a hole had opened near the front door but above water level. With his bare arms, Katherine's father reached through. Time and again, he pushed away the beams floating dangerously close.

His quick thinking saved the house. "But for months after he suffered agony as the doctor probed and worked over his torn and lacerated arms and hands, for they were filled with glass, splinters, and other foreign matter which swept by on the waters of the storm," Katherine said. Her father carried scars on his hands the rest of his life.

Katherine's kitten was not the only little one rescued that night. Another cry for help came in the early morning hours. A couple was spotted staggering along through the muddy, churning waters, carrying their lifeless six-week-old baby. Their house was gone and now they fought their way through the flood to try to reach a safe place.

When they were pulled inside, it seemed as though

the tiny baby was dead. But Katherine's mother wasn't about to give up.

"My mother took him and saw that there was still a spark of life," Katherine recalled. "She crawled on her hands and knees through the darkness into the northeast room where, from an overturned bureau and cabinet, she pulled a knitted woolen petticoat and a broken bottle of blackberry cordial.

"Making her way back in the pitch black dark she stripped the baby of its wet clothing and wrapped it in the woolen garment and placed the now dry and purring kitten next to the baby's body for warmth."

Then the baby's mom took some of the sweet, slightly alcoholic drink into her mouth and transferred it, drop by drop, to her baby's mouth, making sure no glass from the broken bottle passed through her lips.

Katherine said, "Gradually the tiny cold body grew warm and soon a wailing infant demanded food."

One tiny kitten had helped save a baby.

GET TRACKING!

The Galveston hurricane struck in early September, during peak **hurricane season** in the North Atlantic. The season runs from the first of June through November 30.

While people in Galveston couldn't track the storm, today's citizen scientists can visit NOAA's National Hurricane Center, which includes a page where you can track big storms across the globe: https://www .nhc.noaa.gov.

You can also download a blank tracking map: https://www.nhc.noaa.gov/AT_Track_chart.pdf.

A **hurricane watch** puts people on alert. When a tropical storm draws closer, a **hurricane warning** is issued, sometimes days in advance. There's a good reason for the advance warning: It takes time to evacuate large cities or coastal areas.

Historically, 97 percent of intense storms have occurred within these June through November dates. That's because conditions then are the most likely to create large storms.

However, there's nothing magical about those dates. According to NOAA, "All it takes is the right combination of atmospheric conditions and warmer ocean waters for a tropical cyclone to form, regardless of the date."

CHAPTER 6
Harry to the Rescue

When fourteen-year-old Harry Maxson made it home late Saturday afternoon, his mother and younger brother and sister were anxiously waiting for him. Harry's father arrived later, his new raincoat torn to shreds by the wind. And Harry found dozens of neighbors and friends there too. The house was packed!

The Maxson house was solid and well built. It seemed much safer than the smaller homes around it. It stood two stories tall, with four brick fireplaces anchoring it to the ground. "It was as if huge nails had been driven through the house from top to bottom," said Harry. "Before the storm was over we had about a hundred people in our house."

With the swift onslaught of the storm, families

living close to the beach had little time to evacuate. They had to make life-and-death decisions quickly. Even houses that seemed safe one minute were suddenly inundated by the terrific force of the water and swept away. Other houses shattered when floating timber and debris rammed into their walls, tearing them from their foundations.

Throughout the evening, Harry's mother moved from room to room, trying to reassure and comfort everyone. But she was worried about her next-door neighbors, who were expecting a new baby. She didn't think they were safe and asked Harry to go next door and bring the couple over to their house.

When Harry arrived, he found that his neighbor had just given birth to a baby boy. There was no way a new mom could wade through the fast-moving flood, made even more dangerous by fence posts, tree limbs, boards, and beams.

Harry had to come up with a solution—and fast.

"I returned home to get a ladder that some of the

men and myself used as a stretcher for the mother. The water at that time was about a waist high in her cottage, and the wind was getting terrific. It was with the greatest of difficulty that we moved her into our house and a comparatively safe bed."

While Harry rescued his neighbor, his dad was engaged in a desperate struggle to save the house from the pressure of the rising water. "Father anticipated what would happen to the house if the water got above the second floor level. It would float off," said Harry.

Soon, Harry, his dad, and some of their neighbors began to cut holes in the floor of each room. "We had no tools in the house, so we used pocket knives and butcher knives," Harry explained. "Each family was huddled together in corners under tables, so if the house went down they could all hang together."

Just as in Katherine Vedder's house, the main entrance posed a problem. Harry's house had double stained-glass-window front doors. To keep them from blowing in, Harry's father held one side closed, and a

neighbor held the other shut. The men also took a table leaf from the dining room table and braced it under the front door handle to give added support to the door.

Each time a gust of wind struck, the house rattled something fierce. Flying timbers rammed into it like cannonballs. The houses and cottages around them were being ripped from their foundations. Telephone poles and trees toppled like toothpicks, tossed into the salty water surging through the city.

At about one in the morning, Harry's father sent him to the kitchen to open a window a few inches and listen for anyone calling out for help. Harry asked others to leave the kitchen so he could listen better.

He knelt by the window. "I heard what I didn't want to hear, a woman yelling, 'For God sake come and save us, our home is falling to pieces.' I shut the window as quickly as I could and tried to forget that woman's voice . . . it made me shake all over."

Harry didn't *want* to go out in the storm, but he couldn't ignore those cries for help. He asked several of

the men to help him. Only one, a young newly married truck driver named Bill, was brave enough to go with the teen. Harry told his father they were leaving but didn't dare say anything to worry his mom.

Harry and Bill set out. They found a downed telephone pole floating along, and held on to it as they fought the rushing water. As they came closer to the house, they spotted the woman who had shouted for help perched precariously on the rooftop. She called out, telling them there were thirteen babies and children and about two dozen adults trapped in the attic.

Each gust of wind tore off part of the house, which had landed on railroad tracks. The house was crumbling fast. Time was running out.

Drawing nearer, Harry yelled to the people inside and asked each man to carry out a child. At first, there was silence. People were too scared to move.

Then one man emerged. He was African American, rescuing a white baby. One brave man was showing the way. Harry said, "I thanked him loud enough for all

to hear and here they came—all the men with a baby each and some of their wives."

The bedraggled party set out, single file, each one grabbing on to the person in front. When Harry arrived with the first group, he found his mother in the kitchen making hot coffee and baking biscuits. He didn't record what she said, but she must have been relieved and proud of her brave son.

Then Harry went back for the next group. Everyone made it to the Maxsons' home alive.

Railroad tracks and railway cars in the aftermath of the Galveston hurricane.

WHAT CATEGORY STORM WAS THE GALVESTON HURRICANE?

In the United States, we use a scale called the **Saffir-Simpson Hurricane Wind Scale** to categorize hurricanes. The scale, developed in the 1970s, ranks storms from 1 to 5, based on a hurricane's maximum sustained, or constant, winds. The higher the category, the greater the hurricane's wind force and the potential danger the storm may cause.

A Category 5 storm has sustained winds greater than 156 mph. Winds in Category 4 are 130 up to 156 mph. Category 3 hurricanes range from 111 to 129 mph. Winds in Category 2 storms fall between 96 and 110 mph. And winds in Category 1 storms range from 74 to 95 mph.

Although the scale was not in use in 1900, based

on records and Isaac Cline's reports, experts believe Galveston was a Category 4 storm. Visit NOAA to read more about hurricane categories: https://www.nhc.noaa.gov/aboutsshws.php.

CHAPTER 7
Voices from the Storm

Annie: Just did get away!

Twenty-two-year-old Annie Smizer McCullough was a newlywed, proud of her house; her husband, Ed; and her garden. Early on Saturday, neighbors had gone to the beach to watch the big waves.

Annie and Ed lived on K Avenue and Eighth Street, not far and "near level with the beach," Annie recalled years later. Ed's cousin, Henry, a young teen, was staying with them. Annie was so worried about her roses, she asked Henry to dig them all up and stick them in a tub so they wouldn't get washed away.

But when Ed came back from an errand on Saturday, the family had more to worry about than rosebushes. As the weather worsened, they realized their house was far from safe. They decided to first head for the

local African American school, East District School, on Tenth and Broadway. It wasn't far. So while Ed and Henry took the mule and the cart to pick up Annie's mother and other Smizer family members, Annie decided she'd just walk on over.

"When I got to corner of 9th and Broadway . . . the wind was so strong, and those waves comin', so I stopped. I didn't try to cross. Somebody picked me up, carried me across the street," said Annie.

But East District was just a frame building. When a neighbor came by with a big wagon used for delivering pianos, he announced he was heading for Rosenberg School, over on Tenth and I, which was larger and made of bricks. Annie and her family crowded on along with other friends. At times the water was so deep, the wagon was floating. The mules had to swim. Adults held on to children tightly.

"When we [hit] Rosenberg School, water hadn't come on there, but the *wind*! Ooh," exclaimed Annie more than sixty years later, recounting the tale to her

Many families sought refuge in public schools during the hurricane. The all-Black East District School was destroyed in the storm. Annie and Ed McCullough barely escaped being killed when part of the Rosenberg School, pictured here, collapsed.

great-niece Izola Collins. "Those men that was in the school, all they could do was stand up against those doors, try to hold them closed, keep them from blowin' open. . . . Upstairs, people was hollerin' and cryin', hunting their folk, couldn't find them. Oh, it was an awful thing! You want me to tell you. But no tongue can tell it!"

And then Ed urged Annie to move from one long hall to another. Suddenly, lightning struck the building's chimney. Bricks crashed down into the hall—instantly killing more than a dozen people. It was right in the hall, in the exact spot where Ed and Annie had been.

Annie never forgot it. "Just did get away!"

Milton: The House Fell on Us

On Saturday afternoon, about four o'clock, a young man named Milton Elford escaped from his house, with his parents and young nephew, Dwight. They made their way to a solid home in the neighborhood

with a brick foundation. It was on higher ground and they hoped it would be safe.

As the storm roared, Milton's family clung to one another, along with fifteen or sixteen other people. Everyone clustered in one room.

"About 5 [o'clock] it grew worse and began to break up the fence, and the wreckage of other houses was coming against it," Milton wrote his brothers later. "We had it arranged that if the house showed signs of breaking up I would take the lead, and pa would come next, with Dwight and ma next."

Milton went on, "All at once the house went from its foundation and the water came in waist-deep, and we all made a break for the door, but could not get it open. We then smashed out the window and I led the way."

Too late. Milton said, "I had got only part way out when the house fell on us."

Everything happened fast. "I was hit on the head with something and it knocked me out and into the water head

Fifty-one people are reported to have died in this structure. Buildings that collapsed on people seeking shelter caused many deaths, including the members of Milton Elford's family.

first," Milton said. "I do not know how long I was down, as I must have been stunned. I came up and got hold of some wreckage on the other side of the house."

Milton was alone. He couldn't see anyone else. Not his parents or nephew. No one. "We must have all gone down the same time." Only he had come up. Milton could only guess the others had been thrown down under a wall or floor and pinned there. "It was just a wonder I did not get killed."

Milton had no choice: He had to keep going. He pushed his way out of the window, hoping his family would be right behind. Half swimming, half walking, he fought to get free of debris. He tried to keep from getting struck and dragged under again. At last he was out of the house. Partly running, partly swimming, Milton somehow made his way from one pile of debris to another.

"The street was full of tops and sides of houses, and the air was full of flying boards." Milton worried about getting trapped or hit or buried.

After about five blocks, Milton noticed the water beginning to go down. By now, it was about three in the morning.

It was too dark to see. Shivering and heartsick, Milton could only wait for dawn.

Arnold: Clinging to a Tree

Arnold R. Wolfram worked at a fruit and produce store in Galveston. Late Saturday afternoon, he headed home to his wife and children, about twenty blocks away. As he struggled to avoid flying glass and debris, Arnold came up with a brilliant idea. He'd just bought a new pair of shoes. Stepping into a doorway, he took them out of the package and tied them around his head for protection.

"At the corner I suddenly stopped in horror. A little Western Union messenger boy, a lad of about ten years, had fallen from his wheel [bicycle] into the street and was being swept by the water towards the sewer drain.

"Even as I started toward him, he was just going

into the whirlpool marking the spot of the drain. I caught him just in time, and dragged him up on the sidewalk."

Arnold recognized the boy as the son of neighbors. "I shouted to him above the roar of the wind and rain that I would take him home." Arnold's voice was lost in the gale, but he motioned for the young messenger to put his shoes around his head too.

"We were now forcing our way in the very face of the storm, which had become a raging tempest. It was almost impossible to shout above the din, and I realized then that we were facing death," said Arnold.

"The wind and rain were wreaking havoc everywhere, poles and wires were snapping, making passage down the street doubly dangerous; windows were crashing in; flimsy structures and parts of roofs were swirling swiftly down the river which had, just a few hours before, been a beautiful esplanaded street; and the water was rising higher every minute."

The next street had become a raging river. Arnold

Arnold Wolfram and his young neighbor clung to a tree to escape being swept away in a scene much like this one of raging floods during Hurricane Carol in Connecticut in August of 1954.

and the boy managed to swim across. On the other side, they spotted a man clinging to a fence, weak and exhausted. Before they could reach him, the man lost his grip and was swept away.

They kept on. The water now reached the boy's

armpits. As they waded across another street, the current surged. "We were both suddenly swept from our feet and rushed pell-mell into a tree. I struggled up to the surface all the while holding frantically to the tree," said Arnold.

Arnold looked around and was relieved to see the boy clinging on too. The two climbed higher up into the branches, shivering and holding on to the trunk for dear life. "The air was full of flying wood and slate and glass and the water was hurling everything imaginable at our perch," Arnold said. "During this time, we sat in our tree and prayed that we might be spared."

The moon peeked out behind the clouds. In its pale light, Arnold watched a terrifying scene unfold. A man and woman drifted toward them, clinging to the roof of a house. That makeshift raft crashed right into the tree. The man floated away on one part. The woman screamed and held out her hand. Arnold leaned out to grab her, but she was swept away.

"Our own situation was becoming more desperate," he said. Debris kept slamming against the tree, which wasn't very big. Arnold worried it would be torn up by the roots and they would be thrown into the deluge. They were exhausted and cold, and getting weaker by the minute. He wasn't sure how long they could hang on.

And then Arnold saw a way out. Some debris floated toward them and became lodged between the tree and the porch of the nearest house. Arnold's neighbors lived there. Arnold figured that if they moved fast, he and the boy could climb onto the debris and get to safety.

They made it! The neighbors welcomed the survivors with warm, dry clothes and hot food. It was now about midnight. The young messenger dropped off to sleep, but Arnold couldn't rest. He wanted the water to go down; he wanted to look for his wife and children.

He wanted this terrible night to be over.

Louise: "Wait!"

Seven-year-old Louise Bristol lived with her mom and siblings on Avenue C. This was a part of town closer to the bay and the Texas mainland, and farther from the Gulf beach. Louise was the baby of the family. Her sister, Lois, was eight years older and her brothers, John and William, were in their early twenties.

Louise's mom was a widow who struggled to make ends meet. She'd taken out a mortgage to enlarge the house so she could rent out rooms to boarders. Her home was her only way to support her family.

Even though they were farther from the Gulf shore, the floods still reached their neighborhood. At first, Louise was excited. "I remember seeing the water come down the street and being so delighted that we didn't have far to go to the beach. It was right there at the front door and then it began to get bigger and wider and was coming into the garden that my mother had."

Then, as Louise saw the garden disappear underwater,

she began to understand the danger. And by the time one of her older brothers reached home, the water was up to his chest.

Like Harry Maxson's father, Louise's mother was worried her house might crumble from the pressure of the flood. Louise said, "She got an axe and chopped holes into every floor of every room downstairs in the hallway and the kitchen and the dining room. So the water would come up into the house and hold the house on the ground."

The family gathered upstairs, bringing what they could from the kitchen cabinets. The house began to shake. At one point, Louise's sister screamed and pointed at a corner of the wall. It had separated from the ceiling and was moving up and down with each gust of wind.

Louise's mother didn't seem surprised. "She realized that the house was going to pieces around us," said Louise. "She knew that the back end had already gone off, because we heard the crash."

Now it was only a matter of time. They could see a lamp on in the house across the street, which was sturdier than theirs. Louise's mother had an idea. She took sheets off the bed and got ready to tie her children together. Her idea was that Louise's two brothers, who were strong swimmers, could pull the rest of the family across to the other house on a floating mattress.

Louise's fifteen-year-old sister urged her mom to hold off. "My mother would say, 'Let's go now.' My sister would say, 'Wait,'" said Louise.

"If we hadn't waited I'm sure we never would have made it across."

WHAT'S IN A NAME?

You might have noticed that, unlike Hurricane Katrina, Harvey, or Maria, the Galveston hurricane doesn't have a name.

That's because hurricanes weren't given names until 1953, when female names were used; starting in 1979, male and female names were used for Atlantic storms. NOAA's National Hurricane Center doesn't control the naming but follows a procedure established by the World Meteorological Organization, an agency of the United Nations.

The lists of names are recycled every six years, unless a name is retired and not used again. A name is retired if the storm is especially costly or deadly. To date, the most retired names happened in 2005. In addition to Katrina, that year saw Dennis, Rita, Stan, and Wilma. Each year's list contains twenty-one

What's in a Name?

names. If there are more storms than that in any given year, names are taken from the Greek alphabet.

To see a list of hurricane names, visit the National Hurricane Center: https://www.nhc.noaa.gov/aboutnames.shtml.

Is your name on the list?

CHAPTER 8

The Cline Brothers:
Drifting Out to Sea

By Saturday evening, more than fifty people had gathered in an upstairs room in Isaac Cline's house. At seven thirty, Isaac and Joseph had witnessed a sudden surge of four feet. The force of the water wreaked havoc on the houses near them, turning walls and roofs and furniture into battering rams against the Cline home.

Even a lighthouse on a rock couldn't hold out against the terrific beating. Joseph Cline tried to prepare the others for what he feared was about to happen.

"I urged them, if possible, to get on top of the drift and float upon it when the dangerous moment came," said Joseph. "As the peril became greater, so did the crowd's excitement. Most of them began to sing; some

of them were weeping even wailing; while, again, others knelt in panic-stricken prayer."

And then it did happen.

Around eight thirty, the house began to topple over into the water. Joseph sprang into action. "I seized the hand of each of my brother's two children, turned my back toward the window, and, lunging from my heels, smashed through the glass and the wooden storm shutters, still gripping the hands of the two youngsters," he said.

Joseph had one goal in mind: to land on a wall resting on top of the water and not be crushed beneath the house as it fell. "The momentum hurled us all through the window as the building, with seeming deliberation, settled far over. It rocked a bit and then rose fairly level on the surface of the flood."

The plan worked. Joseph held on to Allie May, who was twelve, and Rosemary, eleven. "It was raining in torrents, and through winds of terrific force came flying pieces of timber. The clouds had broken in spots,

and the dim light of the moon made it possible for us to see for a short distance over the mass of drift about us," said Joseph.

Joseph called out; no one answered. Then, just as the house began to break up completely, Joseph spotted Isaac and his youngest girl, six-year-old Esther, clinging to a drift a hundred feet away.

Isaac had been pushed under the water. As he groped for the surface, he'd brushed against Esther. He kept hold of her and managed to get to the surface and stay afloat by clinging to some debris. Cora Cline and her unborn child were lost, along with most everyone else who had been with them inside the house.

Now the survivors had to stay alive. It wouldn't be easy.

Throughout that long night, Isaac and Joseph, along with Isaac's three young daughters, struggled to keep afloat, clinging to one piece of wreckage after another. They would settle on some boards or planks that seemed safe. But before long, each makeshift raft would start to sink under their weight.

Some houses, like Isaac Cline's, capsized and disintegrated. This house on Avenue N was toppled on its side from the force of the water.

"We remained close together, climbing and crawling from one piece of wreckage to another," recalled Joseph.

In this way they floated, shivering and terrified. Minutes, then hours, went by. At one point, they were swept into the Gulf of Mexico into complete darkness. Would they drift so far out to sea they would be beyond reach? Would their raft hold together?

They were in luck. The wind shifted, blowing them back to Galveston Island. The brothers sat upright,

trying to shelter the girls on their laps and protect them from flying timbers and drifting debris.

Once, incredibly, the family's dog appeared. The retriever sniffed each person in turn. Then, despite Joseph's best efforts to hold him, he jumped off the float again. Joseph realized the loyal dog was looking for his mistress, Cora, the only family member missing.

"I made a lunge for him, but he dodged, outran me, and plunged over the side of our drift. We never saw him any more," said Joseph.

The bulky wreckage was keeping the Cline family safe. At the same time, it made their unlikely lifeboat extremely dangerous to others. And soon they found themselves coming closer and closer to one house. Joseph heard people calling for help from inside.

He knew they were not bringing help, but destruction. In the next moment, their debris float struck the house with a crashing blow. The house began breaking apart.

"My brother was struck and knocked down by

one of the hurtling timbers," Joseph said later. After making sure Isaac was all right, Joseph noticed a little girl struggling in the water and plucked her out of the flood. In the darkness, he thought it was one of his nieces. But no, it was a survivor from the house. They later learned her name was Cora too. Now they were six drifting in the night.

Finally, about an hour before midnight, they floated near a house still standing on solid ground. This time, their raft lodged without damaging the structure.

"Tired and unspeakably battered, we climbed through an upstairs window into a room from which the roof and ceiling had been blown away," said Joseph. "Just under the floor of the room, the black waters of the Gulf were lapping. After having fought a frantic battle of body and mind for three hours, we dragged ourselves wearily inside."

Grateful to be alive, they joined other survivors in the house. They huddled together, hoping for this longest night to end.

Galveston survivors woke up to devastation after the storm.

Part Three
AFTER

Sunday Dawn & On

CHAPTER 9
Voices of Survivors

Katherine

Dawn. The wind had calmed. The waters were receding. But daylight brought unimaginable scenes of horror.

Everywhere they turned, Katherine Vedder and her family found chaos, death, and destruction. Nearly 3,000 homes had been completely swept out of existence; many more were damaged. And while the actual number of deaths can never be known, most historians estimate that at least 8,000 people were killed.

When Katherine's mother looked out the window on Sunday morning, the first thing she saw was the body of an African American child, tangled in the debris in their yard. Katherine and her mom would never forget that heartbreaking sight.

Only three houses still stood in Katherine's entire neighborhood. Katherine's brother called out, "'Papa, where are the Peeks?'"

They looked over to the spot where their neighbors' house had been—the house Katherine's father had thought was sturdier than their own, the house he had planned to go to for refuge if theirs didn't survive.

"Not a plank nor brick remained," said Katherine. "Not even a trace of the foundation. Richard Peek, his wife, eight children, and two servants were gone." Their bodies were never found.

The Vedder home was too damaged to live in, so the family set out on the grim walk to Katherine's grandparents, hoping they had survived. It took five hours to get through what had once been a thriving city. Katherine's father carried her much of the way. Debris blocked their passage almost everywhere.

"No streets or roads were visible. The wreckage piled high obscured every familiar landmark," recalled Katherine. "We picked our way where we could,

sometimes in ankle-deep water and mud, sometimes in water waist deep where great holes had been created by the current."

They came across many bodies: a small white child wrapped in a quilt, a nun who had tied several children to her body, a Black man caught in the mud with his bicycle. People who had tried to run, to get to higher ground, to swim, or even to ride a bicycle to safety. All lost. At one point, Katherine's mother broke down and wept.

Katherine's grandparents lived in the center of town, farther from the beach. Fortunately, they'd come through fine, and their house had weathered the storm. It was eleven days before Katherine's parents returned home to see what could be salvaged. Her mother found three dozen pieces of her wedding china, buried in the soft mud and without a chip on them.

Afterward, Katherine and her siblings were sent to New York to live with her other grandparents while the family home was being repaired. She later returned to

live in Galveston. Katherine grew up to study music in college. She married, and became active in the Galveston Historical Society.

Katherine never forgot that night and the rescue of her kitten and the baby. Years later, traveling on a bus, she found herself sitting next to a young woman. When the woman learned Katherine was from Galveston, she mentioned that her grandmother had also lived through the storm.

The young woman said, "'You know, my grandmother told me the most fantastic story. She told me about a home down the island where a lot of people spent the night of the storm and there was a little baby that was brought in just about dead and the lady who lived in the home saved the little baby. . . . Isn't that the most remarkable thing?'"

Katherine replied, "'Well, you don't know how remarkable it is, because it was in my home that the baby was saved and it was my mother who saved him.'"

And, of course, the kitten helped too.

Arnold

At midnight on Saturday, Arnold Wolfram had managed to save himself and a boy from his neighborhood by clambering over floating debris to reach the porch of a house. After eating and getting a change of clothes, the boy dropped off to sleep.

Not Arnold. All he could think of was his wife and four children at home. Had they survived?

At first light on Sunday morning, he set out to find them. His first inkling of the extent of the desolation came almost instantly. Stepping into the water that still covered the street, his foot hit something soft. Reaching under the water, Arnold realized he had stepped on a dead body. "I turned away sick and horrified, but as I walked on, again and again, I saw bodies of men, women and children, everywhere."

Arnold quickened his pace, trying to make his way through the wreckage, his fears rising. Finally, he reached his own block. "I dreaded to look but finally did—Oh my God, where would I find my loved

ones—for I saw that my home was tilted crazily, the roof crushed in.

"I stood stunned, sickened to the very core of my being. Finally I started forward for I knew that no matter what I might find on reaching the house, I had to search those ruins for all I had held dear."

Then Arnold heard someone call his name. A friend had come to look for him and reported that Arnold's wife and children were safe. They'd escaped from the house when it started to sway and shake and managed to survive inside a grocery store on the next corner.

Arnold and his family lost much of what they owned but eventually were able to rebuild their house. Nearly forty years later, when he was almost eighty-one, Arnold reflected, "The little lad whom I saved is now grown and married and has a very good business in another state but we still correspond. . . . All my children have grown up, married, and have children of their own. And I even have some few great-grandchildren.

"But with all the changes of the years, that one night has always remained most vivid in my mind."

Annie

Annie Smizer McCullough and her husband, Ed, had barely escaped with their lives when part of the Rosenberg School collapsed. When the moon came out and the water began to run off, they headed for the courthouse, which became a makeshift shelter for many.

Izola Collins's maternal grandfather, Ralph "Papa" Scull, brought his family to the courthouse too. Izola's mother, Viola, was twelve. She had one especially vivid memory of the storm. Viola recalled leaving home to go to the courthouse on Saturday as the storm worsened. "She told me emphatically, that as Papa called to her to go, she looked up and saw a huge wave, bigger than she had ever seen, rolling toward them."

Many in Galveston flocked to public buildings

A survivor amid the wreckage. Entire blocks on the Gulf side of Galveston were destroyed. Most buildings were damaged, leaving thousands homeless.

during the hurricane. A Black laborer named Henry Johnson had moved to Galveston just before the storm and lived in a boardinghouse. When it struck, he escaped to the Union Passenger Depot, a sturdier brick building. The boardinghouse was totally destroyed. Like thousands of others, Henry was left homeless.

Annie and Ed McCullough stayed at the courthouse for a week after the storm. There they met a white man who offered the young couple a place to stay. Along with Ed's mother and two brothers, Annie and Ed moved into the house's servants' quarters until they could go to relatives in Hallettsville, Texas. Before then, however, "These white people just turned their place over to us," remembered Annie.

Not everyone was kind, though. And racism had not gone away. Izola Collins interviewed her neighbor, Joseph "Joe" Arnold Banks, whose grandfather had lived through the hurricane. Joe's grandfather said that as he and others were fleeing the rising waters in a wagon, they tried to rescue a white woman in the

A young survivor happy to be alive.

water. But because the people in the wagon were Black, the woman pulled back and refused.

The courthouse sheltered all who came. Joe Banks's grandfather remembered that at least for a short time, people there faced the hurricane together.

Milton

Milton and his parents and young nephew had been caught together in a house that collapsed. Milton was the only one who made it out. Sunday dawn found him bruised, shocked, and sore. "As soon as it was light enough I went back to the location of the house, and not a sign of it could be found, and not a sign of any house within two blocks, where before there was scarcely a vacant lot."

He had five dollars in his pocket and the clothes he was wearing. "It seems that I have been dazed," Milton Elford wrote to his brothers on Thursday, five days later. "I have not been able to collect my thoughts until today. I have not found any of the remains yet."

Milton wasn't the only traumatized survivor wandering helplessly in the midst of the rubble of what had been prosperous Galveston. Where houses had stood, full of laughter and family life, there was only destruction. Nothing looked the same. The city—or what had been the city—was nearly gone.

"There are hundreds of houses in one heap, and you can scarcely recognize a single piece," Milton wrote. "For three to five blocks wide and for about four miles, solid blocks of dwellings and hotels and the residence part of the city, there is not a vestige—not a board. It is all swept clean and banked up in a pile reaching all around from bay to beach."

There was little time to grieve. Milton was soon put to work uncovering the remains of the storm's thousands of victims and burying them. He still hoped to find his family and give them a proper burial.

"I have been helping clear away the debris . . . where we are most likely to find them," Milton told his brothers. "There are hundreds of men working there but the

work moves on slowly . . . It is an awful sight. Every few minutes, somewhere within a block of us they find dead bodies, and often where there is one there are more. Yesterday we took out twelve from one spot. It was a large house, and they had gathered there for safety, and all died together, wedged in between ceiling and floor."

Galveston was under martial law, with white soldiers patrolling to prevent looting and stealing. African American men in particular were pressed into service to handle the grisly task of removing the bodies of victims. They weren't allowed to refuse. "The law would come to your house," remembered Annie Smizer McCullough.

It was gruesome work. Yet the heat, odor, and fear of disease made it imperative to act as soon as possible. With such overwhelming numbers of victims, some bodies had to be burned. Other corpses were hauled out to sea. There was no chance to mourn or to have proper

funerals. No chance for the survivors to say goodbye. The chaos made it more difficult to track friends or family, or compile a complete list of the dead.

"It is the most awful thing of the kind that has ever happened in history," said Milton. "Hundreds of families have gone down, and not a sign of anything left of them."

With all the destruction around him, Milton couldn't stop thinking of what he might have done differently, how he might have saved his family. He replayed the final terrible moments as the house collapsed and the water rushed in; he thought of the people wild with fright, the water rising higher and higher as they fought to get out.

But the end was the same. Milton's parents and nephew were gone. At least, Milton told his brothers, "It was all over in a second. I am satisfied they did not fear death in the least, and I do not believe they suffered." That was his only consolation.

Louise

Since Louise Bristol was only seven, her mother tried to protect her from the horrible sights and smells in the aftermath of the storm. Louise wasn't allowed to leave the house. She knew things were bad, though.

Her two older brothers were pressed into service to remove the dead. "They were told they must help and then they were told they had to dig," Louise recalled. "There was no identification and no prayers said or anything else, the bodies were just put in the ground. There were so many of them that they couldn't find any more ground to bury them. They took them out to sea and then they washed back in again, so they had to be burned."

Louise was also old enough to understand that the hurricane had made life much harder for her mom, who'd lost so much. Their house was almost completely destroyed.

"We went out to the porch to look at our house,

because the back end of it had completely collapsed and it was in the yard next door. Everything, cook stove, the two bedrooms with all the furniture and all the dining room furniture and everything was in the yard next door.

"I can remember crying the next day. We had plenty to eat, because she'd [my mother had] gotten all the food upstairs. But I was crying because it was raining in my beans and I couldn't stop it from raining. I remember a silly little thing like that."

Louise later worked for the railroad and married, becoming a mother, grandmother, and great-grandmother. She often visited public schools to talk about history and the Galveston hurricane. She died in Houston in 1987 at the age of ninety-four.

Harry

"What a wreck it left," said fourteen-year-old Harry Maxson. "Houses split half in two, others gone entirely

and cisterns everywhere with all kinds of furniture, bales of cotton and most everything floating all around."

He never got the names of everyone saved in his parents' home that night. But Harry guessed that, all told, they'd sheltered about 150 people, along with several dogs, cats, and even pet birds.

In the aftermath, Harry's mother was trying to feed these homeless survivors. The chief of police arranged for Harry to pick up some extra food supplies—canned salmon, potatoes, flour, and lard.

They ate canned salmon for ten days. After that, Harry said, he never wanted to eat it again.

On Sunday afternoon, Harry walked around town looking for his friends from school. Some had made it. Others were missing or had died. "About 35th and Avenue P or Q, I saw a lot of men starting small fires and before I knew what had happened I had been conscripted to help bury or burn the dead," he said.

"It was too gruesome to describe the condition some of these bodies were in. In less than an hour I looked up

Horse-drawn carts for food delivery are protected by armed guards in the aftermath of the disaster.

and saw Col. McCaleb, an officer of the Local Militia. He said, 'Harry, you're big enough, but too young to be doing this kind of job.' He wrote me out a pass and told me to go home which I was awfully glad to do."

But before he got home, Harry came across the bodies of twin boys, about five years old, still clinging to each other. He fetched a shovel and buried them. Not far away, he saw the corpse of a woman, with a man sitting next to her. The man had been looking for his wife all day.

Harry said, "I tried to get him to go on, but he wanted to stay and help me lay her away . . . he just kept mumbling her name. After getting the grave dug large enough, I found a corrugated washing board and he helped me lay her in her grave so tenderly. It was pitiful! I put the washboard on her face and refilled the grave. Then he thanked me and walked south toward the gulf. I never saw him again."

Brave Harry Maxson lived until he was eighty-one.

When he died in April of 1967, his written account of the storm was discovered among his personal papers.

He closed his recollections this way: "Many of my friends on hearing I passed through the Big 1900 Galveston Storm wanted to hear all about the details—and it was such a long sad story, I made the habit of telling it only once a year and that, of course, would be on Thanksgiving Day."

BE PREPARED!

While people in Galveston had no warning, experts today recommend that families have a preparation kit for emergencies, whether it's a hurricane, wildfire, flood, blizzard, or public health crisis. It's always good to be prepared.

There are different kinds of emergencies. Sometimes, families must leave home immediately to escape danger. Other times, it might be possible to bring a few belongings with you. While our possessions mean a lot, the most important thing is safety. It's critical to follow the guidance of local police, firefighters, or other officials whose job is to keep citizens safe.

And even if the adults in your home are the ones who assemble a preparation kit, everyone has a role to play. You should listen carefully to directions, and if the emergency means your family should stay home, you

should know where supplies are and follow directions about using them.

FEMA, the Federal Emergency Management Agency, a part of the United States government, has an Emergency Supplies Checklist for Kids online with ideas for a scavenger hunt to help your family build a kit.

Most experts advise including flashlights, batteries, candles and matches (only for adults to use), a first aid kit, toothbrushes and toothpaste, pet food, water, a pair of shoes, and clothes for three days, among other supplies.

Check it out at: https://www.fema.gov/media -library-data/35f3ff58f7cc6a2047fdb1e8bae8466b /FEMA_checklist_child_508_071513.pdf.

CHAPTER 10
Too Many Bodies

After Isaac Cline's house fell over into the surging seas, the Cline brothers had been swept into the Gulf of Mexico, balanced precariously on debris. It was all they could do to keep Isaac's three daughters from falling into the water. Luckily, when the wind blew them back to town, they were able to clamber into a house to wait out the rest of the storm.

The girls had survived, but their mother had died. The body of Cora Cline wasn't found for days, and could be identified only by her diamond engagement ring.

On Sunday morning, the Clines ventured out. Like everyone else, they were shocked by the number of victims. Piles of debris ten feet deep stretched on

and on for blocks. Sand covered what had once been streets.

Joseph stood on top of a pile of wreckage and surveyed the wasteland around him. "Not a house was left standing in the area ravaged by the flood, nor could a single street be outlined by the eye. The exact number of the dead was never known, because so many of the bodies were washed away."

There was one bright spot for Joseph. In the middle of the night, he'd plucked from the flood a seven-year-old also named Cora. The little girl told Joseph she lived in San Antonio, Texas, and had been visiting Galveston with her mom and brother. Joseph left Cora in the care of the people in the house where the Clines had spent the last hours of the storm.

Several days later, Joseph happened to overhear a grief-stricken man searching for his lost family. He had come from San Antonio to try to find them.

"Acting upon a sudden impulse, I drew nearer

and asked him if he knew a little girl named Cora Goldbeck," Joseph said. "I shall never forget his face, lined with dread and horror, as he replied, 'She is my daughter.'

"'Then your daughter is safe,' I told him." Though Cora Goldbeck survived, her mother and brother were lost.

Joseph had a footnote to this story. "Many years later, a sequel to this episode brought great happiness to my wife and to me. Miss Cora Goldbeck, a young lady of nineteen, visited us in our home at Corpus Christi [Texas], where she had come in person to thank me for saving her life. The lovely little girl had become a beautiful young woman." Cora lived to be ninety-four years old.

Cora Goldbeck and her father were lucky to find each other. Locating relatives, victims, and survivors after the storm was difficult. So many people had died—sometimes entire families—that it wasn't possible to identify them.

There were just too many.

Outsiders who came to Galveston after the hurricane were overwhelmed by the devastation. Thomas Monagan was one of the first people from off the island to arrive. He worked for an insurance company. He and some colleagues set out on Sunday from Dallas to assess the damages their company would need to cover.

Thomas and his group couldn't get the entire way by train because of damage to the tracks, so they found a sailboat to take them across the bay to Galveston Island. They spotted furniture, debris, and even dead bodies floating in the water. It was dark when they got close to the city, so they anchored offshore on Sunday night.

The very first man they met on Monday morning told them hundreds of bodies were already being burned. Thomas didn't believe it. Surely, the man must be exaggerating. "But we investigated and found it to be true. The authorities were piling up the bodies on the debris and setting fire to the whole mass."

The mortuaries had filled quickly, but there were still thousands of victims. "So they had brought in abandoned barges to the wharf and loaded on them hundreds of bodies as they were pulled from the wreckage of destroyed buildings," said Thomas. "Most of these were badly discolored and unrecognizable. They tied sash weights to their legs and threw them into the bay and came back for another load."

The horrors didn't end there. "We walked over the island, speechless at the sight of the prosperous city laid in waste."

In this desperate situation, where could people turn for help?

Today, after natural disasters, the federal government provides help through FEMA, the Federal Emergency Management Agency. Nonprofit organizations such as the American Red Cross also step in to help. And in 1900, the woman who founded the American Red Cross was still alive. Her name was Clara Barton.

Born in 1821, Clara was almost seventy-nine when the deadliest hurricane struck. Nearly forty years earlier, she had rushed to nurse soldiers on Civil War battlefields. And she established the American Red Cross in 1881. Disaster relief was what she knew best.

Despite her age and ill health, Clara came to Galveston's aid. She and six helpers arrived on September 15, about a week after the hurricane, when smoke from piles of burning rubble and bodies still enveloped the city. Clara stayed for two months, often directing operations from a couch in her hotel room when she didn't feel well.

Clara and her team set up a local chapter of the Red Cross and organized people into sections to help with temporary shelter, clothing, orphaned children, and a soup kitchen. Clara Barton's reputation also helped bring awareness to Galveston's plight.

Newspapers carried stories about the deadly hurricane and the devastated survivors. Ordinary people in America and in other countries too contributed money

and goods. Donors in the state of New York contributed more than $90,000. Seven-year-old Louise Bristol remembered getting a new outfit in a box of clothes from the north.

African American organizations responded as well. H. C. Bell, of Denton, Texas, served as Grand Master of the Colored Odd Fellows, a civic group. He appealed for gifts to benefit all victims: "'To the Lodges and Members of the Grand United Order of Odd Fellows in Texas: Dear Brethren—The greatest calamity that has ever visited any city in America visited Galveston on the 8th . . . leaving in its wake thousands of dead and helpless people of our race, together with the white race.

"'It is our duty to help, as far as we are able, to relieve the suffering condition of the citizens of Galveston. It goes without saying that the white citizens of Texas have always contributed freely to ameliorate and alleviate suffering humanity; it is, therefore, our bounden duty, and, indeed, this is a most fitting opportunity

for us, as members of the greatest negro organization in the world, to show to our white fellow-citizens of Texas the charitable spirit that has always characterized Odd Fellows.'"

Rebuilding the city of Galveston was a slow process. A Central Relief Committee set up a subcommittee to repair and construct new houses. Close to $300,000 was used for new housing, which in today's dollars is about ten million.

In May of 1902, the housing subcommittee reported that more than four hundred cottages had been completed at a cost of about $300 each: "'Contracts were made for building three-room cottages (as fast as men and materials were available) on lots belonging to families whose residences had been entirely destroyed. No distinction was made between the races.'" Cash contributions also helped about eleven hundred families repair or rebuild their houses.

Since preference was given to people who already owned their homes, poorer families and those who

After the storm, thousands were left homeless and forced into makeshift structures such as this.

rented Galveston's alley houses, many occupied by Black residents, were often left out. Some people simply decided to leave. Historians estimate about 2,000 people moved away from Galveston, while others constructed makeshift dwellings.

While Galveston worked to try to meet immediate needs, the hurricane prompted action for the future. This was the deadliest natural disaster in American history and it could not be allowed to happen again.

First, Galveston tried to protect houses by raising the land where most residents lived, by about eight feet above sea level. Then, to help protect the city from storm surges in future storms, Galveston built a thick concrete seawall seventeen feet high along the Gulf shore. The Galveston Seawall, completed in 1904 (and since extended from about three miles to ten miles), is listed on the National Register of Historic Places.

In 1915, another hurricane struck Galveston. Although there was some damage, the concrete barrier held back the storm surge.

In Cuba, it was now clear that Father Gangoite had been correct; the ban on Cuban weather cables was removed.

Joseph Cline married Ula Jackson in 1901, when he was thirty-one. He remained in the weather service in Dallas, Texas, but never forgot the Galveston storm and its "night of horror."

Isaac Cline tried to pick up the pieces of his life and make a future for himself and his three daughters. In 1901, Willis Moore, still in charge of the Weather Bureau, transferred Isaac to New Orleans. There, Isaac devoted himself to trying to understand hurricanes and became a national expert on these deadly storms. He did not remarry.

As for the city of Galveston, it never reclaimed its former glory. And the survivors of the deadliest hurricane in America would never be the same.

EPILOGUE

Hurricanes: Yesterday, Today, and Tomorrow

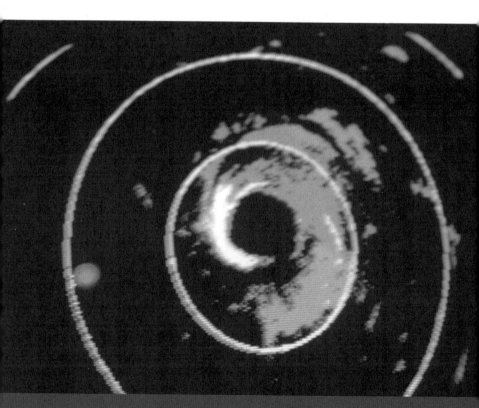

Aircraft radar display of the center of Hurricane Frederic in 1979, which caused an estimated 1.7 billion dollars in damage.

Other Deadly Hurricanes of the Past

Hurricanes are the most expensive, frequent, and deadly natural disasters in the world. These giant whirlwinds have terrified human beings for as long as we have existed—and now, in the twenty-first century, with warming ocean temperatures, hurricanes have the potential to become even more dangerous.

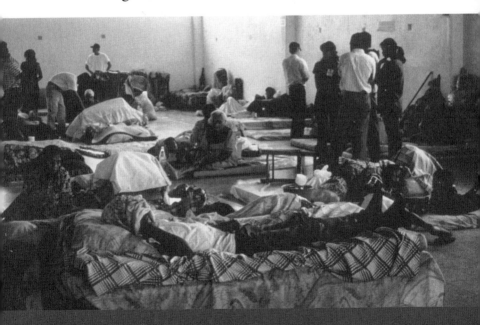

Shelter for the homeless in the wake of Hurricane Mitch, a Category 5 storm that struck Honduras in October of 1998, causing more than 7,000 deaths and more than five billion dollars in damage.

The Galveston hurricane, in which more than 8,000 people lost their lives, remains the worst natural disaster causing loss of life in the United States. But world history is full of examples of horrific and deadly storms.

In 1737, a cyclone struck India, killing more than 300,000; in 1865, again in India, another cyclone killed 50–70,000 people. In 1897, more than 175,000 people died as a result of a cyclone in Bengal, which is now Bangladesh.

The aftereffects of storms often bring more deaths, when food supplies and water sources are disrupted. In 1876, a storm in Bengal killed 100,000 people, with the same number dying later from hunger and disease.

Atlantic hurricanes have also caused tremendous loss of life. Twenty-two thousand people died during a hurricane in the Caribbean in 1780. In 1928, the Okeechobee hurricane killed 1,500 people in the Caribbean before striking Florida, where 3,000 more people lost their lives.

Other hurricanes have caused massive amounts of damage even though their death tolls have not been as horrific. A chart in the back of this book lists the ten most damaging hurricanes in the United States to date.

Hurricane Katrina, 2005

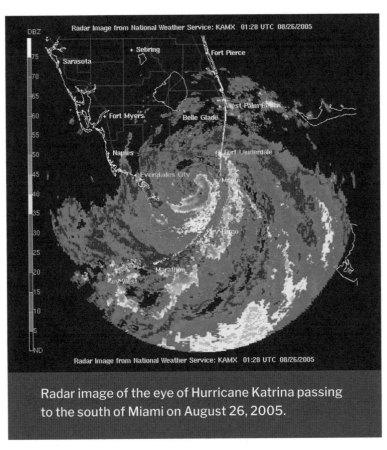

Radar image of the eye of Hurricane Katrina passing to the south of Miami on August 26, 2005.

Despite better hurricane tracking, we continue to experience deadly hurricanes in the United States and in the U.S. territory of Puerto Rico. On Monday, August 29, 2005, Hurricane Katrina slammed into New Orleans and the Gulf Coast. Like the Galveston hurricane in 1900, the storm's path took it across the Gulf of Mexico.

Two days before, at five o'clock on the morning of Saturday, August 27, the National Hurricane Center had released an advisory that the Category 3 Hurricane Katrina, which had already hit Florida as a Category 1 storm, was gaining strength.

As Katrina traveled across the warm waters of the Gulf, the storm intensified just as the Galveston hurricane had. At one point, wind gusts reached more than 170 miles per hour. Katrina made landfall again on Monday morning as a Category 3 storm, causing damage to beachfront areas in Mississippi and Alabama, as well as Louisiana, where it caused the most damage and loss of life.

The inside of a school cafeteria in Mississippi after Hurricane Katrina in 2005, with mud left on tables and stools after the water receded.

Katrina will always be remembered for its devastating impact on the vibrant, historic city of New Orleans and its residents, many of whom are people of color. Much of the city is below sea level. It was not the hurricane's winds, but rainfall and the hurricane's storm surge that resulted in disaster. Water overwhelmed the city's levee system—barriers designed to contain the waters of nearby Lake Pontchartrain and Lake Borgne.

On Monday afternoon, about 20 percent of the entire city was submerged; by the next day, about 80 percent was underwater.

While an evacuation order had been issued for New Orleans, many people accustomed to storms battering their city simply didn't realize the severity of the situation and didn't leave. Others had no means to evacuate. Hospitals and nursing homes struggled to respond.

As the waters rose and overwhelmed the levees, disaster unfolded. Some residents were stranded on

Barbershop in New Orleans damaged by Katrina.

rooftops, desperate for rescue by helicopter or boat. Local emergency services couldn't keep up.

With no place to shelter, about 9,000 people (and later as many as 15,000 to 20,000) converged on the Louisiana Superdome, a large domed stadium. Local officials were overwhelmed. Federal government relief efforts were inadequate and slow. Meanwhile, desperate families suffered in terrible conditions in the Superdome, without adequate water, food, medicine, or supplies.

The horror of Katrina and the suffering it caused for so many families became a symbol of the failure of government preparedness. Thousands of survivors were forced to relocate, moving to other cities to try to remake their lives.

Hurricane Katrina ranks alongside Hurricane Harvey in 2017 as the costliest hurricane in America; each caused a staggering $125 billion in damage. But the greatest tragedy of Katrina was the loss of life:

Only steps are left of this structure after Hurricane Katrina struck Mississippi.

More than 1,800 people died. Americans were angry and devastated and they raised important questions about why this tragedy happened. They also asked: More than one hundred years after Galveston, how can we better protect all people against deadly storms?

Hurricane Maria, 2017

Hurricane Katrina isn't the most recent deadly hurricane. On Wednesday, September 20, 2017, a Category 5 hurricane called Maria hit the U.S. territory of Puerto Rico, along with other islands, especially Dominica and St. Croix. Causing more than ninety billion dollars in damage to houses, roads, and utilities, Maria is the third-costliest hurricane in U.S. history—with high winds and floods devastating much of Puerto Rico—behind Hurricane Katrina in 2005 and Hurricane Harvey, which hit Texas, also in 2017, and caused widespread flooding and sixty-eight deaths.

However, unlike Galveston, where most deaths occurred during the storm, many of the deaths from Hurricane Maria occurred afterward, and weren't included in the original official death toll. There are several reasons for this.

Hurricane Maria knocked out the island's power system, which was not robust. NOAA estimated that 80 percent of Puerto Rico's utility poles and transmission

lines were damaged. The system also took a very long time to repair.

By the end of January of 2018, several months after the storm, only 65 percent of Puerto Rico's 3.4 million residents had power. This meant that for months after the storm, most residents had no electricity, water, or phone service. These conditions caused severe problems, and also led to illness and death. People could not refrigerate medicine, contact relatives or emergency services, or get to the doctor.

As a result, Maria proved even more deadly than Hurricane Katrina. Reports of those who died because of the hurricane have varied, but most experts attribute more than 2,900 deaths to the disaster.

WANT TO BECOME A METEOROLOGIST OR CLIMATOLOGIST?

Meteorologists use math and science to help predict the weather. They work in many different kinds of organizations, from large agencies like NOAA to local television stations. You might see weather forecasters on the nightly news. Other scientists study storms or climate change. They do research, provide forecasts, and apply their skills to new satellite technologies and weather models. To learn more, visit: https://www.environmentalscience .org/career/meteorologist.

The Future: Hurricanes and Global Warming

Hurricanes have always been a part of Earth's climate system. However, scientists have determined that intense hurricane activity has increased in the North Atlantic over the last fifty years.

Why? The reason is human-caused **global warming**.

The global climate crisis has been caused by burning fossil fuels, like oil and coal, to run factories, cars, and airplanes. As they burn, these fuels emit carbon dioxide, which gets trapped in the Earth's atmosphere. This creates a **greenhouse effect**. It's called that because these gases trap the sun's radiation and make the Earth warmer, the same way a glass greenhouse creates warmth for plants.

Global warming is an example of a greenhouse effect. Because the atmosphere is warmer, glaciers and pack ice melt into the oceans, which also have higher temperatures. Sea levels rise, and coastal areas and cities are in more danger from storm surges and flooding.

Climatologists who study the effects of global

warming conclude that while there might not be more frequent hurricanes, these deadly storms will probably have stronger winds and bring more rain. For instance, in 2017, Hurricane Harvey dropped more than forty inches of rain in four days on Texas, causing widespread flooding and dozens of deaths in the Houston area.

NOAA predicts that worldwide, intense tropical cyclones in Categories 4 and 5 will increase throughout the twenty-first century.

Hurricanes are here to stay. But we can take action to lessen the threat to people, birds and animals, and entire cities. The challenge of creating a society based on renewable energy and creating a world not dependent on fossil fuels lies before us.

It is the greatest challenge of all.

THE GREAT GALVESTON HURRICANE FACTS & FIGURES

Date: Saturday, September 8, 1900

Place: Galveston, Texas

City population: 37,789

Estimated winds: 130–140 mph

Storm surge: 15 feet or higher

Estimated deaths: 8,000 or more (true number unknown)

Damage: $20 million (equivalent to about $700 million today)

Houses destroyed: 2,636

People left homeless: More than 4,000

Aftermath: Over the next ten years, the city built a ten-mile-long seawall, about seventeen feet high and sixteen feet at the base. About 500 city blocks were raised an average of eight feet.

In 1915, Galveston was hit by another hurricane. The seawall held and within the city only six people perished.

More for Young
Weather Scientists

GLOSSARY

AIR PRESSURE

Also called atmospheric pressure, the pressure of the atmosphere exerted on the Earth.

BAROMETER

Instrument to measure barometric or air pressure.

EYE

Area in the center of a tropical cyclone with low air pressure and calm winds.

EYEWALL

A ring of spiraling clouds and winds whirling around the eye of a storm.

GLOBAL WARMING

A gradual increase in the atmosphere's temperature.

GOES

NOAA's Geostationary Operational Environmental Satellite.

GREENHOUSE EFFECT

The trapping of the sun's warmth in the lower atmosphere, caused by release of gases like carbon dioxide from burning fuels such as gas and coal.

HURRICANE

A tropical cyclone with winds over 74 mph in the North Atlantic, Northeast Pacific Ocean east of the International Date Line, or the South Pacific Ocean east of 160 degrees.

HURRICANE SEASON

Time of year, June 1 to November 30, when storms are most likely to form in the North Atlantic.

Glossary

HURRICANE WARNING

An announcement that a hurricane is expected.

HURRICANE WATCH

An announcement that a hurricane may possibly be approaching.

METEOROLOGY

Science concerned with the atmosphere and forecasting weather.

NOAA

National Oceanic and Atmospheric Administration, part of the U.S. government.

RADAR

Radar stands for RAdio Detection And Ranging. In use since World War II, this technology helps weather science detect precipitation and forecast storms.

SAFFIR-SIMPSON HURRICANE WIND SCALE

A scale of 1 to 5 used to indicate a storm's intensity and the likelihood of storm damage.

From NOAA:

CATEGORY	WIND SPEED (MPH)	DAMAGE
1	74–95	Very dangerous winds will produce some damage
2	96–110	Extremely dangerous winds will cause extensive damage
3	111–129	Devastating damage will occur
4	130–156	Catastrophic damage will occur
5	>156	Catastrophic damage will occur

Glossary

SEAWALL

A wall or embankment used as a barrier to protect people and things on land from erosion or water coming from the sea.

STORM SURGE

An abnormal rise in sea level with water pushed onto land by the force of a severe storm.

SWELL

A series of waves generated by distant weather systems.

TROPICAL CYCLONE

General meteorological term used to describe storms that form in the tropics with winds that circulate around a center.

TROPICAL DEPRESSION

A tropical cyclone with a maximum sustained wind speed of 38 mph or less.

TROPICAL STORM

A tropical cyclone with wind speeds of 39–73 mph.

TROPICAL WAVE

An area of low pressure and storms moving east to west.
May also be called easterly wave or African easterly wave.

TROPICS

Region of the globe surrounding the equator.

TYPHOON

A severe storm, with winds over 74 mph, that
forms in the Northwest Pacific Ocean, west of the
International Date Line.

WEATHER SATELLITE

An object that orbits above the Earth and monitors
weather and climate, using sophisticated imaging
equipment. Geostationary satellites appear to hover in
place, as they move at the same speed and direction as
the Earth's rotation.

TEST YOUR KNOWLEDGE
Fill in the Correct Words

_____: The center of a hurricane, with calm winds.

_____: A tropical cyclone with winds 74 mph or more in the North Atlantic, Northeast Pacific Ocean east of the International Date Line, or the South Pacific Ocean east of 160 degrees.

_____: A rise in sea level pushing water onshore in a severe storm.

_____: A severe storm, with winds over 74 mph, that forms in the Northwest Pacific Ocean, west of the International Date Line.

_____: Instrument to measure air pressure.

_____: A ring of spiraling clouds and winds whirling around the eye of a storm.

_____: Science concerned with the atmosphere and forecasting weather.

_____: Scale used to measure a hurricane's intensity.

ANSWERS:
EYE
HURRICANE
STORM SURGE
TYPHOON
BAROMETER
EYEWALL
METEOROLOGY
SAFFIR-SIMPSON HURRICANE WIND SCALE

HURRICANE WORD UNSCRAMBLE

LELSW

YCLENOC

LTICRPOA

YTAOGREC

The Deadliest Hurricanes Then and Now

ANSMTIU

PEAMSOETHR

PHONYTO

LSEITLAET

LEWYELA

ANSWERS: SWELL, CYCLONE, TROPICAL, CATEGORY, TSUNAMI, ATMOSPHERE, TYPHOON, SATELLITE, EYEWALL

MORE HURRICANE ACTIVITIES

Make a Barometer

Weather forecasters use barometers to measure air pressure. Visit Scholastic online to make your own.

» https://www.scholastic.com/teachers/articles /teaching-content/barometer

Track a Hurricane

Follow along with a NOAA lesson plan to track a hurricane.

» https://aambcelebrating200.blob.core.windows. net/celebrating200-prod/media/edufun/book /FollowthatHurricane.pdf

Get a Hurricane Tracking Chart

Download and print a hurricane tracking chart from the National Hurricane Center at NOAA.

» https://www.nhc.noaa.gov/AT_Track_chart.pdf

Perform a Hurricane Katrina Damage Assessment Activity

Using maps and aerial photography images online.

» https://oceanservice.noaa.gov/education/lessons/katrina.html

SAMPLE ORAL HISTORY QUESTIONS

Stories matter! Often, oral history interviews are conducted by recording the interview with audio or video. Afterward, someone writes up the interview; this is called a transcript. You can also make your own oral history question sheet and leave blanks to write the person's responses. Try to capture their words exactly. Here are some ideas for an oral history interview with a grandparent.

Please state your full name and date of birth.

Where were you born and what are the names of your parents and siblings?

The Deadliest Hurricanes Then and Now

What was your house like when you were a child and what did you like to do with your family?

What is your favorite memory from when you were young?

Where did you go to school and what did you dream of doing?

When did you get married and to whom?

Have you lived through a difficult time in your life or a big storm or hurricane?

How did you get through hard times? What gives you hope?

What advice do you have for young people today?

TIMETABLE OF
MAJOR U.S. HURRICANES

Throughout recorded history, hurricanes and cyclones have proven deadly in many parts of the world. Here are a few of the most destructive and deadly to strike the continental United States, Hawai'i, and Puerto Rico.

The United States started giving storms female names in 1953; by 1978, both male and female names were used for Pacific storms. The system was adopted in 1979 for Atlantic storms. Naming procedures are set by the UN's World Meteorological Organization.

AUGUST 27, 1667

Hurricane is reported by white settlers in Jamestown, Virginia.

The Deadliest Hurricanes Then and Now

SEPTEMBER 23, 1815

The Great September Gale strikes New England.

OCTOBER 29, 1867

Hurricane strikes the Virgin Islands and Puerto Rico, killing 1,000.

AUGUST 27–28, 1893

Hurricane kills up to 2,500 in South Carolina.

AUGUST 8–19, 1899

Three thousand die in an East Coast hurricane.

SEPTEMBER 8, 1900

More than 8,000 die in Galveston, Texas, hurricane and flood.

SEPTEMBER 28, 1926

A destructive hurricane devastates Miami, Florida.

SEPTEMBER 21, 1938

The surprise Great New England Hurricane kills more than 600.

Timetable of Major U.S. Hurricanes

AUGUST 25–31, 1954
Hurricane Carol strikes the East Coast, inflicting severe damage.

AUGUST 19, 1955
Hurricane Diane strikes New England.

SEPTEMBER 7–10, 1965
Hurricane Betsy causes major damage in Florida and Louisiana.

AUGUST 17, 1969
Hurricane Camille attacks coastal Mississippi and Louisiana.

JUNE 14–23, 1972
Hurricane Agnes causes floods in the mid-Atlantic.

SEPTEMBER 10–25, 1989
Hurricane Hugo hits islands in the Caribbean as well as the southeast U.S.

The Deadliest Hurricanes Then and Now

AUGUST 24, 1992

Hurricane Andrew breaks the 1989 record for damage set by Hugo.

AUGUST 29, 2005

Hurricane Katrina becomes the U.S. hurricane causing the most damage to that date.

AUGUST 24, 2017

Hurricane Harvey ties Katrina for damage, with heavy floods in Texas.

SEPTEMBER 20, 2017

Hurricane Maria strikes Puerto Rico, causing the third-most damage.

NOAA NATIONAL HURRICANE CENTER
LIST OF THE COSTLIEST

NOAA satellite image of Hurricane Andrew.

This is a list of the top ten costliest tropical cyclones to strike the mainland United States. To see the full

list and a table with figures adjusted for inflation, visit: https://www.nhc.noaa.gov/news/UpdatedCostliest .pdf.

(Updated 1/26/18)

HURRICANE	YEAR	CATEGORY	DOLLARS OF DAMAGE
Katrina	2005	3	125 billion
Harvey	2017	4	125 billion
Maria	2017	4	90 billion
Sandy	2012	1	65 billion
Irma	2017	4	50 billion
Ike	2008	2	30 billion
Andrew	1992	5	27 billion
Ivan	2004	3	20.5 billion
Wilma	2005	3	19 billion
Rita	2005	3	18.5 billion

EXPLORE MORE
Internet Resources and Lesson Plans

Education World Hurricane Lesson Plans
https://www.educationworld.com/a_lesson/lesson
/lesson076.shtml

Galveston Hurricane Slideshow
https://rosenberg-library.org/special-collections
/the-1900-storm-a-slideshow

**NEA—Activities and Lesson Plans
for K–5 Students**
http://www.nea.org/tools/lessons/hurricane-season
-grades-k-5.html

NOAA—Galveston Hurricane of 1900

https://celebrating200years.noaa.gov/magazine/galv _hurricane/welcome.html

NOAA—National Hurricane Center

https://www.nhc.noaa.gov

NOAA—Explore Hurricanes in History

https://www.nhc.noaa.gov/outreach/history

SELECTED BIBLIOGRAPHY

Books

Beasley, Ellen. *The Alleys and Back Buildings of Galveston: An Architectural and Social History.* College Station, TX: Texas A&M University Press, 1996.

Bixel, Patricia B., and Elizabeth Hayes Turner. *Galveston and the 1900 Storm.* Austin, TX: University of Texas Press, 2008.

Cline, Joseph L. *When the Heavens Frowned.* Gretna, LA: Mathis Van Hort and Co., 1946.

Collins, Izola. *Island of Color: Where Juneteenth Started.* Bloomington, IN: AuthorHouse, 2004.

Emanuel, Kerry. *Divine Wind: The History and Science of Hurricanes.* Oxford and New York: Oxford University Press, 2005.

Greene, Casey E., and Shelly Henley Kelly, eds. *Through a Night of Horrors: Voices from the 1900 Galveston Storm.* College Station, TX: Texas A&M University Press, 2000.

Halstead, Murat. *Galveston: The Horrors of a Stricken City.* Forgotten Books, 2016. (Reproduction of 1900 book, originally published by American Publishers' Association.)

Larson, Eric. *Isaac's Storm: A Man, a Time, and the Deadliest Hurricane in History.* New York: Vintage Books, 1999.

Lester, Paul. *The Great Galveston Disaster.* Good Press, 2019. (Reproduction of 1900 book.)

McComb, David G. *Galveston: A History*. Austin, TX: University of Texas Press, 1986.

Roker, Al. *The Storm of the Century: Tragedy, Heroism, Survival, and the Epic True Story of America's Deadliest Natural Disaster: The Great Gulf Hurricane of 1900*. New York: William Morrow, 2015.

Schumacher, Michael. *November's Fury: The Deadly Great Lakes Hurricane of 1913*. Minneapolis: University of Minnesota Press, 2013.

Weems, John Edward. *A Weekend in September*. College Station, TX: Texas A&M University Press, 2002.

Articles, Newspapers, and Websites

Cline, Isaac M. *Monthly Weather Review*, Vol. 28, No. 9, September 1900, 373.

———. "West India Hurricanes," *Galveston News*, July 16, 1891.

Galveston & Texas History Center. 1900 Storm. https://www.galvestonhistorycenter.org /research/1900-storm.

Lienhard, John H. *Engines of Our Ingenuity*, Episode 865: "Raising Galveston." University of Houston College of Engineering. https://uh.edu/engines /epi865.htm.

Spillane, Richard. "The Wrecking of Galveston." *New York Times*, September 11, 1900.

SOURCE NOTES

Source notes tell us where a quotation came from, such as an oral history, interview, newspaper article, or book. In nonfiction, facts and research are important, so authors also use source notes to let readers know where they have obtained specific facts or details. The notes here are organized by chapters. Paying attention to source notes helps us become better readers, researchers, and writers too.

Prologue
"I saw a roof . . .": Harry I. Maxson in Greene and Kelly, *Through a Night of Horrors*, 129.

Before You Begin
"I remember passing . . .": Collins, *Island of Color*, 7.

About the People in This Book
Mary Louise Bristol (Hopkins): Hopkins obituary, *Galveston Daily News*, November 21, 1987, https://www.newspapers.com /image/?clipping_id=19318369&fcfToken=eyJhbGciOiJIUzI1NiIsIn

The Deadliest Hurricanes Then and Now

R5cCI6IkpXVCJ9.eyJmcmVlLXZpZZXctaWQiOjExNTA4MTcyL-
CJpYXQiOjE1ODEwMjk3MzcsImV4cCI6MTU4MTExNjEzN30.
VUp_MmrvKtmLQnLOXv7hFXg7Nv0sVSq8K8rrkHnXjt0.

Milton Elford: Find a Grave, https://www.findagrave.com /memorial/48421992/john-elford.

Katherine Vedder (Pauls): Find a Grave, https://www.findagrave.com /memorial/71991068/katharine-pauls.

Arnold R. Wolfram: Find a Grave, https://www.findagrave.com /memorial/87069814/arnold-rudolph-wolfram.

Chapter 1

"The hurricane which visited . . .": I. M. Cline, "Monthly Weather Review."

"It was a perfect . . .": Katherine Vedder Pauls in Greene and Kelly, 180.

Galveston in 1900: Greene and Kelly, 3.

Cline address: Larson, *Isaac's Storm*, 7.

"the only area . . .": Collins, 17–18.

Hurricane formation: https://spaceplace.nasa.gov/hurricanes/en/.

heights of ten or eleven feet: Emanuel, *Divine Wind*, 7.

the word *hurricane*: Ibid., 18.

Chapter 2

Brazos River: Roker, 79.

Elevation: Lienhard, "Raising Galveston."

"It would be impossible . . .": I. M. Cline, "West India Hurricanes."

Cuba weather observers: Roker, 89–93.

"'We are today . . .'": Larson, 111.

"If Gangoite's prediction . . .": Ibid., 96.

Source Notes

"The usual signs . . .": I. M. Cline, "Monthly Weather Review."

Storm Definitions: https://phys.org/news/2015-03-cyclone-hurricane -typhoon-violent-phenomenon.html.; Emanuel, 18–21.

Chapter 3
"On the dark, cold winter . . .": J. L. Cline, *When the Heavens Frowned*, 1.

"I applied myself . . .": Ibid., 34.

Swells: Ibid., 133.

"Unusually heavy swells . . .": I. M. Cline, "Monthly Weather Review."

"'The weather bureau . . .'": Larson, 143.

"Friday evening . . .": Sarah Hawley in Greene and Kelly, 28.

"Gulf rising . . .": I. M. Cline, "Monthly Weather Review."

"indicate the great intensity . . .": Ibid.

Torricelli: http://chemed.chem.purdue.edu/genchem/history/torricelli .html.

lowest barometer: https://www.guinnessworldrecords.com/world-records /lowest-barometric-pressure?fb_comment_id=724903447587744_1561 623120582435.

Chapter 4
"The wreck of Galveston . . .": Spillane, "Wrecking of Galveston."

Cline house: Larson, 7.

"like a lighthouse . . .": J. L. Cline, 52.

"At this time . . .": I. M. Cline, "Monthly Weather Review."

"The water rose . . .": Ibid.

Winds: Emanuel, 88.

Chapter 5

"About half past three . . .": Katherine Vedder Pauls in Greene and Kelly, 180.

"The house rose . . .": Ibid., 181.

Galveston in 1900: Greene and Kelly, 3.

"handed us . . .": Katherine Vedder Pauls in Greene and Kelly, 181.

"I called out . . .": Ibid.

"But for months . . .": Ibid., 182.

"My mother took him . . .": Ibid.

"Gradually the tiny body . . .": Ibid.

"all it takes . . .": https://www.noaa.gov/stories/tropical-storms-and -hurricanes-in-winter-and-spring.

Chapter 6

"It was as if . . .": Harry I. Maxson in Greene and Kelly, 130.

"I returned home . . .": Ibid., 130–31.

"Father anticipated . . .": Ibid., 131.

"We had no tools . . .": Ibid.

"I heard what I didn't . . .": Ibid., 132.

"I thanked him . . .": Ibid., 133.

Chapter 7

"near level . . .": Collins, 279.

"When I got . . .": Ibid., 279–80.

"When we [hit] . . .": Ibid., 280.

"Just did get away!": Ibid., 281.

"About 5 [o'clock] it grew worse . . .": Milton Elford in Halstead, Galveston, 212.

"All at once . . .": Ibid., 212–13.

"I had only got . . .": Ibid., 213.

"I was hit on the head . . .": Ibid.

"We must have all gone . . .": Ibid.

"The street was full . . .": Ibid.

"At the corner . . .": Arnold Wolfram in Greene and Kelly, 119.

"I shouted to him . . .": Ibid.

"We were now forcing . . .": Ibid., 120.

"We were both suddenly . . .": Ibid., 121.

"The air was full . . .": Ibid.

"I remember seeing . . .": Mary Louise Bristol Hopkins in Greene and Kelly, 170.

"She got an axe . . .": Ibid., 171.

"She realized that the house . . .": Ibid.

"My mother would say . . .": Ibid., 172.

Chapter 8
"I urged them . . .": J. L. Cline, 53–54.

"I seized the hand . . .": Ibid., 54.

"It was raining in torrents . . .": Ibid.

"We remained close together . . .": Ibid., 56.

"I made a lunge for him . . .": Ibid., 57.

"Tired and unspeakably battered . . .": Ibid., 59.

Chapter 9
Death toll: https://www.galvestonhistorycenter.org/research/1900-storm.

"'Papa, where are . . .'": Ibid.

"Not a plank . . .": Ibid.

"No streets or roads . . .": Ibid.

"'You know, my grandmother . . .'": Ibid., 185.

"I turned away . . .": Arnold Wolfram in Greene and Kelly, 122.

"I dreaded to look . . .": Ibid.

"The little lad . . .": Ibid., 123.

"She told me . . .": Collins, 272–73.

Henry Johnson: Beasley, *Alleys and Back Buildings*, 69.

"These white people . . .": Collins, 281.

"As soon as it was light . . .": Halstead, 214.

"It seems that I have . . .": Ibid., 211.

"There are hundreds . . .": Ibid., 212.

"I have been helping . . .": Ibid., 211.

"The law would come . . .": Collins, 282.

"It is the most awful . . .": Halstead, 214–15.

"Hundreds of families . . .": Ibid., 215.

"It was all over . . .": Ibid.

"They were told . . .": Mary Louise Bristol Hopkins in Greene and Kelly, 172–73.

"We went to the back porch . . .": Ibid.

"What a wreck it left . . .": Harry I. Maxson in Greene and Kelly, 134.

"About 35th and Avenue P . . .": Ibid., 135.

"I tried to get him . . .": Ibid., 136.

"Many of my friends . . .": Ibid., 139.

Chapter 10

"Not a house was left . . .": J. L. Cline, 60.

"Acting upon a sudden . . .": Ibid., 61.

"Many years later . . .": Ibid., 62.

Cora Goldbeck: https://ancestors.familysearch.org/en/L7B1-KC1/cora-audrey-goldbeck-1892-1987.

"But we investigated . . .": Thomas Monagan in Greene and Kelly, 103.

"So they had brought . . .": Ibid.

"We walked over . . .": Ibid., 104.

Donations: Larson, 244–45.

"'To the Lodges . . .'": Lester, *The Great Galveston Disaster*, 261.

"'Contracts were made . . .'": Beasley, 70.

"night of horror.": J. L. Cline, 134.

Epilogue

NOAA: https://www.nhc.noaa.gov/news/UpdatedCostliest.pdf.

Deadly cyclones: Emanuel, 263–64.

PHOTO CREDITS

Images; 96–97: National Archives (27-S-23b-306); 99, 107, 120: Library of Congress; 123: NOAA; 124: Debbie Larson/NWS/NOAA; 126: NOAA; 128: Barbara Ambrose/NODC/NCDDC/NOAA; 129, 131: Carol M. Highsmith's America, Library of Congress; 159: NOAA; 181: NOAA National Environmental Satellite, Data, and Information Service (NESDIS).

INDEX

Page numbers in *italics* refer to illustrations.

Index

One of the deadliest hurricanes in modern times was Hurricane Katrina. This NOAA satellite image of Katrina was taken on August 28, 2005, when the storm was at its peak intensity.

ABOUT THE AUTHOR

Deborah Hopkinson is an award-winning author of picture books, middle grade fiction, and nonfiction. Her nonfiction titles include *We Must Not Forget: Holocaust Stories of Survival and Resistance*; *We Had to Be Brave: Escaping the Nazis on the Kindertransport*; *Titanic: Voices from the Disaster*, a Sibert Medal Honor Book and YALSA Award for Excellence in Nonfiction finalist; *Courage & Defiance: Stories of Spies, Saboteurs, and Survivors in World War II Denmark*, a Sydney Taylor Notable Book, NCTE Orbis Pictus Recommended Book, and a winner of the Oregon Book Award and Oregon Spirit Award; *Dive! World War II Stories of Sailors & Submarines in the Pacific*, an NCTE Orbis Pictus Recommended Book and Oregon Spirit Award

Honor Book; and *D-Day: The World War II Invasion That Changed History.*

Deborah lives with her family near Portland, Oregon, along with an assortment of pets that includes two canine office companions (Brooklyn and Rue); one cat (Beatrix); three chickens (Daisy, Chuckles, and Georgina); canaries named for #GOT characters; and an assortment of finches and fish. When she's not traveling the country to talk about history with students, Deborah is at the gym or attempting to create a garden. She also reads a lot. Visit her online at www.deborahhopkinson.com and follow her on Twitter at @Deborahopkinson and on Instagram at @deborah_hopkinson.

THE DEADLIEST

HURRICANES THEN AND NOW

Contents

Contents

Preface

Bubbles lie at the intersection between finance, economics, and psychology. Recent explanations of large-scale asset price movements have leaned toward placing psychology first in the list, not only for episodes from the dim past but also for most events in the crisis years of 1997, 1998, and 1999. The evidence that will be developed in this book, however, indicates that the early bubbles at least were driven by fundamentals. They stem from the more basic intersection of finance and economics, with psychology at most in the background.

This book is about the three most famous bubbles—the Dutch tulipmania, the Mississippi Bubble, and the South Sea Bubble—all of which have served as examples of private capital markets gone haywire. On the contrary,

• The high prices of rare bulbs in the tulipmania—emphasized in most stories as the prima facie evidence for its madness—is a standard feature of markets in newly developed varieties, as is a rapid price decline.

- Even now, rare bulb varieties carry a price equal in value to a substantial house.
- Little economic distress was associated with the end of the tulipmania.
- The stories that we have now stem mainly from a single source resulting from a moralistic campaign of the Dutch government.
- The speculation in common bulbs was a phenomenon lasting one month in the dreary Dutch winter of 1637. A drinking phenomenon held in the taverns, it occurred in the midst of a massive outbreak of bubonic plague and had no real consequence.
- The Mississippi Bubble was a large-scale money printing operation and a government debt-for-equity swap.
- The South Sea Bubble was also a debt-for-equity swap, although less well-grounded.
- Both bubbles were grandiose macroeconomic schemes launched or aided by high government officials and supported by the entire apparatus of the governments of England and France.
- Nevertheless, they are now interpreted as prime examples of the madness possible in *private* financial markets and of the need for government control and regulation.

Acknowledgments

This book results from my research on the early bubbles undertaken over the years. As its basis, it combines two papers, "Tulipmania" (*Journal of Political Economy*, 1989) and "Famous First Bubbles"(*Journal of Economic Perspectives*, 1990), and a conference volume chapter, "Who Put the Mania in the Tulipmania?" (in E. White, ed., *Crashes and Panics: The Lessons From History*, Homewood: Dow-Jones Irwin, 1990). I am grateful to Robert Flood, Herschel Grossman, Robert Hodrick, Salih Neftci, Stuart Parkinson, David Ribar, Rudiger Dornbusch, and James Peck for useful discussions, to Guido Imbens for resourceful research assistance, and to Marina van Dongen and Klaas Baks for helpful translations. Librarians at Harvard's Houghton, Kress, Arnold Arboretum, and Grey Herbarium Libraries and at the Massachusetts Horticultural Society provided valuable guidance. George Stigler at the *Journal of Political Economy* provided extensive editorial comment in developing the basic paper on tulipmania on which this book is based, and Joseph Stiglitz and Timothy Taylor at the *Journal of Economic Perspectives* as well as several anonymous referees both for journal review and for this book also contributed helpful suggestions. I have benefited from the comments of participants in workshops at Brown University, the Board of Governors of the Federal Reserve, CUNY, Columbia University, Queens University, UCLA, MIT, the IMF, and Northwestern.

I

The Bubble Interpretation

The Dutch tulipmania, the Mississippi Bubble, the South Sea Bubble—these are always invoked with every outbreak of great financial instability. So implanted are they in our literature, that they are now used more as synonyms for financial instability than as references to the particular events themselves. Along with words such as *herding* and the newly popular *irrational exuberance*, they now dominate the policymaking, academic rhetoric, and market commentary on the crisis years of 1997, 1998, and 1999.

In general, these events are viewed as outbursts of irrationality: self-generating surges of optimism that pump up asset prices and misallocate investments and resources to such a great extent that a crash and major financial and economic distress inevitably follow. Only some bizarre self-delusion or blindness could have prevented a participant from seeing the obvious, so these episodes are called forth almost as a form of ridicule for such losers.

This book presents the fundamental history of the three famous bubbles. But it is necessary first to come to grips with the meaning of the class of words spawned by these events to understand how these events from so long ago serve the modern regulatory rhetoric. In this small introductory glossary—and I hope not too excessive a detour—I will first work through the meaning of these words and critique them. Then I will present and discuss the definition of the word *bubble* that can be found in the authoritative literature on the subject. Finally, I will return to the important role as rhetorical weapons played by the three most famous bubbles by looking at how even the *Financial Times* employed them to interpret the events of October 1998.

The Meanings of a Few Words

Bubbles

The classic word for these phenomena is *bubble*. Bubble is one of the most beautiful concepts in economics and finance in that it is a fuzzy word filled with import but lacking a solid operational definition. Thus, one can make whatever one wants of it. The definition of *bubble* most often used in economic research is that part of asset price movement that is unexplainable based on what we call fundamentals. Fundamentals are a collection of variables that we believe should drive asset prices. In the context of a particular model of asset price determination, if we have a serious misforecast of asset prices we might then say that there is a bubble.

This is no more than saying that there is something happening that we cannot explain, which we normally call a random disturbance. In asset pricing studies, we give it a name—*bubble*—and appeal to unverifiable psychological stories.

Psychological state of mind is not a measurable concept, especially years after an event. It does, however, provide a convenient way of explaining some phenomena in the market that cannot otherwise be explained. Our existing or favorite models of fundamentals often cannot explain important observed phenomena in asset markets. We know that market psychology or *market sentiment* can be important, so we blame the inadequacy of our fundamental model vis-à-vis actual outcomes on unmeasurable market psychology.

Herding

Although used frequently these days to explain large capital flows, *herding* is a vague word, projecting the feeling that speculators are cattle, some kind of prey. The rigged image here is that investors go grazing passively from one place to another, following a leader, without scouting out the grass themselves. In particular, the herding concept arises in the context of large amounts of funds flowing into emerging markets.

Of course, herding is not an irrational act. If it is known that someone is good at analysis and that person makes a move, it is reasonable to follow. The problem is that those who call on herding as an explanation for the movement of funds by a large number of institutions or individuals into a particular market never provide any evidence of on what basis investors are making decisions. That we see large amounts of funds flowing in together at one time and flowing out together at another does not mean that herding is going on—that is, that one or two smart people are doing the analysis and that everyone is following blindly. Everyone may be doing analysis. Alternatively, fund managers may delegate the serious research and analytical effort to a trusted research organization, which in turn advises many clients. That the individual fund manager does not have a research department does not mean he is acting blindly.

The future is always shrouded in fog: we never know what is coming, and yet we have to allocate investment resources according to our best guess at the future. To fill the gap, we have theories. Once in a while, a convincing theory emerges that allows us to visualize the future "better" than before. That is what economic research is about: generating concepts that we can use to interpret observed phenomena and perhaps to forecast phenomena. Every once in a while, a theory becomes dominant and perhaps convincing. Keynesianism was a convincing theory once, and governments *herded* on the basis of Keynesian policy prescriptions. These tended to fail in their more overblown forms, after which governments shied away from such policies and imposed (*herded* around) stringent anti-inflationist policies. No one says, though, that we observed herding behavior on the part of governments during the 1960s and 1970s when they bought into Keynesianism and during the 1980s and 1990s when they got out en masse.

Irrational Exuberance

This is a term recently invoked by Alan Greenspan, chairman of the Board of Governors of the Federal Reserve. It was simply part of a claim, as of December 1996 when the Dow was at about 6500, that the stock markets might be getting it wrong and that he might know better what the right level of stock prices should be (i.e., he gave a new name to the divergence of market prices from a theory of where they should be). He concluded that there might be irrationality afoot.

Three years later, with the stock market fifty percent higher, in testimony on February 23, 1999, Mr. Greenspan was asked whether he thought there was still irrational exuberance. His reply was "That is something you can only know after the fact." Thus, he removed all meaningful content from the concept.

Two Other Definitions of Bubble

To place a final emphasis on how tenuous and unusable the meaning of bubbles can be, let us focus on a pair of definitions of *bubble* that can be found at various stages in the economics literature.

The premodern definition of a bubble is from Palgrave's *Dictionary of Political Economy* (1926): "Any unsound undertaking accompanied by a high degree of speculation." This is basically the *irrational exuberance* definition of a bubble. By this definition, we cannot know if we have a bubble until after it bursts. Commercial undertakings accompanied by a high degree of speculation may actually turn out to be quite successful. It is only after we find out that a commercial undertaking did not work that we can conclude it was unsound and then call it a bubble. This concept is as empty as Greenspan's.

It is always possible that a scheme might succeed—if it does, it would then be described as brilliantly audacious. With the future often very uncertain, the only way that we can operate according to a purposeful plan is to postulate theories that allow us to forecast the future, given the current state of the world. These theories may be based on past experience but perhaps also on new phenomena that we observe.

If the theory is convincing, it will attract commercial and speculative activity. To return to the herding concept, speculators really gather around theories, not each other. If someone enters with a convincing story and structure of thought for organizing otherwise confusing phenomena, he will attract speculative capital. For instance, we know that the Internet stocks are a gamble, but they are backed by a theory of an epochal change in technology that will alter the entire economic structure. Normally careful governments are pushing this view to the extent that high officials even claim to have invented the Internet.

When there is a large technological shift, great uncertainty exists about what the future will bring. We do not know how the economic system will absorb all these changes, so naturally investment in many commercial undertakings suddenly becomes speculative, even in the old established businesses that may suffer if the theory comes true. These are almost required gambles on the future. If there is a convincing theory about the Internet, we have to bet on it. We must allocate part of our portfolio to it. Otherwise, we might miss out on the next big winner or, even worse, be backing a loser. Therefore, we truly cannot know if the speculation was unsound until after the fact.

In his popular book on manias and bubbles, Kindleberger's definition of a *bubble* is as follows: "A bubble is an upward price movement over an extended range that then implodes." This is an empirical statement about the pattern of asset prices. A sort of chartist view of bubbles, this prescribes that we simply give a name to that particular price pattern. Such patterns can be observed in the data, so according to this definition, we cannot deny that a particular historical episode—for example, tulipmania or Mississippi Bubble—was a bubble. However, with this definition, there can be no necessary conclusion that this pattern reflects any irrationality or excess or was not based a priori on fundamentals, the usual reason for calling an event a bubble.

How These Bubbles Are Used to Sway Opinion

The concept of a bubble is a fuzzy one, which is why the concept itself can be debated incessantly. To short-circuit this poor definition, anyone aiming to explain current market phenomena in terms of bubbles is likely to cite the most famous historical examples—that is, to list phenomena such as the Dutch tulipmania, the Mississippi

Bubble, and the South Sea Bubble that everyone agrees were outbursts of irrationality. By analogy, it is easier to claim that there must be irrationality in the current episodes.

As an example of how these famous bubbles are always cited in periods of market stress, we can refer to the lead editorial of the *Financial Times*, usually the most careful of the financial press, which reviewed the IMF's *World Economic Outlook/Capital Markets Interim Report* of December 1998:

• "When everyone rushes in the same direction, it is hard for financial speculators to stand aside and recall the lessons of past stampedes."

• "Stories of the Dutch tulipmania in 1636 or the South Sea Bubble eighty-four years later might have left derivatives traders cold this summer; but the Mexico crisis of 1994–1995 certainly should have created a warning tremor. In an update to its October *World Economic Outlook,* the International Monetary Fund draws special attention to this failure to learn" (*Financial Times,* "The Madness of Crowds," December 22, 1998).

In this editorial, the *Financial Times* uses the Dutch tulipmania as the historical template for the global financial crisis of October 1998. How accurate is its interpretation of the tulipmania and of the statements of the IMF's report? The Interim Report did discuss how risk control works in the financial markets. Usually, when we think of risk control, we do not think in terms of panic, exuberance, or irrationality. We think of correct, prudent behavior on the part of financial institutions. Indeed, that was the gist of the Interim Report: standard risk control procedures require that when some disturbance hits, banks have to adjust their credit positions. It is exactly such prudent behavior that makes all the contagion explainable. The thrust of the report was not that there was irrationality, panic, or mania. Rather, the report was a fundamental explanation of how the process worked, a documentation of the interconnections among financial markets. These risk control procedures are, in fact, *imposed* by industrial country regulators as a way of managing market and credit risk.

• "When the crowd tried to reverse direction after August 17, as Russia defaulted on its debt, many comforting systems for limiting risk broke down. This was because, like the seventeenth century tulip speculators, they relied on continuous orderly markets for closing unsuccessful positions. When everyone panicked the computerized strategies only exacerbated market turmoil" (*Financial Times*, "The Madness of Crowds," December 22, 1998).

I have spent a great deal of time studying the tulip speculation, and I have never seen any reference to tulip speculators' relying on continuously orderly markets. This is just something that the *Financial Times* editorial writer made up. There can be no more stark example of how the tulipmania episode is used: it is simply a rhetorical device to put across an argument. The story is now on such a mythological level that anyone feels the ability to embellish it, however falsely, to make a point.

For what reason is the tulipmania generally invoked? The argument is always that the existence of tulipmania proves that markets are crazy. A curious disturbance in a particular modern market can then be attributed to crazy behavior, so perhaps the market needs to be more severely regulated. Thus, these early episodes are the dream events for those who want to control the flow of capital.

The Famous Bubbles

History is a rhetorical weapon to be used in influencing modern policy outcomes. In particular, the invocation of bubbles is one such use of history. We now turn to the histories of the early bubbles to track down what they actually imply about the behavior of the private capital markets.

I aim here to supply market fundamental explanations for the three most famous bubbles: the Dutch tulipmania (1634–1637), the Mississippi Bubble (1719–1720), and the closely connected South Sea Bubble (1720). Though several authors have proposed market fundamental explanations for the well-documented Mississippi and South Sea Bubbles, these episodes are still treated in the modern view as spectacular outbursts of crowd irrationality. This interpretation is attributable to the influence of Charles Mackay's ([1841] 1852) famous descriptions of the frenzied speculative crowds that materialized in Paris and London in 1719 and 1720.

I concentrate most on the tulipmania because it is the event that most modern observers view as obviously crazy. I briefly discuss the historical background from which the tulipmania emerged, review the traditional version of the tulipmania, and trace the sources of the traditional version. To understand the nature of tulip markets, we must focus on how the reproductive cycle of the tulip itself determined behavior during the mania.

Data on seventeenth-century tulip prices and markets are too limited to construct "market fundamentals" on the supply and demand for tulip bulbs. I simply characterize the movement of prices for a variety of bulbs during and after the mania and compare the results to the pattern of price declines for initially rare eighteenth-century bulbs. This evidence can then be used to address the question of whether the seventeenth-century tulip speculation clearly exhibits the existence of a speculative mania.

I conclude that the most famous aspect of the mania, the extremely high prices reported for rare bulbs and their rapid decline, reflects normal pricing behavior in bulb markets and cannot be interpreted as evidence of market irrationality.

The Mississippi and South Sea Bubbles are the other two examples that appear on everyone's short list of spectacular financial collapses. They provide the most popular synonym for speculative mania. Based on the innovative economic theories of John Law, essentially what we now call Keynesian theories, both involved financial manipulations, monetary creation, and government connivance on a scale that was not matched again until this century, but which have now become commonplace. I will describe the nature of the asset markets and financial manipulations that occurred in these episodes and cast these also as market fundamentals.

II

The Tulipmania
Legend

Gathered around the campfires early in their training, fledgling economists hear the legend of the Dutch tulip speculation from their elders, priming them with a skeptical attitude toward speculative markets. That prices of "intrinsically useless" bulbs could have risen so high and collapsed so rapidly seems to provide a decisive example of the instability and irrationality that may materialize in asset markets. The Dutch tulipmania of 1634–1637 always appears as a favorite case of speculative excess, even providing a synonym in our jargon for a speculative mania.

As a nonessential agricultural commodity, the tulip could have been reproduced rapidly and without limit, should its relative price have increased. Since market fundamental prices under any reasonable explanation should not have attained recorded levels, the tulipmania phenomenon has made it more likely that a sizable body of economists will occasionally embrace a rational or irrational "bubble hypothesis" in debates about whether bubbles have emerged in other episodes.

1   A Political and Economic Background

The introduction of the tulip market into the Netherlands and the tulipmania occurred in the midst of
the Eighty Years' War of independence between the
Dutch and the Spanish.[1] Spanish possession of the Low
Countries had arisen through marriage; both the old
Burgundian possessions in the Low Countries and Spain
had been melded with Hapsburg territories in Central
Europe in this manner. In trying to centralize and make
organizational sense of this amalgamation of territories,
the Hapsburgs attempted to impose administrative
reforms that initiated the Dutch rebellion in 1567. This
war was waged continuously, with Spain using the
Spanish Netherlands (Belgium) as a base to attack the
United Provinces until the Twelve Years' Truce was
arranged in 1609. The Spanish were thwarted in their
attempts to subjugate the Netherlands, which con-
solidated its territory and eventually seized control of
most of international shipping. During this phase of the
war, the English and Dutch formed an alliance, under

which the English defeated of the Spanish Armada in 1588.

In 1618, the Thirty Years' War broke out in Europe, aligning the Hapsburgs and the Holy Roman Empire, including the Spanish, on the Catholic side against various Protestant powers in Central Europe. The Thirty Years' War was particularly destructive of the populations and economies of Central Europe, with many principalities in the Holy Roman Empire losing one-third of their populations. The map from Rich and Wilson (1975, 42) indicates the population declines to the east of the Netherlands in this period.

With the expiration of the Twelve Years' Truce in 1621, the Spanish-Dutch Eighty Years' War revived as a continuing parallel of the Thirty Years' War and did not end until just before the general peace of 1648. In every year of the war, the Dutch fielded armies as large as 100,000 men during campaigning seasons and supported large fleets, though the population of the Netherlands was no more than 1.5 million. The Dutch provided much of the strategic planning and finance for the Protestant effort, with France negotiating and financing the successive interventions of Denmark and Sweden on the Protestant side in the 1620s and 1630s.

From 1620 to 1645, the Dutch established near monopolies on trade with the East Indies and Japan, conquered most of Brazil, took possession of the Dutch Caribbean islands, and founded New York. In 1628, the Dutch West India Company captured in a Caribbean naval action the

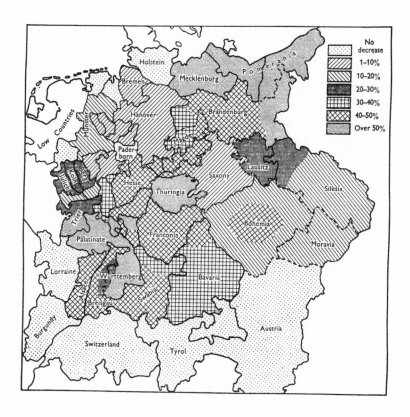

Legend:
- No decrease
- 1–10%
- 10–20%
- 20–30%
- 30–40%
- 40–50%
- Over 50%

entire year's output of silver and gold from Spain's American possessions, amounting to between 11.5 and 14 million guilders, or about $90 million in today's gold prices.[2] In 1635, the Dutch formed a military alliance with Richelieu's France, which eventually placed the Spanish Netherlands in a precarious position. In 1639, the Dutch completely destroyed a second Spanish Armada of a size comparable to that of 1588. As an outcome of the war,

Spain ceased to be the dominating power in Europe, and the Netherlands, though small in population and resources, became a major power center because of its complete control over international trade and international finance. The Dutch were to seventeenth-century trade and finance as the British were to nineteenth-century trade and finance.

Of course, this period was not one of uninterrupted triumph. Notably, in the years 1634–1637, the Dutch suffered several setbacks. From 1635 to 1637, the bubonic plague ravaged the Netherlands. In July 1634, the Empire completely defeated Swedish forces in the Battle of Nordlingen, forcing a treaty on the German Protestant principalities in the May 1635 Peace of Prague and releasing Spanish resources for the war against the Dutch. Along with the growing war weariness in the Netherlands, these events forced France to enter the Thirty Years' War militarily with the Dutch alliance in 1635. Initially unprepared, the French suffered major setbacks, culminating in an Imperial invasion of northern France in August 1636. The war did not again turn in favor of the Dutch until the capture of the important Spanish fortress of Breda in October 1637.

The expansion of Dutch political power depended on the rapid development of the Dutch economy. The Netherlands was a largely urbanized society engaged in manufacture, trade, and finance; the rest of Europe consisted of peasant societies. The major Dutch industries were shipbuilding, fisheries, transport, textiles, and finance. During the seventeenth century, most ships in European merchant fleets were built by the Dutch; and the Dutch merchant fleet outnumbered the fleets of all the other maritime nations of Europe combined. The Dutch dominated transport in grains, precious and common metals, and salt and other bulk goods; as an entrepôt, the Netherlands provided a natural location for European markets in all major commodities.

Sophisticated finance mechanisms evolved with the establishment of the commodity markets. Amsterdam became the dominant market for short- and long-term credit; and markets in stocks, commodity futures, and options materialized early in the seventeenth century.[3] Trading of national loans of many countries centered in Amsterdam, as did a market in the shares of joint stock companies. The East India Company, founded in 1602, gradually gained control over East Asian trade and consistently paid out large dividends. The West India Company, founded in 1622, was given the right to undertake ventures in the Western Hemisphere, including the incipient takeover of the Atlantic slave trade.

At the time of the tulip speculation, the Netherlands was a highly commercialized country with well-developed and innovative financial markets and a large population of sophisticated traders. Its participation in innumerable risky ventures had proven so successful that the era is considered the golden age of the Netherlands.

The Traditional
Image of Tulipmania

Descriptions of the tulip speculation always are framed in a context of doubt about how the Dutch, usually so astute in their speculations, could have been caught in such an obvious blunder. Modern references to the episode depend on the brief description in Mackay ([1841] 1852). The tulip originated in Turkey but diffused into Western Europe only in the middle of the sixteenth century, carried first to Austria by a fancier of the flower. The tulip was immediately accepted by the wealthy as a beautiful and rare flower, appropriate for the most stylish gardens. The market was for durable bulbs, not flowers. As in so many other markets, the Dutch dominated that for tulips, initiating the development of methods to create new flower varieties. The bulbs that commanded high prices produced unique, beautifully patterned flowers; common tulips were sold at much lower prices.

Beginning in 1634, nonprofessionals entered the tulip trade in large numbers. According to Mackay, individual bulb prices reached enormous levels. For example, a single Semper Augustus bulb was sold at the height of the speculation for 5500 guilders, a weight of gold equal to $33,000 evaluated at $300/oz. Mackay provided neither the sources of these bulb prices nor the dates on which they were observed, however.

Mackay emphasized the lunacy of the event through a pair of anecdotes about a sailor who mistakenly ate valuable bulbs and an unsuspecting English traveler who experimented with them by peeling off their layers. The implausibility of a Dutch businessman leaving a highly valuable bulb lying about for a loutish sailor to eat for lunch or for a presumptuous English experimenter to dissect escaped him. He also described some barter transactions for acquiring rare bulbs so that the monetary expenditure could be translated into units of goods more meaningful to the modern (1841) reader.

Mackay then shifted to the final speculative frenzy, stating that large amounts of foreign funds entered the country to add to the speculation, and people from all classes hurriedly liquidated other assets to participate in the tulip market. However, he presented no evidence of the sources and quantity of these foreign funds.

Finally and inexplicably, the frenzy terminated; and, overnight, even rare bulbs could find no buyers at 10 percent of their previous prices, creating a long-term economic distress, according to Mackay. No evidence of immediate post-collapse transaction prices of the rare bulbs was produced by Mackay, however. Rather, Mackay cited prices from bulb sales from 60 years, 130 years, or 200 years later as indicators of the magnitude of the collapse and of the obvious misalignment of prices at the peak of the speculation. Moreover, Mackay provided no evidence of the general economic context from which the speculation emerged.

3

Where Does the Tulipmania Legend Come From?

Given its strategic position in current views of tulipmania, it is vital to investigate from which sources Mackay constructed his version of the speculation. While at one point Mackay includes a minor citation to Johann Beckmann, he plagiarized most of his description from Beckmann with a little literary embellishment.[4]

Beckmann, the original source of the sailor and dissector anecdotes referred to in the previous chapter, cites Blainville (1743) as his source for the story about the Englishman. A careful reading of Blainville, however, turns up only a one-sentence report that a tulip speculation occurred from 1634–1637 in what is otherwise a baroque travel log of Haarlem. Indeed, Blainville's description of his travels through Holland was a diary of a tour made in 1705, seventy years after the speculation. For the sailor story, Beckmann mentions that the incident occurred while John Balthasar Schuppe (1610–1661) was in Holland, without other reference. However, the context of the paragraph in which the story appears seems to indicate that it happened after the tulip speculation. Mackay, who greatly dramatizes both stories, cites Blainville as the source for both, obviously without having researched beyond Beckmann's accounts.

Beckmann carefully reported his sources of information about the functioning of the markets and bulb sales prices, using notably the dialogues between Gaergoedt and Waermondt ("Samenspraeck Tusschen Waermondt ende Gaergoedt: Flora," 1637), hereafter denoted G&W, and Munting's (1672, 1696) discussions of this episode. G&W is a series of three pamphlets in dialogue form that provides details about the markets and numerous prices of various bulbs, taken mostly from the final day of the speculation. These pamphlets were motivated by a moralistic attack against speculation by the authorities, as were all of the numerous pamphlets that appeared immediately after the end of the episode.[5]

Munting was a botanist who wrote a 1000-folio volume on numerous flowers. Though Mackay claims that the volume was devoted to the tulipmania, only the six pages allocated to tulips discuss the episode. Mackay must have recorded Beckmann's reference to Munting without examining the Munting text at all. All the price data described in Munting can be found in the G&W dialogues, so we must conclude that this is Munting's primary source.

The popular version of the tulipmania, to the extent that it is based on scholarly work, follows a lattice of hearsay fanning out from the G&W dialogues.

A more careful line of research has had little impact on our current interpretation of the tulip speculation. Solms-Laubach's (1899) history of tulips in Europe provides an extensive description of the available literature on tulips, including the G&W dialogues. Most of his price data originates in G&W, but he also explores records left by notaries of tulip contracts written during the mania.

Van Damme documented the tulipmania in a series of short articles written from 1899 to 1903.[6] This series consists of reprints of G&W, reproductions of some pre-collapse pricing contracts, and details of bulb auctions from just before the collapse and from six years after the end of the speculation. Since many of the prices in G&W are also on the earlier auction list, it provides a key confirmation of the validity of the prices in the G&W dialogues.

Posthumus (1927, 1929, 1934), the only economist in this literature, extended the available data by compiling and reproducing more of the notaries' contracts. Most of his discussion, however, again depends on price information in the G&W dialogues and on information compiled by Van Damme.

Finally, Krelage (1942, 1946) extensively describes the markets, though the prices that he reports for the speculation period also seem to come from G&W. Krelage (1946) does provide tulip price lists from sales in 1708 and 1709 and a 1739 bulb catalogue. In addition, he compiles a time series of prices for a large variety of hyacinth bulbs during the eighteenth and nineteenth centuries.

Even this line of research accomplishes little more than gathering additional price data, and those data that we have are not organized in a systematic time series. Posthumus attempts to analyze the functioning of the futures markets that materialized at the end of the speculation. But in spite of his efforts, we have inherited the concept of the tulipmania as the most famous of bubbles, accompanied by no serious effort to describe what might constitute the market fundamentals of the bulb market.

4   Establishment Attitudes toward Futures Markets and Short Selling: The Source of the Pamphlets

In his history of the Dutch Golden Age, Schama (1987) discusses the forces that led to the successful development of the Dutch economy in the seventeenth century.[7] He structures his description around a perceived tension in the ruling oligarchy between "speculation" and safe "investment." The oligarchy and its magistrates sought a balance between "safe" and "unsafe" areas of economic activity, knowing that sustained economic well-being depended on secure enterprises while growth depended on a willingness to undertake risky new ventures.

Safe areas of economic and financial activity were those regulated by public authorities such as the City Chamber of Marine Insurance, the Wisselbank, and the trade in commodities through the Baltic Sea, which the Dutch effectively monopolized. Riskier though still vital areas of economic activity were the more distant trades in the hands of the Dutch East India Company and the Dutch West India Company. The East India Company was enormously successful, earning large profits for its shareholders. The West India Company, more an instrument in the military contest with Spain and Portugal, performed poorly.

Trading activity in company shares on the bourse was yet a riskier financial activity. Such trades involved spot transactions, stock options, and futures trades. Soon after active trading in East India Company shares was initiated in 1606, organized bear raids were conducted on share prices under the direction of the noted speculator Isaac Le Maire. These involved short sales of stock and the spreading of negative rumors about the affairs of the company, a tactic employed to this day.

Reaction to these practices led to an edict in 1610 that prohibited such manipulative activities. Most notably for our purposes, the edict banned "windhandel" or "trading in the wind," trading in shares not currently possessed by the seller. Sales for future delivery were permitted to people who actually owned shares. Future sales that were not obviously for such hedging purposes were prohibited. The authorities continually regarded futures trading as immoral gambling, and the edict was reiterated and extended with the renewal of war with Spain in 1621, again in 1630, and most notably in the midst of the tulipmania in 1636.

The authorities did not prosecute people for participating in proscribed futures contracts. They simply refused legal enforcement of such contracts. In a process known as "an appeal to Frederick" (the Stadholder or

Prince), a buyer of a prohibited futures contract could repudiate it with the backing of the courts. Thus, the futures trades and short sales frowned upon by the authorities could continue as long as contracts could be privately enforced. A repudiation might lead to the exclusion of an established trader from the bourse and a consequent loss of trading profits in the future, so a buyer would not likely repudiate a moderate loss on a futures contract. If the loss were sufficient to bankrupt and impoverish a trader, he would be likely to repudiate however.

To the authorities, the tulip speculation represented an obviously unsafe financial speculation in which a legitimate business had suddenly degenerated into a bizarre form of gambling. The futures trading, which was the center of the activity, was clearly banned by the edicts; and in the end, the courts did not enforce deals made in the taverns where such trading occurred, all of which were repudiated. It is incomprehensible that anyone involved in the fluctuating associations of the taverns would have entered such unenforceable agreements in the first place unless they were merely part of a game.

According to Schama, the speculation frightened the Dutch elite with a demonstration of how quickly a seemingly safe activity could convert itself into undisciplined gambling. It was, in their view, money run amok—a kind of anarchy in which all the conventions and rules for virtuous and sober commercial conduct had been thrown to the wind (p. 359).

The ruling elite implemented a propaganda drive against such behavior, described by Shama as follows:

The magistrates of the Dutch towns saw niceties of equity as less pressing than the need to de-intoxicate the tulip craze. . . . But they still felt impelled to launch a didactic campaign in tracts, sermons, and prints against the folly, since its special wickedness had been leading the common people astray. To the humanist oligarchs, the tulip mania had violated all their most sacred tenets: moderation, prudence, discretion, right reason and reciprocity between effort and reward. (Pp. 361–362)

The objectives of this campaign were to channel speculative proclivities into the safe areas of economic activity. Not surprisingly, the safe areas coincided with those controlled by the ruling elite. Among the numerous anti-speculative pamphlets launched during this reaction were the G&W dialogues.

5   The Bubonic Plague

External to the bulb market, one extraordinary event in the period 1634–1637 may have driven the speculation. From 1635 to 1637, the bubonic plague ravaged the Netherlands, killing 17,193 people in Amsterdam alone in 1636 (one-seventh of the population). It also caused 14,502 deaths in Leiden in 1635 (33 percent of the 1622 population); and it killed 14 percent of the population of Haarlem, the center of the tulip speculation, from August to November 1636, the moment when the trading in common and cheap varieties took off.

The plague had marched westward with the dynamics of the armies in Germany starting in 1630.[8] Plague also broke out from 1623 to 1625, from 1654 to 1655, and from 1663 to 1664, killing in Amsterdam one-ninth, one-eighth, and one-sixth of the population, respectively.

Van Damme (1976) quotes C. de Koning, who states that the plague began in 1635 and forced the city authorities to take drastic health measures:

These and other precautions could not prevent the progress of the outbreak that caused 5723 to die during August, September, October and November, 1636, so many that the number of graveyards was too small. So great was the misery and sorrow of citizens and inhabitants that the best description would only be a weak image of the great misery of those unhappy days, which is why we will end the story by thanking the almighty God for saving us from this great terror from which our forefathers suffered so much. In the midst of all this misery that made our city suffer, people were caught by a special fever, by a particular anxiety to get rich in a very short period of time. The means to this were thought to be found in the tulip trade. This trade, so well known in the history of our country, and so well developed in our city should be taught to our fellow citizens as a proof of forefatherly folly. (Pp. 129–130)

Of the plague in Haarlem, Van Damme notes that "one can presume that the tulip futures speculation reached its peak when the plague was worst." De Vries (1976) claims that the plague outbreak of 1635–1636 "perhaps by spreading a certain fatalism among the population kicked off the most frenzied episode of the mania" (226).

The population of the Netherlands faced an increased probability of imminent death, either from plague or Spanish invasion, from 1635 to 1637, coincident with the tulip speculation, and a decline in the probability afterward. Although the plague outbreak may be a false clue, it is conceivable that a gambling binge tied, as we will see, to a drinking game emerged as a response to the death threat.

6   The Broken Tulip

An understanding of the tulip markets requires some information about the nature of the tulip. A bulb flower, the tulip can propagate either through seeds or through buds that form on the mother bulb. Properly cultivated, the buds can directly reproduce another bulb. Each bulb, after planting, eventually disappears during the growing season. By the end of the season, the original bulb is replaced by a clone, the primary bud, which is now a functioning bulb, and by a few secondary buds. Asexual reproduction through buds, the principal propagation method, produces an increase in bulbs at a maximum annual rate of from 100 to 150 percent in normal bulbs.[9]

A bulb produced directly from seed requires seven to twelve years before it flowers. The flowers appear in April or May and last for about a week. The amount of time required before the secondary buds flower depends on the size of the bulb produced from the bud. Hartman and Kester (1983) state that the time before flowering of a bulb less than 5 cm. in diameter is three years, of a bulb from 5 to 7 cm. is two years, and of a bulb greater than 8 cm. is one year.

In June, bulbs can be removed from their beds but must be replanted by September. To verify the delivery of a specific variety, spot trading in bulbs had to occur immediately after the flowering period, usually in June.

Tulips are subject to invasion by a mosaic virus whose important effect, called "breaking," is to produce remarkable patterns on the flower, some of which are considered beautiful. The pattern imposed on a particular flower cannot be reproduced through seed propagation; seeds will produce bulbs that yield a common flower, since they are unaffected by the virus. These bulbs may themselves eventually "break" at some unknown date but into a pattern that may not be remarkable. A specific pattern can be reproduced by cultivating the buds into new bulbs.

As another effect, the mosaic virus makes the bulb sickly and reduces its rate of reproduction. Although seventeenth-century florists thought that breaking was a normal stage in the maturing process of breeder bulbs (the stock of bulbs vulnerable to attack by the virus), theories arose that broken tulips were diseased. For example, La Chesnee Monstereul (1654), contrasting the theory of breaking as "self perfection" with a disease theory, noted that broken bulbs had smaller bulb and stem sizes and that they never produced more than three buds.

Smith (1937, 413) states that broken bulbs do not "proliferate as freely" as undiseased plants but that this weakening need not cause broken bulbs to succumb, giving as an example the broken Zomerschoon, which has been actively cultivated since 1620. Van Slogteren (1960) claims that the mosaic virus may cause total loss of a plant or a 10–20 percent reduction in propagation rates.

Almost all bulbs traded in the tulipmania have by now completely disappeared. For example, the Royal General Bulbgrowers Society's (1969) classification of thousands of actively grown tulips mentions such important bulbs of the tulip speculation as Admirael Liefkens, Admirael van der Eyck, Paragon Liefkens, Semper Augustus, and Viceroy only as historically important names. The only bulbs still grown were the Gheele Croonen and Lack van Rijn, despised in the 1630s as common flowers except at the height of the speculation. Currently, even these bulbs are grown only by collectors.

The high market prices for tulips, to which the current version of the tulipmania refers, were for particularly beautiful broken bulbs. Single-colored breeder bulbs, except to the extent that they could potentially break, were not valued; and all important tulip varieties in the first two centuries of European cultivation were diseased. Broken bulbs fell from fashion only in the nineteenth century.[10] Indeed, since breaking was unpredictable, some have characterized tulipmania among growers as a gamble, with growers "vying to produce better and more bizarre variegations and feathering."[11]

Though it is now known that the mosaic virus is spread by aphids, methods of encouraging breaking were not well understood in the seventeenth century. G&W

suggested grafting half a bulb of a broken tulip to half a bulb of an unbroken tulip to cause breaking (van Slogteren 1960, 27). La Chesnee Monstereul (1654, 163) states that the art of "speeding transformation" was controversial among florists. D'Ardene (1760, 198–217) devotes a chapter to breaking in tulips, shedding little light on methods to encourage breaking.

7   The Bulb Market, 1634–1637

The market for bulbs was limited to professional growers until 1634, but participation encompassed a more general class of speculators by the end of 1634. A rising demand for bulbs in France apparently drove the speculation.

In France, it became fashionable for women to array quantities of fresh tulips at the tops of their gowns. Wealthy men competed to present the most exotic flowers to eligible women, thereby driving up the demand for rare flowers. Munting (1696, 911) claims that at the time of the speculation, a single *flower* of a particular broken tulip was sold for 1000 guilders in Paris. This was a final demand price for a consumption good and not the asset price of the bulb.

Market participants could make many types of deals. The rare flowers were called "piece" goods, and particular bulbs were sold by their weight. The heavier bulbs had more outgrowths and therefore represented a collection of future bulbs. The weight standard was the "aas," about one-twentieth of a gram. For example, if a Gouda of 57 azen (plural of aas) were sold for a given price, the sale contract would refer to a particular bulb planted at a given location. Once markets developed in common bulbs, they were sold in standardized units of 1000 azen or 1 pound (9728 azen in Haarlem, 10,240 azen in Amsterdam). Purchase contracts for "pound" goods would not refer to particular bulbs.

A purchase between September and June was necessarily a contract for future delivery. Also, markets materialized for the outgrowths of the rarer bulbs. The outgrowths could not be delivered immediately, as they had to attain some minimum size before they could be separated from the parent bulb to assure the viability of the new bulb. Hence, the contracts for outgrowths were also for future delivery.

Formal futures markets developed in 1636 and were the primary focus of trading before the collapse in February 1637. Earlier deals had employed written contracts entered into before a notary. Trading became extensive enough in the summer of 1636—the peak of the plague— that traders began meeting in numerous taverns in groups called "colleges" where trades were regulated by a few rules governing the method of bidding and fees. Buyers were required to pay one-half stuiver (1 stuiver = 1/20 guilder) out of each contracted guilder to sellers up to a maximum of 3 guilders for each deal for "wine money." To the extent that a trader ran a balanced book over any length of time, these payments would cancel out. No margin was required from either party, so bankruptcy constraints did not restrict the magnitude of an individual's position.

Typically, the buyer did not currently possess the cash to be delivered on the settlement date, and the seller did not currently possess the bulb. Neither party intended a delivery on the settlement date; only a payment of the difference between the contract and settlement price was expected. So, as a bet on the price of the bulbs on the settlement date, this market was not different in function from currently operating futures markets. The operational differences were that the contracts were not continuously marked to market—that is, repriced according to daily price fluctuations, required no margin deposits to guarantee compliance, and consisted of commitments of individuals rather than of an exchange. A collapse would require the untangling of gross, rather than net, positions.

All discussions of the tulipmania openly criticize the activity of buying or selling for future delivery without current possession of the commodity sold or an intention to effect delivery. They attack futures markets as a means of creating artificial risk and do not consider their role in marketing existing risks.

It is unclear which date was designated as the settlement date in the "college" contracts. No bulbs were delivered under the deals struck in the new futures markets in 1636–1637 prior to the collapse because of the necessity of waiting until June to exhume the bulbs. It is also unclear how the settlement price was determined.

Beckmann (1846, 29) states that the settlement price was "determined by that at which most bargains were made," presumably at the time of expiration of a given contract. Again, this is the standard practice in current futures markets.

Serious and wealthy tulip fanciers who traded regularly in rare varieties did not participate in the new speculative markets. Even after the collapse of the speculation, they continued to trade rare bulbs for "large amounts."[12] To the extent that rare bulbs also traded on the futures markets, this implies that no one arbitraged the spot and futures markets. Taking a long position in spot bulbs required substantial capital resources or access to the financial credit markets. To hedge this position with a short sale in the futures market would have required the future purchaser to have substantial capital or access to sound credit; substantial risk of noncompliance with the deal in the futures market would have undermined the hedge. Since participants in the futures markets faced no capital requirements, there was no basis for an arbitrage.

During most of the period of the tulip speculation, high prices and recorded trading occurred only for the rare bulbs. Common bulbs did not figure in the speculation until November 1636.

Posthumus (1929, 444) hypothesizes the following timing of events:

I think the sequence of events may be seen as follows. At the end of 1634, the new nonprofessional buyers came into action.

Towards the middle of 1635 prices rose rapidly, while people could buy on credit, generally delivering at once some article of value; at the same time the sale per aas was introduced. About the middle of 1636 the colleges appeared; and soon thereafter the trade in non-available bulbs was started, while in November of the same year the trade was extended to the common varieties, and bulbs were sold by the thousand azen and per pound.

8   Some Characterization of the Data

To a great extent, the available price data are a blend of apples and oranges. I cannot separate the prices determined in the colleges, in which bankruptcy constraints seem not to have been imposed, from those that may have been more seriously binding on the transactors. Moreover, I cannot separate the spot from the futures deals, although all transactions after September 1636 must have been for future delivery. One natural way to separate these categories is to split the sample between "piece" goods and "pound" goods. Posthumus claims that there was a class difference between those trading in piece goods and those trading in pound goods, even in the colleges. Members of the middle classes and capitalized workers such as the weavers disdained the pound goods and traded only in the rarer bulbs.

In charts 1 through 16, I depict the "time series" in guilders/aas or guilders/bulb that I have been able to reconstruct for various bulbs. These charts consist of data gathered from auctions, contracts recorded with notaries,

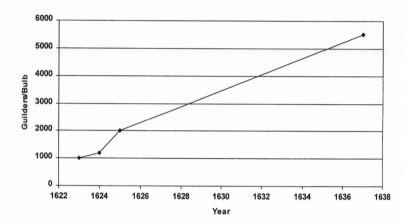

Chapter 8

Chart 1
Semper Augustus

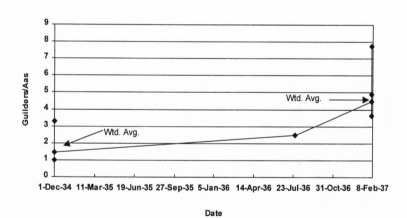

Chart 2
Admirael van der Eyck

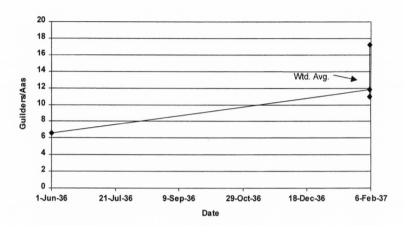

Chart 3
Admirael Liefkens

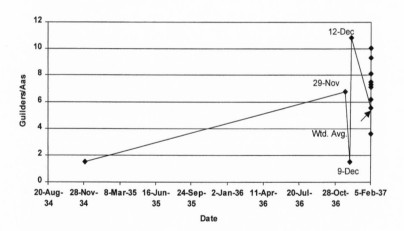

Chart 4
Gouda mature bulbs

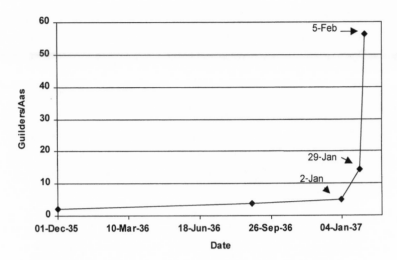

Chart 5
Gouda buds

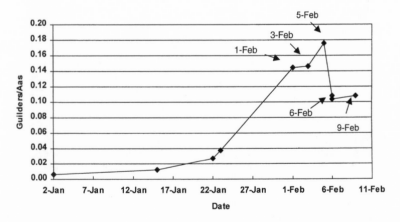

Chart 6
Switsers

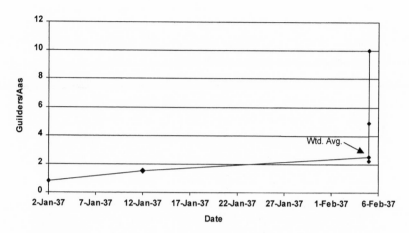

Chart 7
Scipio

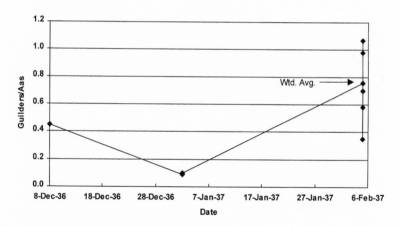

Chart 8
Gheele ende Roote van Leyden

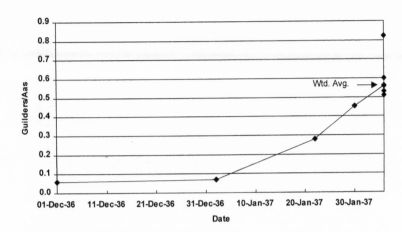

Chart 9
Oudenaerden

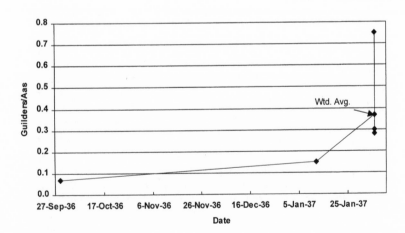

Chart 10
Groote Geplumiceerde

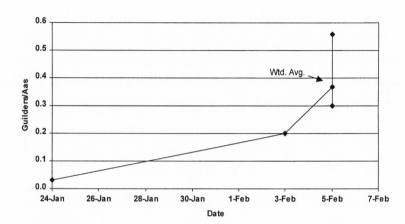

Chart 11
Macx

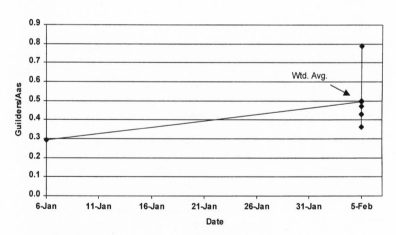

Chart 12
Nieuwberger

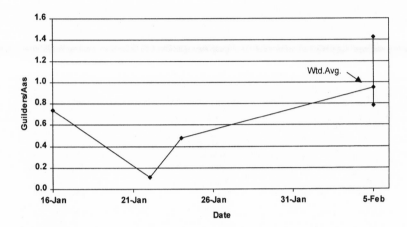

Chart 13
Le Grand

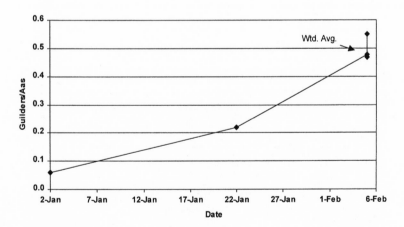

Chart 14
Coorenaerts

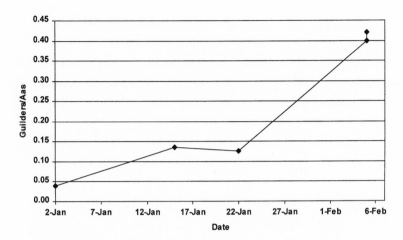

Chart 15
Centen

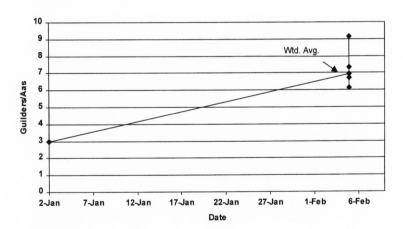

Chart 16
Viceroy

and the G&W dialogues. Data for Oudenaerden, Scipio, Nieuwberger, Macx, Groote Geplumiceerde, Coorenaerts, Centen, Witte Croonen, Gheele ende Roote van Leyden, and Switsers are in terms of guilders/aas for standardized weights of pound goods. Data for Semper Augustus, Admirael van der Eyck, Admirael Liefkens, Viceroy, and Gouda, are for individual bulbs that vary in weight from one to many hundred azen. Chart 4 indicates prices for mature Gouda bulbs; chart 5 is for Gouda of very low weights, ranging from 1 to 7 aas, which I have interpreted as bud prices.

The last observations for each series, except for the Switsers, were recorded on February 5, 1637, apparently the peak of the mania. For that date, there are usually several price observations for each flower, but their order of appearance in the charts has no meaning. Specifically, the charts do not indicate a price explosion at an infinite rate on February 5. I have connected the price lines to the weighted average of prices for February 5.

The bulbs that can be included among "piece" goods are Admirael Liefkens, Admirael van der Eyck, Gouda, Semper Augustus, and Viceroy. Among these, the Gouda can be considered a standard, since we have the longest price series for this bulb, starting at the beginning of the speculation. The bulbs that can be included among the "pound" goods, that is, bulbs trading in 1000 aasen or pound lots are Centen, Coorenaerts, Gheele ende Roote van Leyden, Groote Geplumiceerde, Le Grand, Macx, Nieuwburger, Oudenaerden, Switsers, and Witte

Croonen.[13] Other bulbs are more difficult to classify, encompassing different deals in which either odd weights or standard weights appear.

Generally, the pound goods sold at much lower prices per aas than the piece goods. However, in the last few months of the speculation—at the time of the outbreak of plague in Haarlem—their prices increased much more rapidly than did those of the piece goods. Prices of Coorenaerts, Gheele ende Roote van Leyden, Le Grand, Macx, Oudenaerden, Switsers, and Witte Croonen rose up to twentyfold within one month. Over a much longer period, the prices of the piece goods doubled or perhaps tripled.

The exception to the relatively slow price movement for rarer bulbs is for the prices of Gouda buds shown in chart 5. Apparently, buds attracted speculation of the same sort as the common varieties. However, the very sharp rise comes from a single observation of 56 guilders per aas for a 4 aas bulb on the last day of the speculation, February 5. Through January 29, the price data for Gouda buds were about the same as for mature bulbs—14 guilders per aas on January 29 and 5 guilders per aas on January 2 for buds compared to mature bulb prices of 10.8 guilders per aas on December 12 and a range between 3.6 and 10 guilders per aas on February 5. This fourfold increase in Gouda bud price is of the same order of magnitude as the price jumps for several of the common bulbs in the last week or two of the speculation—for example, Switser, Centen, and Macx.

9   Post-Collapse Tulip Prices

The tulip speculation collapsed after the first week of February 1637, but there is no explanation for this timing. A general suspension of settlement occurred on contracts coming due—that is, contracts were not rolled over.

On February 24, 1637, delegates of florists meeting in Amsterdam proposed that sales of tulips contracted on or before November 30, 1636 should be executed. For later contracts, the buyer would be given the right to reject the deal *on payment of 10 percent of the sale price* to the seller. This may be the source of the claims in Mackay that bulbs could not sell at 10 percent of their peak prices. The authorities did not adopt this suggestion.

On April 27, 1637, the States of Holland decided to suspend all contracts, giving the seller of existing bulbs the right to sell contracted bulbs at market prices during the suspension. The buyer in the contract would be responsible for the difference between this market price and whatever price the authorities eventually deter-mined for contract settlement. This decision released the growers to market the bulbs that would emerge in June.

The disposition of further settlement then becomes murky. Posthumus (1929, 446–447) states that many cities followed the example of Haarlem where in May 1638, the city council passed a regulation permitting buyers to terminate a contract on payment of 3.5 percent of the contract price.

Even the pre-collapse legal status of the futures contracts was unclear. Early price manipulation and bear raids in East India Company shares led to legal bans on short sales on the Amsterdam exchange in 1610. Whether the ban applied to traders on the new tulip futures market is unclear. Ultimately, the courts did not uphold any contracts for tulips, but local attempts at settlement were made.

With the end of large-scale bulb trading after February 1637, records of transaction prices virtually disappeared. Prices no longer were publicly recorded, and only an occasional estate auction of an important florist would reveal the magnitude of prices. Prior to 1634, only a handful of prices are available from recorded sales contracts: a pair of bulbs from 1612 reported by Posthumus (1929) in his contract numbers 3 and 4; a 1625 sale of three bulbs; and a 1633 sale of a pair of bulbs, both reported in Posthumus (1934). Even the series in chart 1 for the Semper Augustus is based on undocumented stories emanating from the historical authority Wassenaer in the 1620s, as reported by Solms-Laubach (1899, 77), among others.

Fortunately, van Damme (1976, 109–113) reports prices from a post-collapse estate auction in 1643. In the estate auction of the bulb dealer J. van Damme (no relation), fl. 42,013 were raised through the sale of bulbs. This amount reflects a bulb value comparable to the fl. 68,553 derived from the February 1637 estate auction from which we have received most of the tulipmania peak price data.

This total was not broken down into individual bulb prices. For those few bulbs sold in which the estate held a fractional interest, however, the sales prices were reported (van Damme 1976, 111). The prices were as follows:

1 Tulpa Meerman	fl. 430
1 Vrouge Brantson	fl. 25
1 General Rotgans	fl. 138
1 Verspreijt	fl. 582
1 Vroege Brantson	
$^1/_4$ of 1 English Admiral	

In addition, the records detailing the settling of the estate's accounts contains a list of 1643 cash expenditures for bulbs purchased in 1642. These prices were as follows:

$^1/_2$ pound Witte Croonen	fl. 37 st. 10
1 Admirael van der Eyck	fl. 225
1 English Admiral outgrowth	
1 English Admiral	fl. 210

Table 9.1
Post-Collapse Bulb Prices in Guilders

Bulb	Jan. 1637	Feb. 5, 1637	1642 or 1643	Annual % Depreciation[1]
1. Witte Croonen (one-half pound)	64.	1668. (avg.)	37.5	76
2. English Admiral (bulb)		700. (25 aas bulb)	210.	24
3. Admirael van der Eyck (bulb)		1345. (wtd. avg.)	220.*	36
4. General Rotgans (Rotgansen)		805. (1000 azen)	138.	35

*Adjusted downward fl. 5 to account for the English Admiral outgrowth.
[1] From February 1637 peak.

Individual bulbs then could still command high prices six years after the collapse. Four bulbs whose prices were listed individually also appear among the bulbs traded in 1636–1637: Witte Croonen, English Admiral, Admirael van der Eyck, and General Rotgans (Rotgansen). Witte Croonen were pound goods, and the others were piece goods. Table 9.1 presents a comparison of 1636, 1637, and 1642 or 1643 prices.

Even from the peaks of February 1637, the price declines of the rarer bulbs, English Admiral, Admiral van der Eyck, and General Rotgans, over the course of six years was not unusually rapid. We shall see below that they fit the pattern of decline typical of a prized variety.

10   Bulb Prices in
       Later Centuries

Eighteenth-Century Tulip Prices

Though a few prices are available from the years immediately after the collapse, a gap of about seventy years
arises in detailed tulip price data. While price data disappeared, at least the names of the important tulips
from the speculation remained current thirty-two years
after the collapse. Van der Groen (1669) mentions the
important tulips that a fashionable garden might hold.
Among them were Vroege Bleyenberger, Parragon
Grebber, Gheel and Roote van Leyden, Admirael van
Enchuysen, Brabanson, Senecours, Admirael de Man,
Coorenaerts, Jan Gerritz, Gouda, Saeyblom, Switsers,
Parragon Liefkens, and Semper Augustus.

High tulip prices are available only for much later
periods, and these are an order of magnitude lower
than those quoted during the speculation. Van Damme
(1976) reproduces numerous announcements of bulb
sales and auctions printed in such periodicals as the

Table 10.1

Guilder Prices of Tulip Bulbs Common to 1637, 1722, and 1739 Price Lists

Bulb	Jan. 2, 1637	Feb. 5, 1637	1722	1739
1. Admirael de Man	18.	209.		0.1
2. Gheele Croonen	0.41	20.5		0.025*
3. Witte Croonen	2.2	57.		0.02*
4. Gheele ende Roote van Leyden	17.5	136.5	0.1	0.2
5. Switsers	1.	30.	0.05	
6. Semper Augustus	2000. (7/1/25)	6290.		0.1
7. Zomerschoon		480.	0.15	0.15
8. Admirael van Enchuysen		4900.	0.2	
9. Fama		776.	0.03*	
10. Admirael van Hoorn		65.5	0.1	
11. Admirael Liefkens		2968.	0.2	

Note: To construct this table, I have assumed a standard bulb size of 175 azen. All sales by the bulb are assumed to be in the standard weight, and prices are adjusted proportionally from reported prices. When more than one bulb price is available on a given day, I report the average of adjusted prices.
*Sold in lots of 100 bulbs.

Haarlemscher Courant in the latter half of the seventeenth century, but there is no record of prices generated in the auctions.

Table 10.1 reports prices for bulbs from January 2, 1637; February 5, 1637; 1722; and 1739. These prices come from several sources. Krelage (1946) reproduces tulip lists from auctions on May 17, 1707, in the Hague (542) and on May 16, 1708, in Rotterdam (541), on which a participant fortuitously annotated the final sales prices. While the 1707 auction list contains eighty-four different bulb names and that of 1708 contains twelve, no bulb name of the hundreds commonly traded in 1637 appears in the lists. Krelage reproduces only the first page of the 1708 price list. The entire list was sold to British buyers with the breakup of Krelage's library, and I have been unable to examine it.

Bradley (1728) reproduces the 1722 bulb catalogue of a Haarlem florist. The majority of the hundreds of bulbs in this catalogue were offered at prices less than one guilder, and only one, Superintendent Roman, sold for 100 guilders. The list, however, does contain prices for twenty-five bulbs that appeared in the 1637 tulip speculation.

Krelage (1946) also reproduces a 1739 Haarlem price catalogue of hyacinth and tulip bulbs. Of its several hundred different bulbs, only six names match those of bulbs traded in 1637. Interestingly, it offers Semper Augustus bulbs for 0.1 guilders.

Even starting in January 1637, before the peak of the speculation, the price decline is remarkable. Prices fall to levels of 1 percent, 0.5 percent, 0.1 percent, or 0.005 percent of the January 1637 values over a century. Also noteworthy is the convergence of prices of all individually sold bulbs to a common value, regardless of the initial bulb values.

Table 10.2 contains prices of bulbs common to the 1707 auction and either the 1722 or the 1739 price lists. While this was not a period known for a tulip speculation or crash, prices display the same pattern of decline. Bulbs appearing on an auction list were for recently developed rare varieties that commanded relatively high prices. None of the bulbs on the 1739 list carried a price greater than eight guilders, while most prices were much lower. Rare and valuable bulbs would not have appeared on a standard dealer's list. Conversely, auctions would not have bothered with common, inexpensive bulbs. Because the 1637 rare bulbs had become common by 1707, it is not surprising that their names had disappeared from auction lists.

By the time they appeared in a general catalogue, they had diffused sufficiently to become relatively common. Again, in thirty-two years, prices declined to 3 percent, 0.25 percent, 0.35 percent, or 0.04 percent of their original values, repeating the pattern of decline of the bulbs from the tulipmania. Indeed, the valuable bulbs of 1707 even converged approximately to the same prices as the valuable bulbs of 1637.

We now have a pattern in the evolution of prices of newly developed, fashionable tulip bulbs. The first bulbs, unique or in small supply, carry high prices. With time, the price declines rapidly either because of rapid reproduction of the new variety or because of the increasing introduction of new varieties. Anyone

Table 10.2
Guilder Prices of Tulip Bulbs, 1707, 1722, and 1739

Bulb	1707	1722	1739	Annual % Depreciation 1707–22	1722–39
1. Triomphe d'Europe	6.75	0.3	0.2		
2. Premier Noble	409.		1.0	19*	
3. Aigle Noir	110.	0.75	0.3	33	
4. Roi de Fleurs	251.	10.0	0.1	22	27
5. Diamant	71.	2.5	2.0	22	
6. Superintendent		100.	0.12		40
7. Keyzer Kazel de VI		40.	0.5		26
8. Goude Zon, bontlof		15.	10.0		2
9. Roy de Mouritaine		15.	2.0		12
10. Triomphe Royal		10.	1.0		14

Sources: Krelage (1946) and Bradley (1728).
* 1707–1739.

who acquired a rare bulb would have understood this standard pattern of anticipated capital depreciation, at least by the eighteenth century.

To apply this pattern to the post-collapse period, I treat as rare all eighteenth-century bulbs selling for at least 100 guilders (Premier Noble, Aigle Noir, Roi de Fleurs, and Superintendent. For example, Roi de Fleurs would be counted as rare when its price was fl. 251 in 1707. By 1722, its price was fl. 10, so it would no longer be considered rare. The price declined between 1707 and 1722 by 96 percent, and the average annual decline was 21.5 percent. This 21.5 percent annual decline was averaged with similarly computed declines for other rare bulbs to produce an overall average.

Prices for these bulbs declined at an average annual percentage rate of 28.5 percent. From table 9.1, the three costly bulbs of February 1637 (English Admiral, Admirael van der Eyck, and General Rotgans) had an average annual price decline of 32 percent from the peak of the speculation through 1642. Using the eighteenth-century price depreciation rate as a benchmark also followed by expensive bulbs after the mania, we can infer that any price collapse for rare bulbs in February 1637 could not have exceeded 16 percent of peak prices. Thus, the crash of February 1637 for rare bulbs was not of extraordinary magnitude and did not greatly affect the normal time series pattern of rare bulb prices.

Eighteenth-Century Hyacinth Prices

As further evidence of this standard pattern in bulb prices, I now turn to the market for hyacinths. Krelage supplies prices of hyacinths during the eighteenth and nineteenth centuries. Hyacinths replaced tulips at the start of the eighteenth century as the fashionable flower, and once again a large effort arose to innovate beautiful varieties. A speculation similar to that for tulips occurred from 1734 to 1739, leading to the production of reprints of G&W as a warning against unconstrained financial contracting. Table 10.3 indicates the magnitude of the price declines for a few of the more expensive bulbs during the hyacinthmania. The price decline to as low as 10 percent of 1735 prices in some cases was of similar magnitude to the 1637 crash for common tulip bulbs.

Krelage provides long price series for many hyacinths after their introduction. In table 10.3, I have mainly selected the price patterns for bulbs carrying particularly high prices at the time of introduction. Note that the pattern is similar to that for prized tulips in the seventeenth and eighteenth century. Within three decades, prices of even the highest priced bulbs usually fell to 1–2 percent of the original price. Both originally highly priced and inexpensive bulbs converged to a price of from 0.5 to 1 guilder. The average annual rate of price depreciation for bulbs valued at more than 100 guilders (8 observations) was 38 percent, somewhat faster than the depreciation rate for tulip bulbs. For bulbs valued at

Table 10.3
Hyacinth Price Patterns (Guilders)

Bulb	1716	1735	1739	1788	1802	1808
1. Coralijn*	100	12.75	2	0.6	—	—
2. L'Admirable	100	—	1	1.	—	—
3. Starrekroon	200	—	1	0.3	—	0.3
4. Vredenrijck	—	80	16	1.5	—	—
5. Koning Sesostris	—	100	8	1.	1	—
6. Staaten Generaal	—	210	20	1.5	2	—
7. Robijn	—	12	4	1	1	0.5
8. Struijsvogel	—	161	20	—	—	—
9. Miroir	—	141	10	—	—	—

Bulb	1788	1802	1815	1830	1845	1875
10. Comte de la Coste	200	50	1	0.75	0.5	0.15
11. Henri Quatre	50	30	1	3	5	1
12. Van Doeveren	50	—	1	2	1.2	0.75
13. Flos Niger	60	20	10	—	0.25 (1860)	
14. Rex rubrorum	3	1.5	0.3	1	0.35	0.24

Source: Krelage, 645–655.
*Krelage (645) notes that the Coralijn bulb originally sold for 1000 guilders, though he does not include a year.

between 10 and 80 guilders, the annual price depreciation averaged 20 percent.

Modern Bulb Prices

In modern times, new flower bulb varieties can also be highly valuable. Typically, however, new varieties are reproduced in mass by the bulb's developer and marketed at relatively low prices only when a large quantity of bulbs has been produced. Hence, prices for prototype bulbs are usually unavailable. In the few cases where a prototype bulb does change hands, transaction prices are not announced. Information provided in 1987 by officials at the Bloembollencentrum in Haarlem indicates, however, that new varieties of "very special" tulip bulbs sold for about 5000 guilders ($2400 at 1987 exchange rates) per kilo. A small quantity of prototype lily bulbs was sold for 1 million guilders ($480,000 at 1987 exchange rates, $693,000 at 1999 consumer prices), namely, the price of a fine house, a car, a suit of clothes, several tons of wheat, rye, butter, and so forth. Such bulbs can now be reproduced rapidly with tissue growth techniques, so they also would be marketed at relatively low prices.

11   Was This Episode a "Tulipmania"?

I now examine whether the evidence demands a mania interpretation for the tulip price movements. First, I will dispose of two nagging issues: (1) the absence of descriptions of economic distress in accounts of the period not engaged in antispeculative moralizing, and (2) the claims that the disappearance of renowned bulbs or their extreme price declines over long time periods signal the lunacy of the event. Next, I will isolate the aspect of the speculation for which the evidence provides no compelling explanation, the trading in common bulbs in the period from January 2, 1637, to February 5, 1637.

Where Was the Purported Economic Distress?

Economic histories of the important events and institutions in the Netherlands during this period are detailed, but they hardly mention the tulip speculation. For example, volumes IV and V of *The Cambridge Economic History of Europe* (Rich and Wilson 1975, 1977) do not

mention tulips, though the seventeenth-century Dutch
are the leading players in these narratives. The period is
characterized as a sequence of Dutch commercial and
financial triumphs, and economic distress seems not to
have materialized in the Netherlands until after the
Thirty Years' War ended in 1648. Cooper (1970, 100) does
mention the tulip speculation, in one sentence, as an
example of the speculative proclivity of the Dutch during
this period. Schama (1987) provides a detailed discussion
of the events based primarily on Posthumus and Krelage,
but he does not depart from the standard interpretation
of the mania.

It is not difficult to understand why general economic
studies of this period take little notice of "economic distress" arising from the speculation. Because the longer-
term price rise occurred only in the rare bulbs, no
significant agricultural resources were devoted to expand
their cultivation. Krelage (1946, 498) states that all florists
in Haarlem maintained their gardens within the city
walls until the second half of the eighteenth century.
Gardens could be small, since concentrations of large
numbers of identical flowers were not valued highly,
unlike current fashion.

Because the spectacular price rise in the common
bulbs occurred only after the bulbs were in the ground in
September 1636, rises in these prices could also have
had little effect on the allocation of resources during
1636–1637. To the extent that the speculation had
any impact, it would have had an effect only through the

distribution of wealth. Little wealth was actually transferred, however; the fees paid out by buyers in the colleges must have evened out over the course of many transactions, though the "wine money" may have indicated a transfer to tavern owners. In addition, after the collapse, only small settlements were required; and of these, few were made. Even the period of uncertainty about the percentage of settlement required could have had little impact; people with little credit to begin with would not have been affected by a cut off of credit until the contracts were straightened out.

Kindleberger, in his new edition of *Manias, Panics, and Crashes* (1996), which dominates the popular mind on the history of bubbles, added a chapter on tulipmania, which had not been in previous editions, to critique my view that the tulipmania was based on fundamentals. He argued that in fact there were signs of continuation of the tulip exuberance because the share prices of the Dutch East India Company doubled between 1630 and 1639, which is three years after the end of the mania. (In nine years, the Dow has quadrupled; but this is not necessarily the sign of irrationality.) But most of this occurred after 1636, rising from 229 in March 1636 to 412 in 1639, nearly a doubling in three years. Of course, the Spanish armies were on the march in 1636, which would have had some effect on East India shares, and by 1639 had been pushed away. When a second Armada that threatened East India trade was destroyed in 1639, things looked

rather good again. Trolling for an impact on the real
economy from the tulipmania, Kindleberger (1996) then
stretches the timing for possible distress from tulipmania
into the 1640s: "This perspective undermines one of
Garber's points that there could have been no tulipmania because there was no depressed aftermath. In fact the
Dutch economy slowed down to a degree in the 1640s
before putting on a tremendous spurt from 1650 to 1672"
(101).[14]

Bulb Prices Decline Fast: It Is in Their Nature

That the valuable tulips of 1634–1637 later either disappeared or became common is typical of the market
dynamics for newly developed bulb varieties, as indicated by price patterns for eighteenth-century tulip and
hyacinth bulbs and for modern bulbs. As the bulbs propagate, their prices naturally fall with expanding supply;
however, the original bulb owner's bulb stock increases.
The discounted value of bulb sales can easily justify
extremely high prices for the unique bulb of a new
variety. Even the magnitudes of prices for valuable bulbs
and their patterns of decline are not out of line with later
prices for new varieties of rare bulbs. Single bulbs in
the eighteenth century commanded prices as high as
1000 guilders. In this context, the 1000–2000 guilder
price of Semper Augustus from 1623 to 1625 or even its
5500 guilder price in 1637 do not appear obviously
overvalued.

The Common Bulbs

The only facet of the speculation for which an explanation does not emerge from the evidence is the one-month price surge for *common* bulbs in January 1637, when prices rose up to twentyfold. After February 9, 1637, the first price observation for a common bulb, the Witte Croonen, is available only in 1642.

Claims that prices dropped to less than 10 percent of peak values after the crash must have originated in the officially proposed 3.5 percent contract settlement fee. This did not necessarily reflect the true price decline but simply provided a means of relieving buyers of most of their losses. For example, suppose that a futures contract had established a price of fl. 500 for a bulb but that its settlement price had been fl. 350 after the collapse. This is a substantial loss of fl. 150 that may even have wiped out the buyer if the contract had been taken seriously. Instead, the official proposal would have required a payment on the lost bet of fl. 17.5, but we learn nothing of the post-collapse price of the underlying bulb from the proposed settlement percentage. Because they never cite a specific transaction price (none exist from trades immediately after the crash), authors citing massive price falls must have inferred them from the percentages proposed for contract buyouts, to the extent that they researched the issue at all.

Table 9.1 contains the price data for one-half pound of Witte Croonen bulbs. From February 1637 to 1642, the price depreciated at an annual rate of 76 percent. As an eighteenth-century benchmark rate, I have used 17 percent per year, the average rate of depreciation of all bulbs priced between fl. 10 and fl. 71 in table 10.2. Assuming that after February 1637 Witte Croonen depreciated at this benchmark rate, the price must have collapsed in the crash to 5 percent of its peak price to have attained a 1642 price of fl. 37.5. Thus, Witte Croonen prices rose by about twenty-six times in January 1637 and fell to one-twentieth of their peak value in the first week of February. The eighteenth-century benchmark pattern of price depreciation, however, would have justified a peak price of fl. 84; so the January price is not out of line.

That a precipitous price decline for common bulbs occurred is confirmed by observations on Switsers in chart 5. The peak price for this bulb of 0.17 guilders/aas was attained on February 5, the apparent peak of the market. Data from notarized contracts on February 6 and 9 indicate a sudden decline to 0.11 guilders/aas. This represents a substantial decline from the prices of the first five days of February, but it still substantially exceeds the prices attained on January 23 and is not of the same order of magnitude as the collapse indicated above for Witte Croonen.

Since already valuable bulbs rose by no more than 200–300 percent over a longer duration, the increase and collapse of the relative price of common bulbs is the remarkable feature of this phase of the speculation. Even if detailed, day-to-day information about market events for this period were available, we would be hard pressed to find a market fundamental explanation for these relative price movements. It is clear that the "colleges" generated these prices, although they are echoed in some written contracts. As noted earlier, the college futures markets suffered from a lack of internal control over the nature of contracts, which might have encouraged a speculation of this sort. These markets consisted of a collection of people without equity making ever-increasing numbers of "million dollar bets" with one another with some knowledge that the state would not enforce the contracts. This was no more than a meaningless winter drinking game, played by a plague-ridden population that made use of the vibrant tulip market.

In any case, the price movements of the common bulbs have little to do with the image of the tulipmania that we have inherited from Mackay and his myriad followers, which was all about the astoundingly high prices and bizarre deals for single rare bulbs.

Indeed, discussions on how strange the tulipmania was have until recently centered on the rare bulbs, especially on one often cited, particularly bizarre trade mentioned in Mackay. On this trade, Krelage (1942, 67) states:[15]

In popular articles about the tulipmania the story of a transaction where a whole list of different goods up to a total value of fl 2500 or fl 3000 was paid for a single Viceroy bulb lives on. Even in a foreign book of academic quality it is assumed without further research that this transaction was indeed carried out.

The story however relates to a non-existent transaction. The key can be found in a pamphlet[16] discussing the "wind trade" [i.e., futures speculation] which states "as a wonder for reference of future generations" that in 1636 one could buy "all the following goods for the value of one flower [bulb]

2 lasts of wheat	448 guilders
4 lasts of rye	558
4 well-fed oxen	480
8 well-fed pigs	240
12 well-fed sheep	120
2 oxheads of wine	70
4 tons of 8 guilder beer	32
2 tons butter	192
1000 pounds cheese	120
1 bed with accessories	100
1 stack of clothes	80
1 silver chalice	60
Total	2500 guilders

Add to this a ship to carry all these goods worth fl 500. And one has got fl 3000 for which one cannot buy the best tulip bulb (so the florists say)."

The intent of this statement is to give the reader an idea of the real value of the money spent on a single bulb. Someone, retelling the story, added that this transaction, which he must have considered as actually having taken place, must have involved a Viceroy because one of those bulbs sold, according to other records, for fl 3000. Since that day the story goes around.

Krelage adds that no other records are available of transactions with such different goods and questions whether any seller would want this kind of transaction in a time when food was not scarce.

As an example of yet another author of a "foreign book of academic quality," Kindleberger cannot resist passing on the myth: "Other down-payments consisted of tracts of land, houses, furniture, silver and gold vessels, paintings, a suit and a coat, a coach and dapple gray pair; and for a single Viceroy (rare), valued at Fl. 2500, two lasts (a measure which varies by commodity and locality) of wheat and four of rye, eight pigs, a dozen sheep, two oxheads of wine, four tons of butter, a thousand pounds of cheese, a bed, some clothing, and a silver beaker" Kindleberger (1996, 100–101, crediting Schama and Krelage, 67).

Even a serious historian, Schama (1987, 358), citing the very page from Krelage quoted above, completely ignores the context to emphasize only a bizarre transaction that, according to Krelage, never happened. He even feels free to weave his own fiction around the story: "In all liklihood it was a farmer who paid fl. 2500 for a single Viceroy in the form of two last of wheat and four of rye, four fat oxen, eight pigs, a dozen sheep, two oxheads of wine, four tons of butter, a thousand pounds of cheese, a bed, some clothing, and a silver beaker."

The wonderful tales from the tulipmania are catnip irresistible to those with a taste for crying bubble, even when the stories are so obviously untrue. So perfect are they for didactic use that financial moralizers will always find a ready market for them in a world filled with investors ever fearful of financial Armageddon.

III

The Macro Bubbles

A Preliminary View: The Mississippi and South Sea Bubbles

The financial dynamics of these speculations assumed remarkably similar forms. Government connivance was at the heart of these schemes. Each involved a company that sought a rapid expansion of its balance sheet through corporate takeovers or acquisition of government debt, financed by successive issues of shares, and with spectacular payoffs to governments. The new waves of shares marketed were offered at successively higher prices. The purchasers of the last wave of shares took the greatest losses when stock prices fell, while the initial buyers generally gained.

Adam Anderson (1787, 123–124) presents a remarkably lucid description of such speculative dynamics in which a sequence of investors buy equal shares in a venture:

A, having one hundred pounds stock in trade, though pretty much in debt, gives it out to be worth three hundred pounds, on account of many privileges and advantages to which he is entitled. B, relying on A's great wisdom and integrity, sues to be admitted partner on those terms, and accordingly buys three

hundred pounds into the partnership. The trade being afterwards given out or discovered to be very improving, C comes
in at five hundred pounds; and afterwards D, at one thousand
one hundred pounds. And the capital is then completed to two
thousand pounds. If the partnership had gone no further than
A and B, then A had got and B had lost one hundred pounds.
If it had stopped at C, then A had got and C had lost two
hundred pounds; and B had been where he was before: but D
also coming in, A gains four hundred pounds, and B two
hundred pounds; and C neither gains nor loses: but D loses six
hundred pounds. Indeed, if A could shew that the said capital
was intrinsically worth four thousand and four hundred
pounds, there would be no harm done to D; and B and C would
have been obliged to him. But if the capital at first was worth
but one hundred pounds, and increased only by subsequent
partnership, it must then be acknowledged that B and C have
been imposed on in their turns, and that unfortunate thought-
less D paid the piper.

Should we, as outside observers, interpret such a sequence of transactions and prices as a bubble? The in-
trinsic value of the venture from the point of view of the
new investors is the crux of the matter.

First, if the original investor falsely claimed that the
venture promised great dividends, though as yet unreal-
ized, he would be committing fraud. The new investors,
however, would be basing their decisions on their perception of market fundamentals. This is a situation of
asymmetric information in which one player has an
incentive to dissemble.

Second, the original investor might use some of
the proceeds from the stock sales to pay high dividends
to the early investors. This would provide concrete

evidence of the great prospects of the venture to new investors. Of course, this twist on the original fraud is known as a Ponzi scheme; but since the "pigeons" are acting on their view of market fundamentals, there is still no bubble.

Third, the great future earnings may actually material-ize, thereby satisfying all investors. This result is typical of the early stages of successful companies; and the sequence of stock issues at increasing prices would neither surprise a modern investment banker nor raise the eyebrows of the SEC. In this case, the promised market fundamentals would actually materialize.

Fourth, the projected future earnings, though based on the best available evidence, may fail to materialize. If the evidence of failure appears suddenly, the share price will suffer a precipitous decline, causing late buyers vocifer-ously to regret their purchases. Hindsight will readily identify the blind folly of the investors and, if it is extreme enough, perhaps categorize the event as a bubble. In fact, the traditional definition of a bubble, as in Palgrave (1926, 181), is "any unsound commercial undertaking accom-panied by a high degree of speculation." If the under-taking appeared sound at the start, however, and only looks foolish in hindsight, economists should classify this event as being driven by market fundamentals.

Finally, all investors may understand perfectly well that the venture has no chance of paying large dividends but that a sequence of share buyers at ever increasing prices is available. Investors buy in on a gamble that they will not be in the last wave of buyers. The modern economics literature refers to this scenario as a bubble or chain letter. We now consider whether the Mississippi and South Sea episodes can fit only in the last category.

13

John Law and the
Fundamentals of the
Mississippi and
South Sea Bubbles

John Law's Financial System

Both the Mississippi and South Sea Bubbles can best be understood in the context of the monetary theory and system created by John Law.[17] Law is not well known today, but Schumpeter (1954, 295), for example, is unreserved in praising him: "He worked out the economics of his projects with a brilliance and, yes, profundity which places him in the front ranks of monetary theorists of all times."

Law sketched a monetary theory in an environment of unemployed resources. In such an environment, he argued ([1705] 1760, 190–191), an emission of paper currency would expand real commerce permanently, thereby increasing the demand for the new currency sufficiently to preclude pressure on prices. To finance a great economic project, an entrepreneur needed only the power to create claims that served as a means of payment. Once financed, the project would profit sufficiently from the employment of previously wasted resources to justify the public's faith in its liabilities.

Economic policy advocates and their ideas, good or bad, float to the surface only when they provide a convenient pretext for politicians to impose their preferred schemes. Law's idea got its chance in France in 1715. France had been bankrupted by the wars of Louis XIV. In a situation recently repeated by Russia in 1998, France had repudiated part of its internal debt, forced a reduction in interest due on the remainder, and was still in arrears on its debt servicing. High taxes, combined with a tax system full of privileges and exemptions, had seriously depressed economic activity.

The French economic environment was well suited for Law's scheme, and he quickly convinced the Regent to permit him to open a conventional, note-issuing bank in June 1716, the Banque Generale. In August 1717, Law organized the Compagnie d'Occident to take over the monopoly on trade with Louisiana and on trade in Canadian beaver skins. This line of business is the source of the word "Mississippi" in characterizing Law's system.

To finance the company, Law took subscriptions on shares to be paid partly in cash but mostly in government debt. He then converted the government's debt into long-term *rentes*, offering the government an interest-rate reduction.

The idea was to establish a solid "fund of credit," a certain cash inflow that, when capitalized, could be leveraged to undertake the grand commercial schemes that lay at the heart of Law's economic theory. The nature of Law's scheme was that finance of the operation came first; expanded commercial activity would result naturally once the financial structure was in place.

In effect, the French privatized the treasury under Law's plan and had only to wait for the general commercial expansion promised by Law's theory to materialize and to support the market prices of the company's shares.

14 John Law's Finance Operations

The Compagnie d'Occident did increase its commercial activity, obtaining the tobacco monopoly in September 1718 and the Senegalese Company for trade with Africa, that is, the slave trade, in November 1718.[18] In January 1719, the Banque General was taken over by the regent and renamed the Banque Royale, with a note issue guaranteed by the crown. Law remained in control of the new bank. In May 1719, he acquired the East India Company and the China Company; and he reorganized the entire conglomerate as the Compagnie des Indes, an organization that monopolized all French trade outside Europe.

On July 25, 1719, the Compagnie purchased the right to mint new coinage for fifty million livres tournois to be delivered in fifteen monthly payments. The *livre tournois* was the unit of account and was officially valued at weights of gold or silver that varied during Law's regime. To finance this expenditure, Law issued 50,000 shares at 1000 livres per share to cover this acquisition, requiring share buyers to hold five previously issued shares. Share prices rose to 1800 livres.

In August 1719, the Compagnie bought the right to collect all French indirect taxes for a payment to the government of 52 million livres per year. The takeover of the administration of the tax system was in line with Law's views that a simplified fiscal regime would benefit commerce and reduce the costs of collection. Law thought that taxes should be broad-based and few, with no exemptions or privileges. He set about reorganizing the personnel of the tax system, because a reduced collection cost would be a source of company profit. In October 1719, he took over the collection of direct taxes. Share prices rose to 3000 livres.

Finally, Law determined to refund most of the national debt through the Compagnie des Indes, an amount with a face value of 1.5 billion livres. The face value of the entire debt was estimated by Harsin (1928) at about two billion livres; the market value of the debt was well below the par value because of previous defaults and arrearages.

To finance the debt acquisition, Law undertook a sequence of three stock sales on September 12, September 28, and October 2, 1719. In each offering, the Compagnie sold 100,000 shares at 5000 livres per share payable in ten equal monthly payments. Payment could be made either at par in *rentes* or in the notes of the Banque Royale. Thus, by August 1720, enough would have been raised to acquire the face value of the debt.

Of the 540,000 shares then outstanding of the Compagnie des Indes, the King held 100,000 shares and therefore was counted a powerful backer of the scheme. In addition, the Compagnie itself held 100,000 shares that it could sell. Researchers of the Mississippi and South Sea episodes treat the quantity of own shares held by the companies as significant. There was a limitation on authorized share issues, so shares held by the company provided a source of cash to fuel company finance activities as prices rose.

Acquiring the debt would create a huge "fund of credit," a steady income flow from the government, which could be used as equity against any potential commercial venture of the Compagnie. Simultaneously, the Compagnie would reduce the interest paid by the state to 3 percent per year. After these operations, share prices rose to 10,000 livres in October 1719.

The shares outstanding would then have had a market value of 5.4 billion livres, somewhat less than four times the face value of the rentes that were the most tangible assets of the Compagnie. For perspective, Law estimated the national wealth of France at 30 billion livres.

Law attained maximum power in January 1720 when he was made France's Controller General and Superintendent General of Finance. As an official, he now controlled all government finance and expenditure and the money creation of the Banque Royale. Simultaneously, he was the chief executive officer of a private firm that controlled France's overseas trade and the development of its colonies, collected France's taxes, minted its coins, and held the bulk of France's national debt. The king was a principal shareholder of the firm. It must have been obvious to all that the Compagnie would find few government or financial obstacles to its undertaking any commercial scheme that it chose. Surely no economist has since had a better set of conditions for testing a major economic theory than that possessed by Law.

Figure 14.1 illustrates the Mississippi bubble. The phase of price increase is associated with the expanding activity of the Compagnie at this time.

In the end, however, the commercial scheme chosen was to print money. Starting with the July 1719 stock issue, the Banque Royale had increased its note issue to facilitate the stock sales. Each government authorization of a share expansion simultaneously authorized a note emission.

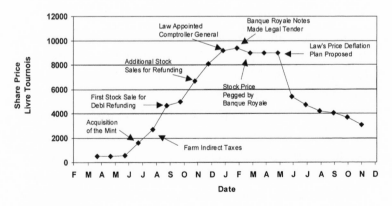

Figure 14.1
Daily South Sea Share Prices, 1720

For example, with only 159 million livres in notes previously authorized, the Banque received authorization to emit 240 million livres on July 25, 1719. A further 240 million livre expansion was associated with the September and October share sales. Additional note issues of 360 million and 200 million livres occurred on December 29, 1719, and February 6, 1720, respectively, without new share issues. For comparison, Harsin (1928) estimates the total specie stock of France at about 1.2 billion livres. The money creation was used to provide loans to buyers of the shares. This reduced the number of floating shares, replacing them with bank notes. Because Law regarded shares as a superior form of currency, this did not increase the "money supply" in his view.

The ultimate control on such wealth surges through rising valuation is the attempt by shareholders to convert their capital gains into current goods or gold. The surge of goods supply needed to meet this demand did not currently exist and in Law's theory would be realized in amounts adequate to match demand stemming from high share values only after the fruition of the projects. Even if there was a chance for his operations to pay off, the short-term finance of his operations through the monetization of the shares was to be the fatal financial flaw of the scheme.

By the end of January 1720, share prices had begun to fall below 10,000 livres because of increasing attempts to convert capital gains into a gold form. The falling price of shares threatened Law's ability to use his "fund of credit" to begin a commercial expansion.

In January 1720, Law began to act against the use of specie in payments by prohibiting payments above 100 livres in metallic money. On February 22, 1720, the Compagnie took over direct control of the management of the Banque Royale; and the Banque Royale's notes were made legal tender for payments above 100 livres. Simultaneously, the King sold his 100,000 shares back to the Compagnie at 9000 livres per share. Of this amount, three hundred million livres would be deposited in the King's accounts in the Banque immediately with the rest to be paid over ten years. The Compagnie then ceased supporting the price of its shares with banknotes, precipitating a sharp price decline. Thus, the most powerful insider bailed out near the peak of the speculation.

Law criticized unsophisticated shareholders trying to convert shares to the concrete form of gold because there was not enough gold in the kingdom to satisfy such an attempt. Law stated that the shares had high value only if they were regarded as a capital investment, to be bought and sold infrequently, held by people content to receive their yields as a flow of dividends that he claimed was somewhat higher than the prevailing interest rate.[19]

On March 5, 1720, share prices were pegged at 9000 livres: the Banque Royale now intervened directly to exchange its notes for Compagnie stock. Effectively converting shares into banknotes with a denomination of 9000 livres, this policy was a realization of Law's theory that a commercial enterprise could finance itself with emissions of circulating debt. Until its termination on May 21, 1720, the pegging scheme generated legal tender note expansions of 300 million, 390 million, 438 million, and 362 million livres on March 25, April 5, April 19, and May 1, respectively, to absorb sales by shareholders. The Banque's legal tender note circulation doubled in about one month.

This also was a doubling in the money stock, because the circulating metallic stock of money had by then disappeared. In an effort to drive out metallic currency and to maintain the facade of note convertibility, Law had simultaneously imposed a series of drastic devaluations of specie in terms of livre tournois. As a result of this dramatic monetary expansion, the average monthly inflation rate from August 1719 through September 1720 was 4 percent, with a peak of 23 percent in January 1720. The index of commodity prices increased from 116.1 in July 1719 to 203.7 in September 1720 (Hamilton 1936–37). Figure 14.2 depicts how the sequence of bank note issues drove the currency supply and the price level.

Deciding that the price of shares had been fixed at too high a level, Law proposed a drastic deflation on May 21, 1720.[20] Share prices would be reduced from 9000 to 5000 livres in seven stages, ending on December 1. Banque notes would be reduced in value to 50 percent of their face value—that is, he would force a restructuring on

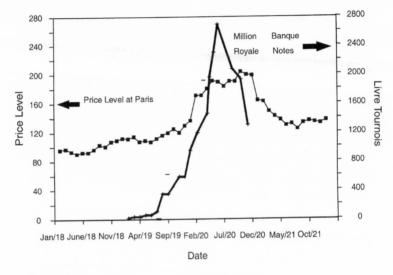

Figure 14.2
Mississippi Bubble Money and Price Data

holders of the Banque Royale's liabilities. Under this plan
by December, only 2.3 billion livres in paper asset values
(1.3 billion in Banque notes and 1 billion in stock) would
remain. This reduction was actually accomplished by
various other means. Law's plan simply to write down
the value of the Banque notes in terms of livre tournois
was abandoned when he was thrown from office at the
end of May 1720. He was, however, quickly reappointed
and presided over the deflation.

By October 1720, only 1.2 billion livres of notes
remained in circulation (of a peak of 2.7 billion) and 1.2
billion livres of specie reappeared. Specie was rapidly
revalued to the definition that it had at the start of 1720.

By December 1720, the price level had fallen to 164.2. Thus, the period starting in February 1720 represents an initial period of share price pegging by the Banque—that is, the monetization of shares—followed by the purposeful monetary and share price deflation undertaken by Law.

The price of the Compagnie's shares fell to 2000 livres in September 1720 and to 1000 livres by December. Law's enemies were now in a position to impose policies hostile to the Compagnie, notably a confiscation of two-thirds of the shares outstanding. The share price fell to 500 livres by September 1721, approximately its value in May 1719.

15   A Rehash of Mississippi Market Fundamentals

Should economists sum up the increasing stock prices of the Compagnie des Indes only as the "Mississippi bubble"? After all, behind the price rise lies Law's program to revitalize the French economy through financial innovation and fiscal reform. Law's theory was plausible and even has many modern manifestations, and he was an effective propagandist. Investors also could readily observe Law's astounding rise to power. At each stage, as the implementation of the economic experiment became ever more likely, they had to factor the possibility of success into the share prices of the Compagnie des Indes.

The downward slide of share prices is even easier to understand, given the radical shifts in monetary policy and the intimate connection of Compagnie shares to Banque Royale note emissions. The final fall to original share values was driven by Law's fall from power and the accession of his enemies, who aimed to dismantle the Compagnie.

That Law's promised expansion never materialized does not imply that a bubble occurred in the modern sense of the word. After all, this was not the last time that a convincing economic idea would fracture in practice. One respectable group of modern economists or another have described Keynesian economics, supply side economics, monetarism, fixed exchange-rate regimes, floating exchange-rate regimes, and the belief in rational expectations in asset markets as disastrously flawed schemes. Indeed, elements of the first three were primary components in Law's scheme.

Only after the experiment had been run could investors have known that the idea was flawed. That they referred to the ensuing collapse and their after-the-fact foolishness as a bubble should not confuse economists' interpretation of the event. According to the modern definition in economics, the event is easily explainable on the basis of market fundamentals. For a finance operation to be successful always requires a certain degree of sustained confidence from investors. Finance serves as the spearhead of corporate rationalization. In any leveraged buyout or corporate acquisition, high securities prices come first and are followed only gradually by expanded revenues. If investors suddenly lose confidence, they may turn a potentially profitable project into a bankruptcy if it is financed with short-term funding.

Law's scheme was more audacious than the normal Wall Street operation in that he was attempting a corporate takeover of France. But Law's principle was also that finance came first; the financial operation and the expansion of circulating credit was the driving force for economic expansion. From a modern perspective, this idea is not flawed. It is the centerpiece of most money and macroeconomics textbooks produced in the last two generations and the lingua franca of economic policymakers concerned with the problem of underemployed economies. Indeed, recent pressure on the Bank of Japan to monetize long-term government bonds is a scheme that Law would have found familiar.

Law's mistake was that he recognized the accelerating price inflation as inconsistent with the prediction of his theory. His launching of the deflation was similar to any modern restructuring effort to eliminate an excessive debt overhang. Because of the programmed share price fall and the ensuing declines forced by his removal from power, his experiment is tarred with the perjorative "bubble." When modern economic policymakers' reach exceeds their grasp, they simply accommodate the ensuing tenfold price inflation and get the Nobel prize.

16   Law's Shadow: The South Sea Bubble

Following Law's scheme to refinance the French debt, the South Sea Company launched a similar plan to acquire British government debt in January 1720.[21] The financial operations of the British scheme, however, were much simpler than those of Law: the South Sea Company was not involved in large-scale takeovers of commercial companies or of government functions such as the mint, the collection of taxes, or the creation of legal tender paper money.

The British debt in 1720 amounted to approximately £50 million of face value. Of this, £18.3 million was held by the three largest corporations: £3.4 million by the Bank of England, £3.2 million by the East India Company, and £11.7 million by the South Sea Company. Redeemable government bonds held privately amounted to £16.5 million; these could be called by the government on short notice. About £15 million of the debt was in the form of irredeemable annuities: long annuities of between seventy-two and eighty-seven

years and short annuities of twenty-two years in
maturity.[22]

The Refunding Agreement

In 1720, the assets of the South Sea Company consisted
of monopoly rights on British trade with the South Seas—
that is, the Spanish colonies of America—and its holdings
of government debt. These were treaty rights to trade on
a small scale and especially to export slaves. It was well
known that British trade with Spanish America was
effectively blocked by the Spanish and in any case
unprofitable, so only the holdings of government debt
are important to the economic story. After competitive
bidding between the South Sea Company and the Bank
of England, the bill permitting the South Sea Company
to refund the debt had its first passage in Parliament on
March 21, 1720. To acquire this right, the company agreed
to pay the government up to £7.5 million if it managed
to acquire the £31 million of debt held in noncorporate
hands.

To finance the debt acquisition, the Company was
permitted to expand the number of its shares, each of
which had a par value of £100. For each £100 per year of
the long and short annuities acquired, the company could
increase the par value of its shares outstanding by £2000
and by £1400, respectively. For each £100 par value
of redeemables acquired, it could increase its stock issue
by £100.

Quantities of shares were designated in terms of total par value issued. Most research on the episode has continued this convention and has emphasized the difference between the market and par value of shares. The company was free to set the exchange rate between shares and debt. It valued the shares exchanged at well above the par value, leaving it an excess of authorized shares that it was free to market. Scott (1911) labeled these surplus shares the company's "profits" from the conversion. The curious view that a company's holdings of its own shares represents an asset has been replicated in recent examinations of the South Sea Company; for instance, Dickson (1967, 160) lists the company's holdings of its own stock among its assets.

The interest to be paid by the government on the debt acquired by the company was 5 percent per year until 1727 and 4 percent per year thereafter. This would imply a substantial reduction in the annual debt servicing costs of the government.

The Purchase of Parliament

Conditional on the passage of the refunding act, the South Sea Company paid bribes to leading members of Parliament and favorites of the king totaling £1.3 million (Scott 1911, 315). Moreover, in the sequence of stock subscriptions through August 1720, numerous members of Parliament and of the government participated; and most received large cash loans from the company on their shares. For example, 128 members of Parliament acquired shares in the first cash subscriptions for shares, 190 in the second subscription, 352 in the third subscription, and 76 in the fourth subscription. The total par value of shares acquired by them was £1.1 million. For peers, the participation was 58 in the first subscription, 73 in the second subscription, 119 in the third subscription, and 56 in the fourth subscription. The total par value for peers was £548,000. Prior to the refunding operation, the par value of South Sea shares outstanding was £11.7 million; and this was increased to £22.8 million by the end of the speculation. Thus, people in powerful positions in Parliament took 17 percent of the additional shares created. In addition, as Dickson (1967, 108–109) explains, 132 members of Parliament received £1.1 million and 64 peers received £686,000 in loans against shares. Members of the government acquired £75,000 of shares at par value in these subscriptions.

While these bribes add a sinister appearance to the episode, they were not themselves a signal of impending fraud. At the time, bribery was not an unusual practice for a company seeking favors from a Parliament well positioned to block any profitable venture unless its members received their cut.

Indeed, that Parliament and the government supported the refunding so enthusiastically must have served as a signal that official cooperation in South Sea's ventures had been purchased. To the extent that members of Parliament held shares, they would have no interest in thwarting any commercial projects that the company might propose in the future. Given Law's influential theories of commercial expansion, the equity in the South Sea Company could then have been leveraged to undertake those commercial projects that would drive the economy to a higher employment equilibrium. The income generated, accruing to the company without hindrance of Parliament, could in theory then have justified the initial value of the equity—provided that there were such projects.

17 South Sea Finance Operations

Figure 17.1 depicts the movement of South Sea share prices during the speculation. Starting at about £120 per £100 par value share in January 1720, prices moved upward as the refunding proposal was negotiated. With the passage of the refunding act on March 21, prices jumped from about £200 to £300.

To finance the contracted bribes and to make loans to shareholders, the Company offered two subscriptions of shares for cash on April 14 and April 29. In the first subscription, 22,500 shares were issued at a price of £300 per share; one-fifth of the price was required immediately in cash with the remainder due in eight bimonthly installments. In the second, 15,000 shares were subscribed at a price of £400; one-tenth was required immediately in cash, with the remainder due in nine payments at three- or four-month intervals. From these issues, the company immediately realized about £2 million to pay its bribe commitments.

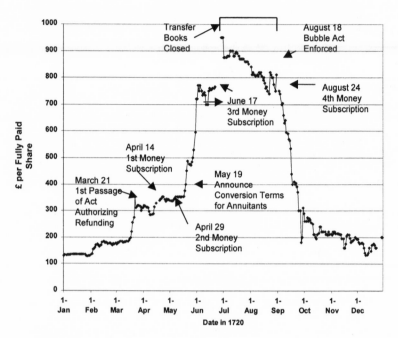

Figure 17.1
Daily South Sea Share Prices, 1720. Data courtesy of Larry Neal.

The first debt conversion aimed at convincing the holders of the irredeemable annuities to agree to an exchange for South Sea shares. Subscriptions began on April 28. The company announced its conversion terms on May 19, allowing holders of the debt one week to accept or reject the conversion terms, which depended on the type of annuity. As an example, the holders of £100 long annuities were offered £700 par value of stock (7 shares) and £575 in bonds and cash. At the time of the offer, South Sea shares were selling for about £400, so the value of the offer was about £3375 for a long annuity. Scott (1911, 311) estimates the market value of the annuity at about £1600 prior to the conversion attempt. Since annuity holders would not lose unless share prices fell below £146, the offer was highly attractive.

All government creditors who had subscribed prior to the announcement assented to the company's terms. According to Dickson (1967, 130–132), the company therefore absorbed about 64 percent of the long annuities and 52 percent of the short annuities outstanding in this subscription. As it became clear that the company would succeed in accumulating most of the outstanding debt, share prices rose rapidly to £700.

To permit it sufficient cash to engage in market price manipulation and to make loans to its shareholders, the company undertook a third cash subscription on June 17, 1720, in which it sold a par value of £5 million (50,000 shares) for a market price of £1000 per share. Purchasers had to pay one-tenth down in cash (£5 million), with the remainder to be paid in nine semi-annual payments. Share prices immediately jumped from £745 to £950. The final cash subscription occurred on August 24. The company sold 12,500 shares with a par value of £1.25 million at a price of £1000 per share. One-fifth was required immediately in cash, with four additional payments at nine-month intervals. From June 24 to August 22, the transfer books of the company were closed in preparation for a dividend payment, so the market prices depicted in figure 17.1 for this period were future prices.[23]

Finally, the company offered two additional subscriptions for government bonds; terms for subscribing the remaining irredeemables and the redeemables were announced on August 4 and August 12, respectively. Of the outstanding £16.5 million in redeemables, £14.4 million were exchanged for 18,900 shares of stock. At market prices of £800 per share, this amounted to a price of £105 per £100 bond. Redeemables were callable by the government, so this price, although seemingly low in comparison to the irredeemables, was generally acceptable. The remaining irredeemables were to be exchanged for varying amounts of stock and cash. By means of all the debt conversions, the South Sea Company acquired 80 percent of the public's holdings of the irredeemables and 85 percent of the redeemables.

The Price Collapse

South Sea share prices collapsed from about £775 on August 31 to about £290 on October 1, 1720. Shares outstanding or to be issued to the public after subscribers were entered on company registers numbered 212,012. Thus, the market value of all shares on August 31 was £164 million and about £103 million of that total evaporated in one month, an amount exceeding twice the value of the original, burdensome government debt.

Researchers of the episode like Dickson (1967, 148–152), Scott (1911, 324–328), and Neal (1988) are vague about the reason for the speed and magnitude of the decline, though they generally attribute it to the appearance of a liquidity crisis. The South Sea speculation had triggered a simultaneous upsurge in the prices of other existing companies along with the creation of numerous "bubble companies." The emergence of these companies, many of which were fraudulent, generated most of the amusing anecdotes that have been transmitted to us about this speculation. Many of the companies born in the 1720 speculation were quite sound, however, notably the Royal Assurance Company and the London Assurance Company. The channeling of capital into these companies alarmed the directors of the South Sea Company, who, having paid a high price to buy the Parliament, did not wish to see potential South Sea profits dissipated by the entry of unauthorized commercial corporations. Consequently, Parliament passed the Bubble Act in June 1720 to ban the formation of unauthorized corporations or the extension of existing corporate charters into new, unauthorized ventures.

When the Bubble Act was enforced against some of the company's competitors on August 18, 1720, immediate downward pressure was placed on the price of shares of the affected companies. Because the shares were mostly held on margin, general selling hit the shares of all companies, including South Sea shares, in a scramble for liquidity. Simultaneously, there was an international scramble for liquidity with the final collapse of Law's Compagnie des Indes in September 1720 and of a Dutch speculation. Liquidity may have been drained from

English markets by these international events. Neal and Schubert (1985) provide evidence on large-scale capital movements during this period.

With the collapse of share prices, the South Sea Company faced the hostility of its shareholders who had participated in its debt and cash subscriptions. Parliament quickly turned against the company, eventually forcing it to sell off part of its debt holdings to the Bank of England. Parliament eventually stripped the directors of the company and several government officials of their wealth (£2 million) and directed the payment of the proceeds to the South Sea Company. Adjustments were also made to redistribute shares among the different waves of subscribers, so that losses to later subscribers were reduced. Finally, Parliament forgave payment of the £7.1 million that the company had contracted on receipt of the conversion privilege.

Fundamentals of the South Sea Company

At the beginning of September 1720, the market value of South Sea shares was £164 million. The visible asset supporting this price was a flow of revenue from the company's claim against the government of £1.9 million per year until 1727 and £1.5 million thereafter. At a 4 percent long-term discount rate, this asset had a value of about £40 million. Against this, the company had agreed to pay £7.1 million for the conversion privilege and owed £6 million in bonds and bills for a net asset value of £26.1 million. In addition, the company's cash receivables were £11 million due on loans to stockholders and £70 million eventually due from cash subscribers. Thus, share values exceeded asset values by more than £60 million. Given the dubious value of the company's cash claims, share values exceeded tangible net assets by five times or more.

What intangible assets could have justified this value of the company? Again, the answer lies in Law's prediction of a commercial expansion associated with the accumulation of a fund of credit. The company succeeded in gathering the fund and obviously had the support of Parliament in its ventures. On this basis, Scott (1911, 313–314) believed that a price of £400 was not excessive.

It may be added too that the great need of commerce in the first quarter of the eighteenth century was a sufficiency of capital, and so it is scarcely possible to estimate adequately, under the different conditions of the present time, the many promising outlets there were then for the remunerative employment of capital. In fact capital, organized in one single unit, might be utilized in many directions, where no single fraction of the same capital could find its way, and therefore some premium on South Sea stock was justified and maintainable. . . . Thus, it will be seen that the investor, who in 1720 bought stock at 300 or even 400, may have been unduly optimistic, but there was at least a possibility that his confidence would be rewarded in the future.

The experiment was terminated with the liquidity crisis and the withdrawal of parliamentary support while it was still in its finance stage. In retrospect, anyone projecting commercial returns high enough to justify the higher prices of South Sea shares was probably too optimistic. Nevertheless, the episode is readily understandable as a case of speculators' working on the basis of the best economic analysis available and pushing prices along by their changing view of market fundamentals.

19   Conclusion

The jargon of economics and finance contains numerous colorful expressions to denote a market-determined asset price at odds with any reasonable economic explanation. Such terms as *tulipmania, bubble, chain letter, Ponzi scheme, panic, crash,* and *financial crisis* immediately evoke images of frenzied and irrational speculative activity. Lately, the same terms, or modern versions of them—*herding, irrational exhuberance, contagion,* and *self-generating equilibrium*—have been used by media, academics, and policymakers to paint the crises of 1997, 1998, and 1999.

These words are always used to argue the irrationality of financial markets in particularly volatile periods. Many of these terms have emerged from specific speculative episodes, which have been sufficiently frequent and important that they underpin a strong current belief that key capital markets generate irrational and inefficient pricing and allocational outcomes.

The proponents of such arguments can hardly ever resist the invocation of three famous bubbles—the Dutch tulipmania, the Mississippi Bubble, and the South Sea Bubble. That such obvious craziness happened in the past is taken as the only necessary explanation for modern events that are otherwise hard to explain with their favorite economic theories.

Before we relegate a speculative event to the fundamentally inexplicable or bubble category driven by crowd psychology, however, we should exhaust the reasonable economic explanations. Such explanations are often not easily generated due to the inherent complexity of economic phenomena, but bubble explanations are often clutched as a first and not a last resort. Indeed, "bubble" characterizations should be a last resort because they are non-explanations of events, merely a name that we attach to a financial phenomenon that we have not invested sufficiently in understanding. Invoking crowd psychology—which is always ill defined and unmeasured—turns our explanation to tautology in a self-deluding attempt to say something more than a confession of confusion.

Fascinated by the brilliance of grand speculative events, observers of financial markets have huddled in the bubble interpretation and have neglected an examination of potential market fundamentals. The ready availability of a banal explanation of the tulipmania, compared to its dominant position in the speculative pantheon of economics, is stark evidence of how bubble and mania characterizations have served to divert us from understanding those outlying events highest in informational content. The bubble inter-pretation has relegated the far more important Mississippi and South Sea episodes to a description of pathologies of group psychology. Yet these events were a vast macroeconomic and financial experiment, imposed on a scale and with a degree of control by their main theoretical architects that did not occur again until the war economies of this century. True, the experiment failed, either because its theoretical basis was fundamentally flawed or because its managers lacked the complex financial skills required to undertake the day-to-day tactics necessary for its consummation. Nevertheless, investors *had* to take positions on its potential success. It is curious that students of finance and economists alike have accepted the failure of the experiments as proof that the investors were foolishly and irrationally wrong.

An observation that the tulipmania and the Mississippi and South Sea Bubbles predispose us to advance bubble theories of asset pricing provided the point of departure of this study. If small strata of particular episodes underpin the belief that bubbles may exist, it is desirable to undertake a detailed study of these events, most of which have not been examined from the perspective of market fundamental theories of asset pricing, to assure that other reasonable explanations have not been overlooked.

In the end, one can take one's pick: market fundamental explanations of events or bubble and crowd psychology theories. It is my view that bubble theories are the easy way out—they are simply names that we attach to that part of asset price movements that we cannot easily explain. As tautological explanations, they can never be refuted. The goal here is to find explanations with some measure of economic and refutable content.

Appendix 1

The Tulipmania in the Popular and Economics Literature

Chroniclers of the tulip speculation, and modern writers who cite it, take for granted that it was a mania, selecting and organizing the evidence to emphasize the irrationality of the market outcome.

In the twentieth century, a strong intellectual influence on participants and observers of the financial markets has been exerted by Mackay's version of the tulipmania, although he devoted only seven pages of text to it. Bernard Baruch wrote an introduction to Mackay's book, whose reprinting he had encouraged, emphasizing the importance of crowd psychology in all economic movements. Dreman (1977), who also stresses psychological forces in asset price determination, uses the tulipmania as a prototype of market mania. Relating the same anecdotes as Mackay, Dreman employs the tulipmania as a constant metaphor in discussions of succeeding major speculative collapses. He states (52):

If, for example, my neighbor tried to sell me a tulip bulb for $5,000, I'd simply laugh at him. . . . The tulip craze, like the manias we shall see shortly, created its own reality as it went along. It is ludicrous to pay as much for a flower as one pays for a house. . . .[24]

Whenever large and rapid fluctuations of asset prices occur, the popular media recall the tulipmania. For example, when gold prices jumped in 1979, a *Wall Street Journal* (Sept. 26, 1979) article stated, "The ongoing frenzy in the gold market may be only an illusion of crowds, a modern repetition of the tulip-bulb craze or the South Sea Bubble." The October 19, 1987, stock market crash brought forth similar comparisons from the *Wall Street Journal* (Dec. 11, 1987); and *The Economist* (Oct. 24, 1987) explained the event as follows:

The crash suffered by the world's stockmarkets has provided a beginning and middle for a new chapter updating Charles Mackay's 1841 book "Extraordinary Popular Delusions and the Madness of Crowds" which chronicled Dutch tulip bulbs, the South Sea bubble. . . . It was the madness of crowds that sent the bull market ever upward. . . . It is mob psychology that has now sent investors so rapidly for the exits. (P. 75)

Malkiel (1985) cites Mackay extensively in his chapter "The Madness of Crowds," including the anecdote about the sailor and the claim that the collapse led to a prolonged depression in Holland. In reference to other speculative episodes, he asks:

Why do such speculative crazes seem so isolated from the lessons of history? I have no apt answer to offer, but I am convinced that Bernard Baruch was correct in suggesting that a study of these events can help equip investors for survival. The consistent losers in the market, from my personal experience, are those who are unable to resist being swept up in some kind of tulip-bulb craze. (Pp. 44–45)

Galbraith (1993) simply repeats Mackay's story about the tulipmania without any effort at serious research to include succeeding developments in knowledge on the topic. Krugman (1995) could not resist invoking the tulipmania in discussing emerging market capital flows.

On a more serious note, the pre–1950s academic literature written by major professional economists contains little direct reference to the tulipmania. *Palgrave's Dictionary of Political Economy* (1926, 182) includes a paragraph on tulips in its section on bubbles, citing Mackay. In earlier editions of his cubist study of manias, Kindleberger (1978) catalogued a long sequence of financial panics and manias and provided a descriptive pathology of their dynamics; but he did not include the tulipmania among those episodes examined in detail because "manias such as . . . the tulip mania of 1634 are too isolated and lack the characteristic monetary features that come with the spread of banking" (6). In his article on "bubbles" in *The New Palgrave Dictionary of Economics* (Eatwell, Milgate, and Newman 1987), however, Kindleberger includes the tulipmania as one of the two most famous manias. In the most recent edition of his book on manias, Kindleberger (1996) added a chapter critiquing earlier papers that I had written on tulipmania.

The tulipmania made its first appearance in serious economics journals with the development of capital theory in the 1950s and the discovery of the potential existence of multiple, dynamically unstable asset price paths. Samuelson (1957, 1967) presents the tulipmania metaphor and associates it with "the purely financial dream world of indefinite group self-fulfillment" (1967, 230). Samuelson (1957) uses "tulipmania" interchangeably with "Ponzi scheme," "chain letter," and "bubble."

Students of Samuelson, in a flurry of research activity concerning the "Hahn problem," employ the tulipmania as an empirical motivation. Shell and Stiglitz (1967) state, "The instability of the Hahn model is suggestive of the economic forces operating during 'speculative booms' like the Tulip Bulb mania." Burmeister (1980, 264–286) summarizes these models.

The advent of the "sunspot" literature generated a revival of references to tulips as a motivation for the line of research. For example, Azariadis (1981, 380) argues that "the evidence on the influence of subjective factors is ample and dates back several centuries; the Dutch 'tulip mania,' the South Sea bubble in England, and the collapse of the Mississippi Company in France are three well-documented cases of speculative price movements that historians consider unwarranted by 'objective' conditions." More recently, Azariadis and Guesnerie (1986) state, "And the reading of economic historians may suggest that these factors (sunspots) have some pertinence for the explanation of phenomena like the Dutch tulipmania in the seventeenth century and the Great Depression in our own" (725).

Under the topic "tulipmania" in *The New Palgrave Dictionary of Economics* (Eatwell, Milgate, and Newman 1987), Guillermo Calvo does not refer to the seventeenth-century Dutch speculative episode at all. Rather, he defines tulipmania as a situation in which asset prices do not behave in ways explainable by economic fundamentals. He develops examples of rational bubbles, both of the explosive and "sunspot" varieties. In the finance literature, the emergence of empirical anomalies has also generated references to tulipmania as bubble and fad explanations have regained respectability. In his presidential address to the American Finance Association, van Horne (1985), embraces the possibility of bubbles and manias and, as an example, refers explicitly to the tulipmania, where a "single bulb sold for many years' salary."

Appendix 2

The Seventeenth-Century Tulip Price Data

Table A2.1 contains price data for various tulips. For each type of bulb, the observations are ordered by date; they include the price paid, the weight in aas of the bulb, the price per aas, and the data source. I have gathered the data from different sources of uneven reliability.

Some sources are marked with numbers to indicate the numbering of notarized contracts reported by Posthumus in *Economisch-Historisch Jaarboek* (1927, 1934). Because these were carefully drawn contracts sworn before notaries, they are the most reliable data, representing serious transactions that did not occur in the colleges. Furthermore, many are dated before the peak of the speculation in January–February 1637. Presumably, the contracts drawn from June to September were for spot delivery. The delivery dates for the winter contracts are unclear. A few contract prices reported in Krelage (1946) are labeled as "Krelage–46–p482."

Next in order of reliability are the bulbs labeled "Children," which I have taken from *Economisch-Historisch*

Jaarboek (1927). These bulbs are taken from a price list labeled "List of some tulips sold to the highest bidder on February 5, 1637, in the city of Alkmaar. These tulips were sold to the benefit of the children of Mr. Wouter Bartelmiesz at a total amount of Fl. 68,553." A facsimile of this list is also reproduced in Krelage (1946, 488). Again, the delivery date and terms of payment are not clear from the available information. Also, the February 5 date seems at odds with the collapse date, which G&W claim occurred on February 3. However, as recorded auction prices, the list represents some actual transactions.

Lower in order of reliability are the numerous prices reported in G&W. G&W is in the form of a long and moralistic dialogue between Gaergoedt (Greedy Goods) and Waermondt (True Mouth) about the nature of the markets and the price dynamics during the speculation. The third dialogue, "Prijsen der Bloemen," presents a list of about 250 bulb transactions, including prices and weights, but it does not report the dates of the sales. Fortunately, since a great deal of overlap appears between the G&W prices and the "Children" prices, the author of G&W must have had access to the "Children" list in constructing the G&W list. Thus, I used the February 5 date of the "Children list to date the reported prices in the G&W list, including those G&W flowers not reported in the "Children" list. Moreover, finding many of the G&W flowers listed among verifiable transactions generates some confidence that the G&W author did not simply make up the prices reported in the third dialogue.

In discussing the rapidity of price movement during the speculation, G&W present the prices of twenty bulbs observed at two different times in the speculation, claiming the earlier prices were taken from four to six weeks prior to the later prices for each bulb. However, they do not indicate the dates on which the later transactions occurred. Fortunately, most of the later transactions for these bulbs are among the bulbs in the "Children" list or in the extensive G&W list described above. Since these bulbs are the only "time series" reported in G&W, it is important to include them. Thus, I have presumed that the later transaction for each bulb occurred on February 5, 1637, and that the earlier transaction occurred on January 2, 1637, five weeks earlier. This explains why so many January 2–February 5 pairs appear in the list in table A2.1.

Finally, the list contains several transactions listed in Munting (1672, 1696) and in Krelage (1942) that I could not find among the above sources. Unfortunately, Krelage reports the price per aas involved in particular transactions and not the price and weight of the transacted bulb.

Table A2.1
Basic Tulip Price Data

Date	Tulip	Price	Weight	Price/Aas	Source	Place
01-Jun-36	Admirael Liefkens	6.6	1	6.6000	18	Haarlem
05-Feb-37	Admirael Liefkens			11.8000	Krelage, 49	
05-Feb-37	Admirael Liefkens	4,400	400	11.0000	G&W	
05-Feb-37	Admirael Liefkens	1,015	59	17.2034	Children	Alkmaer
02-Jan-37	Admirael de Man	15	130	0.1154	G&W	
02-Jan-37	Admirael de Man	90	1,000	0.0900	G&W	
05-Feb-37	Admirael de Man	250	175	1.4286	G&W	
05-Feb-37	Admirael de Man	800	1,000	0.8000	G&W	
05-Feb-37	Admirael de Man	175	130	1.3462	G&W	
05-Feb-37	Admirael van Enchuysen	5,400	215	25.1163	G&W	
05-Feb-37	Admirael van Enchuysen			28.0000	Krelage, 49	
05-Feb-37	Admirael van Enchuysen	900	8	112.5000	G&W	
05-Feb-37	Admirael van Hoorn	230	1,000	0.2300	G&W	
05-Feb-37	Admirael van Hoorn	200	440	0.4545	G&W	
01-Dec-34	Admirael van der Eyck	80	80	1.0000	7	Haarlem
01-Dec-34	Admirael van der Eyck	66	20	3.3000	7	Haarlem

Date	Name	Guilders	Aces	Guilders/Ace	Source	Location
27-Jul-36	Admirael van der Eyck	2.5	1	2.5000	17	Haarlem
05-Feb-37	Admirael van der Eyck			4.5000	Krelage, 49	Alkmaer
05-Feb-37	Admirael van der Eyck	1,620	446	3.6323	Children	Alkmaer
05-Feb-37	Admirael van der Eyck	1,045	214	4.8832	Children	Alkmaer
05-Feb-37	Admirael van der Eyck	710	92	7.7174	Children	Amsterdam
01-Dec-36	Bleyenburch (Laeten)	350	4 tulips		57	Amsterdam
28-Dec-36	Bleyenburch (Laeten)	120	104	1.1538	65	
05-Feb-37	Blijenburger (Vroege)			3.5000	Krelage, 49	Alkmaer
05-Feb-37	Blijenburger (Vroege)	1,300	443	2.9345	Children	Alkmaer
05-Feb-37	Blijenburger (Vroege)	900	171	5.2632	Children	Alkmaer
05-Feb-37	Bruyne Purper	2,025	320	6.3281	Children	
05-Feb-37	Bruyne Purper			10.3000	Krelage, 49	
05-Feb-37	Bruyne Purper	1,100	50	22.0000	G&W	
05-Feb-37	Bruyne Purper	1,300	60	21.6667	G&W	
10-Jul-12	Caers op de Candelaer	24			3	Haarlem
02-Jan-37	Centen	40	1,000	0.0400	G&W	
15-Jan-37	Centen	72	530	0.1358	van Damme, 106	Amsterdam
22-Jan-37	Centen	380	3,000	0.1267	32	
05-Feb-37	Centen	400	1,000	0.4000	G&W	
05-Feb-37	Centen	4,300	10,240	0.4199	G&W	

Table A2.1 (continued)

Date	Tulip	Price	Weight	Price/Aas	Source	Place
02-Jan-37	Coorenaerts	60	1,000	0.0600	G&W	
22-Jan-37	Coorenaerts	220	1,000	0.2200	32	Amsterdam
05-Feb-37	Coorenaerts	550	1,000	0.5500	G&W	
05-Feb-37	Coorenaerts	4,800	10,240	0.4688	G&W	
10-Jun-36	English Admiral	3	1	3.0000	13	
05-Feb-37	English Admiral	700	25	28.0000	G&W	
05-Feb-37	Fama	605	130	4.6538	Children	Alkmaer
05-Feb-37	Fama	700	158	4.4304	Children	Alkmaer
05-Feb-37	Fama	440	104	4.2308	Children	Alkmaer
02-Jan-37	Generalissimo	95	10	9.5000	G&W	
05-Feb-37	Generalissimo	900	10	90.0000	G&W	
02-Jan-37	Gheele Croonen	24	10,240	0.0023	G&W	
05-Feb-37	Gheele Croonen	1,200	10,240	0.1172	G&W	
08-Dec-36	Gheele ende Roote van Leyden	260	578	0.4498	Krelage, 73	
02-Jan-37	Gheele ende Roote van Leyden	46	515	0.0893	G&W	
02-Jan-37	Gheele ende Roote van Leyden	100	1,000	0.1000	G&W	
05-Feb-37	Gheele ende Roote van Leyden	700	1,000	0.7000	G&W	

Date	Variety				Source	City
05-Feb-37	Gheele ende Roote van Leyden	140	400	0.3500	G&W	
05-Feb-37	Gheele ende Roote van Leyden	550	515	1.0680	G&W	
05-Feb-37	Gheele ende Roote van Leyden	235	240	0.5800	Krelage, 49	
05-Feb-37	Gheele ende Roote van Leyden	70	357	0.9792	G&W	
12-Nov-36	Ghemarm. de Goyer	36	1 bulb	0.1961	Krelage, 73	
04-Feb-37	Ghemarm. de Goyer	250	1,000		van Damme, 21	
05-Feb-37	Ghemarm. de Goyer			0.2500	G&W	
05-Feb-37	Gouda			7.5000	Krelage, 49	
01-Dec-34	Gouda	45	30	1.5000	7&Krelage, 49	Haarlem
01-Dec-35	Gouda	2.1	1	2.1000	24	Haarlem
29-Aug-36	Gouda	3.75	1	3.7500	20	Haarlem
25-Nov-36	Gouda	446	66	6.7576	30	Haarlem
09-Dec-36	Gouda	600	400	1.5000	35	Haarlem
12-Dec-36	Gouda	520	48	10.8333	Laubach, 87	
02-Jan-37	Gouda	20	4	5.0000	G&W	
29-Jan-37	Gouda	100	7	14.2857	33	Haarlem
05-Feb-37	Gouda	3,600	1,000	3.6000	Munting & G&W	
05-Feb-37	Gouda	1,500	244	6.1475	Children	Alkmaer
05-Feb-37	Gouda	1,330	187	7.1123	Children	Alkmaer
05-Feb-37	Gouda	1,165	160	7.2813	Children	Alkmaer

Table A2.1 (continued)

Date	Tulip	Price	Weight	Price/Aas	Source	Place
05-Feb-37	Gouda	1,165	156	7.4679	Children	Alkmaer
05-Feb-37	Gouda	1,015	125	8.1200	Children	Alkmaer
05-Feb-37	Gouda	765	82	9.3293	Children	Alkmaer
05-Feb-37	Gouda	635	63	10.0794	Children	Alkmaer
05-Feb-37	Gouda	225	4	56.2500	G&W&30	Haarlem
29-Sep-36	Groote Geplumiceerde	140	2,000	0.0700	28	Amsterdam
12-Jan-37	Groote Geplumiceerde	300	2,000	0.1500	G&W	
05-Feb-37	Groote Geplumiceerde	300	400	0.7500	71	Haarlem
05-Feb-37	Groote Geplumiceerde	280	1,000	0.2800	Children	Alkmaer
05-Feb-37	Groote Gepulmiceerde	300	1,000	0.3000	G&W	
15-Jan-37	Jan Gerritsz	230	288	0.7986	van Damme, 104	
05-Feb-37	Jan Gerritsz	734	1,000	0.7340	G&W	
05-Feb-37	Jan Gerritsz	210	263	0.7985	Children	Alkmaer
05-Feb-37	Jan Gerritsz (Swijmende)	210	925	0.2270	Children	Alkmaer
05-Feb-37	Jan Gerritsz (Swijmende)	51	80	0.6375	Children	Alkmaer
05-Feb-37	Julius Caesar	1,300	187	6.9519	G&W	
18-Dec-35	Latour	27	16	1.6875	9	Haarlem

Date	Name				Source	City
05-Feb-37	Latour	390	450	0.8667	G&W	Haarlem
16-Jan-37	Le Grand	90	122	0.7377	Krel-46-p482	Amsterdam
22-Jan-37	Le Grand	21	185	0.1135	32	Haarlem
24-Jan-37	Le Grand	480	1,000	0.4800	31	Alkmaer
05-Feb-37	Le Grand	500	350	1.4286	Children	
05-Feb-37	Le Grand	780	1,000	0.7800	G&W	Haarlem
24-Jan-37	Macx	12	400	0.0300	31	Amsterdam
03-Feb-37	Macx	400	2,000	0.2000	75	Alkmaer
05-Feb-37	Macx	300	1,000	0.3000	Children	Alkmaer
05-Feb-37	Macx	300	1,000	0.3000	Children	
05-Feb-37	Macx	390	700	0.5571	G&W	Amsterdam
06-Jan-37	Nieuwburger	125	425	0.2941	65	
05-Feb-37	Nieuwburger	500	1,000	0.5000	G&W	
05-Feb-37	Nieuwburger	390	495	0.7879	G&W	Alkmaer
05-Feb-37	Nieuwburger	235	500	0.4700	Children	Alkmaer
05-Feb-37	Nieuwburger	430	1,000	0.4300	Children	
05-Feb-37	Nieuwburger	180	495	0.3636	G&W	
01-Dec-36	Oudenaerden	600	10,240	0.0586	57	Amsterdam
02-Jan-37	Oudenaerden	70	1,000	0.0700	G&W	

Table A2.1 (continued)

Date	Tulip	Price	Weight	Price/Aas	Source	Place
22-Jan-37	Oudenaerden	1,430	5,120	0.2793	32	Amsterdam
30-Jan-37	Oudenaerden	2,200	4,864	0.4523	Krel-46-p482	Haarlem
05-Feb-37	Oudenaerden	600	1,000	0.6000	G&W	
05-Feb-37	Oudenaerden	370	450	0.8222	Children	Alkmaer
05-Feb-37	Oudenaerden	530	1,000	0.5300	Children	Alkmaer
05-Feb-37	Oudenaerden	510	1,000	0.5100	G&W	
05-Feb-37	Oudenaerden	5,700	10,240	0.5566	G&W	
17-May-33	Parragon Schilder	50	1 Bulb		34-2	Amsterdam
05-Feb-37	Parragon Schilder	1,615	106	15.2358	G&W	
16-Dec-36	Petter	172	360	0.4778	van Damme, 103	
05-Feb-37	Petter	900	800	1.1250	G&W	
05-Feb-37	Petter	730	1,000	0.7300	Children	Alkmaer
05-Feb-37	Petter	705	1,000	0.7050	Children	Alkmaer
05-Feb-37	Petter	730	1,000	0.7300	G&W	
05-Feb-37	Rotgans	805	1,000	0.8050	Children	Alkmaer
05-Feb-37	Rotgans (Violette Gevlamde)	725	1,000	0.7250	Children	Alkmaer
05-Feb-37	Rotgans (Violette Gevlamde)	375	500	0.7500	Children	Alkmaer

Date	Name					City
18-Dec-35	Saeyblom van Coningh	30	7.5	4.0000	9	Haarlem
05-Feb-37	Saeyblom van Coningh	320	220	1.4545	G&W	
05-Feb-37	Saeyblom, beste	1,000	1,000	1.0000	G&W	
05-Feb-37	Schapesteyn	235	95	2.4737	Children	Alkmaer
05-Feb-37	Schapesteyn	375	246	1.5244	Children	Alkmaer
02-Jan-37	Scipio	800	1,000	0.8000	G&W	
12-Jan-37	Scipio	1,500	1,000	1.5000	28	Amsterdam
05-Feb-37	Scipio	100	10	10.0000	G&W	
05-Feb-37	Scipio	400	82	4.8780	Children	Alkmaer
05-Feb-37	Scipio	2,250	1,000	2.2500	G&W	
01-Jul-23	Semper Augustus	1,000	1 bulb		Krelage, 32	
01-Jul-24	Semper Augustus	1,200	1 bulb		Posthumus	
01-Jul-25	Semper Augustus	2,000	1 bulb		Krelage, 33	
05-Feb-37	Semper Augustus	5,500	200	27.5000	Munting	
02-Jan-37	Switsers	60	10,240	0.0059	G&W	
15-Jan-37	Switsers	120	9,728	0.0123	34	Haarlem
22-Jan-37	Switsers	280	10,240	0.0273	32	Amsterdam
23-Jan-37	Switsers	385	10,240	0.0376	Krelage, 51	
01-Feb-37	Switsers	1,400	9,728	0.1439	75	Amsterdam

Table A2.1 (continued)

Date	Tulip	Price	Weight	Price/Aas	Source	Place
03-Feb-37	Switsers	6,000	40,960	0.1465	38	Amsterdam
05-Feb-37	Switsers	1,800	10,240	0.1758	G&W	
06-Feb-37	Switsers	1,100	10,240	0.1074	34-6	Amsterdam
06-Feb-37	Switsers	1,060	10,240	0.1035	34-5	Amsterdam
09-Feb-37	Switsers	1,100	10,240	0.1074	40	Haarlem
02-Jan-37	Viceroy	3,000	1,000	3.0000	G&W	
05-Feb-37	Viceroy	4,203	685	6.1358	Children	Alkmaer
05-Feb-37	Viceroy	3,000	410	7.3171	Children	Alkmaer
05-Feb-37	Viceroy	2,700	295	9.1525	G&W	
05-Feb-37	Viceroy	6,700	1,000	6.7000	G&W	
10-Jul-12	Vlaems	450	38,912	0.0116	4	Haarlem
02-Jan-37	Witte Croonen	128	10,240	0.0125	G&W	
05-Feb-37	Witte Croonen	300	1,000	0.3000	G&W	
05-Feb-37	Witte Croonen	3,600	10,240	0.3516	G&W	
05-Feb-37	Witte Croonen			0.2700	Krelage, 49	
05-Feb-37	Zomerschoon	1,010	368	2.7446	G&W	

Notes

1. The discussion of political and economic history is based on Rich and Wilson, *The Cambridge Economic History of Europe*, vols. 4 and 5 (Rich and Wilson 1975, 1977); Braudel (1979), vol. 3; Attman (1983); and Cooper, *The New Cambridge Modern History of Europe*, vol. IV (1970).

2. See Attman (1983, 35). The guilder was the unit of account. It was denoted by the sign fl. (florin) and was divided into 20 stuivers. The stuiver was further subdivided into 16 pennings. The guilder was a bimetallic unit, equivalent to 10.75 grams of fine silver from 1610–1614, 10.28 grams from 1620–1659, and 9.74 grams thereafter. See Posthumus (1964, cxv) and Rich and Wilson (1977, 458). Its gold content was 0.867 grams of fine gold in 1612, 0.856 grams in 1622, 0.77 in 1638, and 0.73 in 1645. This was a devaluation of gold content of 16%. See Posthumus (1964, cxix). Prices of foodstuffs, metals, and fibers did not display significant secular movements from 1600 through 1750; so given the orders of magnitude of bulb price changes that we will observe, we can take the price level as approximately constant in interpreting nominal prices during this 150-year period.

3. See Penso de la Vega ([1688] 1957) for a description of the variety of securities and the sophistication of market manipulation on the Amsterdam exchange.

4. Beckmann wrote originally in German at the end of the eighteenth century; only the fourth English edition (1846) of his book was available to me.

5. For a list of these pamphlets, see the references in Krelage (1942, 1946).

6. These were published in *the Weekblad voor Bloembollencultur* and are reprinted in Van Damme (1976).

7. The discussion in this section is based on Schama (1987, 323–371), and on the translation of Penso de la Vega (1688, xii–xix).

8. See Prinzing (1916) on the epidemics of the Thirty Years' War. See also Cooper (1970, 76).

9. See Mather (1961, 44).

10. See Doorenbos (1954, 1–11).

11. See Mather (1961, 100–101).

12. See Posthumus (1929, 442).

13. Gheele Croonen and Witte Croonen apparently were not broken tulips, though they were multicolored. However, it is not clear whether all the other "pound good" tulips were broken.

14. In his discussion on economic distress in the tulipmania, Malkiel asks, "And what of those who had sold out early in the game? In the end, they too were engulfed by the tulip craze. For the final chapter of this bizarre story is that the shock generated by the boom and collapse was followed by a prolonged depression in Holland. No one was spared" (1996, 38). Unfortunately, there was no depression in Holland. Malkiel prefers to propagate the myth handed down by Mackay to seriously researching the topic.

15. I thank Guido Imbens and Klaas Baks for this translation.

16. Krelage cites "Clare ontdeckingh der ghener, die haer tegenwoordigh laten noemen Floristen" (Hoorn: Zacharias Cornelisz, 1636) as the source.

17. This section is intended as a brief outline of the vast Mississippi scheme. For a recent fascinating view of the scheme and its implementation, see Antoin Murphy's excellent *John Law* and also his biography of Richard Cantillon. Larry Neal (1990) provides a general description of the development of the financial markets in England, the Netherlands, and France in the eighteenth century, along with an analysis of the South Sea and Mississippi bubbles.

18. This outline of Law's experiment is based on descriptions in Harsin (1928), Faure (1977), and Murphy (1986).

19. See Harsin's (1928, 180) citation of Law's *Deuxieme Lettre sur le nouveau system des finances*.

20. Murphy (1997, 235) argues that Law was pushed into the share price fixing phase during a temporary loss of control.

21. I have taken the factual information in this section primarily from Scott (1911), Carswell (1960), and Dickson (1967).

22. Neal (1988) discusses the nature of these annuities.

23. Neal (1988) argues that the peak price was £950 on July 1. Scott (1911) indicates a peak price of £1050, but this apparently includes the announced stock dividend of 10 percent. Following Neal, I have used the peak price of £950.

24. Dreman clearly neglected to inquire about current bulb prices in Haarlem before he wrote.

References

Anderson, A. 1787. *An Historical and Chronological Deduction of the Origin of Commerce,* vol. 3. London: J. Walter.

Attman, A. 1983. *Dutch Enterprise in the World Bullion Trade.* Goteborg: Almqvist and Wicksell.

Azariadis, C. 1981. "Self-Fulfilling Prophecies." *Journal of Economic Theory* 25:380–396.

Azariadis, C., and R. Guesnerie. 1986. "Sunspots and Cycles." *Review of Economic Studies* 53 (Oct.):725–737.

Beckmann, J. 1846. *History of Inventions, Discoveries, and Origins,* vol. 1, 4th ed. London: Harry G. Bohn.

Bradley, R. 1728. *Dictionarium Botanicum: Or, a Botanical Dictionary for the Use of the Curious in Husbandry and Gardening.* London.

Braudel, F. 1979. *The Perspective of the World.* Vol. 3, *Civilization & Capitalism, 15th–18th Century.* New York: Harper and Row.

Burmeister, E. 1980. *Capital Theory and Dynamics.* Cambridge: Cambridge University Press.

Carswell, J. 1960. *The South Sea Bubble.* London: Cresset Press.

"Clare ontdeckingh der ghener, die haer tegenwoordigh laten noemen Floristen." 1636. Hoorn: Zacharias Cornelisz.

Cooper, P. 1970. *New Cambridge Modern History*. Vol. IV, *The Decline of Spain and the Thirty Years' War*. Cambridge: Cambridge University Press.

D'Ardene, J. 1760. *Traité des Tulipes*. Avignon: Chambeau.

de Vries, J. 1976. *The Economy of Europe in an Age of Crisis, 1600–1750*. Cambridge: Cambridge University Press.

Dickson, P. G. M. 1967. *The Financial Revolution in England: A Study in the Development of Public Credit*. London: Macmillan.

Doorenbos, J., "Notes on the History of Bulb Breeding in the Netherlands." *Euphytica* 3, no. 1 (February 1954):1–11.

Dreman, D. 1977. *Psychology and the Stock Market*. New York: Anacom.

Eatwell, J., M. Milgate, and P. Newman, eds. 1987. *The New Palgrave Dictionary of Economics*. Dictionary oillan.

Faure, E. 1977. *La Banqueroute de Law*. Paris.

Galbraith, J. K. 1993. *A Short History of Financial Euphoria*. New York: Viking.

Garber, P. 1989. "Tulipmania." *Journal of Political Economy* (April): 535–560.

———. 1990a. "Famous First Bubbles." *Journal of Economic Perspectives* (May): 35–54.

———. 1990b. "Who Put the Mania in Tulipmania?" In E. White, ed., *Crashes and Panics: The Lessons from History*. Homewood, IL: Dow-Jones Irwin.

Hamilton, E. 1936–37. "Prices and Wages at Paris under John Law's System." *Quarterly Journal of Economics* 51:42–70.

Harsin, P. 1928. *Les Doctrines Monetarires et Financieres en France*. Paris: Librairie Felix Alcan.

Hartman, H., and D. Kester. 1983. *Plant Propagation*. Englewood Cliffs, NJ: Prentice-Hall.

International Monetary Fund. 1998. *World Economic Outlook and International Capital Markets, Interim Assessment.* Washington, DC: IMF.

Kindleberger, C. 1978. *Manias, Panics, and Crashes.* New York: Basic Books.

Kindleberger, C. P. 1996. *Manias, Panics, and Crashes: A History of Financial Crises,* 3d ed. New York: Wiley.

Krelage, E. H. 1942. *Bloemenspeculatie in Nederland.* Amsterdam: P. N. van Kampen & Zoon.

———. 1946. *Drie Eeuwen Bloembollenexport,* Vol 2. s'Gravenhage.

Krugman, P. 1995. "Dutch Tulips and Emerging Markets." *Foreign Affairs* 74:28–44.

La Chesnee Monstereul. 1654. *Le Floriste François.* Caen: Mangeant.

Law, J. [1705] 1760. *Money and Trade Considered: With a Proposal for Supplying the Nation with Money.* Glasgow: Foulis.

"Liste van Eenige Tulpaen . . ." [1637] 1927. In *Economisch-Historisch Jaarboek,* vol. XII, 96–99. Reprint, Haarlem: Adriaen Roman.

Mackay, C. [1841] 1852. *Extraordinary Popular Delusions and the Madness of Crowds,* vol. 1, 2d ed. London: Office of the National Illustrated Library.

Malkiel, B. 1985. "The Madness of Crowds." In *A Random Walk Down Wall Street,* 4th ed. New York: Norton.

Malkiel, B. G. 1996. *A Random Walk Down Wall Street.* New York: Norton.

Mather, J. 1961. *Commercial Production of Tulips and Daffodils.* London: WH&L.

Munting, A. 1672. *Waare Oeffening der Planten.* Amsterdam.

———. 1696. *Naauwkeurige Beschryving der Aardgewassen.* Leyden.

Murphy, A. E. 1986. *Richard Cantillon, Entrepreneur and Economist.* Oxford: Clarendon Press.

——. 1997. *John Law: Economic Theorist and Policy-Maker.* Oxford: Clarendon Press.

Neal, L. 1988. "How the South Sea Bubble Was Blown Up and Burst: A New Look at Old Data." University of Illinois Working Paper, August.

——. 1990. *The Rise of Financial Capitalism.* Oxford: Cambridge University Press.

Neal, L., and E. Schubert. 1985. "The First Rational Bubbles: A New Look at the Mississippi and South Sea Schemes." BEBR Working Paper 1188, University of Illinois, Urbana-Champaign, September.

Palgrave, R. H. 1926. *Dictionary of Political Economy.* London: MacMillan.

Penso de la Vega, J. [1688, Amsterdam] 1957. *Confusion de Confusiones,* English trans. Boston: Baker Library.

Posthumus, N. W. 1926, 1927, 1934. "Die Speculatie in Tulpen in de Jaren 1636–37." *Economisch-Historisch Jaarboek.*

——. 1929. "The Tulip Mania in Holland in the Years 1636 and 1637." *Journal of Economic and Business History* 1 (May).

——. 1964. *Inquiry into the History of Prices in Holland.* Leiden: E. J. Brill.

Prinzing, F. 1916. *Epidemics Resulting from Wars.* Oxford: Clarendon Press.

"Register den de Prijsen der Bloemen . . . Derde Samenspraeck." [1637] 1926. In *Economisch-Historisch Jaarboek,* vol. XII. Reprint, Haarlem: Adriaen Roman.

Rich, E. E., and C. H. Wilson, eds. 1975. *The Cambridge Economic History of Europe.* Vol. IV, *The Economy of Expanding Europe in the Sixteenth and Seventeenth Centuries.* London: Cambridge University Press.

——. 1977. *The Cambridge Economic History of Europe.* Vol. V, *The Economic Organization of Early Modern Europe.* London: Cambridge University Press.

The Royal General Bulbgrowers Society. 1969. *Classified List and International Register of Tulip Names.* Haarlem.

"Samenspraeck Tusschen Waermondt ende Gaergoedt: Flora." [1637] 1926. In *Economisch-Historisch Jaarboek*, vol. XII. Reprint, Haarlem: Adriaen Roman.

Samuelson, P. A. 1957. "Intertemporal Price Equilibrium: A Prologue to the Theory of Speculation." *Weltwirtschaftliches Archiv* 79, no. 2:181–219; reprinted in J. Stiglitz, ed., *The Collected Scientific Papers of Paul A. Samuelson*, vol. 2. Cambridge: The MIT Press, 1966.

———. 1967. "Indeterminacy of Development in a Heterogeneous-Capital Model with Constant Saving Propensity." In K. Shell, ed.,*Essays on the Theory of Optimal Economic Growth*. Cambridge: The MIT Press.

Schama, S. 1987. *The Embarrassment of Riches*. New York: Alfred Knopf.

Schumpeter, J. 1954. *History of Economic Analysis*. New York: Oxford University Press.

Scott, W. 1911. *The Constitution and Finance of English, Scottish, and Irish Joint Stock Companies to 1720*, vol. 2. Cambridge: Cambridge University Press.

Shell, K., and J. Stiglitz. 1967. "The Allocation of Investment in a Dynamic Economy." *Quarterly Journal of Economics* 81, no. 4 (November):592–609.

Smith, K. 1937. *Textbook of Plant Virus Diseases*. London: J&A Churchill.

Solms-Laubach, H. Graf. 1899. *Weizen und Tulpe und deren Geschichte*. Leipzig: Felix.

"Tweede Samenspraeck Tusschen Waermondt ende Gaergoedt." [1637] 1926. In *Economisch-Historisch Jaarboek*, vol. XII. Reprint, Haarlem: Adriaen Roman.

van Damme, A. 1976. *Aanteekeningen Betreffende de Geschiedenis der Bloembollen, Haarlem 1899–1903*. Leiden: Boerhaave Press.

van Horne, J. 1985. "Of Financial Innovations and Excesses." *Journal of Finance* 40, no. 3 (July):621–631.

van Slogteren, E. 1960. "Broken Tulips." In *The Daffodil and Tulip Yearbook*, 25–31. London: Royal Horticultural Society.

Index